QIGONG FEVER

DAVID A. PALMER

Qigong Fever

Body, Science, and Utopia
in China

COLUMBIA UNIVERSITY PRESS
NEW YORK

Columbia University Press
Publishers Since 1893
New York
© 2007 David A. Palmer

Library of Congress Cataloging-in-Publication Data

Palmer, David A.
    Qigong fever : body, science, and utopia in China / by David Palmer.
      p. cm.
    Includes bibliographical references and index.
    ISBN 0-231-14066-5 (alk. paper)
    1. Qi gong. 2. Qi gong—Social aspects. 3. Qi gong—Political aspects. 4.
Falun gong exercises. I. Title.

    RA781.8.P36 2007
    613.7'14—dc22

                                 2006049025

To Kristofer Schipper

CONTENTS

ACKNOWLEDGEMENTS

Let me begin by expressing my gratitude to my beloved family—my wife Chen Li, our daughters Danielle and Solenne, my parents John and Christiane, and my grandfather Claude. Thanks to their unflagging support and patience, their love and their material assistance, this project, throughout each of its phases, was made to feel worthwhile.

This work is an abridged, revised and updated version of my book *La fièvre du qigong*, published by the Ecole des Hautes Etudes en Sciences Sociales.[1] I owe a deep debt of gratitude to my mentors, colleagues and collaborators, whose advice, support and encouragement throughout the period of research and writing can be credited for bringing this project to fruition. First and foremost is my doctoral thesis director at the Ecole Pratique des Hautes Etudes, Kristofer Schipper, whose insights and methodological advice enabled me to build a coherent and meaningful historical narrative out of the data, which, I hope, will be seen as a contribution to the history of religion in modern China. I also extend my thanks to Ken Dean, my first mentor at McGill University, for inspiring me to pursue a career in research on Chinese religion, and to Tobie Nathan of the Georges Devereux Centre for Ethnopsychiatry at the Université de Paris-VIII for encouraging me to experience personally the dense links between healing, culture and politics in China. The advice and steadfast support of Danièle Hervieu-Léger and Jean-Paul Willaime were instrumental in helping me to engage with broader debates in the sociology of religion, while Yves Chevrier and Jean-Luc Domenach provided the same in relation to the history and sociology of modern Chinese politics. Special thanks are also due to Christophe Jaffrelot for his efforts to ensure the diffusion of my work to broader audiences.

Several Chinese friends, colleagues and *qigong* masters and practitioners provided me with invaluable data, interviews and

1 Palmer 2005a.

other assistance during my years in China, but wisdom dictates that under current conditions they remain unnamed. Catherine Despeux and Livia Kohn supplied me with hard-to-find references and sources, which were notably helpful in connecting the *qigong* story to earlier developments. I am also grateful to David Ownby for sharing sources on Falungong and for his constant encouragement and useful feedback. The comments of Frank Dikötter and anonymous reviewers were most helpful for improving the English edition.

I am grateful to Vincent Goossaert, Feng Congde, Christiane Pignan, John Palmer, Joan Bakker and Fabienne Jagou for proofreading various versions of the manuscript, in French or in English, to Adam Chau for his precious suggestions on translating Chinese terms, to Caroline Gyss-Vermande and Joubine Eslahpazire for their logistical support, as well as to the painstaking efforts of the staff of the Editions de l'EHESS, Hurst and Columbia University Press. Any errors that remain are, of course, my entire responsibility.

I have benefited greatly from my interactions with other scholars in France, the United States, Britain and Hong Kong, whom I would like to thank for their insights, their questions, their encouragement and often their assistance, including, in alphabetical order, Elizabeth Allès, Eileen Barker, Joe Bosco, Jean-Pierre Cabestan, Adam Yuet Chau, Ned Davis, Stephan Feuchtwang, Ji Zhe, Marc Kalinowski, Arthur Kleinman, John Lagerwey, Richard Landes, Liu Xun, Nathalie Luca, Gordon Melton, Peter Ng, Leslie Orr, Michael Penn, Elizabeth Perry, Bill Powell, Jean-Louis Rocca, Vivienne Shue, Elijah Siegler, C.B. Tan, Franciscus Verellen, Mayfair Mei-hui Yang. I also thank lecture audiences and conference participants, whose questions and comments helped me to shape and refine my arguments, at the Academia Sinica, CERI, the Chinese University of Hong Kong, CNRS (Groupe de Sociologie des Religions et de la Laïcité), Concordia University, the Ecole des Hautes Etudes en Sciences Sociales, the Ecole Pratique des Hautes Etudes, the European Association for Chinese Studies, the French Centre for Research on Contemporary China, Harvard University, Hong Kong University, Hong Kong Baptist University, the London School of Economics and Political Science, the Macau Ricci Institute, Oxford University, the Santa Barbara College of Oriental Medicine, Stanford University, the Université de Paris-VIII, the University of California at Santa Barbara and the Université de Montréal.

I extend my appreciation to the publishers of *China Perspectives*, *Extreme Orient Extreme Occident*, *Social Compass*, *Asian Anthropology* and *China Cross Currents*, as well as Les Indes Savantes and ABC-CLIO, for their permission to reproduce here segments of articles or chapters previously published in their journals and in volumes edited by John Lagerwey and James Miller.[2]

Funding and institutional support for this research and writing came from several sources, beginning with a doctoral fellowship from the Social Science and Humanities Research Council of Canada from 1996 to 1999, a fellowship from Sichuan University in 1999–2000, grants from the Ecole Pratique des Hautes Etudes, the Centre National de la Recherche Scientifique (Groupe de sociologie des religions et de la laïcité), the French Centre for Research on Contemporary China and the Antenne expérimentale franco-chinoise en sciences humaines et sociales. I was able to translate the book into English in 2003–4 on a post-doctoral fellowship at the Sociology Department of the London School of Economics and Political Science, and to complete the editing work while posted by the Ecole Française d'Extrême-Orient (EFEO) to its centre at the Institute of Chinese Studies of the Chinese University of Hong Kong in 2004–5. I am most grateful to Nikolas Rose, chair of the sociology department at the LSE, to Jenny So, director of the Institute of Chinese Studies of CUHK, and to Franciscus Verellen, director of the EFEO, for providing me with ideal conditions and support for completing the work.

DP

---

2 Palmer 2001b, 2002, 2003a, 2003b, 2005b and 2006.

ABBREVIATIONS

BQRS	Beijing Qigong Research Society (*Beijing qigong yanjiuhui*)
CCP	Chinese Communist Party (*Zhongguo gongchandang*)
COSTIND	Commission of Science, Technology and Industry for National Defence (*Guofang keji gongye weiyuanhui*)
CQRS	China Qigong Science Research Society (*Zhongguo qigong kexue yanjiuhui*)
CSICOP	Committee for the Scientific Investigation of Claims of the Paranormal
CSQS	China Sports Qigong Research Society (*Zhongguo tiyu qigong yanjiuhui*)
CSSS	China Somatic Science Society (*Zhongguo renti kexue xuehui*)
IQSF	International Qigong Science Federation (*Guoji qigong kexue lianhehui*)
NAST	National Association for Science and Technology (*Quanguo kexue jishu xiehui*)
PLA	People's Liberation Army (*Zhongguo renmin jiefangjun*)
TQSC	Tantric Qigong Specialised Commission (*Zangmi qigong zhuanye weiyuanhui*)

INTRODUCTION

A few years before the founding of the People's Republic of China in 1949 a group of Communist cadres in the mountains of the South Hebei Liberated Zone discovered an ancient technique that, at almost no cost, could bring health and vigour to the sickly and impoverished masses. It was a simple set of exercises that anyone could learn: every day stand still for half an hour, control your breath, concentrate on the *yongquan* acupoints at the centre of the soles of your feet, recite the mantra 'My organs move, my mind is still'. The cadres called this and other sitting, lying and stretching exercises *qigong* (pronounced 'Chee-gong')—a name that literally means 'breath training'.

Within a decade the nation's leaders were practising *qigong* at their exclusive seaside resort of Beidaihe, and *qigong* clinics were founded in hospitals around the country. By the late 1980s, every morning at dawn millions of people came out into the parks and sidewalks to practise the miraculous technique. Elderly men and women could be seen standing still, facing clumps of bushes, eyes closed, their hands forming a circle below the abdomen. In the yards of residential compounds practitioners drew arcs in the air with their stretched arms, following the rhythm of taped traditional Chinese music. In parks students recited mantras, sitting on stones in the lotus position. *Qigong* healers grasped the air, removing pernicious *qi* from the sick. Others hugged trees, while people in trance rolled on the ground, crying, shouting, laughing, and still others danced or kicked like kung fu artists. In sports stadiums charismatic *qigong* masters held mass healing sessions for audiences in the thousands. Researchers invited masters into their laboratories, to detect and measure the mysterious power of *qi*. China's leading nuclear scientist raved about an imminent scientific revolution of historic implications, as *qigong* contained the key to the power of life.

Qigong fever was still in the air when, on a rare sunny day in the spring of 1994, as I sat on the steps under the massive Mao statue that overlooks People's Road in Chengdu, an old man approached me and introduced himself as Professor Wang. He took me as his student and, for the next few years, taught me the *qigong* method of the 'Supreme Mystery of the Venerable Infant', which involved study of Laozi's *Book of the Tao and its Virtue*, standing meditation and gentle gymnastic exercises which embody the forms of the hexagrams of the *Book of Changes*.

This encounter occurred as I was trying to lay the groundwork for an ethnographic field research project by learning several *qigong* methods, visiting various groups, and searching for a suitable setting for a formal study. As an aspiring anthropologist I hoped to plunge deeply into the Otherness of Chinese culture, and *qigong* appeared to me as a good technique for penetrating the Chinese mind and experience through participant observation. At the same time, as a mass movement of revitalised traditions and urban religiosity in a socialist state, *qigong* raised many questions which warranted social scientific investigation.

However, as my involvement with *qigong* deepened such a study became increasingly difficult to carry out. The effects of *qigong* practice were powerful. I entered mental states I had never previously imagined. The limits of my body and of my world seemed to dissolve. I felt imbued with a powerful energy that could make anything possible. I no longer thought in words, but in forms and symbols which seemed to leap out of my head, my hands and my abdomen. I could see my thoughts like visible and living objects, as real and palpable as the material things in the outside world. The boundary between the real and the imaginary was vanishing. I read classical Chinese texts with a new perspective, and plunged into ancient Chinese mysticism.

But I did not truly enjoy most of the time I spent with *qigong* enthusiasts. The main subject of conversation was the miraculous cures attributed to *qigong*, and the paranormal powers of masters. The latter seemed to be motivated by an inordinate thirst for money and/or personal fame. In one extreme case, a master calling himself Celestial Imprint asked me for the equivalent of US$1000 for a half-day secret initiation. His disciple told me it would be a good investment: I could make a fortune teaching his method overseas. Others were also interested in working with me, either for immediate financial gain, or for more long-term benefits, such as my collaboration in establishing a branch of their organisation in a Western country.

To expect me to reciprocate for the masters' contribution to my research was natural. Clearly I would be led into deeper involvement in their networks, a prospect that left me hesitant: the *qigong* exercises were taught by individuals or organisations to which I did not wish to affiliate myself, and were couched in an ideology which, often, I did not subscribe to. I realised these networks and discourses were modern productions, inseparable from the political and social configuration of the People's Republic of China. It became necessary to make a distinction between: (1) the body technologies, many of which originated in ancient times; (2) the modalities of their transmission by specific social organisations; and (3) the ideology carried by the latter. Seeing the *qigong* movement as made up of these three components is a basic premise of this study.

This distinction made, it became clear that to follow the *qigong* movement from a general and historical perspective might be more fruitful.[1] State policies, the interventions of influential and charismatic individuals, and mass training networks created the setting within which millions of unique, individual trajectories and therapeutic encounters came together as a movement. Although the field research had provided me with an intimate experience of the *qigong* subculture, which has guided my analysis, I distanced myself from the *qigong* milieu and turned to collecting documentary sources for reconstructing the history of the *qigong* movement in socialist China.[2]

As I collected my materials in the late 1990s *qigong* was increasingly the subject of media controversy around the alleged 'quackery' and 'pseudo-science' of many masters and their teachings, leading to a decline in the movement and a sense of crisis in *qigong* circles. One master, Li Hongzhi, claimed the disarray was the result of people's fascination with *qi*, which he asserted was but a lower form of energy—and that one should cultivate *gong*, an even higher cosmic power that could be attained only though moral rigour and the practice of his Great Law of the Dharma Wheel: Falungong. His followers, who numbered in the tens of millions, were not content to do their morning exercises inconspicuously, like the practitioners of other methods: the Great Law was the only path to salvation,

1 I am indebted to my doctoral advisor, Kristofer Schipper, for suggesting this approach.
2 See appendix for a discussion of these sources.

and adepts had the urgent mission of saving as many people as possible by exposing them to their master's book.

In April 1999 an obscure college magazine in Tianjin published an article claiming that Falungong practice could trigger mental illness. Followers did not take the criticism lightly: six thousand of them turned up at the magazine offices, demanding the offending issue be removed from circulation. The editor refused and a handful of the protesters were arrested. The rest decided to take their grievance to the country's supreme leaders. At dawn on 25 April ten thousand practitioners quietly converged around Zhongnanhai, the 'Forbidden City' of the nation's Communist leaders—a large compound next to Tiananmen in which, only a few years earlier, some *qigong* masters had been special guests, teaching longevity techniques to the aging leaders of the Long March generation. It was the largest popular protest since the 1989 Tiananmen student movement, and only weeks from its tenth anniversary.

President Jiang Zemin responded with a ruthless crackdown on Falungong. Since then Party leaders and the master of the Dharma Wheel have been caught in a standoff, with cycles of arrests and protests succeeding each other. The former call for vigilance against the 'evil cult', while the latter calls for the criminal prosecution of the 'demonic' Jiang for instigating the 'genocide' of thousands of Falungong disciples killed in work camps, torture chambers and organ-harvesting laboratories.

This book tells the story of how these body techniques, launched within socialist state institutions in the 1950s, became the carriers of urban China's most popular form of religious expression in the 1980s, then led to a powerful and enduring challenge to the legitimacy of China's political leadership in the late 1990s. In doing so the book will try to show how *qigong* evolved from a therapeutic practice into a mass expression of charismatic religiosity, before laying the stage for a political conflict. It will also describe the development of the *qigong* category from the late 1940s to the end of the 1990s, tracing the shifting combinations of practices and concepts which came to be associated with *qigong* in a changing ideological and political context, and will end with an analysis of Falungong's rupture, first with the *qigong* movement, then with the Chinese state.

In the 1950s and early 1960s traditional body technologies were reformulated and institutionalised as part of the Communist state's project of developing the health of the masses and of extracting and transforming all useful elements of traditional culture in the service of building a New China. The choice of the term *qigong* by Party cadres in 1949 reflected an ideological project: to extract Chinese body cultivation techniques from their 'feudal' and religious setting, to standardise them, and to put them to the service of the construction of a secular, modern state. As such, *qigong* is an invented tradition.[3] The object of its construction was to present *qigong* from a purely technical angle, to reconstitute the history of these techniques in isolation from their religious, political and social context, and to classify them according to a rational schema. The techniques were thus divided into 'hard' forms (*ying qigong*) derived from martial arts, often with a dramatic component (swallowing a broken glass bottle, breaking bricks or stones with one's hand, lifting a car with one's tongue etc.), and 'soft' forms (*ruan qigong*).[4] The latter were grouped into 'still' forms (*jinggong*), which include meditation, concentration and visualisation techniques practised in a sitting, standing or lying state, and 'active' forms (*donggong*), derived from the slow-motion gymnastics of *daoyin*.

During the Cultural Revolution *qigong* was officially banned, but informally a mass practice model was born in Beijing. In the 1980s *qigong* became an outlet for a cultural shift from political utopianism to individual empowerment and subjectivity, and became a pathway to inner freedom and alternative worlds, often expressed in a religious idiom and symbolism, within the interstices of the state.

Qigong was touted as a cheap and powerful healing technology, as a 'somatic science' that could lead to revolutionary discoveries of ways to harness the powers of the human mind, and as a secularised training system that contained the key to the mysteries of traditional Chinese wisdom without the dross of religion or superstition. And yet while these modernising discourses lent legitimacy to *qigong*, practitioners plunged into the legends and symbols of Buddhist magicians and Taoist immortals, dabbled in talismans and divination, and often experienced, through trance states, visions of popular demons and deities. The indeterminacy of *qigong*, as a type

---

3   On the notion of 'invented tradition', see Hobsbawm and Ranger 1983.
4   Despeux 1997: 268.

of body practice that allows one to pass in a breath from physical fitness exercises to mystic visualisations or apocalyptic militancy, opened a space for the massive spread of a body-centred religiosity under the rubric of health, sports and science, outside the supervision of the official Bureau of Religious Affairs. At its height in the late 1980s the *qigong* movement may have attracted over one hundred million practitioners in some form or another—over 20 per cent of the urban population—making it the most widespread form of popular religiosity in post-Mao urban China. During this period, breathing and meditation techniques were disseminated to a degree perhaps never before seen in Chinese history. China was gripped by what was popularly called '*qigong* fever' (*qigong re*).

Though still promoted by Party leaders, *qigong* in this period increasingly escaped state control and became a locus for alternative networks of masters and practitioners. Like other social movements in post-Mao China, the *qigong* milieu was part of an emerging but still tenuous space for autonomous social associations which could be maintained only through the personal patronage of state leaders and the corollary risk of being drawn into factional politics. In the 1990s these networks gave birth to large-scale commercial and cultic groups. Hundreds of charismatic *qigong* healers and masters rose to fame and built organisations with enough followers, in the two cases of Zhonggong and Falungong, to rival with the 70-million-strong Chinese Communist Party (CCP): the largest mass organisations independent of government control in China. In the case of Falungong, the *qigong* training became a vehicle for resistance to the state and to the destructuring and corruption of a rapidly-changing society.

The *qigong* movement and its offshoot, Falungong, expressed and combined, in unexpected and sometimes explosive ways, some of the processes and discourses of cultural, social and political transformation that moulded China through the second half of the twentieth century: state-building, nationalism, scientism, utopianism, capitalism and transnational networks—discourses and processes that reflect the tensions and paradoxes of Chinese modernity. Each phase in the evolution of Chinese socialism—from its period of utopian state-construction to its post-revolutionary and market-driven phases—witnessed the appearance of different uses of traditional body technologies and, through them, a different relationship between the individual body and the body politic.

Central to these transformations was the appearance of a particular form of charisma, which mediated bodily experience and utopian expectations.

QIGONG AS A TECHNOLOGY OF THE BODY

This book is not a study of the therapeutic efficacy of *qigong*, nor is it a discussion of the mystical realities that can be explored through *qigong* practice. *Qigong* adepts may well be disappointed that this book deals only with 'superficial' social phenomena and ignores the 'essential reality' of *qigong*. I do not deny the health benefits of moderate *qigong* exercise, nor the powerful experiences and insights that can be triggered during practice, but the same type of experience, and perhaps deeper insights, can be found by practising similar techniques in other traditions, such as *Taijiquan* or Taoist inner alchemy. What, then, is specific about *qigong*? This book will argue that what makes *qigong* special is not so much the techniques in themselves, which are also practised in many other traditions and movements that do *not* identify themselves as part of *qigong*, but rather the meanings *qigong* practitioners give to them, the reasons they want to practise them, and the social relationships created between people who promote, who teach, who learn, who practise, who don't practise, and who oppose *qigong*. The meanings, the goals and the social relations created around *qigong* practices are not quite the same as those that have emerged around similar or even identical body techniques among Taoist inner alchemists seeking immortality, Buddhist monks seeking deliverance from rebirth, sectarians seeking millennial salvation, martial artists seeking combat invincibility, Confucians seeking composure, or Western spiritual sojourners seeking their true self. The meanings and social relations formed around these techniques are different today than they were in past centuries, and they are different in post-Mao China than in the post-modern West.

Qigong advocates often claim that *Taijiquan*, Taoist inner alchemy, Buddhist meditation etc. are actually forms of *qigong*, but such a claim would be rejected or strongly qualified by representatives of those traditions. The names and meanings given to body technologies are points of contention, linked to the historical, social and even political situatedness of practitioners. To practise *qigong*, then, is not only to practise certain traditional body techniques, but also to participate in the elaboration of meanings and of social relations around the goals and ideals of the *qigong* movement.

It is important, then, to make a distinction between the body techniques practised under the name of *qigong*, and *qigong* as a specific form of ideological and social organisation of such practices. Many of the gymnastic, breathing and meditation techniques defined as *qigong* were widely practised in Chinese society before 1949, but were not known under that name, nor grouped under a single category. They were practised in a diversity of contexts, and embedded in a variety of systems of representations and social organisations: monastic institutions, sectarian groups, martial arts networks, literati circles and medical lineages. It was only in 1949 that *qigong* became a global category which aimed to include all Chinese breathing, meditation and gymnastic techniques. As noted by Jian Xu,

> In a certain sense, the various forms of *qi* exercises designated by the modern term *qigong* always resided at the centre of Chinese culture, even though they were never regarded as self-sufficient cultural practices, but instead as ancillary to other cultural practices. ... Masters and students who transmitted knowledge of *qi* techniques usually did so in the name of a religion, or of a school of medicine or martial arts. It was unthinkable to study *qi* just for the sake of its form and techniques and not in the service of other goals.[5]

The general terms 'longevity techniques', 'immortality techniques' or 'self-cultivation techniques' have been used by modern Western scholars in their studies of these practices at various periods. I prefer not to use the former two because they refer to the purported goal of the techniques, which has varied in different contexts and periods, and I find the notion of 'self-cultivation' problematic given that many traditions practise the techniques as means to *transcend* the self and merge with the Tao. When used in a more limited sense of individual cultivation as opposed to collective rituals, the term 'self-cultivation' obscures the social role of master–disciple transmission or, in the case of *qigong*, of mass group practice, as essential contexts in which the techniques produce experiences and inner transformation for practitioners.

Here the term 'traditional body technologies' will be used to designate the body practices as such. Speaking of 'technologies of the

---

5   Xu, Jian 1999: 968.

body' mirrors the 'technologies of the self' described by Foucault in his history of self-cultivation regimens in the West, from classical antiquity to the present, 'which permit individuals to effect by their own means or with the help of others a certain number of operations on their own bodies and souls, thoughts, conduct, and way of being, so as to transform themselves in order to attain a certain state of happiness, purity, wisdom, perfection or immortality'.[6] However, as explained above, I prefer not to speak of the 'self' as the goal of the technologies under discussion in the Chinese context.

Each of the three words in the term 'traditional body technologies' needs further elaboration. Speaking of the 'body' with its connotations of a binary distinction between the mind and the flesh is highly problematic when dealing with Chinese traditions, which have not objectified a physical body separate from mental functions or even the individual's social persona.[7] For want of a better word, the term 'body' is used here in a non-dualistic sense, closer to Chinese conceptions, as englobing all interconnected human functions, including thinking, feeling, moving, breathing, desiring, ingesting, digesting and so on.

The term 'technology' is used in this context to refer collectively to a range of techniques of the body, which are, and have been for centuries, the subject of specialised and highly elaborate discourses linking different body techniques to each other, as well as to cosmologies and intentional paths of life. Body technologies involve sets of movements and forms which aim for the attainment of specific goals, and are transmitted through a training process which forms the basis of a tradition.[8] They are *individual* practices that usually involve the self-disciplined control of diet, posture, breathing and thoughts. They are also *social* practices in which techniques and interpretive frameworks are transmitted from a master to disciples, and in which the powers gained from practice are used for a variety of ends within specific social and historical contexts.

Finally, the term 'traditional' is used here to emphasise that the technologies themselves are known by their practitioners and by the broader public to have their roots in pre-modern Chinese tradition: they are not body technologies imported from the West

---

6 Foucault 1988a: 18.
7 For a discussion of the problem with the word 'body' in Chinese culture, see Brownell 1995: 15.
8 See Mauss's classic definition of 'body techniques': Mauss 1979 [1935]: 120.

or invented from scratch. Throughout history Chinese body technologies have been transmitted in different social settings, and have been used for various purposes within different cosmologies.[9] The dances and ecstatic healing practices of ancient Chinese shamanism were probably the source of later traditions of body cultivation.[10] Invisible forces represented as demons and winds were later reconceptualised as cosmic breath (*qi*).[11] During the warring-states period (475–221 BC) gymnastics and breath-training were practised as forms of health cultivation, and were described in philosophical works, notably the *Laozi* and *Zhuangzi*, as means of attaining unity with the Tao. Other texts mentioned body cultivation among the techniques for attaining immortality.[12] In classical China the proper training of the body through fasting and meditation was a prerequisite to participation in rituals, which, to Confucius, aimed to foster social cohesion through the harmonious movement of bodies. The emperor's body was seen as the centre of the ordering of the cosmos: the appropriate movements of his body through the space of the realm and following the cycles of the seasons were essential to preserving the cosmic order. The empire was seen as an extension of the emperor's body: the disorderly conduct of the emperor would cause chaos in the realm; natural disasters and calamities were seen as signs of the moral degeneracy of the emperor's body.[13] The correspondence between the body of the emperor and the body politic was formalised in the medical theories of the Han dynasty, which applied the principles of government to the flows of *qi* in the body: the same Chinese word *zhi* refers to healing and government.

From the first century CE onward Taoism developed a rich repertoire of body technologies, ranging from the meditations on oneness of the Heavenly Masters movement to the Shangqing and Lingbao sects' visualisations of the divine landscape of the inner body.[14] The inner alchemy tradition sought to refine the elixir of immortality through the manipulation and combination of cosmic

---

9   On the changing configurations of Chinese body technologies, see Maspero 1971 [1937].
10   See Eliade 1968.
11   See Unschuld 1985: 29–50.
12   On the techniques of the 'men of recipes' (*fangshi*), see Robinet 1990: 39.
13   See Schipper 1993; Lagerwey 1997: 102; Zito and Barlow 1994; Zito 1997.
14   Robinet 1979.

energies in the body. Body technologies were also practised by Taoist priests as a key to the mastery and efficacy of rituals conducted for local families and communities.[15] Buddhism introduced yogic meditation from India, practised as a means of nurturing awareness of ultimate reality and, in the case of tantrism, of nurturing and controlling divine powers.[16] The Shaolin and Wudang traditions of martial arts, among others, developed the use of body technologies for combat.[17]

By the Song dynasty body technologies had become widespread in many segments of society. Meditation by 'sitting in tranquillity' became a popular practice of Confucian literati,[18] while salvationist groups disseminated body cultivation techniques among the common people. These groups, which often espoused apocalyptic beliefs, commonly used the transmission of body techniques—including mantra recitation, breath control, sitting meditation, healing techniques and martial arts—as a method of recruitment and expansion. Practice of the techniques could reinforce sectarian identity; the body became a vehicle for the nurturing and transmission of eschatological beliefs.[19] Martial arts became more important in the popular repertoire in the nineteenth century, as increasing social chaos and banditry led to the multiplication of community self-defence groups. In the Boxer rebellion of 1899–1900 certain forms of martial arts were believed to confer invincibility against Western military technology.[20]

By the early twentieth century body technologies were practised among both common people and the élites, and diffused in a wide variety of contexts—they were even a fundamental part of training for the Chinese opera and acrobatic performance, which are closely related to the martial arts; were employed in the sexual disciplines of the 'arts of the bedchamber' and of 'dual cultivation';[21] and were popularised through the standardised forms of *taijiquan*.[22]

15 For a summary and references on the scholarship on Inner Alchemy and Taoist Body Cultivation, see Kohn 2004. On Chen Yingning's modern interpretations of inner alchemy in Republican China, see Liu, Xun 2001.
16 Strickmann 1996.
17 Shahar 2001.
18 Gernet 1981.
19 Overmyer 1976: 188–91; Naquin 1976: 26–32; Naquin 1985.
20 See Esherick 1987: 50–3; and Cohen 1997: 16–30, 99–118.
21 Gulik 2003 [1961]; Wile 1992.
22 See Despeux 1981; Wile 1996; Frank 2006.

Redemptive societies such as the Fellowship United in Goodness (*Tongshanshe*), the Heavenly Virtues Teachings (*Tiandejiao*), and the Red Swastika Society, which had millions of adherents in the Republican era, included traditional body technologies among their standard practices of inner cultivation (*neigong*). The techniques varied greatly, but in most cases involved breath training as a basic foundation. They were usually steeped in religious symbolism, and were transmitted secretly from master to disciple: mastering the arts of body cultivation was part of being initiated into an esoteric tradition. The process of initiation could last many years, as in the case of the Taoist priesthood, or could take only moments, as in some salvationist movements which taught a secret mantra as a sign of membership. But in all cases body technologies were never an end in themselves: they were always but one element of other social practices and conceptual systems: religion, government, medicine, mysticism, ritual, monasticism, defence or millennial salvation. There was no single category to encompass the various forms of what are here called 'body technologies', much less a self-conscious community or unified network of practitioners who could recognise each other in their common practice of these techniques.

The status of body technologies began to change in the first half of the twentieth century with the introduction of Western values and the construction of a modern state. The new institutions privileged a mechanical, disembodied ordering of the world: traditional body technologies were irrelevant to the ends of the modern bureaucracies, armies and schools that mediated knowledge and power in the emerging society. And yet body techniques could find a niche within new social structures that atomised the individual body and privileged material technologies leading to rational ends. Marginalised, body cultivation techniques became visible, and could be conceptualised as a distinct category that would recast them either as a modern technology for the mass development of healthy bodies, or as a vehicle for a nationalist or mystical resistance to an alienating modernity, or, as would happen in the *qigong* boom of the 1980s, both at the same time.

Such a process began during the Republican era (1911–49), when some authors, especially Jiang Weiqiao and Chen Yingning, popularised sitting meditation and other practices through widely circulated books that sought to eliminate the obscure esoteric language in which the techniques had traditionally been couched, and to present them in the idioms of psychology, physiology and physics.[23] Attempts to modernise and nationalise Chinese martial arts also prefigured many of the developments traced here in the story of *qigong*.[24] But it was under the Communist regime that traditional body technologies became a distinct category. In its secular, technical, rational expression *qigong* has attempted a modern reformulation of the traditions through new combinations of techniques, new ideological constructions and new models of transmission and collective practice. The technologies are traditional, but the *qigong* movement which diffused them in the second half of the twentieth century is a product of the Chinese socialist project of modernisation.

THE SOCIAL WORLD OF QIGONG

Qigong is most commonly practised in the form of standardised sets of exercises called *gongfa* in Chinese, which literally means '*qigong* method'. Each *gongfa* had a name, such as 'Xianggong' ('aromatic *qigong*') or 'Zhinenggong' ('intelligent *qigong*'), and was associated with a charismatic *qigong* master, who was the author or inheritor of the method. Although a *gongfa* technically referred to a set of exercises, in practice each *gongfa* was the basis of a training network linking the master to hundreds, thousands or even millions of practitioners. Each *gongfa* was transmitted to the mass of practitioners by networks of trainers in local practice points throughout a region, the country and often even abroad. In this study the term 'denomination' will be used to designate the networks of practitioners and trainers who practised and taught the *gongfa* of a specific master.[25] As networks, they involved both vertical communication between the master, his disciples and trainers, and the practitioners, as well as horizontal communication between network members.

The leading figures among those who practised, studied and promoted traditional Chinese body technologies under the name *qigong* described themselves as the '*qigong* circle' or '*qigong* sector' (*qigong jie*)—a term used in socialist China to designate an offi-

---

23   On Jiang Weiqiao's contribution to the birth of modern *qigong*, see Kohn 2002. On Chen Yingning, see Liu, Xun 2001.
24   Morris 2004: 185–245.
25   Thanks to Adam Chau for suggesting using this term.

cially-recognised community that periodically meets to collaborate in the implementation of state policies and campaigns, such as
the 'cultural sector', the 'religious sector', the 'commercial sector'.
The '*qigong* sector' is the legal, public face of a larger social space
here called the '*qigong* milieu': a nebula of networks and associations which, with the encouragement of Party, Army and scientific
leaders, expanded massively in the 1980s.[26] The *qigong* milieu was a
space of relative freedom in which, between 1979 and 1999, many
types of popular activities and networks flourished: the group practise sessions in public parks, the therapeutic encounters and healing
sessions, the training workshops, the academic conferences and the
ritualised meetings of state-sponsored associations; the interconnected networks of *qigong* associations, organisations and institutions; and the popular *qigong* magazines and books through which
qigong discourse was elaborated, debated and diffused. Within the
qigong milieu people exercised their bodies and minds, practised
divination and laboratory experiments, and discussed subjects as
varied as Buddhism, Taoism, the scientific method, health maintenance and the progress of Chinese culture. Thousands of masters competed in an emerging market for *qigong* health, healing
and spiritual arts, each proposing his own package of exercises and

---

[26] I speak of the '*qigong* milieu' in a manner analogous to Hubert Seiwert's
description of the 'sectarian milieu' in Chinese religious history (Seiwert 2003:
365–6) and to the use of the term 'cultic milieu' by sociologists of Western esoteric movements and new religious movements. The notion of the cultic milieu
was introduced by Colin Campbell in a 1972 article, in the context of academic
debates on the distinction between 'sects' and 'cults'—these terms being used in
a non-pejorative, sociological sense. Without engaging in this debate, which does
not easily apply to China, it is useful to consider Campbell's contribution, which
focuses our attention on the immediate social context out of which such types
of groups emerge: 'Given that cultic groups have a tendency to be ephemeral and
highly unstable, it is a fact that new ones are being born just as fast as the old ones
die. There is a continual process of cult formation and collapse which parallels the
high turnover of membership at the individual level. Clearly, therefore, cults must
exist within a milieu which, if not conducive to the maintenance of individual
cults, is clearly highly conducive to the spawning of cults in general. Such a generally supportive cultic milieu is continually giving birth to new cults, absorbing the
debris of the dead ones and creating new generations of cult-prone individuals to
maintain the high levels of membership turnover. Thus, whereas cults are by definition a largely transitory phenomenon, the cultic milieu is, by contrast, a constant
feature of society. It could therefore prove more viable and illuminating to take
the cultic milieu and not the individual cult as the focus of sociological concern'
(Campbell 1972: 121–2).

theories. Debates raged on the effects and powers attributed to *qigong*. The groups within the *qigong* milieu were characterised by extreme diversity and fragmentation, but this centrifugal tendency was countered by, firstly, a mystical and syncretistic outlook that encouraged tolerance and mutual receptivity, and secondly, a sense of cultural marginality bordering on the heterodox, leading to a common consciousness of the need to justify themselves in relation to the ridicule that could be directed at them from the standpoints of conventional Western scientism and orthodox Marxism. These counter-centrifugal tendencies facilitated the circulation of people and ideas between diverse groups.[27] The training and practice networks founded by hundreds of masters may well have formed China's greatest collection of popular associations during the period, and 'probably the greatest mass movement in modern China that was not under direct government control'.[28] The story of *qigong* presented in this book, then, is that of the birth, expansion, division and contraction of the *qigong* milieu in China, and of the formation, development and collapse or breaking away of denominations from within the milieu.

The *qigong* movement was born during the Mao era, reached its zenith in the post-Mao reform years of Deng Xiaoping, and imploded under Jiang Zemin. The changing forms and fortunes of the movement are inseparable from the transformations of Chinese socialism during the second half of the twentieth century. Owing to the peculiar structure and dynamics of Chinese socialist society, a few key Chinese terms have been translated in the text, which should now be explained for readers unfamiliar with contemporary China. Until the mid to late 1990s the basic social unit for most urban Chinese was the *danwei* or 'Unit', typically a large walled compound containing a factory, a state-owned enterprise, or a government administration, together with, for the Unit employees, residential apartment blocks, a kindergarten and primary school, a vegetable and meat market, a workers' club, a dining hall, a barber shop, a clinic and other amenities. Unit members typically lived, worked, played and even did most of their daily shopping within the walls of the Unit compound. Each Unit was ruled by a

27 See Campbell 1972: 122.
28 Zhu and Penny 1994: 3.

cadre of managers and Party officials collectively known as _lingdao_ or 'Officials'. Officials were personalised incarnations of Party and state power, whose influence went far beyond their bureaucratic functions. They controlled the distribution of resources within the Unit, the promotion, demotion and work assignment of members, and the allocation of scarce residential space. They were expected to care paternally for the Unit members, solve disputes between them, and even act as matchmakers for unmarried youth. In a nutshell, Officials exercised considerable power over the lives of the Unit members, in a context of limited resources and opportunities. Each Unit was a subsidiary of a higher-level Unit, extending up to central government ministries and ultimately to the State Council; each Official was thus subject to higher-ranking Officials, extending ultimately to the supreme leaders of the CCP Politburo. The relationships between Officials at different hierarchical levels and from different Units, and between Unit members and Officials, were characterised by the cultivation of informal alliances and factions which struggled over the distribution of power and resources, and often subverted official lines of authority. The cultivation of such informal _guanxi_ or 'Connections' followed subtle, ritualised patterns of the reciprocal exchange of gifts, favours and banquets, creating mutual obligations between people at different levels of the hierarchy, or from different Units, who had access to different resources.[29]

The _qigong_ milieu was as much a part of this system as any other sector of Chinese society, and the story of the _qigong_ movement is to a great extent the story of how _qigong_ enthusiasts navigated the system of Units, Officials and Connections to promote _qigong_, establish _qigong_ associations, and advance the movement's ideals. In such a system there were no legal associations independent of the state. Besides the state-controlled mass associations such as the Women's Federation and the Trade Unions, the only legal social associations were those officially sponsored and supervised by a government Unit, which took on responsibility for any misconduct by the association.[30] In a sense the association thus became an extension of the sponsoring Unit. A 'state-sponsored _qigong_ association' is thus

---

29 For studies of _danwei_ and _guanxi_ dynamics, see Walder 1986; Yang 1994; Lü and Perry 1997; Evasdottir 2004.

30 On the types of social association in China, see Heberer 2002; also Ding 1998 for a more detailed discussion.

an association which, through the cultivation of Connections, was sponsored and officialised by a higher-level government Unit.

As a 'social movement' *Qigong* was characterised by social mobilisation, in which there was increased communication and common action between people from different backgrounds, social spheres and regions, on a national and even global scale, as they promoted their common goals. What started with decentralised, non-coordinated initiatives in the mid to late 1970s quickly took on a life of its own and acquired organisational capacity within a few years, with a core network of influential political leaders, scientists and masters who were able to assume leading roles within the movement and to articulate and promote a common vision and discourse. The social goals upheld by the movement included improving the health of the masses, bringing about a renaissance of traditional Chinese culture, and triggering a Chinese-led scientific revolution which would lead to a paranormal utopia. Another, more mundane goal of the movement was to promote the interests and legitimacy of *qigong* researchers, masters and groups within the state system, and to defend them in the face of other ideological and political networks opposed to the *qigong* movement. As a cultural and social, rather than political movement, the *qigong* movement operated outside of regular political channels, but as an interest group, it penetrated deeply into political power circles. *Qigong* does not, then, correspond to conventional sociological definitions of social movements as finding existence in opposition to the state and expressing themselves primarily through protest actions.[31] While *qigong* is clearly both social and a movement, it offers a fascinating case for questioning assumptions about a fundamental dichotomy between the 'state' and 'society'. Rather, *qigong* illustrates the full spectrum of possibilities presented to social organisations and movements in socialist China, from a paradigm of 'interpenetration' between the state and social groups, to one of 'polarisation' and conflict, as exemplified when Falungong broke away from the *qigong* movement, becoming a distinct social movement of its own, committed to the moral regeneration of Chinese society and to the promotion and defence of its own ideology, followers and influence.[32]

[31] See for example Touraine 2002; Tarrow 1994.
[32] For a discussion of the applicability of sociological theories of social movements to *qigong*, see Palmer forthcoming a.

POWER, UTOPIA, CHARISMA AND FEVER

The first time the term *qigong* appeared was in a Tang dynasty (618–910) Taoist text, with the meaning of 'breath techniques'. A few centuries later, under the Song (960–1279), the word was used in two documents, with the meaning of 'efficiency of the breath'.[33] Thereafter, occurrences of the term were extremely rare until the beginning of the twentieth century, when it appeared in a handful of titles.[34] But only after 1949 did *qigong* became a general and autonomous category, universally used in Chinese medical, scientific and popular discourse, and englobing most traditional breathing, meditation, visualisation and gymnastic practices, to which, over the years, would be added martial, performance, trance, divination, charismatic healing, and talismanic techniques, as well as the *Book of Changes*, the study of paranormal phenomena, and UFOs.

The term *qigong* evokes a palette of images and concepts. *Qi* is often translated as 'breath', and *gong* as 'work', which explains the choice of the term *qigong* to designate breathing techniques. But let us examine the nuances of the characters as they are used in *qigong* circles. *Qi* is understood as the animating energy of the universe, a substance which circulates in and through the body. In its standard usage, the term derives from the theory of Chinese medicine; but it also leads to further associations with traditional Chinese cosmology. In practice it is said that *qi* can be mentally directed (*xingqi*), projected to the exterior of the body (*faqi*), and extracted from other objects (*chaiqi*); it can involuntarily leak from the body (*xieqi*); and it can even be stolen from other persons (*touqi*). It can be applied to create an energy field (*qichang*) between practitioners

---

33 On the etymology of the term *qigong* and for the references of its first uses, see Despeux 1997: 267.

34 These include a book on martial arts by Zun Wozhai, *Subtle Explanations of Qigong* (*qigong miaojie*), as well as a work by Dong Hao, *Qigong Therapy* (*qigong liaofa*) (Despeux 1997: 267). The word *qigong* also appears in the *Precise Explication of the Work of the Power of Intention* (*yiqigong xiangjie*) by Wang Zhulin, which describes how to make one's intention (*yi*) follow the breath (*qi*) and conduct it through the body (Li Zhiyong 1988: 404–5; Wang Buxiong and Zhou Zhirong 1989: 500–1). In 1934 the Xianglin hotel of Hangzhou published *A Special Treatment for Tuberculosis: Qigong Therapy* (Hu Meicheng 1981: 42). Also in the 1930s Fang Gongpu founded the Gongpu institute for *qigong* therapy, the first clinic to have the *qigong* name in modern history. Fang also published *Record of Qigong Therapy Experience* in 1938 (Li Zhiyong 1988: 409).

united in the same space, which is said to increase the efficacy of *qigong*.

Gong is a term associated with the martial arts tradition: composed of the two characters 'work' and 'force', *gong* is related to *gongfu*, an untranslatable word which refers to the virtuosity of the martial artist: a perfect mastery of the body and mind which is the fruit of a rigorous training discipline culminating in the manifestation of magical powers. *Gong* is inseparable from the essential substance of a person, of a person's moral character; it manifests itself in the struggle against evil or against an enemy. *Gong* is sometimes understood as the magical power of a person with a high level of *gongfu*, which can be projected towards other people (*fagong*); in this case, it is another way to refer to the emission of *qi*. *Gong* can also emanate from a person or an action, inducing the emergence of *gong* in the person with whom it is in contact: one can then speak of 'power-inducing audiotapes' (*daigong cidai*) or 'power-inducing lectures' (*daigong baogao*). The character *gong* is also found in the word *gongneng* which means 'function', a term which takes a specific meaning in *qigong*, often referring to the 'Extraordinary Powers of the human body' (*renti teyigongneng*)—the magical or paranormal powers said to appear at a high level of *qigong* practice. In the same sense, the expression *shengong*, 'divine power', is sometimes used to designate the miraculous aspects of *qigong*. *Qigong* practice is often abbreviated as *liangong*, a formulation which can connote the training or exercise of the magical power of *gongfu*, in order to enter into a '*qigong* state', a state of profound relaxation which can resemble hypnosis.[35] Another term used to speak of this training, at a higher level, is *xiulian*, often translated as 'cultivation', the spiritual discipline needed to forge the elixir of immortality, which evokes the Taoist traditions of inner alchemy (*neidan*).[36]

The concepts of *qi*, *gong* and 'Extraordinary Powers' can be compared to the Western notion of charisma, derived from Christian conceptions of divine grace and theorised as a universal category by Max Weber in his sociology of authority and of religion, which

---

35 Cf. Despeux 1997: 275. On the physiological relaxation response provoked by practices similar to *qigong*, see Benson 1975, 1996.
36 I am grateful to Adam Chau, whose thoughtful comments have helped me refine this discussion of the meanings of the terms related to *qigong*.

he defined as 'the extraordinary quality' of a person gifted with a superhuman, supernatural or unusual force or ability which is inaccessible to common people.[37] In *qi* and *gong* we have a similar type of power, but which is not restricted to the 'elect' or, by secular extension, the 'genius'—although such a notion is present as well—but one which can potentially be nurtured, cultivated, manipulated, even circulated by anyone, at will.

In the case of individuals with the ability to project *qi* or induce *gong* in others, creating an 'energy field' between themselves and multitudes of followers, we can speak of a 'somatised' charisma which is felt in the bodily sensations of flows of *qi* and healing experiences.[38] In *qigong* the body becomes not only a locus of 'charismatic' power, but also a site for utopian experiences—in which, by entering states of heightened or altered consciousness, the practitioner may enter alternative inner worlds which can be correlated to utopian visions and critiques of the outer world of mundane life and society. Here, utopia can be broadly defined as an imagined 'other' world in which hopes and desires are realised, be it in the next life or in this world, in the past or in the future. Thus understood, utopia is the common basis of millennialism, apocalypticism, modernism and communism, and provides a key to understanding, as will appear in the story of *qigong*, how traditional body technologies could facilitate shifts from one type of utopia to another in socialist China.

The social implications of such experiences can be understood in reference to Weber's categorisation, which stresses the collective dimension of charismatic authority, which, to exist, depends on its being freely and voluntary accepted by those who partake of it. The eruption of charisma would thus be facilitated by the existence of shared feelings and cultural references. Thus, while Weber contrasted the creativity and innovation of charismatic authority with the more inert nature of traditional and legal-rational authority, anthropologists Stephan Feuchtwang and Wang Mingming have reworked his scheme by stressing that the ruptures and bursts of collective enthusiasm released through charisma should not be seen in opposition to tradition, but are in fact rooted in traditional hopes for transformation which present themselves as the memory of an idealised past:

37 Weber 1995: 320.
38 On somatisation, see Kleinman 1986.

Every traditional authority contains a strand of hope for transformation, which legitimises an alternative to existing authority, or for innovation even though it presents itself as restoration. Charisma is the name for the innovative and restorative potential of tradition. It is a potential realised in explosions of social movement and invention when internal and external disturbances and dissatisfactions sharpen boundaries between a present that does not live up to traditional expectations which are 'remembered'. What is remembered is a past when mythology says those expectations were really fulfilled. Such utopian explosions occur on the boundaries between an 'us' who know this and a 'them' or a 'world' which as yet does not.[39]

'*Charisma pure and simple*', argue Feuchtwang and Wang, '*is the splitting away from religious traditions of their utopian expectations of the extraordinary*.'[40] At moments when more static forms of custom fail to meet expectations, charismatic traditions come to the fore. Modernity doubly enhances such potentialities, first by widening the gulf between present reality and traditional ideals, and second, by intersecting mythical or messianic time with the linear historicity of utopian progress. Thus '*modern charisma is the joining of traditional expectations of the extraordinary with a sense of time as homogenous, empty and secular, producing utopian expectations*.'[41]

The *qigong* movement is a perfect case in point. The conflation of a magicalised fantasy of the past with the dreams of utopian scientism, in a context of the breakdown of tradition, produced the burst of *qigong* 'fever' in the late 1980s, and then, ten years later, the conflation of sectarian apocalypticism with post-revolutionary nostalgia ignited the Falungong conflagration. Practices and experiences of the body grounded these visions in subjective perception, facilitated the passage from one to the other, and gave concrete sensation to the affective relations between practitioners and their masters. The *qigong* movement thus presents a fascinating case of 'bio-social' charisma, or the collective generation, experience and conflicts over a peculiar type of power within bodies, between bodies and within the state.

Commentators termed the *qigong* movement a *re*, a 'fever'— one of the countless cultural crazes which swept post-Mao China in the 1980s and 1990s, ranging from 'culture fever' to 'Mao fever' to 'stock market fever'. The 'fever' can be situated somewhere between

39 Feuchtwang and Wang 2001: 19.
40 Feuchtwang and Wang 2001: 21. Italics in original.
41 Feuchtwang and Wang 2001: 21. Italics in original.

the political campaigns or 'movements' (*yundong*) of the Mao era, and the fully commoditised consumer fads of capitalist societies: a 'fever' is a form of collective effervescence in China's post-totalitarian phase which occurs when official policies and informal signals sent from above correspond with, open the space for, and amplify popular desire, which appropriates these spaces in unexpected ways, simultaneously complying with, appropriating, disrupting and mirroring the projects of state hegemony. Thus, in *qigong*, the official campaign to promote science and technology as the foundation of Deng's Four Modernisations, was enthusiastically taken up by the *qigong* milieu and recast as a call to encourage the mass propagation of breathing exercises as a stage in China's cultural and scientific renaissance. As 'moments when an entire cultural area (often all of urban China, sometimes the nation as a whole) is unified by a common activity', as described by Ellen Hertz,[42] fevers create a social sphere in which all the actors operate within the roughly corresponding spatial and temporal frames of the nation and its historicity.

What defines *qigong* in the People's Republic of China as distinct from both other configurations of traditional body technologies, and from other social movements, then, is its alignment of traditional expectations of miraculous powers with the unfolding of the utopian project of modernity and scientism at every juncture of socialist China's history, producing the conditions, as defined above, for a nation-wide charismatic 'fever'.

QIGONG AND CHINA'S RELIGIOUS QUESTION

Although rooted in ancient traditions, *qigong* is a decidedly modern phenomenon, and although purportedly a set of secular body techniques, it can be seen as a form of *religious* practice centred on the body. The body becomes the locus for a new understanding of religious traditions, one which seeks to be compatible with a scientific worldview, and to reconcile the contradictions between tradition and modernity. And while traditional technologies of the body flourished in a secular culture, they served to propagate religious concepts and practices under new guises, contributing to a post-secular resurgence of religiosity outside of formal institutions.

---

42 Hertz 1998: 82. See pp. 71–93 for a discussion of the notion of the 'fever' in relation to the stock-trading craze of the early 1990s.

Treating *qigong* as a religious phenomenon would be strongly disputed by most *qigong* groups. Indeed, although *qigong* freely draws from the symbolic trove of Chinese religion, *qigong* discourse asserts its scientific and moral superiority over religion. Likewise, orthodox Buddhist and Taoist institutions generally do not recognise *qigong* as religion. Although several state agencies were involved in shaping and supervising the *qigong* sector, the Religious Affairs Bureau was never one of them. And yet, when Falungong began to draw widespread public attention, it was obvious that, in spite of the master's denials, there was *something* religious about the movement, the faith of its adherents and its collective behaviour. Despite its origins in a secularising project, *qigong* had become increasingly religious with the passage of time.

Owing to conventional definitions of 'religion' used by scholars and officials in China and abroad, the religious aspect of *qigong* largely escaped their attention until the Falungong confrontation. Inadequate conceptual tools still make it difficult to identify the specifically religious dimension of *qigong*, to understand why and how it affected the dynamics of the *qigong* movement, and to situate the *qigong* movement in relation to the broader landscape of religion in China and to comparable movements around the world.

Before the twentieth century, China did not have a concept of religion as an institution distinct from other domains of social and cultural life. The Chinese word *zongjiao* was first used in 1902 to translate a Western concept of religion, itself modelled on Protestant Christianity, seen as private belief in a doctrine based on a sacred text, with its ministers, its places of worship and its exclusive congregations, all distinct from secular institutions.[43] With its ethical teachings and transcendental orientation, this type of religion was defined in opposition to the magical practices of 'superstition' (*mixin*),[44] and confined to the realm of the private faith of individuals and their congregational worship. This definition, which would form the basis of official Chinese policy toward religion throughout the twentieth century, under both Nationalist and Communist regimes, excluded both the ritual architecture of the overthrown dynastic state, with its Emperor as mediator between Heaven and Earth, and its Confucian mandarinate as moral exemplars and of-

---

43 On the origins of the term *zongjiao*, see Bastid-Brugière 1998.
44 On the contested definitions of religion and superstition in Nationalist China and their implications for state policy, see Nedostup 2001; Goossaert 2003.

ficiators at the state cults, as well as most of the beliefs and rituals commonly practised by the Chinese people: the communal temple cults, festivals and healing practices which had neither doctrine nor ecclesiastical institution, and which, though they called on Buddhist, Taoist and other specialists to provide ritual services, were fully autonomous and not affiliated to religious institutions. To gain legality and protection against iconoclastic anti-religion and anti-superstition campaigns, Buddhist and, to a lesser extent, Taoist reformers were able to reinvent their traditions, alongside Protestantism, Catholicism and Islam, as officially recognised 'church'-style religions which defined themselves in opposition to the 'superstitions' of communal temple cults.[45] China's new religious regime allowed for the construction of a secular state by confining 'religion' to a restricted domain without social relevance and, in the PRC, managed by rigid state-supervised associations with little room for innovation, while most popular expressions of religiosity resurfaced and evolved under the rubric of superstition, theoretically illegal but often tolerated to varying degrees.

The *qigong* movement, however, is an interesting exception in that, for about twenty years until the mid 1990s, and in the face of sceptical polemics, it successfully defined itself and was generally recognised as pertaining to health, science and sports—neither religion nor superstition. But in the end, it was groups identified with *qigong*, and notably Falungong, which were targeted by Marxist and Buddhist critics who retrieved the category *xiejiao* or 'heretical teaching'—usually translated as 'evil cult'—from the old discourses of imperial orthodoxy, and correlated it with Western and Japanese cult scares fanned by the Jonestown, Waco and Aum Shinrikyo massacres.[46]

Since religion is a highly contested term in China, in relation to which *qigong* advocates and practitioners respond in different ways, it would not be useful for the purposes of this study to attempt to impose some outside definition of religion which would help us to classify some groups as religions and others as not;[47] the very characteristic of *qigong* is its indeterminacy, which allows the same body

---

45 Nedostup 2001, 108–19. On the main Buddhist reformers, see Goldfuss 2001 on Yang Wenhui; Pitman 2001 on Taixu.

46 See Palmer forthcoming b.

47 For a discussion of various academic definitions of religion and their applicability to Falungong, see Porter 2003: 35–44.

technologies to be invested with more or less religious significance, depending on the person, the group, the place or the time. Rather, this study will try to trace how certain universal subjective dispositions which we might call 'religiosity'—be it rooted in mundane hopes for the avoidance of disease and misfortune, in aspirations for self-realisation, or in the search for transcendental salvation or wisdom—are nurtured, channelled and find expression in various types of social formations with a range of political implications. As a subjective disposition, religiosity disregards artificial boundaries between the private and the social, between the religious and the secular, between personal pain and political judgements.

The Chinese state's policy of controlling religious organisations and restricting their development has weakened the institutional framework of religion in China, forcing religiosity to find expression in extra-institutional forms. In times of momentous change in China, religiosity has not disappeared as predicted by Marxists, but has found outlets adapted to new social and political conditions. *Qigong* is thus a product of this 'institutional deregulation of belief'[48] which is a global characteristic of modernity, a phenomenon which has affected the Chinese religious landscape as much as in the West, albeit as a result of a different historical process.

Since the early twentieth century the destruction, especially in the cities, of ancestral cults, temple worship and communal festivals, through which Chinese people's social identities were constructed, has created atomised bodies, 'modern' individuals cut off from their ancestral filiations. The weakening and destruction of traditional religious practices has accelerated the emergence of a modern religiosity characterised by individual, voluntary engagement.[49] At the same time, traditional body technologies, owing to the simplicity of their transmission and their indeterminate status, were one of the few potential outlets of religiosity to survive in the cities, perfectly adapted for individuals entering a post-revolutionary modernity. After the Cultural Revolution, while the spread of other forms of religious practice and community was still difficult, *qigong* could rapidly propagate and integrate itself into the urban fabric of society.

The question, then, is to look at the forms of expression religiosity has taken in the contemporary Chinese context of institutional

48   Hervieu-Léger 2001: 126.
49   See Hervieu-Léger 1998.

weakness, and their social and political ramifications. The *qigong* movement's evolution toward ever greater religious colouration can be analysed with the aid of French sociologist of religion Danièle Hervieu-Léger's conceptualisation of modern religiosity as involving the construction of 'chains of memory' which involve the embodiment of a continuity with the past through an authorised tradition. Hervieu-Léger draws our attention to the creation of such an authorised tradition through which individuals can be linked to the chain of memory: the 'ideological, practical and symbolic device by which the (individual and collective) consciousness of belonging to a specific chain of memory is constituted, maintained, developed and controlled'.[50] This leads her to pose the question of 'the factors which produce, in concrete historical circumstances, the emergence of these religious traits, their crystallisation, and ultimately their organisation in the form of a "religion"'.[51]

Qigong is a case in point: what was initially promoted as a simple gymnastic method in the early 1950s became the locus of a mass explosion of religiosity in the 1980s and 1990s. From the existence of beliefs and practices unevenly diffused in Chinese culture, *qigong* became a point of condensation of specific practices and concepts related to the body and health, stories of divination and of miraculous healing, apocalyptic expectations, and Buddhist and Taoist symbols. Through these practices adepts sought to embody a chain of memory extending ever further into the distant past. Masters, intellectuals and state-sponsored associations and official institutions set about elaborating authoritative traditions and established mechanisms to create, manage and propagate specific forms

50 Hervieu-Léger 1993: 119. Hervieu-Léger thus defines the term 'religion'. Her concept of the 'chain of memory' (*lignée croyante*) is elaborated in the context of a discussion of the definition of the noun 'religion', in an attempt to move beyond the tired debate among social scientists between substantive and functional definitions of religion. For the purposes of this book, however, I have preferred not to engage in the debate on the definition of 'religion', which remains an open and highly contested question in the Chinese context, and ultimately irresolvable as long as the term conflates descriptive and normative meanings as well as subjective states and institutional forms. Rather, then, I have preferred to focus, following Hervieu-Léger's conceptualisation, on the processes by which subjective dispositions of what I prefer to call 'religiosity' find organised social forms of expression. To affix the label of 'religions' to these social forms of expression, in this case *qigong* groups, does not entirely do justice to their indeterminate nature as arguably simultaneously religious and not religious.

51 Hervieu-Léger 1993: 116.

of *qigong*, establish norms of legitimacy, and struggle against other rival, 'fake' or 'evil' forms of *qigong*.

Hervieu-Léger's definition allows us to see how the *qigong* movement recreated a tradition, the memory of which could be incorporated through body technologies, how different versions of this tradition became crystallised in various schools and methods, and how the institutionalisation and control of these traditions—and by extension, of the people who were embodying them through their practice—became crucial issues as the *qigong* movement began to display social influence. It also sheds light on the process of identity formation through technologies for embodying cultural memory. It points to the process by which a medicalised and secularised category shifted towards practices and beliefs which marked an increasing return to what has been called the Chinese sectarian tradition, culminating in the emergence of Falungong.

LIMITS OF THIS STUDY

Institutionalised *qigong* was founded in March 1949; the repression of Falungong in July 1999 brought about the end of the *qigong* sector as it had existed since 1979. This study thus covers the fifty years between 1949 and 1999. Discussion is limited to mainland China, leaving out the new forms *qigong* has taken after spreading to Hong Kong, Taiwan and the West.

This book deals with the *general* configuration of the *qigong* movement, overlooking regional differences as well as the great diversity of practices and denominations. It would have been impossible to describe each method and group; I can only attempt to present a broad picture of the movement as a whole. Three denominations—Zangmigong, Zhonggong and Falungong—are presented in some detail,[52] as examples that can give the reader an idea of the range of organisational strategies existing within the *qigong* milieu, without pretending to provide an exhaustive presentation of the entire spectrum of possibilities.

The case of Falungong presents an additional difficulty. Both Falungong and *qigong* circles agree in claiming that the former does not belong to the latter. On that basis it would have been possible to exclude Falungong from this study. Indeed Li Hongzhi's move-

52   See chapters 7 and 8.

ment has its own characteristics in terms of practice and ideology which, in many respects, represent a radical break with *qigong*. It also has its own history which, since 1996 and especially 1999, has increasingly followed a trajectory different from that of the *qigong* milieu. An in-depth analysis of Li Hongzhi's writings would in itself require an entire book.[53] But given that Falungong was founded as a *qigong* method, that its first years of growth took place within the *qigong* fold, that its evolution is strongly marked by the problems that were dividing the *qigong* sector in the mid 1990s, and that the anti-Falungong campaign was fatal to the *qigong* movement, it has been necessary to include its essential aspects. It is impossible to understand the last years of the *qigong* movement without taking a close look at Falungong, just as it is impossible to understand Falungong without locating its roots in the *qigong* movement. But the significant events and changes in Falungong since the 1999 repression campaign are not dealt with here.[54]

Another question this book will not answer is whether *qi* exists and whether the Extraordinary Powers of *qigong* are true. *Qi* is at the core of a great diversity of practices which aim to cultivate it, manipulate it, and cause it to circulate between people and objects. Whether this is true or not will not concern us here. But that tens of millions of Chinese have cultivated this '*qi*', and even done many things to cultivate it, and in the process built and changed relationships between minds, bodies and people, is undoubtedly true. These changing configurations of relationships, particularly in the social sphere, are what interest us here. On the one hand, this angle reflects the analytical questions of a social scientist, which are different from those which may be asked by a biologist, a physicist or a philosopher interested in the fundamental question of what *is* this *qi*, anyway? On the other hand, even if we accept the holistic cosmology underlying most *qi* practices, we might then wish to extend our awareness beyond the body-mind and its immediate environment and cosmic connections, to society as a whole; and in evaluating the effects of *qigong* practices, be interested in the types of transformations they bring to the social body.

53　See Penny forthcoming.
54　See Ownby forthcoming.

1

THE BIRTH OF MODERN QIGONG, 1949–64

Modern *qigong* was launched in the 'Liberated Zone' of Southern Hebei on 3 March 1949, when cadre Huang Yueting proclaimed the adoption of the name *qigong* to designate a set of body training exercises which a team of clinicians had been researching under his leadership in the previous few years. The creation of *qigong* was a political act: while destroying the 'feudal' social and symbolic context of traditional masters, the new medical institutions sought to reclaim their knowledge of body techniques and to train a new corps of 'medical workers' to teach and practise them in a socialist institutional setting.[1] This chapter describes the birth and early years of *qigong* as a component of socialist China's medical system.

During the first five years of the new regime, from 1949 to 1954, traditional Chinese medicine was institutionalised by the expanding state, which modernised its transmission and practice. The first *qigong* clinical research teams worked within the new institutions. From 1954 to 1959, benefiting from a political turn against Western medicine and from the massive expansion of Chinese medicine, specialised *qigong* institutions were established and grew rapidly. The Great Leap Forward, from 1959 to 1961, favoured the large-scale dissemination of *qigong*. Finally, the years 1962 to 1964 saw a slowing down of activity, until *qigong* was finally banned just before the Cultural Revolution.

The CCP's attitude toward traditional healing underwent significant changes since the Party's early days in the first decades of the twentieth century. The first Chinese Marxists, though not especially interested in medical issues, were, as a logical consequence of their modernist orientation, opposed to the traditional healing traditions

---

[1]   On the anticlerical aspects of *qigong*, see Palmer 2002a.

associated with the old society.[2] In 1929 the Party discussed a policy proposal to abolish the old medicine in order to develop modern medicine and hygiene.[3] But after the experience of the Soviets in Jiangxi and Shaanxi, the Long March, and the deepening of the Party's rural roots in the 1930s, the CCP's attitude began to change: far from the cities, the Red Army had to resort to traditional therapists for medical care. A conscious policy was formulated in the 'Liberated Areas' in the 1940s to make use of local medical resources within a 'scientific orientation'. Mao called on modern-trained doctors to unite with traditional therapists, who were closer to the people, and to 'help them to reform'. Traditional doctors were thus no longer seen as enemies of progress. Essential in the field, where there were no modern medical institutions, they could be used and reformed along the lines of the scientific medicine which would gradually and naturally replace traditional healing. Local Party and Army leaders were thus free to call on traditional doctors for the care of injured and ill soldiers and officials.[4]

Such was the context in which official *qigong* was born. The innovation occurred in the administrative region of Southern Hebei, a base for anti-Japanese operations since the beginning of the Sino-Japanese war, and incorporated into the Huabei 'Liberated area' in 1948.[5] In this region the Party administration was unable to provide adequate medical treatment to the large number of sick and wounded cadres and soldiers. Guo Xianrui, a local Party leader who would later become deputy mayor of Beijing and honorary chairman of the Beijing Qigong Research Society, heard that a certain healer from Wei county had successfully cured young Party cadre Liu Guizhen from a host of illnesses.

Born in 1920, Liu, who had joined the anti-Japanese resistance at the age of twenty, worked as a clerk for the local Communist administration. Sick and weakened by years of gastric ulcers, insomnia and 'neurasthenia', he went back to his native village in Wei county in 1947, where he met old master Liu Duzhou, who taught him the traditional callisthenics of the 'Inner Cultivation Exercise' (*neiyang-*

2   For in-depth accounts of Chinese communist policy toward Chinese medicine, see Agren 1975; Croizier 1968, 1973, 1975; Taylor 2002.

3   Agren 1975: 41.

4   On the use of Chinese medicine in CCP-controlled areas prior to 1949, see Taylor 2001, 2005.

5   Che Guocheng and Ke Yuwen 1997: 21.

gong).[6] After 102 days of practice Liu Guizhen's ulcer was cured, and his other ailments improved. On returning to his work post he enthusiastically reported on the method's efficiency to Cheng Yulin, the Party Secretary of Xingtai district, who passed the news on to Guo Xianrui and Wang Yuechen, leaders of the liberated area government. The leaders charged him with experimenting with clinical applications of the method, and encouraged him to return to his village to become a disciple of Liu Duzhou, in order to learn fully the *neiyanggong* method, and gave him an extra ration of rice to cover his expenses.[7] Guo Xianrui learned the method himself, practising it for half an hour each day.

Liu Guizhen—who, during this time, had become a member of the CCP[8]—thus became a sixth-generation inheritor of the *neiyanggong* tradition. Cheng Yulin assigned him to teach the method in the local cadres' sanatorium, and organised a research team of local hospital officials to conduct systematic research on the practice and effects of *neiyanggong*.[9] The group set to work on the task of extracting the method from its religious and 'superstitious' setting. The method was compared with techniques described in classical medical texts, its concepts were reformulated, and its mantras 're-formed': for example, the mantra 'The Claw of the Golden Dragon Sitting in Meditation in the Chan Chamber' was changed to 'I Practise Sitting Meditation for a Better Health'.[10] Based on this research and on Liu Guizhen's clinical experiences at the sanatorium, three exercise methods were developed: *neiyanggong*, a breathing method practised in the sitting or lying position; *qiangzhuanggong* or the 'Work of Strength and Robustness', a breathing method in the lotus position; and *baojiangong*, the 'Work of Health Preservation', which combines breath training with self-massage techniques.[11]

The group also discussed the general name that would be given to the methods they had developed. Among the suggestions they considered were 'spiritual therapy' (*jingshen liaofa*), 'psychological

---

6   Liu Duzhou was in the fifth generation of the line of transmission of the method. For genealogies of the method's transmission from the mid seventeenth century to Liu Guizhen, see Wang Buxiong and Zhou Zhirong 1989: 511; and Despeux 1997: 269.

7   Li Zhiyong 1988: 418; JSK (I).

8   ZG 118: 4; JSK (I).

9   Che Guocheng and Ke Yuwen 1997: 21; JSK (I).

10   Lan Sheng 1999: 4.

11   Hu Meicheng 1981: 42; Liu Guizhen 1981 [1957].

therapy' (*xinli liaofa*) and 'incantation therapy' (*zhuyou liaofa*).[12] Finally they settled for '*qigong* therapy' (*qigong liaofa*), which Liu Guizhen explained in the following words:

> The character '*qi*' here means breath, and '*gong*' means a constant exercise to regulate breath and posture; that is to say, what popular parlance calls to practise until one has mastery [*you gongfu*]; to use medical perspectives to organise and research this *qigong* method; and to use it for therapy and hygiene, while removing the superstitious dross of old; so it is thus called *qigong* therapy.[13]

Liu Guizhen proposed a typology of the techniques covered by the name *qigong*. He defined *qigong* as integrating the 'triple discipline' (*santiao*) of the body, breath and mind. This made possible the grouping, under a single category, of techniques which previously had not necessarily been associated, and established a norm that would later influence all Chinese research on *qigong*, as well as most *qigong* methods. For example, many denominations today include both gymnastic methods as well as meditation forms in the lotus position—a combination of techniques which was not commonly found in body technologies prior to 1949.

On 3 March 1949 Huang Yueting formally proclaimed the adoption of the term '*qigong*' at a meeting on health in Southern Hebei, during which reports on *qigong* clinical treatments were presented.[14] A few months before the founding of the People's Republic, therefore, the birth of modern *qigong* was announced by a local Party leader in an official meeting. By transmitting *neiyanggong* to Liu Guizhen, popular master Liu Duzhou had done more than teach the method to a personal disciple: the Communist Party's new government, of which Liu Guizhen was the instrument, became the inheritor of the tradition. By authorising and supervising Liu Guizhen's training, and by collecting, reformulating, renaming and proclaiming the method in a manner conforming to its ideology, the Party gave itself, through *qigong*, a modern instrument for the training and healing of bodies. Body cultivation technique thus passed from the popular domain of superstition to the official and legitimate domain of health policy.

---

12   On the term *zhuyou*, see Fang 2001.
13   Liu Guizhen 1957: 1.
14   Che Guocheng and Ke Yuwen 1997: 21.

INSTITUTIONALISATION OF CHINESE MEDICINE, 1949–54

At the end of the 1940s, after decades of civil war, the country's medical system was in ruins. As soon as the CCP took power it was faced with the pitiful state of the nation's health system. There were only 12,000 scientifically-trained doctors—one doctor for every 26,000 people—almost all of whom were concentrated in the cities. On the other hand, traditional doctors were estimated to number 400,000.[15]

The new government carried out the Party's policy: integrate the traditional doctors into China's new health system until they could be replaced by modern medical professionals. While previous republican regimes had attempted—unsuccessfully—to ban or restrict Chinese medicine,[16] traditional doctors were now told that their days of suffering under the imperialists were finished, and that they were now free to unite to serve the people. However, they would have to abandon their conservative prejudices, learn science, and work with doctors of Western medicine to improve their technical competence. Chinese medicine would learn the scientific spirit of Western medicine, and Western medicine would learn the popular and universal spirit of Chinese medicine. In this cooperation, however, Western medicine would have the chief responsibility in improving the level of Chinese medicine.[17] Under the Party's direction, New China would save valuable Chinese traditions from feudal decadence, spur them to new heights of development, and contribute them to the health and welfare of the people. Thus institutionalised and modernised, Chinese medicine could be marshalled to serve the health policy needs of the new state.

Overall, then, Chinese policy from 1949 to 1954 was characterised by the official recognition and institutionalisation of Chinese medicine. The government tried to extract traditional therapists from their old lineages of secret transmission, and integrate them into state-controlled modern health institutions. Traditional doctors, who had previously operated independently and privately, were integrated into specialised medical work units. Chinese medicine research societies were established to stimulate the sharing of

15 Agren 1975: 42; Croizier 1973: 4.
16 Ye Xiaoqing 2002.
17 Croizier 1973: 9; Croizier 1968: 158–9.

knowledge and experience among traditional doctors, who were used to jealously guarding their secret formulas. Learned journals were launched and formal training institutes were set up to increase rapidly the number of medical workers. Fifteen thousand 'unified' clinics and hospitals were built, integrating modern and traditional doctors under one roof.

The nationalisation of the traditional medical profession was justified for pragmatic reasons: the lack of modern medical personnel and the low cost of traditional healing. Though legitimised, Chinese medicine still had a lower status than Western medicine. Traditional doctors were excluded from joining the prestigious Chinese Medical Association, and from practising in the best hospitals in the capital. Recognition of Chinese medicine was seen as a temporary measure, modern medicine—or a new integrated medicine guided by the laws of dialectical materialism—being destined to replace it gradually. Although the Party encouraged modern doctors to make use of indigenous resources, little was done to end their prejudice against traditional medicine.[18]

BEGINNINGS OF THE FIRST QIGONG WAVE, 1954–9

Modern, socialist 'Chinese medicine' at first mainly included the professions of herbalist and acupuncturist. Between 1949 and 1954 *qigong* was not yet recognised or disseminated on a national scale. But its development continued in Hebei province. Liu Guizhen continued his clinical work on *qigong*, first in Xingtai, then in Baoding, and finally in Tangshan, where his political patron Cheng Yulin, who had been promoted to municipal Party secretary, invited him and his team to establish a *qigong* centre at the Tangshan Workers' Sanatorium. One wing, containing ten rooms, was allocated to what would become the world's first specialised *qigong* institution. The provincial health department budgeted for the construction of a new 100-bed ward for the *qigong* sanatorium, where treatment was to be reimbursed by the state. Patients, who came from Beijing, Tianjin and the surrounding area, practised *qigong* for seven hours per day. Most suffered from 'neurasthenia' and gastric disorders. Liu Guizhen's teacher Liu Duzhou was put in charge of the overall *qigong* coaching for patients. In its first year the Tangshan centre

18 Croizier 1968: 166. See also Taylor 2002 for a detailed study of Chinese medicine in the years 1949–53.

held five training and healing workshops for medical personnel from hospitals in the area.[19]

Official support for Liu Guizhen's work should be seen in the context of an ideological turn against Western medicine, which became a casualty of the struggle between 'Reds' and 'Experts'—a conflict which began in 1953 and grew in intensity until its culmination in the Great Leap Forward of 1959–61.[20] In high demand for their rare medical expertise, Western medical doctors, by virtue of their scientific training, were inclined to see their profession as independent from politics. For them, technical issues were more important than political ones when making decisions and considering therapeutic strategies. Such an attitude cast into doubt the Party's capacity to supervise doctors' scientific and technical work. Furthermore, because they had been trained abroad or in missionary colleges, they were tainted by their association with imperialist bourgeois culture.

The institutions of Chinese medicine, on the other hand, as creations of the Communist state, were more docile and grateful to the Party authorities. Though traditional doctors were told to study scientific methods and to share their secrets, they were never subject to intensive criticism or to ideological reform—not because they were free from 'feudal' influences, but because they posed no threat to the new political order. On the contrary, says Croizier, from 1954 onwards newspapers praised them for their correct political attitude. Images of the venerable doctor with his white beard came to symbolise the new regime's love and concern for the healthy elements of the old culture, after long years of indifference and neglect before 1949.[21]

With the growing rift between Maoist China and the Soviet Union, Chinese medicine further benefited from an increasing nationalism and appreciation of native civilisation. The exaltation of the 'cultural heritage of the motherland' was expressed not only in medicine, but also in architecture, theatre and painting. A campaign against several leaders of the state's medical institutions, known for their bias towards Western medicine, coincided with the fall of their allies in the pro-Russian faction in the Party.[22]

---

19 Li Zhiyong 1988: 418; QG 2(1): 48; JSK (I) (2).
20 Croizier 1968: 168–72.
21 Croizier 1968: 174.
22 Croizier 1973: 11; Croizier 1968: 176.

The turn against Western medicine was accompanied by an unprecedented expansion of Chinese medicine. The 'popular' roots of the traditional medicine were emphasised; links with feudalism and Confucianism were played down. Traditional medical theory was standardised in a manner compatible with dialectical materialism. A national Chinese medicine research institute was established in 1955, with branches in most provinces. Medical journals devoted a growing proportion of their pages to articles on Chinese medicine. Acupuncture became a required subject in medical schools, and the most talented graduates were given intensive training. In 1956 specialised colleges of Chinese medicine were founded in Beijing, Shanghai, Guangzhou and Chengdu, as well as hundreds of lesser training schools. Over one hundred specialised hospitals of Chinese medicine were built. The mass media frequently published reports of remarkable cures.[23]

The three years from 1955 to 1958 were thus marked by the large-scale organisation of a vast institutional system of Chinese medicine—a movement which spurred the development of *qigong*.[24] In 1954–5 Liu Guizhen was sent three times to report to the national health authorities in Beijing. Health minister Li Dequan, in a speech reported in the front page of the *People's Daily*, publicly congratulated Liu Guizhen for his work and, at the inauguration ceremony of the China Academy of Chinese Medicine, gave his sanatorium an award of 3,000 yuan, a large sum at the time.[25] A year later Liu was honoured by Mao as an 'All-China Advanced Worker' at the All-China Conference of Heroes of the Masses, and he was received by the highest leaders of the Party including Vice-President Liu Shaoqi (1898–1969), Vice-Premier Li Fuchun (1900–75) and State Council member Chen Yi (1901–72).[26]

In June 1956 the Hebei provincial Health Department assigned Liu Guizhen to open a second, even larger *qigong* sanatorium at the prestigious seaside resort of Beidaihe, where the provincial cadres' sanatorium was henceforth designated as an institution specialised

23 Agren 1975: 42; Croizier 1968: 167–80; Croizier 1973: 10–11.
24 This movement, launched for ideological reasons and spurred by Mao's pronouncements, met with constant resistance from the medical establishment dominated by Western-trained medical professionals. On the internal dynamics of the health policy process in the early PRC, see Lampton 1977.
25 RR, 20 December 1955: 1; GR, 30 August 1995: 5; Che Guocheng and Ke Yuwen 1997: 21; JSK (I).
26 ZG 81: 4; ZGL: 6.

solely in *qigong*.[27] The Beidaihe Qigong Sanatorium would be the principal *qigong* institution in China until 1965, with the responsibility of training *qigong* clinicians for the whole country. Altogether, from its establishment until 1964 the sanatorium treated 3,000 patients and trained 700 *qigong* medical workers. Party leaders, who often went to the Beidaihe resort for political meetings—and who were under considerable mental stress—received *qigong* treatment at the Sanatorium, including Liu Shaoqi, Chen Yi, Li Fuchun, CCP founding member and Supreme Court Chairman Dong Biwu (1886–1975), Long March veteran and Politburo member Lin Boqu (1886–1960), Long March veteran Ye Jianying (1897–1986) and International Trade Minister Ye Jizhuang (1893–1967). Liu Shaoqi is reported to have personally intervened to secure funding for the construction of new buildings and the purchase of equipment for the Sanatorium.[28]

Other, less important Party leaders also became *qigong* enthusiasts and would play an important role in its development. For example, Wang Juemin, the Baoding Municipal Party Secretary, had undergone *qigong* treatment for leg injuries while Liu was based in his city. The injury, which had become gangrenous and threatened to spread to his whole body, significantly improved after a few months of practice, turning Wang Juemin into a passionate promoter of *qigong*. He became something of a celebrity in Hebei, and was consulted on *qigong* by his colleagues in the government.[29]

Benefiting from such political support, *qigong* quickly spread within medical institutions. Seventy *qigong* units were founded by the end of the 1950s, including clinics and sanatoria. One of the most influential was the eighty-bed Shanghai Qigong Sanatorium, founded by Chen Shou (b. 1922).[30] This centre developed the 'Relaxation Qigong' method (*fangsonggong*), based on Jiang Weiqiao's sitting meditation method, which had been popular before 1949.[31] The method involved concentrating on different parts of the body while repeating the character *song* (relax), until one entered a state

[27] JSK [II].
[28] ZG 81: 4; JSK.
[29] Heise 1999: 98; ZGL: 5. During the 1980s Wang Juemin would found the Baoding Qigong Hospital and become a key member of the Baoding Qigong Association (Sumrall 1998: ch. 4).
[30] QG 5(6): 282.
[31] Cf. Despeux 1997: 270; Kohn 2002.

of deep relaxation.[32] Chen Shou, as a young intellectual from a wealthy family, had joined the CCP propaganda work in the liberated areas after graduating from the missionary-run St John's University. Injured in the eye and suffering from nervous and neurological damage as a result of an accidental discharge of his pistol, he had begun practising *qigong* and *taijiquan* in 1955, and after a significant recovery dedicated himself completely to *qigong* work. He networked with masters of traditional body technologies, including Jiang Weiqiao, visited the Tangshan and Beidaihe sanatoria, and sent seven recuperating cadres to Mt Tiantai to study meditation under Taoist master Wu Zhiyuan, before establishing the Shanghai sanatorium in 1957.[33]

Liu Guizhen published a book on his methods, *The Practice of Qigong Therapy*,[34] in 1957. As the first modern work on *qigong*, its influence was considerable; reprinted in 1982, two million copies were printed in total.[35] The book popularised the concept of *qigong*, which would no longer be a specialised term used only in official *qigong* units. The book's presentation of the concept and method of *qigong* practice became a standard model which would be followed in most of the *qigong* literature until the 1990s. Following the publication of Liu's book, a dozen other works were also released between 1957 and 1964.[36]

Famous masters of traditional body technologies were called on to participate in *qigong*'s development. Zhou Qianchuan (1908–71) was assigned to the Shanxi Institute of Chinese Medicine in 1958, where he prepared a book on *qigong*, which explained in simple language the esoteric formulas of the Emei tradition, which he tried to strip of its 'superstitious' garment:

In the past, [*qigong*] was practised by few people, and had superstitious colouration; they used it to fool people and to attract disciples; at the same time, they usurped for themselves the jewel left in heritage by the forefathers of ancient times. Fathers did not transmit to sons, nor husbands to

32 Liu Guizhen 1981 [1957]: 130–2.
33 JSK [III].
34 Liu Guizhen 1981 [1957].
35 QG 5(6): 282.
36 Li Zhiyong 1988: 419–20. See for example Chen Yingning 1963 [1957]; Jiang Weiqiao 1981 [1956]; Jiang Weiqiao and Liu Guizhen 1958; Hu Yaozhen 1959; Qin Chongsan 1959; Zhou Qianchuan 1967 [1959]; Shanghai shi qigong liaoyangsuo 1958; Zhejiang sheng zhongyiyao yanjiusuo 1959.

wives, but in a most conservative way used it as a tool to establish lineages and compete with other sects. As a result, this type of health-preserving and therapeutic medicine, which was compatible with scientific principles, buried its fine essence, and became clothed in superstitious garments, so that people came to perceive it wrongly as empty mystical talk.[37]

Further, Jiang Weiqiao, author of bestselling books on sitting meditation in the early Republican period,[38] now 81 years old, was invited to give a workshop at the Beidaihe Sanatorium in 1957.[39] He and Liu Guizhen co-edited a collection of papers on *qigong* therapy.[40] Chen Yingning, a well-known moderniser of Taoist inner alchemy, was hired by the Zhejiang Provincial Workers' Sanatorium to teach still meditation (*jinggong*) at its newly established department of quiet sitting therapy and rehabilitation, located at scenic Mount Fengping. He gave lectures, directed practice sessions, and prepared pamphlets for publication.[41] In the same year, he was elected to the leadership of the newly formed China Taoist Association, the official state-controlled organisation for Taoists, of which he became Secretary-General in 1961. According to Liu Xun's study of Chen Yingning, Liu Guizhen was said to hold Chen Yingning in high regard, having once stood all night long outside his sleeping quarters at Beijing's White Cloud Monastery, seeking permission for an interview.[42]

The process of *qigong*'s institutionalisation is illustrated by the case of master Dai Junying of the Bronze Bell tradition. This tradition had been transmitted in a lineage of successive masters and disciples until 1956, when its body technologies were incorporated in the new medical institutions. According to legend, the Bronze Bell technique had been founded by Bodhidharma, the sixth-century patriarch known as the creator of Chan Buddhism and of the Shaolin school of martial arts. After the end of the Ming dynasty

37 Zhou Qianchuan 1961: 1–2; see also Zhou Qianchuan 1967 [1959]. Zhou was born in a literati family and studied military engineering in Germany and England. After falling gravely ill, he had become a disciple of Emei monk Yong Yan in 1939, and acquired a reputation as a highly accomplished master (JSK [III]).

38 Jiang Weiqiao 1974 [1917].

39 Ding Shu 1993: ch. 16. Jiang reportedly committed suicide shortly after the workshop, upon learning that his son had been labelled a rightist.

40 Jiang Weiqiao and Liu Guizhen 1958. See also Yin Shizi 1962 [1955]: 19–23; Jiang Weiqiao 1981 [1956]: 12–19.

41 Liu Xun 2001: 75–6. See Chen Yingning 2000: 371–83.

42 Liu Xun 2001: 84 n. 67.

the method was primarily known in Sichuan. Around 1860 the monk Honghong left Mt Emei for Zhejiang, where he transmitted the lineage to Bi Xuejing, who taught it to his son-in-law Chen Chucai, from whom Dai Junying learned it in 1903. Dai started teaching the method in 1926, and founded an association to treat chronic illnesses with the Bronze Bell technique. In 1956, on the invitation of the Zhejiang Health Department, he founded a *qigong* clinic at the provincial hospital of Chinese medicine, and published the results of his clinical *qigong* research in the *Zhejiang Journal of Chinese Medicine* in 1958 and 1959.[43]

The choice of the term *qigong* to designate all such practices was not wholeheartedly accepted by all specialists. Jiang Weiqiao, author of the *Sitting Meditation of Master Yinshi*,[44] which had been so influential in the first half of the century, wrote, 'now everyone calls it *qigong*; actually this name is not suitable, but since it's already in common usage, I can only follow the flow. In past times, it was called the "method for nourishing life [*yangshengfa*]".'[45] Chen Shou, founder of the Shanghai Qigong Sanatorium, warned, 'if we take the character *qi* in *qigong* therapy to mean certain phenomena of the activity of the human body's nervous system, we can easily understand [the choice of the term], but if we insist to say that it's the effect of the mysterious cosmic *qi* in the human body, it will be impossible to throw off the mystical garment, and [*qigong* will be unable to] become a method to heal illnesses and nourish life for the great masses of people.'[46] Chen Yingning emphasised the distinction between his *jinggong*, which required only stillness and natural breathing, and *qigong*, which he defined as based on breath and *qi* training. For Chen, the term *qigong* had become 'excessively complicated' now that techniques ranging from martial arts *qi* training to Taoist inner alchemy and Buddhist visualisations were also being included under the category. He claimed that *jinggong* was more effective, easier to learn, and involved fewer health risks from incorrect practice than *qigong*.[47]

[43]   QG 4(5): 199.
[44]   Jiang Weiqiao 1974 [1917].
[45]   Jiang Weiqiao 1981 [1956]: 12.
[46]   Quoted in GR, 30 August 1995: 5.
[47]   Chen Yingning 2000: 371–83.

GREAT LEAP FORWARD FOR QIGONG, 1959–61

The first wave of *qigong* peaked during the Great Leap Forward, from 1959 to 1961, when the whole notion of a medical science run by a specialised caste of experts was condemned. Just as engineers had to learn from workers and agronomists from farmers, doctors had to study the art of folk healers.[48] The medical question was deemed to be an important front in the struggle between the bourgeoisie and the proletariat.[49] The *Guangming Daily* condemned the 'bourgeois prejudice' which considers medicine to be a science reserved for a small number of experts: medicine comes from the experience of the masses and must mobilise mass participation.[50]

Chinese medicine was promoted as part of Mao's 'popular democratic culture'.[51] Large quantities of secret and folk remedies were collected and published in a movement aiming to promote the medical wisdom of the masses. The press reported countless remarkable cures due to simple remedies, and 'popular experts' were invited into the hospitals and medical schools. Thanks to its identification with non-professional popular culture, Chinese medicine, and by extension *qigong*, became central to the nation's health policy during the Great Leap Forward.[52] Seventy *qigong* units were founded by the end of the 1950s, including clinics and sanatoria. A national conference on *qigong* was held in 1959 and a national *qigong* training course was organised a year later.[53] Several research units began clinical and laboratory trials on the physiological effects of *qigong*. Over 300 articles on *qigong* had been published in medical journals by the early 1960s.[54] *Qigong* was even exported to the Soviet Union, where it was used to treat 500 tuberculosis patients.[55]

At a national meeting on the 'Great Leap Forward for the Cause of Health', held in Beijing in 1959, the Health Ministry praised *qigong*'s contribution to disease prevention and therapy, and gave a

---

48 Croizier 1973: 13. On Chinese medicine during the Great Leap Forward, see Hillier and Jewell 1983: 86–8.
49 Croizier 1968: 184.
50 GM, 3 November 1958: 3.
51 Croizier 1968: 186.
52 Croizier 1968: 187–8; see also GM, 6 December 1958: 1, 2.
53 ZGL: 348–9; ZG 81: 5; JSK [I].
54 JSK [I]; Li Zhiyong 1988: 419–22. See also Tao Bingfu and Yang Weihe 1981 for a compilation of articles published during this period.
55 Heise 1999: 96.

financial award to the Shanghai Qigong Sanatorium.[56] *Qigong* was taught or employed in eighty-six work units in Shanghai. On 25 July 1961 the Health Minister published an article praising the benefits of *qigong* in the *China Youth News*.[57] Clearly, *qigong* was benefiting from the exalted political position of Chinese medicine during the Great Leap.

THE POLITICAL WINDS TURN AGAINST QIGONG, 1962–4

However, at the beginning of the 1960s the official attitude toward Chinese medicine began to cool. From 1961 to 1964 *qigong* activities continued, but didn't expand the way they had in previous years. This can perhaps be linked to the struggle which pitted Mao against the CCP bureaucracy in the wake of the disaster of the Great Leap Forward. *Qigong* became a victim of Mao's campaign against the élite Party leaders who were the political supporters and principal clientele of *qigong*. The Governor and the Party Secretary of Hebei Province, who were the targets of a political campaign, were harshly criticised for practising *qigong*.[58]

At the beginning of 1964 rumours began to circulate against Wang Juemin, the municipal Party Secretary of Baoding, who had become an enthusiastic promoter of *qigong*.[59] It was made known that for a Party secretary to take such an interest in *qigong* was unbecoming. A series of criticisms and interrogations was launched against him, culminating in his punishment in the summer of 1965, which was circulated nationally. Wang was subjected to intense criticism sessions, incarcerated, made to join in forced labour, and in 1967 was starved of food and drink for seven days. He later claimed to have survived thanks to his *qigong* practice. Zhou Qianchuan, who had become a close associate of Wang Juemin, was accused of being a spy who used his strong relationship with this Party secretary to infiltrate and corrupt official circles and to steal state secrets.

No new text on *qigong* was published after 1965. In March that year the *New Physical Education* magazine criticised the abuse of

---

56   Lin Housheng 1988: 37; JSK [III].
57   Wang Buxiong and Zhou Zhirong 1989: 516.
58   JSK [III].
59   See p. 37.

qigong by quacks who took advantage of the healing powers of *qigong*, and condemned *qigong*'s promotion of 'superstitious' concepts of tranquillity and harmony, which were 'completely contrary to our active physical training ... in the interest of contributing even more to the construction of socialism'.[60]

A storm of attacks on *qigong* then flooded the press. *Qigong* was stigmatised as a 'rotten relic of feudalism', 'rubbish of history', 'vitalism' and 'absurd stories'. Liu Guizhen was denounced as the 'creator of the poisonous weed of *qigong*' and as a 'class enemy'. He was expelled from the Party, fired from his position at the Beidaihe Sanatorium, demoted seven ranks in the official hierarchy, and sent to the Shanhaiguan farm for reeducation. In 1969 the staff at the Tangshan clinic were assigned to sweep the streets and clean the public toilets of the city.[61] The Beidaihe Sanatorium was closed, *qigong* activities were stopped, and the staff made to criticise *qigong*. The remaining units were closed during the campaign against the 'Four Olds' in the mid 1960s.[62] Chen Shou was reassigned to a minor clinic, and in 1968 died at the age of forty-six under stress from intense criticism after the beginning of the Cultural Revolution.[63] Zhou Qianchuan died of illness in prison in 1971.[64]

The years 1949 to 1964 represent the first phase in the history of modern *qigong*, the period during which it was born and acquired an institutional form which would reconstitute itself at the end of the 1970s to become the foundation of the *qigong* boom of the 1980s and 1990s.

Modern *qigong* was designed to serve the needs of the new medical institutions of the People's Republic: with *qigong*, traditional body technologies became an instrument of state power. The method elaborated by Liu Guizhen became the model of *qigong* organisation and practice, and was reproduced in medical institutions throughout China. This model differs in many ways from the traditional practice of Chinese body technologies. Conceptual references were reformulated. The effects of practice were described

60　XTY, March 1965: 25–6, quoted in Agren 1975: 43.
61　JSK [III].
62　ZGL: 7.
63　JSK [III].
64　JSK [IV].

in physical and chemical terms, and concepts of yin–yang and *qi* were standardised and materialised as expressions of 'primitive dialectics' compatible with Marxist philosophy. The method of transmission was changed entirely. Useful therapeutic techniques were secularised and extracted from their traditional social and symbolic settings: master–disciple lineages were replaced by cohorts of 'medical workers' operating in institutional settings. Secret transmission was replaced by formal training courses. Instead of becoming the source of esoteric knowledge, practitioners' bodies were used as subjects for clinical research based on biomedical categories. The term '*qigong* master' was not common; the traditional image of the 'master' with its charismatic connotations was replaced by the notion of the modern doctor, the *qigong* 'medical worker' engaged in a scientific enterprise. The old sectarian organisations and medical lineages were replaced by a community of *qigong* specialists who were trained in state health institutions, worked in official settings, met at conferences to exchange their experiences, conducted clinical research, published the results of their work, and held public training classes.

The *qigong* of the 1950s was thus a resolutely modern enterprise, a conscious rupture with the forms of the past. It was thanks to this 'revolutionary' approach that *qigong* could find legitimacy until the mid 1960s. The specialised sanatoria and prestigious urban hospitals in which *qigong* was practised during this period were places reserved for the Party élite. But with its roots in Chinese popular culture, without any link with the capitalist West and its specialist approach to science, requiring no expensive technology, and easy and cheap to teach and learn, *qigong* fit well with the spirit of the Great Leap Forward, which saw a rapid expansion of *qigong* activity and research. Indeed there was a profound affinity between *qigong*, which aims to heal through pure mental effort, and the Great Leap Forward, which promised to propel China to utopia through the simple effect of collective willpower.[65]

The expansion of *qigong* can also be seen in light of a new construction of the body under the socialist regime, expressed by Mao's slogan 'Develop physical culture and sports, strengthen the people's physiques' (*fazhan tiyu yundong, zengqiang renmin tizhi*). Building the new state required a population of strong, healthy bodies which

65 See Friedman 1983: 58.

could increase productivity and defend the nation against its enemies, erasing the label of 'Sick man of East Asia' that the foreign powers had used to deride China. Making physical exercise available to the masses was a way to discipline and strengthen the bodies of the people.[66] The modernisation and expansion of Chinese medicine and of *qigong* could fit into the construction of the socialist body—but not under any conditions. In his oldest surviving piece of writing, 'A Study of Physical Culture', published in 1917, Mao attacked the technique of quiet meditation (*jingzuo*) popular during the Republican period, as instilling passivity: 'there is nothing between heaven and earth that is not activity.'[67] Mao's favouring of active sports may be one reason for the dominance of gymnastic exercises in the *qigong* of the 1950s rather than still meditation, although the latter certainly did not disappear from *qigong*. Rooted in popular practices, but taught in élite medical institutions for Party intellectuals, *qigong* had an ambiguous status in the body politics of the young communist state—an ambiguity which would contribute to its banning at the onset of the Cultural Revolution.

For reasons both practical and ideological, traditional body technologies thus flourished as a branch of institutionalised Chinese medicine in the 1950s. Entirely an instrument of state modernisation and political campaigns, *qigong* during this period did not develop the alternative social networks and ideologies that would emerge in the 1980s. Elements that would spur its massive dissemination had not yet been incorporated to *qigong*: mass practice in parks, healing by external *qi*, charismatic healing sessions, the use of mystical and religious symbols, and the emergence of autonomous organisations and networks. Before the Cultural Revolution *qigong* did benefit from a high degree of official support—because it was practised by élite Party cadres, strictly within the confines of official state institutions. *Qigong* thus acquired legitimacy and a niche within the state system, from which it could expand as a mass movement in the 1980s.

---

66 Brownell 1995: 56–8.
67 Quoted in Miura 1989: 334.

2

POLITICAL NETWORKS AND THE FORMATION OF THE QIGONG SECTOR

GUO LIN AND THE RESURRECTION OF QIGONG

There were no officially sanctioned *qigong* activities in China from 1965 until its rehabilitation in 1978, after the end of the Cultural Revolution. However, one woman, Guo Lin, an artist and cancer victim from Guangdong province who had cured herself by practising *qigong* during the1960s, was brave enough to teach *qigong* to other cancer patients in the parks of Beijing as early as 1970, in the middle of the Cultural Revolution. Her 'New Qigong Therapy' inaugurated a new, collective form of *qigong* teaching and practice that would later be adopted by most *qigong* masters, stimulating a new excitement for *qigong* at the end of the 1970s. Guo Lin can thus be said to have triggered the *qigong* wave of the 1980s.

Born near Zhongshan, Guangdong in 1909, Guo Lin was trained as a young girl in traditional body technologies by her paternal grandfather, a Taoist in Macau, where her family had fled following the 1911 revolution which overthrew the Manchu emperor and established the first Chinese Republic. Later, as a student of landscape painting, she visited several holy mountains; the breathing technique she used when climbing the steep slopes would become the basis for her future *qigong* method. She became an art teacher at various academies in Hong Kong and Shanghai.

In 1949 Guo Lin was hit by uterine cancer, which was treated by hysterectomy. The cancer recurred in 1959 while she was assigned to the new Beijing Painting Academy. The first *qigong* wave was at its peak. Guo Lin remembered the techniques she had learned in her youth, and decided to practise them to treat her cancer.

She took up the Five Animals Frolic,[1] and delved into books on *qigong* theory, Chinese and Western medicine, physiology, pathology, acupuncture and meridian theory. Her cancer was cured after ten years of practice and experimenting. Guo Lin synthesised her experience in the form of a *qigong* method for treating cancer and chronic illness, based on the new technique of 'wind breathing', which modified certain aspects of traditional body technologies and of Liu Guizhen's method. She began teaching her method to people suffering from cancer and chronic illnesses in 1970. Her first student, a worker who suffered from serious heart disease, was cured after practising her *qigong*. Her second student, a factory worker, was cured of his stomach cancer after a year of assiduous practice under Guo Lin's guidance.

Encouraged by these results and by the growing number of people who wanted to learn her *qigong*, she began to teach her method publicly in Dongdan Park in 1971. The word spread; the number of practitioners increased; many recovered their health. She organised the learners into practice groups and taught them the theory and practice of her 'New Qigong Therapy', teaching different techniques to different patients depending on their condition.[2]

Accused of fooling people and of engaging in superstitious activities, Guo Lin was expelled from Dongdan Park. She moved her base to Longtanhu Park, where she was also harassed. Two of her assistant trainers were arrested and imprisoned for twenty days, her home was searched, and her *qigong* materials confiscated.[3] Between 1971 and 1977 Guo Lin was interrogated seven times by the Public Security Bureau, and was criticised on numerous occasions by her work unit. She changed parks several times, moving from Longtanhu to the Temple of Earth, and then to the banks of the Liupukang river.[4] In spite of the harassment, the number of people who came to practise *qigong* with her grew, until she was able to train coaches to lead practice groups in other parks, and an informal organisation of practitioners was created to study and publicise her method. Her

---

1   The Five Animals Frolic (*Wuqin xi*), attributed to the famous Han dynasty surgeon Hua Tuo, involves imitating the movements and bodily dispositions of the tiger, the deer, the bear, the monkey and the crane. See Despeux 1988 for the history and translation of this method.

2   Tao Bingfu 1994: 13; see also Lü Yulan and Cheng Xia 1988: 85–93.

3   Zheng Ping 1994: 302.

4   Tao Bingfu 1994: 14; Zheng Ping 1994: 302.

method was published in mimeograph form in 1975.[5] Interest was so great that she abandoned a plan to emigrate to the United States, where her daughter was living.[6]

Guo Lin began to enjoy the support of Party cadres who had benefited from her method. Gao Wenshan, a retired Navy officer, became an ardent promoter of Guo Lin's *qigong*. Using his official car, he took Guo Lin and her assistants to several work units, looking for a permanent base for teaching and practice. Finally, in 1977, two officials at Beijing Normal University took the risk of offering their campus as a centre for Guo Lin's activities.

Mao had died and the Cultural Revolution had ended. Sensing the new political climate, Guo Lin submitted a report to the health ministry which, summarising seven years of experience teaching *qigong*, claimed that it was a cure for cancer.[7] Her method, which advocated training the mind and the body for the 'mental struggle against cancer', was published as an article in the magazine *Scientific World*.[8] She began to organise regular, formal courses at Beijing Normal University. 'Experience sharing assemblies' were also held, at which practitioners could share and summarise the benefits of the method. Guo Lin was invited to lecture at dozens of universities, factories and official units.[9] Thousands of people began to learn her *qigong* method in parks and public spaces around the country.

The Cultural Revolution had thus failed to eradicate *qigong*. As we shall see in chapter 4, most of the masters of traditional body technologies had simply continued to transmit their techniques secretly. And Guo Lin, who didn't fear teaching in the open, brought a key innovation to *qigong*: by inaugurating group practice in parks, she freed *qigong* from the medical institutions. A new style of *qigong* was born, heavily marked by the mass culture of the Mao era: *qigong* was no longer confined to the institutions of the Party élite, but became a grassroots popular movement. Instead of traditional masters giving secret initiations or professional medical workers providing one-on-one clinical instruction, amateur enthusiasts led free

5 Zheng Ping 1994: 305.
6 Tao Bingfu 1994: 15.
7 Tao Bingfu 1994: 10.
8 Zheng Ping 1994: 305. *Kexue yuandi*, 25 October 1979 (I have not been able to locate this magazine).
9 QG 1(1): 23.

collective practice sessions in public spaces. The standardised set of exercises in Guo Lin's book could be learned by anyone and was replicable anywhere. Guo Lin became something of a celebrity. Her 'New Qigong Therapy' quickly spread to most cities in China and even to several Western countries. Other *qigong* methods were also popularised and spread to all parts of China within less than a year. By the end of the 1970s it was not rare to see more than a dozen different *qigong* methods being practised in the same park on a given morning.

GU HANSEN DISCOVERS THE PHYSICAL NATURE OF 'EXTERNAL QI'

The end of the 1970s was a period of intellectual ferment: a wind of freedom was blowing through the Chinese scientific world. Scientism became the new creed for the development of the country. In this context *qigong* resurfaced, not only as therapy, but also as scientific discovery, indeed as a new form of high technology. After the fall of the 'Gang of Four' the new leadership headed by Deng Xiaoping introduced in 1977 the new policy of the 'Four Modernisations' to guide the development of China: the modernisation of agriculture, of industry, of national defence, of science and technology. The modernisation of science was seen as the most important of the four: indeed, the other three depended on it. On 18 March 1978, at a national party congress on the sciences, which brought together 6,000 delegates, ambitious plans for scientific development were unveiled.[10] Since the 1950s defence had been the highest priority in scientific policy, which was continued under the new plan, with lasers, space research and nuclear fusion being priority projects. As noted by one scholar, 'research priorities were noteworthy more for their state-of-the-art scientific glamour and prestige than for their techno-economic feasibility.'[11] As we shall see, leading figures in the military science community would see *qigong* as the key to directly overcoming the material obstacles to attaining those ambitious scientific objectives. The government also launched a 'patriotic movement for health' to improve the level of health and hygiene of the population,[12] and decided on an 'ac-

10   RR, 12 March 1978: 1.
11   Wang, Yeu-Farn 1993: 83–4.
12   RR, 8 April 1978: 1.

celerated development' of Chinese medicine.[13] *Qigong*, because of its simplicity, its efficacy and its inexpensiveness, fit well with the objectives of the campaign.

As soon as the Cultural Revolution had ended some scientists began research on *qigong*. But unlike the clinicians of the 1950s and the 1960s who studied the effects of the practice of *qigong* on the treatment of different diseases, this new generation of researchers was interested above all on the phenomenon of the 'external *qi*' which the master of *qigong* is said to emit from his hands and body in the direction of a patient or an object.[14] One of the pioneers in this new field of research was Dr Feng Lida, daughter of the Christian warlord General Feng Yuxiang (1882–1948), who had controlled much of north China during the 1920s.[15] She was Vice-Director of the National Navy Hospital when, in 1977, her interest in *qigong* was triggered by the case of a cancer victim who was cured after practising Guo Lin's *qigong*, in spite of having been given only a few months to live. Feng hoped to determine if *qigong* had a scientific basis. She invited *qigong* master Bao Guiwen, who during the 1940s had been a leading disciple of sectarian patriarch and *qi* virtuoso Xiao Changming,[16] to emit external *qi* to objects

---

[13] RR, 2 November 1978: 2.

[14] This technique is mentioned for the first time in the *History of the Jin Dynasty*, and described in *Master Yanling's Book on the Ancient and New Techniques for Swallowing One's Breath*, a text in the Taoist canon which brings together materials of the Tang and previous dynasties (Despeux 1988: 20). Before the period of modern *qigong*, this technique was called 'to pour out the *qi*' (*buqi*). Despeux (1988: 21) points out that this expression is also employed when talismans are used to cure diseases: the talisman contains the *qi* of the master's body, which makes up for the lack of *qi* of the patient (cf. Schipper 1993: 73). The idea resurfaces in the *qigong* of the 1980s, through the notion of 'information objects' (*xinxi wu*), which contained the *qi* emitted by a master and which were employed for therapeutic purposes.

[15] Feng Lida studied acupuncture in Chongqing and Chengdu during the Sino-Japanese war, then followed her parents to the United States, where she studied at the University of California from 1946 to 1948. In 1949 she returned to Communist China and joined its first contingent of students sent to the Soviet Union, where she studied medicine at the University of Leningrad. She returned to China in 1958. In the 1980s she was appointed to a leadership position in the All-China Federation of Women.

[16] Xiao Changming (1895–1944) was the founder of the Heavenly Virtue Teaching (*Tiande shengjiao*), organised as the Society for the Study of Religious Philosophy. In the late 1940s the society moved its headquarters from Huangshan to Hong Kong, while the movement also spread to Taiwan, where one of Xiao's leading disciples, Li Yujie, founded the Heavenly Lord Teaching (*Tiandijiao*) in the 1980s

or substances, and compared the results to those produced by control groups in which an ordinary person would perform the same gestures in front of the same objects or substances. Experiments were conducted on colonic bacilli, typhoid bacilli, dysentery bacilli, white staphylococci, silver staphylococci, contagious viruses and so on. She concluded that external *qi* has the effect of weakening or killing all such micro-organisms. In October 1981 Feng began tests on cancer cells, and concluded that under the effect of external *qi* damage to cancer cells could reach 30 per cent.[17]

In 1979 Gu Hansen, of the Shanghai Institute of Atomic Research, created a sensation by announcing that external *qi* was a measurable physical substance. Afterwards, the concept of external *qi* as a form of matter would be accepted by all the Chinese scientists working on *qigong*. Gu Hansen started her experiments at the end of 1977, independently and without the support of her scientific unit, but in collaboration with the Shanghai Institute of Chinese Medicine, which, under the direction of Lin Hai, had just opened a *qigong* clinic.[18] This is how she recounts the circumstances of her 'discovery':

I study radio electronics, which, originally, has nothing whatever to do with *qigong*. In more than 10 years of work at the Nuclear Research Institute, I devoted myself mainly to the study of devices for the enhancement of micro-signals connected to nuclear electricity. At the end of 1977, by chance, I became acquainted with the therapeutic method of movement by *qi*. With my own eyes, I saw this therapeutic method—without medication, without a needle, and without contact with the body of the patient—succeed in making a paraplegic, paralysed in both legs, able to crouch and to get up. This miraculous event opened new horizons for me, to the extent that I could no longer remain still. I felt I was at the entrance of a new domain—the science of life. Would I have the courage to open this mysterious door?

... I felt my way, I experimented. Given that my work was 'individual and underground' I had to consider, conceive and do everything myself: the difficulties were numerous. How to judge the physical properties of

---

and propagated one of Taiwan's most popular *qigong* forms. On Bao Guiwen, see Fan Shuren 1992. On Xiao Changming and Li Yujie, see Palmer forthcoming c.

17 ZZ 5(9): 653–4; ZZ 5(3): 163–4; ZZ 8(7): 511–13; QDL: 113–16.

18 *Qigong* activities had resurfaced in Shanghai before 1976: in that year, the book *Eighteen Methods of Practising Gong* was published jointly by three medical and sporting units of the city, without the actual use of the term *qigong* (cf. Shanghai shi... 1976).

a phenomenon of *qigong*? How to conceive and to construct the detection devices? How to undertake the experiment in detection? And so on. But the future prospects for the study of *qigong*'s miraculous phenomena greatly attracted me: the point and the time of the *qigong* master's emission of *gong* entirely matched with the changes detected by the device; ... where the point of emission of *gong* produces a sensation of heat, the device detects a fluctuation in the low-frequency modulation of infrared electromagnetic rays; when a feeling of numbness follows the meridians until it reaches the point of emission of *gong*, the device detects a concentration of static electricity or of low frequency magnetic signals; when, before the emission of *gong*, the end of the finger is swollen, when during the emission of *gong* there is a feeling of matter emitted outwards, and when, after the emission of *gong*, the finger contracts, the device detects a micro-particle current. The physical detectors that I used and which were at a distance from the body [of the subject], detected the four types of signals of external *qi* as they are described above. These facts tell us that this invisible and untouchable *qi* possesses an objective physical basis. It is a form (or several forms) of physical movement. It is a particular manifestation of the form of life.[19]

Because the devices available in Shanghai were not advanced enough, the experiments were continued in Beijing, at the Institute of Mechanics of the Chinese Academy of Sciences, with the help of the researchers Hao Jingyao and Lin Zhongpeng. The results were equally encouraging for the researchers.[20] Gu Hansen concluded that the external *qi* was a form of particle current.

The experiments of Gu Hansen would later be acclaimed in the world of *qigong* as a historical moment, when the physical existence of the external *qi* was 'proven' with the help of 'modern devices'. Thus *qigong* apologists Li Jianxin and Zheng Qin wrote in 1996:

10 March 1978 can be considered an extraordinary day. This day marks the start of a new age in the history of *qigong* in China. In collaboration, Gu Hansen, of the Centre for Atomic Research of the Academy of Sciences in Shanghai, and Lin Housheng, of the Shanghai Institute of Chinese Medicine, using modern scientific devices to make preliminary measurements on the external *qi* displaced during *qigong* therapy, detected low frequency, infrared ray modulations. This confirms that the *qigong* practitioner emitted electromagnetic waves containing information. It is

---

19 Gu Hansen 1980a: 4–5. The measuring device was invented by Gu Hansen herself, but she refused to divulge the nature of the experiment to allow other researchers to replicate it (QDL: 224).
20 Lin Hai 2000.

the first time that the physical nature of *qi* was proven. The publication of the results of the experiment created waves within the country, aroused interest and drew the attention of numerous scientists towards *qigong* research. Their heroic undertaking had a determining effect on the rise of *qigong* in contemporary China, allowing it to free itself once and for all of the label of 'superstition' and 'sorcery' so long attached to it.[21]

The research team, directed by Lin Hai, presented a report to the directors of the Shanghai Association for Science and Technology in the autumn of 1978, then in the spring of 1979, presented a demonstration of the experiments to the directors of the State Science Commission, the National Association for Science and Technology (NAST), the Ministry of Health and the State Sports Commission. The report claimed, '*qi* has a material basis and objectively exists', and described seven types of physical manifestation of *qi*. It stressed that foreign countries were also conducting research on *qi*, which could lead to significant advances in physics, chemistry, mathematics, biomedicine and bionics, as well as the theory of Chinese medicine.[22] With the encouragement of General Ye Jianying, who had just overthrown the Gang of Four, putting an end to the Cultural Revolution,[23] Health Minister Qian Xinzhong communicated the 'discovery' to Vice-Premier Fang Yi, responsible for scientific research in the State Council: together, they decided the moment had come to make a formal synthesis of everything that was going on in relation to *qigong*.[24]

THE BEIJING MEETING

On 14 July 1979 Lü Bingkui, director of the ministry of Health's State Administration of Chinese Medicine, chaired a 'meeting for scientific reports on *qigong*' (*qigong kexue huibaohui*) at Beijing's Xiyuan hotel, which was attended by Health Minister Qian Xinzhong, State Sports Commission Director Wang Meng, and several mem-

21 QDL: 224.
22 Lan Sheng 1999: 6; JSK [VI].
23 The Gang of Four refers to the faction led by Mao's wife, Jiang Qing, which took control of the CCP during the 1970s. Four weeks after Mao died on 9 September 1979, Ye Jianying and Hua Guofeng arrested the Gang of Four and their followers, bringing the Cultural Revolution era to an end. They were later sentenced to death or given life sentences.
24 Lin Hai 2000; Lan Sheng 1999: 6.

bers of the State Council: vice-premiers Fang Yi,[25] Geng Biao[26] and Chen Muhua,[27] as well as two hundred scientists, officials and journalists.[28] Research papers on the material nature of external *qi* were presented by Gu Hansen of Shanghai, He Qingnian of Beijing and Fan Zao of the China Academy of Sciences. Zhu Runlong, editor-in-chief of *Ziran* magazine,[29] reported on the phenomenon of children able to read with their ears.[30] Gao Wenshan, director of the cultural section of the political department of the navy, gave a talk on his experience in overcoming cancer by practising Guo Lin's *qigong*.[31] A demonstration of 'hard *qigong*' was performed by masters Hou Shuying and Liu Jinrong; the latter broke stones with his fists and snapped a steel pole with his head. Demonstrations of the material impact of *qi* emission were also made, pointing towards Liu's head, at a distance of 60 cm, an electric detector which was connected to a television set on which, to the wonder of the audience, static charges appeared that were so strong the instrument made loud noises and the recording pen broke. Vice-Premier Fang Yi gave a speech strongly encouraging those present to continue research on *qigong* and on other new fields in the knowledge of the human body.[32]

Five days later 500 people attended a follow-up meeting, which was addressed by former Vice-Premier Tan Zhenlin,[33] and which was recorded by a television crew. At the meeting Tan Gaosheng of the China Academy of Science's Institute of Mechanical Physics spoke of the revolutionary implications of the demonstrations he

---

25 Born in 1916, Vice-Premier and President of the China Academy of Sciences, Chairman of the National Science Commission, and member of the Politburo.

26 Born in 1909, veteran of the Long March, appointed to the Politburo in 1977, Vice-Premier in 1978, General Secretary of the Central Military Commission in 1979, named Minister of Defence in 1981.

27 Born in 1920, Vice-Chair of the Party central core, Vice-Premier of the State Council, Chair of the National Patriotic Movement for Health.

28 Lin Hai 2000; Lan Sheng 1999: 6; JSK [VI]; Tao Bingfu and Yang Weike 1981: 10.

29 *Ziran zazhi*—'Nature Magazine'—not to be confused with the American journal of the same name.

30 See pp. 60–3.

31 Zheng Ping 1994: 303.

32 Lan Sheng 1999: 6; JSK [VI].

33 Lan Sheng 1999: 6. Born in 1902, Tan Zhenlin was Vice-Premier from 1959 to 1967, and member of the Politburo from 1973 to 1982.

had just seen, comparing them to the discoveries of Galileo.[34] These meetings were a historical turning point for *qigong*. By bringing together, under high political patronage, most of the main figures involved in *qigong* training, therapy and research, they gave birth to the '*qigong* sector' (*qigong jie*)—a national network which included not only masters and practitioners, but also scientists. *Qigong* was no longer seen as a mere branch of Chinese medicine, but as a scientific discipline in its own right, specialised in investigating the newly-discovered material substance of external *qi*, which could be controlled and projected by the mind. The reports of children who could read with their ears, and the demonstrations of 'hard *qigong*', suggested a possible link between *qigong* and the paranormal. A new concept of *qigong* was forming: the material substance of external *qi*, controlled mentally through *qigong* practice, could induce paranormal ability. A style of public meeting was also inaugurated, combining, in the presence of Officials, scientific reports, demonstrations of extraordinary power and healing testimonies.

Such ideas might not have been followed up if they hadn't been given the nod by members of the State Council. The Beijing meeting marked what was interpreted as the public rehabilitation of *qigong* by the Party and the government, which confirmed, praised and encouraged its development. This was seen as a green light for the organisation and expansion of *qigong* activities, which, in the space of only a year, began to boom all over China. In September 1979 a first academic conference on *qigong* was organised with the support of the Ministry of Health and the NAST.[35] Lü Bingkui and thirty-three other *qigong* promoters in the scientific community presented a report on the Beijing meeting to the State Science Commission and to Party Secretary Hua Guofeng and the CCP Central Committee, requesting the speedy organisation of *qigong* scientific work, including research institutions, personnel, funding, conferences and training. In response to the report, the State Science Commission on 9 April 1980 called representatives of the Health Ministry, the State Sports Commission and the NAST to a meeting which concluded that *qigong* was an integral component of the nation's medicine; that it had both curative and health-enhancing properties; that research on *qigong* was highly significant to the science of human life; that countries such as the United States,

34 JSK [VII].
35 Despeux 1997: 271.

Canada and India were already conducting similar research and that China should do the same under the leadership of the Bureau of Chinese Medicine of the Ministry of Health; that the *qigong* clinics of the capital's main medical establishments, closed since the Cultural Revolution, should be re-opened; and that *qigong* academic societies should be established throughout the country under the sponsorship of the NAST. These suggestions were approved by Wu Heng, deputy director of the State Science Commission.[36] A sure sign of political approval, Gu Hansen's experiments on external *qi* were reported on China Central Television in January 1980,[37] and published in *Ziran* magazine.[38]

PROPAGATION OF GUO LIN'S METHOD

The first person to benefit from *qigong*'s rehabilitation was Guo Lin. All the obstacles to the teaching and dissemination of her method were removed. Several magazines published features on her *qigong* method.[39] Books and compilations of articles on *qigong* were re-issued, including those by Jiang Weiqiao and Zhou Qianchuan.[40] In July 1980 Guo Lin's book, which had until then been printed informally, was published by an official press.[41]

With such publicity, Guo Lin's method attracted growing numbers of practitioners. Sick people converged on Beijing from all over China and even from abroad, seeking relief through her Qigong Therapy. By 1980 Guo Lin *qigong* was practised in twenty provinces as well as in Hong Kong, Macau, Singapore, Japan, the United States and Canada.[42]

At the same time, a new method appeared, the result of a split in Guo Lin's group. In the summer of 1979 Zhang Mingwu, after a dispute with Guo Lin, founded his own method of 'Qigong Self-Control Therapy'.[43] With a burst of firecrackers, he set up his

---

36   JSK [VII].
37   Lin Hai 2000; JSK [IX].
38   Gu Hansen 1980b and c.
39   QG 1(1): 23.
40   Hu Meicheng 1981: 43; see Jiang Weiqiao 1974 [1917]; Zhou Qianchuan 1967 [1959]; compilations include Tao Bingfu and Yang Weihe 1981; Renmin tiyu chubanshe, 1981.
41   Guo Lin 1980a and b; Zheng Ping 1994: 305.
42   ZGL: 31.
43   On this *gongfa*, see Zhang Mingwu and Sun Xingyuan 1982.

practice point just opposite Guo Lin's in Beijing's Temple of Earth Park. A few months later Zhang Mingwu would become one of the founding members and vice-chairman of the Beijing Qigong Research Society.

THE FIRST STATE-SPONSORED QIGONG ASSOCIATIONS

Official recognition of *qigong* was expressed by the founding on 14 December 1979 of the Beijing Qigong Research Society.[44] This 'mass academic association' (*qunzhong xueshu tuanti*), authorised by the Beijing Association for Science and Technology and actively supported by the Beijing Labour Union, was primarily made up of retired cadres who were *qigong* practitioners, as well as of scientific researchers interested in *qigong*. The Society's founders gave themselves the mission of preserving *qigong* for future generations. Responding to the scepticism of some of their leaders, they answered that *qigong* is a 'jewel of the motherland's culture', with an uninterrupted history of over two thousand years.[45]

As an officially registered 'mass' association, the Beijing Qigong Research Society became the intermediary between *qigong* masters—who were suddenly to be found everywhere—and the state. Several masters of traditional body technologies soon presented themselves to the Society, professing their desire to teach their methods to the public. The Society received forty applications for affiliate status, and practice points for various methods appeared in almost all of Beijing's parks.[46]

In processing the applications, the Society elected to follow the lead of Qinghua University, which had decided on a policy of 'letting a hundred flowers bloom and letting a hundred schools compete', without favouring one method over another:

Any method which is proven by experience to be beneficial and not dangerous is welcome on the Qinghua campus. [The masters of these methods] can teach, train and establish practice points at different places on campus. The masses are free to choose the method they prefer.[47]

44 WH: 606.
45 DF 18: 3.
46 DF 18: 3. See Beijing QigongYanjiuhui 1989 for a selection of papers presenting some of the denominations recognised by the association.
47 DF 18: 3.

Similar state-sponsored associations were soon founded in other cities and provinces—the Zhejiang association became one of the most active. The medical *qigong* institutions from before the Cultural Revolution were re-established: *qigong* clinics in the hospitals were reopened; Liu Guizhen and his colleagues were rehabilitated. The Hebei provincial Health Department proclaimed the reopening of the Beidaihe Qigong Sanatorium on 28 October 1980, and reappointed Liu Guizhen as its director.[48] The restored Sanatorium had 200 beds and a new building for *qigong* teaching.[49]

QIGONG MAGAZINE

A self-conscious community of *qigong* practitioners, therapists and researchers was appearing. The public emergence of the *qigong* sector was signalled by the launch of a national *qigong* magazine in the autumn of 1980, by the Zhejiang Institute of Chinese Medicine. The first issue was prefaced by Lü Bingkui, director of the State Administration Bureau of Chinese Medicine, who declared, 'a new scientific discipline has been added to the field of science and technology: *qigong* science.'[50] The quarterly *Qigong* magazine (which would become a monthly in 1987) became a link between the various specialists, masters and practitioners of *qigong*, and would contribute to the elaboration of a common discourse on *qigong* transcending the particular experiences of readers dispersed throughout the country. The magazine presented various *qigong* methods and masters, the results of clinical and laboratory research on *qigong*, the history and classical concepts of *qigong*, advice on how to practise and the occasional report on paranormal phenomena. The authors of the articles included several scientists from prestigious research centres: the China Academy of Science, the China Academy of Chinese Medicine and the Shanghai Institute of Chinese Medicine. Other frequent contributors worked in the Zhejiang provincial government, the Beijing Therapeutic Instruments Factory and the Beijing Pharmaceutical Plant.

---

48   QG 2(1): 48.
49   Despeux 1997: 270.
50   QG 1(1): 1.

A NATIONAL STATE-SPONSORED QIGONG ASSOCIATION

The medium for the diffusion of information on *qigong* having been created, the only thing the *qigong* sector still needed was an institutional structure. In September 1981 this was accomplished when Liu Guizhen and Guo Lin, as well as 120 masters, scientists and officials attended the first national academic conference on *qigong*, held in Baoding (Hebei), site of Liu Guizhen's first *qigong* clinic, to inaugurate the All-China Qigong Scientific Research Society,[51] a branch of the All-China Society for Chinese Medicine, established with the support of the NAST and the Ministry of Health.[52]

A few months later the new association organised a workshop on 'Modern Science and Qigong' at Qinghua University. Twenty scientists discussed the relationship between traditional *qigong* and modern science, and debated the orientation of future research on *qigong*.[53] With the founding of this national *qigong* scientific association, exclaimed *qigong* chronicler Zheng Guanglu,

[*Qigong*] obtained the formal recognition of the medical establishment and firmly entered the temple of Science. From this moment, the flow of this mysterious *qi* which can't be seen or touched, began to circulate not only in parks and streets, but also began to penetrate institutions of higher education and research laboratories.[54]

QIGONG SCIENCE

While the *qigong* sector thus quietly took shape, the mass media became gripped by the strange phenomenon of children reading with their ears. Indeed, parallel to the formation of *qigong* networks of masters, practitioners and scientists, another community was born, that of scientists engaged in research on the paranormal abilities they called 'Extraordinary Powers of the human body' (*renti teyigongneng*). And when paranormal researchers concluded that there was a link between *qigong* and Extraordinary Powers, they triggered a process

---

51 The term 'medical' was added to the organisation's name after 1985, in order to distinguish it from the new China Qigong Science Research Society (CQRS), founded in 1985. (see p. 75).
52 QG 2(4): 170; Ji Yi 1993: 90.
53 Li Zhiyong 1988: 426; JSK [VIII].
54 ZGL: 52.

that led to the fusion of the two in people's imaginations, turning *qigong* into a method for acquiring Extraordinary Powers: the door thus opened for a mass fascination with strange, miraculous, magical and mystical phenomena under the cover of the 'scientific' concept of Extraordinary Powers. This fascination, in turn, provoked an oppositional movement which equated *qigong* to 'pseudo-science' (*wei kexue*).

The Extraordinary Powers craze began in Dazu county, Sichuan province in 1978 with the discovery of a child who could read with his ears. Two schoolboys, Chen Xiaoming and Tang Yu, were walking to school when, suddenly, Tang pointed his finger at Chen's pocket and accused him of hiding a pack of *Feiyan* brand cigarettes in it. Chen denied it, so Tang grabbed him and pulled the cigarettes from his pocket. Chen was amazed that Tang had guessed the existence of the hidden pack: Tang told him that he hadn't seen it with his eyes, but that the image had directly appeared in his brain.

Tang Yu then became known to his schoolmates for his game of 'guess the characters': they would write Chinese characters or drawings on slips of paper, which they would then roll up into a ball and place inside Tang's ear. Tang would then correctly guess which signs were written on the slips of paper.

Tang's teacher took interest in the phenomenon and summoned him to his office for a game of 'guess the characters'. Tang correctly guessed every sentence written by the teacher and hidden in his ear. News of the strange phenomenon, told by the amazed teacher, spread far and wide: one after another, the People's commune, the county government and the district authorities sent investigators to play 'guess the characters' with Tang, and reported the accuracy of the phenomenon.[55]

Sichuan Daily reporter Zhang Naiming, having heard about the matter, also went to Dazu to find out about this strange boy who could read with his ears. Once again Tang Yu passed the test. Asked how he did it, the boy answered, 'when the [paper] ball is placed into my ear, I feel a tingling, and an image of the characters appears in my head like a film projected onto a screen.'[56] On hearing the report, Provincial Governor (and future Premier of China) Zhao Ziyang ordered the provincial Science Commission to investigate and to support research on the phenomenon if it was verified,

---

55   Liu Huajie 2004: 7; ZGL: 69.
56   Quoted in ZGL: 69.

while Provincial Party Secretary Yang Chao received Tang Yu in person.[57]

Zhang Naiming's report was published as a front page story on 11 March 1979.[58] The article included a photograph of Tang Yu with Yang Chao. The publication of this story in a Party newspaper, openly supported by the most powerful leader of one of China's largest provinces, could only be interpreted as an encouragement to investigate and publish such types of phenomena. The report on Tang Yu—who was now living under special protection in Chengdu's most prestigious hotel, the Jinjiang—was reproduced by the press throughout China.[59] Only days later a second-grade primary school student from the Shijingshan district of Beijing, Jiang Yan, was accompanied by local educational officials and teachers to the China Academy of Science, claiming that she also had the ability to read with her ears.[60] In the following three weeks newspapers in Beijing, Hebei, Anhui, Heilongjiang and Jiangsu provinces also reported cases of children who could read, not only with their ears, but also with their hands, their armpits, their feet, and even after having chewed and swallowed the slip of paper,[61] in most cases on the basis of accounts provided by local Science Commissions and Party branches.[62]

A team of investigators from the Sichuan Medical Institute was sent to investigate Tang Yu's abilities. It concluded, however, that Tang Yu's 'reading with ears' was a hoax. After repeated tests the boy either cheated by using sleight-of-hand, or refused to 'read' when it was impossible to cheat.[63] The same conclusion was also made by the Institute of Psychology of the China Academy of Sciences, which tested Jiang Yan: glass fibres and white powder, which had been enclosed in the folded slips of paper, were detected on the

57 Honglinjin zazhishe, 'Guanyu Tang Yu erduo renzi qianhouqingkuang de diaocha baogao', reproduced in Renti teyigongneng diaocha lianluozu, 1985, 'Renti teyigongneng zhenglun shimo', unpublished report, quoted in Liu Huajie 2004: 8.

58 SR, 11 March 1979: 1.

59 RR, 2 June 1979: 4.

60 TJH.

61 RR, 2 June 1979: 4; ZGL: 70; Dong 1984: 79; Ji Yi 1993: 107; TJH; Yu Guangyuan 2002: 10.

62 Liu Huajie 2004: 102.

63 RR, 2 June 1979: 4; 'Sichuan yixueyuan diaocha baogao', quoted in Yu Guangyuan 2002: 10.

ground and on her legs, proving she had unfolded the papers to 'guess' the characters written on them.[64]

On 5 May 1979, following criticism of the phenomenon by the CCP's Propaganda Chief (and future Party Chairman) Hu Yaobang,[65] the *People's Daily* intervened to put an end to the fascination. As part of the commemoration of the May Fourth Movement,[66] the paper published an editorial which called the phenomenon a 'big joke', stressing that the ear is and has always been an organ for hearing, not for reading. 'It is strange', the author wrote, 'that certain comrades in the scientific institutions and in leadership positions don't go to learn from science and scientists, but take the initiative to applaud conjuring tricks, are full of praise for 'magical ears', and go so far as to order that these children be well nourished.'[67] The Institute of Natural Dialectics, led by the influential economist and Marxist theoretician Yu Guangyuan,[68] held a symposium two weeks later to denounce the anti-scientific nature of such claims.[69] Editorials then appeared in many of the main dailies, repenting for their previous reports and attacking the 'fraud' of children reading with their ears, going against the most elementary notions of scientific materialism.[70] Famous educator Ye Shengtao wrote that it was 'simply a loss of face for China'.[71] The editors of the *Sichuan*

[64]   'Zhongguo kexueyuan xinli yanjiusuo dui Jiang Yan de kaocha qingkuang, 23 April 1979, quoted in Yu Guangyuan 2002: 11; Dong 1984: 81; TJH. Note that these reports were never published, while reports favourable to the existence of such phenomena received widespread media coverage till 1995. (see pp. 166–8).

[65]   Yu Guangyuan 2002: 149; TJH.

[66]   The May Fourth movement refers to student protests against China's signing of the treaty of Versailles in 1919, in which China had conceded special privileges to Japan; the term more broadly refers to the intellectual movement to reject tradition and adopt modern science in order to defend the Chinese nation.

[67]   RR, 5 May 1979: 4.

[68]   Born in 1915, Yu Guangyuan, as the Director of the Science Bureau of the Central Propaganda Department, was the Party's chief supervisor of scientific research from the 1950s till the Cultural Revolution. From the end of the Cultural Revolution to 1982 he was Vice-Minister of the State Science Commission and Vice-President of the China Academy of Social Sciences. He was Director of the Institute for Marxist, Leninist and Mao-Zedong Thought Research from 1979 to 1983, and member of the China Academy of Sciences from 1981. According to Miller, Yu Guangyuan consistently defended professional norms of scientific research and opposed excessively ideological approaches (Miller 1996: 92).

[69]   TJH.

[70]   SR, 6 June 1979: 3; RR, 25 February 1982; Dong 1984: 81–2.

[71]   RR, 2 June 1979: 4.

Daily sent a statement of self-criticism to the Provincial Propaganda Department, admitting that they had paid more attention to the newsworthiness of the story than to its factuality. Yang Chao, also in a letter of self-criticism sent to the Central Propaganda Bureau, then accepted responsibility for authorising the article.[72] Reports of such phenomena then disappeared from the press for half a year.

But the Hong Kong newspaper *Ming Pao* published an attack on Yu Guangyuan's editorial, claiming that opposition to extrasensory perception (ESP) was a sign of scientific ignorance and contrary to the spirit of the Four Modernisations.[73] The argument of a link between parapsychology, which had a long history in the West, and China's modernisation would be taken up by believers in Extraordinary Powers in China, who began systematic research in order to prove their existence and explain them scientifically. A key figure in this movement was Zhu Runlong,[74] one of the chief editors of *Ziran*, who presented a report at the July 1979 Beijing meeting,[75] on two sisters, Wang Qiang and Wang Bin, who could read with their ears:

Altogether, twenty-four experiments were made on the two [girls' ability to] recognise characters with their ears or in their armpits. Over 80 per cent of [their responses] were entirely or partly correct. The twenty-four experiments took place over three days, with over ten participants each day. We had the opportunity to take part, and to observe several of the experiments with our own eyes. We were all sitting in a circle around the two sisters, and the nearest observer was only 40 cm away from them. ... On the samples were written Chinese characters, English words, numbers, pictures etc. The most convincing experiment was the following: each of the two girls put on a glove, through which it was impossible to see the slip of paper [placed inside the glove]; then a string was tied around the opening of the glove [at the wrist], and the hand wearing the glove was placed under the armpit, to test the [girl's] recognition [of the characters]. Under these conditions, the two girls were each able to recognise samples on which characters or figures were drawn.[76]

72   Yu Guangyuan 2002: 149; TJH.
73   MB, 18 June 1979.
74   In the early 1980s Zhu Runlong would become the Secretary-General of the China Somatic Science Research Society and editor-in-chief of the journal *Extraordinary Powers Research*.
75   See pp. 53–6.
76   Quoted in ZGL: 72.

Emboldened by the encouragement of the nation's leaders at the Beijing meeting, believers in Extraordinary Powers endeavoured to prove the truth of their claims. The Dazu County Science, Propaganda and Education offices sent a team to conduct new tests on Tang Yu, which concluded that his powers were real, and that the reason he had failed previous investigations was on account of his being ill with enteritis, which had made him lose his powers.[77] This was followed by a report on a new investigation by journalists from the *Sichuan Daily* and scientific workers from Chengdu, which, on the basis of the testimony of local people and further observation of Tang Yu, 'found the boy's said functions to be objective reality'. The report was published in several newspapers.[78]

In September 1979 *Ziran* published a 'Report on the observation of the recognition of images without visual organs', which presented results of experiments on Wang Qiang and Wang Bin's ear-reading ability. Subsequent issues included a series of articles on children capable of reading with their ears, by researchers from Beijing University, Beijing Normal University and other higher academic institutions. Coverage of these phenomena by a major scientific journal gave significant credibility to such research. Editorials and articles on Extraordinary Powers appeared in almost every issue of *Ziran* throughout the 1980s.[79] Other newspapers didn't hesitate to contradict the *People's Daily's* criticism of such research—an audacity rarely seen in China, and which was encouraged by the absence of a response from the *People's Daily*.[80]

THE LINK BETWEEN QIGONG AND EXTRAORDINARY POWERS

Researchers from Beijing University noticed that the sudden appearance of so many children able to read with their ears had occurred after the children had heard about Tang Yu and tried imitating him, discovering they had the same ability. Could it be that such an ability was latent in all humans? Was there a way to develop this capacity? The researchers trained ten ten-year-old children

---

77 Yu Guangyuan 2002: 12; TJH.
78 TR, 9 December 1979: 4; Dong 1984: 82–3; Yu Guangyuan 2002: 13.
79 See Ji Yi 1991: 82; ZZ 3(3): 163; Gu Hansen 1980b and c; ZZ 3(8): 566–7; Qian Xuesen 1981a; ZZ 4(7): 489–91; ZZ 4(7): 492–6 etc.
80 Yu Guangyuan 2002: 17, 150. GM, 23 January 1980: 3.

in breathing, relaxation and verbal suggestion techniques derived from *qigong*, and discovered that after a short training regime, six of them had acquired the ability to recognise characters or illustrations sealed in cloth bags or in ink bottles. The publication of these results stimulated researchers from other institutions to conduct similar experiments, concluding that after training 40 to 60 per cent of ten-year-old children could display Extraordinary Powers.[81]

In February 1980 *Ziran* magazine organised the first National Academic Conference on Extraordinary Powers of the Human Body.[82] The conference, held in Shanghai, signalled the entry of the term 'Extraordinary Powers of the human body' into the Chinese scientific lexicon. Fourteen children with Extraordinary Powers, including Tang Yu, demonstrated their ability to read with their ears or their armpits. Some *qigong* masters and researchers also attended the conference, leading to lively discussions on the link between Extraordinary Powers and *qigong*. Indeed, while Extraordinary Powers had been discovered by chance in children such as Tang Yu, in other subjects it was *qigong* practice which seemed to have triggered their appearance. For instance, for *qigong* master Qu Hanrong, *qigong* had not only cured his paraplegia, but had also developed his Extraordinary Powers. The participants agreed on the hypothesis that Extraordinary Powers are latent to all humans, and that *qigong* is a method for expressing and cultivating this potential:

In adults, Extraordinary Powers can be developed through *qigong* training; children's Extraordinary Powers can be induced in large numbers. Regarding the induction and training of Extraordinary Powers, this type of function is not a rare phenomenon limited to a few privileged individuals, but corresponds to a physiological potential universal and innate to man. One can conjecture that the phase of birth and perfecting of this type of function lasts from the age of six to seven years until the age of fourteen or fifteen years; if [this phase] is not exploited, the functions will gradually decline and disappear. But *qigong* is a method and a technique that enables these functions to be restored. Of course, not all methods of *qigong* practice can induce Extraordinary Powers.[83]

Meanwhile, researchers were discovering ever stranger paranormal powers. A group at Harbin Industrial University studied the tele-

81 ZZ 3(5): 334–5; ZZ 3(6): 438–9; ZZ 3(9): 683; ZZ 3(10): 741–2.
82 ZZ 3(4): inside cover.
83 QG 2(2): 88.

pathic powers of schoolgirls.[84] In early 1980 the case of a teen-ager from Sihong county, Jiangsu province was reported, whose wrist watch was notoriously wrong, either several hours early or several hours late; but when others wore the watch, it gave the accurate time. Extraordinary Powers researchers took an interest in this phenomenon, which they called 'thought-induced motion' (*yinian zhidong*).[85] Other powers investigated included the ability to see through people's organs like an X-ray; to see a blood sample magnified hundreds of times like a microscope; and to find infor-mation from the past.[86]

Researchers at the Institute of High-Energy Physics of the China Academy of Science and at the Yunnan University Physics Department claimed that the electric signals and energy emitted by children while reading with their ears were over a thousand times higher than those of normal people in a state of mental concentra-tion.[87] In 1980 the scientists at Yunnan University held experiments to train children to develop their Extraordinary Powers. They claimed to have succeeded in training them to read slips of paper hidden on the other side of a wall, at a distance of 10 metres; to lo-cate a coin hidden in a flowerpot; to communicate with each other by telepathy; to pull objects from their grandmother's pocket by the mere use of their mental power; to break the branches of a tree; to cause a flower in a closed jar to bloom; and to move cigarettes, keys, knives and wristwatches with their mind.[88] These experiments were supported and proclaimed as science by a vice-governor and a vice-Party secretary of the province, who called for the creation of a research institute to continue the investigations.[89] Similar experi-ments were reported in Beijing, Wuhan, Xi'an and other cities.[90]

Other scientific and medical units began their own research on *qigong*. Topics included infra-red thermal imaging of asthmatics be-fore and after *qigong* practice; chemical and bacterial composition of saliva before and after *qigong* practice etc.[91] Others, starting with the

84   Yu Guangyuan 2002: 23.
85   ZGL: 73.
86   GR, 27 May 1981: 4.
87   GR, 27 May 1981: 4.
88   ZGL: 74.
89   TJH.
90   ZGL: 74; Yu Guangyuan 2002: 25; Lü Yulan and Cheng Xia 1988: 15–18.
91   Li Zhiyong 1988: 423–4. For a compilation of papers on scientific experi-ments on *qigong*, presented at the All-China Conference on Qigong Science in

premise that external *qi* is a material substance, tried to reproduce the substance with a machine. In 1979 a team of Beijing researchers invented the 'MHZ-792 *qigong*-simulating electronic therapeutic device', which was said to simulate the 'infra-red information' emitted in *qigong* master Zhao Guang's external *qi*. The device was designed for use during the course of therapy with Chinese medicine. In 1980 two more laboratories developed *qi*-emitting devices.[92]

In 1980 three Shanghai hospitals and medical research units discovered '*qigong* anaesthesia', in which a *qigong* master emits external *qi* to patients undergoing thyroid gland surgery and gastrectomies, without any other anaesthesia.[93] Researchers at prestigious Qinghua University attempted to measure the effects of *qigong* with microwave instruments and thermal imaging.[94] Others tried to measure the effects of external *qi* and 'information water'—water onto which external *qi* has been emitted by a master—on the immune system of white mice.[95] *Qigong* was even used to reform criminals, with results measured by administering the Minnesota Multiple-Personality Test before and after the period of *qigong* practice.[96]

POLITICAL DEFENCE OF EXTRAORDINARY POWERS RESEARCH

Research into the paranormal effects of *qigong* practice was enthusiastically promoted by Qian Xuesen, the designer of China's nuclear weapons programme and, as Vice-President of NAST and Vice-Chairman of the National Defence Science and Technology Commission, one of China's most politically influential scientists.[97]

August 1987, see Hu Haichang and Hao Qiyao 1989.

92   Li Zhiyong 1988: 425.

93   Li Zhiyong 1988: 425.

94   ZGL: 138.

95   ZZ 8(1):46–8; ZZ 8(1): 43–5.

96   DF 32: 23–7. Translation ['A First Attempt to Use Zhineng Qigong to Reform Criminals'] published in Zhu and Penny 1994: 79–94.

97   Born in Shanghai in 1912, Qian Xuesen was a graduate of MIT and of Caltech. During the Second World War he worked for the US Air Force as a rocket engineer, and participated in the dismantling of the German rocket production facility at Peenemunde. From 1949 to 1955 he directed the Guggenheim Jet Propulsion Laboratory at the California Institute of Technology. He returned to China in 1955, where he played a leading role in the development of China's nuclear and space programmes (see Wortzel 1999: 211). He was an avid supporter of the 'Draft Plan for Agricultural Development', a mixture of unfeasible projects that provided

Qian called for the creation of a new discipline of 'somatic science' (*renti kexue*), which would study Extraordinary Powers as part of a global programme of research on human body functions.[98] In the summer of 1980 Qian met the editors of *Ziran* magazine, the *Guangming Daily*, the *People's Daily*, the Xinhua News Agency and the *Beijing Science and Technology News*, expressing his support for paranormal research and for the publication of reports on *qigong* and Extraordinary Powers, and urging them to be courageous in the face of attacks that were to be expected in response to new discoveries. Together with Nie Chunrong, Secretary-General of NAST, he invited members of the Association to keep abreast on Extraordinary Powers research, and discussed the possible establishment of a research society devoted to this field.[99]

Following these initiatives by Qian, from mid 1980 to mid 1981 meetings and demonstrations of child prodigies were held in at least a dozen provincial capitals, often in meeting rooms of the provincial CCP headquarters and in the presence of provincial and municipal Party secretaries, governors and mayors, leading to the establishment of local Extraordinary Powers Research Societies.[100] The Beijing Institute of Education summoned several hundred secondary school physics teachers to a demonstration of Extraordinary Powers, while in Yunnan a manual on the 'Principles of Dialectical Materialism' published by the Education Commission was edited to incorporate the new discovery.[101]

The first step leading to the foundation of a nationwide organisation was taken at the second national conference on Extraordinary Powers, held in Chongqing in may 1981 and presided by Yang Chao, the Sichuan provincial Party Secretary, who had triggered the paranormal craze in 1979 with his appearance in newspaper

---

the technical basis for the Great Leap Forward (MacKerras 1998: 99). He was elected as an alternate member of the 9th, 10th, 11th and 12th Politburos of the Party Central Committee (1969, 1973, 1977, 1982). He was Vice-President of the National Defence Science and Technology Commission from 1978 to 1982, along with General Zhang Zhenhuan, who became the Chairman of the China Qigong Science Research Society after his retirement. Qian claimed he did not believe in Extraordinary Powers until he witnessed a demonstration of paranormal powers at the Institute for Aerospace Medical Engineering (Qian Xuesen 1996: 142, 143).

98   Qian Xuesen 1981a and 1981b: 217.
99   Ji Yi 1991: 82; Dong 1984: 88–9; TJH.
100   ZQB, 19 December 1981: 4; TJH.
101   TJH.

photographs alongside Tang Yu, the boy who could read with his ears. Professors from Beijing Normal University showed a video of the Wang sisters emitting light and moving matches from a distance of half a metre, to the cheers and applause of the delegates.[102] Papers by Qian Xuesen and Nie Chunrong, calling for the launch of fundamental research on Somatic Science, were read to an audience of 500 conference participants representing the disciplines of atomic science, physics, radio electronics, optics, acoustics, biophysics, biology, psychology, space flight, neurology, psychiatry, physiology, fundamental medicine, clinical medicine, Chinese medicine, philosophy and natural dialectics.[103] A follow-up meeting held in Shanghai on 9 November elected He Chongyin and Zhu Runlong, the editors of *Ziran*, as Chairman and Secretary-General of the preparatory committee for the future China Somatic Science Research Society, affiliated to NAST.[104] Discussion centred on the Extraordinary Powers controversy. Delegates recognised the utility of healthy debate, but concluded that Extraordinary Powers should not be rejected simply because current scientific theories are unable to explain them. The entire video proceedings of the conference were presented a month later at the Great Hall of the Guangdong Provincial Government.[105] Recognition of the new field of research by the Chinese scientific community was signalled by the publication of an entry on 'Extraordinary Powers' in the 1981 *Yearbook* of the *China Encyclopaedia*.

The beginning of academic exchanges with Western parapsychology researchers also added to the legitimacy of Extraordinary Powers.[106] In October 1981 the State Science Commission invited a delegation of seventeen members of the American Parapsychological Association to investigate Extraordinary Powers in China, where they visited and lectured at Beijing University and several institutes of the China Academy of Sciences, and observed a dozen children with purported Extraordinary Powers.[107] This visit led to

102   GR, 27 May 1981: 4.
103   ZZ 4(7): 489–91; ZZ 4(7): 492–6; Qian Xuesen 1981a; Yu Guangyuan 2002: 26.
104   ZZ 4: 6; ZZ 5(2): 106.
105   TJH.
106   Yu Guangyuan 1982: 34.
107   According to Stanley Krippner, a member of the delegation, 'although some of them performed well under informal conditions, they were not able to demonstrate any convincing extrasensory perception when they used sealed target mate-

Chen Xin and Mei Lei of the Aerospace Medico-Engineering Institute in Beijing being invited to the centennial conference of the Society for Psychical Research at Cambridge University in 1982, where they presented a report on parapsychology in China.[108] Chinese articles on Extraordinary Powers research, including one by Qian Xuesen, were also translated and published in Western parapsychology magazines such as *Psi Research* and the *European Journal of Parapsychology*.[109]

These developments triggered an oppositional movement led by Yu Guangyuan and others, including Zhou Jianren, brother of the famous novelist Lu Xun.[110] A series of anti-paranormal articles appeared in the press, attacking research on Extraordinary Powers as 'a resurgence of superstition', 'the denial of scientific truth', 'abandoning the principles of scientific materialism', and warning against the danger of 'falling into the trap of idealism'.[111] Between 1979 and 1982 Yu Guangyuan published several articles attacking Extraordinary Powers research as 'pseudo-science', claiming that such functions were mere conjurer's tricks in which, contrary to the stage magician who openly tells his audience that his tricks are but the illusion caused by sleight of hand, the Extraordinary Powers master tries to fool the public by claiming that he can truly move objects by mental force.[112] In the journal *Social Science in China* he compared Extraordinary Powers to parapsychology research in the West, which had produced no significant result after a century of effort. The only difference between Extraordinary Powers and parapsychology, he claimed, was that the latter is openly opposed to materialism, while the defenders of Extraordinary Powers are actually 'idealists'[113] in disguise who pretend to be materialists. But in spite of his criticisms, Yu Guangyuan defended the rights of Extraordinary Powers advocates to express their opinions, in order to

---

rial which we had brought with us from the United States and Canada' (Krippner 1984: 207).

108   Krippner 1984: 206–9; Liu Huajie 2004: 202. See Chen Xin and Mei Lei 1988 [1982] for the text of this report.

109   See for example Qian Xuesen 1982.

110   Zhu Xiaoyang 1994 [1989]: 36.

111   Ji Yi 1991: 83.

112   See for example Yu Guangyuan 1982. These and other articles are reproduced in Yu Guangyuan 2002: 10–100.

113   In the Marxist sense, idealism is the philosophical theory, opposed to scientific materialism, which considers that reality exists only in our minds.

stimulate open debate between idealists and Marxists, which would help the latter to improve their debating skills and to deepen their understanding of dialectical materialism.[114]

On 15 September 1981 Zhou Peiyuan, Director of the NAST, declared he was unconvinced by a demonstration he had seen, and that he would oppose the NAST's sponsorship of any Extraordinary Powers Research Society.[115] A few weeks later, under the initiative of Yu Guangyuan, the National Science Commission established a 'contact group for the investigation of Extraordinary Powers', which aimed to coordinate actions against the paranormal craze.[116] On 25 February 1982 the *People's Daily* quoted a call by Yu Guangyuan and Li Chang, Party Secretary of the China Academy of Sciences, to 'put an end to this unscientific propaganda'.[117] The paper also noted that psychologists from the China Academy of Sciences had investigated the phenomenon of children reading with their ears, and concluded that it was a hoax. Another article sarcastically described the 'discoveries' of Extraordinary Powers research since 1979, and summarised the criticisms of several noted scientists.[118] A few weeks later a national conference on debunking Extraordinary Powers was attended by sixty scientists and journalists.[119] Finally, the Propaganda Department of the Party Central Committee intervened to put an end to the controversy on 20 April 1982, with a circular stating that Extraordinary Powers were not a priority area of research, and that there should be 'no publicising, no criticism and no controversy' in the press in relation to Extraordinary Powers.[120] In the *qigong* sector this came to be known as the 'Triple No' policy.

Proponents of Extraordinary Powers research counterattacked with all the political influence they could muster. Qian Xuesen and Lü Bingkui, as well as Zhang Zhenhuan[121] and Wu Shaozu,[122] re-

---

114 Yu Guangyuan 1982: 31, 39–41.
115 TJH.
116 Yu Guangyuan 2002: 2; TJH.
117 RR, 25 February 1982: 3.
118 RR, 25 February 1982: 3.
119 TJH.
120 ZGL: 116; Ji Yi 1991: 83; JG; Yu Guangyuan 2002: 147; TJH.
121 Zhang Zhenhuan (1915–94) joined the revolution in 1935 and became a Party member in 1938. He became a Brigadier-General in the PLA and Vice-President of COSTIND (WH: 559).
122 Born in 1939, Wu Shaozu was elected to the Central Committee of the CCP

spectively Vice-President and Deputy Bureau Director of the Commission for Science, Technology and Industry for National Defence (COSTIND),[123] wrote to the *People's Daily* and to the Propaganda Department in defence of Extraordinary Powers research. Their lobbying reached the highest levels of power: in response to the pressure, Hu Yaobang, who had been behind the media ban on Extraordinary Powers reporting, now allowed a small number of researchers to continue studying Extraordinary Powers and to periodically communicate the results of their findings.[124] As a result of this counter-directive the Propaganda Department modified its policy and in a circular dated 15 June 1982, while reiterating the 'Triple No', authorised the publication of data on Extraordinary Powers research for scientific purposes. Although such publication was meant to be limited to the restricted circle of scientists, the new policy was hailed as a victory by paranormal advocates.[125] From then on Extraordinary Powers were seen in the *qigong* sector as officially legitimised, and Hu Yaobang's action interpreted by advocates as a sign of his support.[126] As we shall see, in practice, with some exceptions, until 1995 the media respected the ban on criticism of Extraordinary Powers, but did not respect the ban on publicising such phenomena. Yu Guangyuan and others stopped writing polemical articles,[127] and wrote letters to Hu Yaobang to express their disappointment at the new policy and to criticise Qian Xuesen's actions.[128]

---

in 1982, and appointed Vice-Minister of COSTIND in 1983. He became Sports Minister in 1988, and was placed in charge of the *qigong* question by the government in the 1990s (see p. 167). He was converted to Extraordinary Powers research after seeing a demonstration of Zhang Baosheng's powers (see pp. 73–5). He is reported to have said that even if ninety-nine demonstrations of Extraordinary Powers are proven to be false, a single true demonstration would be sufficient to justify further research on Extraordinary Powers (JG).

123   COSTIND was established as a merger of the National Defence Science and Technology Commission and two other Party and PLA organs in August 1982, as the agency in charge of the military-industrial complex, until its dissolution in 1998.

124   TJH. Hu Yaobang (1915–89) was a leader of the liberal wing of the CCP. Mass demonstrations of mourning at his death on 15 April 1989 snowballed into the Tiananmen pro-democracy student movement.

125   ZGL: 117; Ji Yi 1991: 83; JG.

126   Qian Xuesen 1988: 205.

127   Yu Guangyuan 2002: 3, 147; He Zuoxiu 2002: 16.

128   Yu Guangyuan 2002: 147.

FASCINATION WITH EXTRAORDINARY POWERS AMONG THE MEDIA, MILITARY AND POLITICAL ÉLITES

Owing to Qian Xuesen's interventions, and to the ideological legitimacy of *qigong* (see chapter 5), the media were now free to report the amazing feats of people with Extraordinary Powers. Li Qingheng, for example, a doctor in a rail ministry hospital, thus popularised the notion of 'electric *qigong*', in which the *qigong* master uses his or her body as a conduit for electric currents. Interviewed on national television, he lit up a light bulb by holding two electric wires in his hands and, again with his hand linked to a wire, cooked mutton on a skewer until white smoke emanated from it.[129]

The applications of *qigong* seemed to be limitless. *Qigong* masters were reported to have been hired by mining companies to detect underground gold deposits,[130] and to have successfully predicted earthquakes.[131] The military applications of *qigong* were tantalising: reports on paranormal research in the Soviet Union and in the United States claimed that the two superpowers were actively studying the uses of parapsychology for spying, for killing enemy troops, for detecting enemy submarines, as a communication system between submarines and naval bases, as protective armour, and as a technique for enhancing the powers of the mind.[132]

The most famous of the Extraordinary Powers masters was Zhang Baosheng, a miner from Benxi (Liaoning), who had been 'discovered' as able to read with his nose following the Tang Yu craze, and was now reported to be able to see through people's bodies and to place objects in closed containers without touching them. The local police called on him to solve criminal cases, and a hospital hired him as a living X-ray machine.

In the spring of 1982 Zhang was invited to Beijing by the preparatory committee of the China Somatic Science Society, which was conducting tests and experiments on eleven individuals with highly developed Extraordinary Powers. The experts, having observed Zhang in action, were convinced of his powers.[133]

129 ZGL: 261–2.
130 Lü Yulan and Cheng Xia 1988: 161–6.
131 ZGL: 86–8.
132 Lü Yulan and Cheng Xia 1988: 211–22. See also Heelas 1996: 97–8.
133 SMK 21:7; Song Shaoming 1988: 209–13.

Zhang Baosheng's reputation spread in Beijing, exciting the curiosity of some high-ranking Party leaders. Healers with Extraordinary Powers were invited into the Zhongnanhai compound to treat the daughter-in-law of General Chen Geng.[134] On 18 May 1982 Zhu Runlong, editor-in-chief of *Ziran* magazine, introduced Zhang to Marshal Ye Jianying, who had masterminded the overthrow of the Gang of Four after Mao's death. Zhang correctly 'smelled' the contents of messages written by Ye on folded slips of paper. From his wheelchair Ye exclaimed his amazement and his support for Extraordinary Powers research.[135] Later, when Ye fell severely ill with respiratory problems, Zhang was urgently summoned to the Marshal's residence, in the presence of senior members of the Politburo and the Central Military Commission. He entered a posture for emitting *qi*, gently stroked Ye's chest, shook the extremities of his right fingers above the Marshal's throat, then opened his palm to reveal a thick and viscous substance. The people present exclaimed it was the phlegm from Ye's throat. After repeating the operation several times, Ye was able to breathe normally again.[136]

Zhang Baosheng was appointed to the No. 507 Institute of Aeronautical Engineering of the COSTIND, in order to research the possible military applications of his powers, and also to keep him from putting them to the wrong uses.[137] He became a favourite of the Party leaders and the most famous of the Extraordinary Powers masters. On 18 September 1986 General Zhang Zhenhuan staged a public demonstration of his abilities for the political and media élite of Guangdong province. Flanked by the Party Secretary and the Chairman of the municipal Congress of People's Representatives, Zhang Baosheng made chocolate sweets disappear before an audience of hundreds of officials and journalists, guessed the serial number of a 5-yuan bill, and removed pills from a closed bottle.[138]

Zhang performed similar demonstrations in other cities. He became a legendary figure, said to be able to set fire to clothes with

---

134   Ji Yi 1993: 108.
135   Zhu Runlong, account published in *Extraordinary Powers Research* and reproduced in ZGL: 79; Ji Yi 1993: 108; Song Shaoming 1988: 214–19; Lü Yulan and Cheng Xia 1988: 6–9.
136   *Baokan wenzhai*, 31 December 1991: 3, quoted in Kane 1993: 162.
137   TJH.
138   Lü Yulan and Cheng Xia 1988: 11–13.

his fingers, and to restore to their original form business cards that had been torn, chewed up and spit out by others.[139] He was reputed to have special access to Zhongnanhai, the headquarters of the top Party leadership, and to have met with Deng Xiaoping in person.

FURTHER INSTITUTIONAL DEVELOPMENT

Meanwhile, state-sponsored *qigong* associations were developing and many of them launched new *qigong* magazines: in August 1982 the Guangdong Qigong Science Research Society founded the magazine *Qigong and Science (qigong yu kexue)*; in 1983 the All-China Qigong Scientific Research Society[140] established the magazine *Chinese Qigong (Zhonghua Qigong)*; in March of the same year the Shanghai municipal government approved the launch of the *Extraordinary Powers Research Journal (Renti teyigongneng yanjiu zazhi)*, edited by Zhu Runlong of *Ziran* magazine; in September 1984 the Beidaihe Qigong Sanatorium[141] launched *Beidaihe Qigong*, which would be renamed *China Qigong (Zhongguo qigong)* in 1986, around the time that the Beijing Qigong Research Society founded the magazine *Oriental Science Qigong (Dongfang Qigong)*.[142] In that year Zhang Zhenhuan estimated the total circulation of the various *qigong* magazines was around 1 million.[143]

From 1983 the government's new scientific policy encouraged the free discussion of scientific issues and condemned the use of highly-charged political labels in scientific debates: terms such as 'spiritual pollution', 'heretical opinions' etc. were not to be used.[144] The new policy was understood as a green light for Extraordinary Powers research and '*qigong* science', which could be pursued without the fear of ideological attacks.

In early 1986 a new national state-sponsored association, which benefited from stronger political support than the earlier one affiliated to the medical authorities,[145] was established. The China Qigong Science Research Society (CQRS) was founded on a

---

139 Song Shaoming 1988; ZGL: 79–85.
140 On the foundation of this organisation, see p. 59.
141 Renamed the Beidaihe Qigong Hospital in 1986 (ZG 81: 4).
142 DF 26: 37.
143 Zhang Zhenhuan 1988b: 17.
144 RR, 18 December 1983: 1.
145 See p. 59.

triumphant note, as Professor Qian Xuesen proclaimed the new scientific and even social revolution:

Our country has a population of one billion. If one out of every 100 people practises *qigong*, that makes ten million. If out of every 100 practitioners, one becomes a teacher, that will add up to 100,000 *qigong* masters. To upgrade these 100,000 *qigong* masters constantly is a truly great thing.[146]

The creation of this academic body was heralded as a turning point in the history of *qigong* and even of science, as *qigong* advocates cried: '*qigong* has left religion and folklore to enter the Temple of Science!'[147] Over two hundred delegates from all parts of China and Hong Kong attended the Society's inaugural assembly on 28–30 April, where Qian Xuesen gave a programmatic keynote speech on the emerging science of *qigong*.[148]

Zhang Zhenhuan was the Society's founder and Chairman. In his speech he explained that the CQRS would be a high-level national organisation, which would have the role of controlling *qigong*'s political direction. It would coordinate the strategies of the various organisations involved in *qigong*, while leaving *qigong* groups and associations the freedom of deciding the means to implement the strategies. Zhang called for *qigong* to be applied to improve agricultural productivity, health standards, school test scores, sporting results and the performance of astronauts. The Society's board of directors comprised representatives of various ministries and officials from different provinces and regions who were interested in *qigong*. The Society aimed to establish branches in each province.[149] Its membership was largely made up of cadres and retired Party officials. Almost half of the 147 delegated to the inaugural assembly were over sixty years old, including past provincial governors, People's Political Consultative Conference vice-chairmen, and representatives of labour and women's federations. The Society's honorary Chairman was Peng Chong, a retired member of the Politburo.

With the objective of federating and controlling the various denominations, the CQRS established a Theories and Methods

---

146   Quoted in TJH.
147   ZGL: 119.
148   See Qian Xuesen 1988: 323–4 for the text of his speech.
149   QG 7(3): 100.

Commission, which was founded at a meeting in Xi'an on 12–19 October 1987. Over 500 delegates, representing denominations from all parts of China, attended the event which was presided over by Zhang Zhenhuan, and which was also addressed by his protégé, master Yan Xin.[150] The denominations were invited to apply for affiliation to the Commission, which would give them a legal status, but would also exert a certain degree of control (more symbolic than real) over them.

One year after the founding of the CQRS, two other national state-sponsored associations were created. The China Sports Qigong Society (CSQS) was established in 1987 by Zuo Lin and Guo Zhouli, under the patronage of the State Sports Commission. The CSQS published the magazine *Qigong and Sports*, which was launched by the United Front Work Department of the Shaanxi Provincial Party Committee.[151]

The other new national association founded in 1987 was the China Somatic Science Society (CSSS). Also headed by Zhang Zhenhuan, with Qian Xuesen as honorary Chairman, the association aimed to federate the community of researchers working on 'somatic science', i.e. Extraordinary Powers.[152] Around half of the 245 members were professional scientists.[153] At the first meeting of the Society's board of directors Zhang Zhenhuan stressed that the Society's establishment was a victory against the adversaries of Extraordinary Powers research:

Since the *Sichuan Daily* published the story on 'reading with ears' on 11 March 1979, many technological workers from around the country have been engaged in research on the Extraordinary Powers of the human body. For eight years, until the foundation of our Society was authorised, [this research] was not easy. This official authorisation marks a new stage in research on the Extraordinary Powers of the human body. Our organisation has been authorised, but our research work is far from finished. The anchor point of science is practice; the quest of scientific workers is truth. True science has no fear, and no force can stop it. In the past, some people have used their power to criticise research on Extraordinary Powers as 'idealist pseudo-science'. Now that the State Commission for Science

150 QG 8(12): 545; QK 58: inside cover; on Yan Xin, see chapter 5.
151 WH: 602, 604. The United Front Work Department (*tongzhanbu*) is a Party organ responsible for federating the various non-Communist social organisations (other political parties, religious associations etc.) around the CCP's leadership.
152 WH: 604.
153 QG 11(5): 236.

and Technology has authorised the establishment of our Somatic Science Research Society, it is not a victory of 'idealism', but it is a victory of true materialism and Marxism, it is a victory of science. In truth, our work is a struggle to defend dialectical materialism, which leads to the victory of the Marxist theory of knowledge, and symbolises the spirit of sacrifice of the quest for scientific truth. ... Qian Xuesen has said: this research will have an effect on the question of the scientific revolution; it can be compared to a second Renaissance; ... it has strategic repercussions for the twenty-first century ...[154]

The CCP Central Committee took this vision seriously, and in 1986 appointed a Leaders' Working Group on Somatic Science made up of representatives from the departments of National Security, Propaganda, COSTIND (Wu Shaozu) and the NAST.[155] The Working Group was responsible for the supervision of the different *qigong* associations and denominations, and of the coordination of the various ministries' actions concerning *qigong*. The Group was at the same time a centre for the pro-*qigong* lobby: Wu Shaozu, tireless promoter of *qigong* and of Extraordinary Powers research, who became Chairman of the Working Group in 1990, hoped that *qigong* would one day have a seat in the State Council. As *qigong* critic He Zuoxiu would later point out, no other scientific discipline in China had a Leaders' Working Group to look after its interests.[156]

While denominations expanded and the national state-sponsored institutions developed, *qigong* spread abroad. *Qigong* associations were established in Hong Kong, the Philippines, Japan and elsewhere. Academic exchanges increased, with visits of professors such as Herbert Benson of Harvard University, famous for his work on the physiological effects of Transcendental Meditation.[157] On 17 May 1987 four hundred delegates from twelve countries attended the first World Qigong Congress, held in May 1987 at Shenzhen University, with the blessing of the State Sports Commission. The assembled participants resolved to create the International Qigong Science Federation (IQSF), based in Xi'an, with Wu Shaozu as its President and the magazine *Qigong and Sports* as its official periodical.

154   Zhang Zhenhuan 1999.
155   SMK 21:7; Chen Guocheng and Ke Yuwen 1997: 23; DF 66: 21–4; JG.
156   He Zuoxiu 2002: 15.
157   QG 5(1): 48; QG 7(1): 44. See Benson 1975 and 1996.

Qigong was also added to the training regimen of professional athletes, in preparation for sporting events such as the 6th and 7th National Games, the 3rd International Swimming Championships and the 1990 Asian Games. For the latter event six *qigong* masters were assigned to assist the Chinese team. Using external *qi* and audiotapes containing *qigong* messages, the masters tended to the athletes' wounds and offered relaxation and rapid recovery sessions.[158]

An important feature of the *qigong* movement was the organisation of academic conferences on *qigong* and somatic science, which strengthened regional, national and international networks based on a common interest in *qigong*, and reinforced its image of a scientific discipline. Academic qualifications were not usually required to present papers. The conferences often featured demonstrations of *qigong* powers by masters. Apart from general regional and national conferences, specialised workshops focused on topics such as the applications of *qigong* in Oriental medicine;[159] the history of physical education in China;[160] the nature of external *qi*; applications of *qigong* in the treatment of nearsightedness;[161] *qigong* and the *Book of Changes*;[162] military applications of *qigong*;[163] and *qigong* and Tibetan tantrism.[164]

Let us take, for example, the activities held in Zhejiang province in 1987. In January the provincial branch of the All-China Society for Chinese Medicine established a medical *qigong* association.[165] On 10–13 March the Zhejiang Qigong Science Research Society was established at a conference of 150 delegates from the academic, health, education, sports and *qigong* sectors, as well as government leaders who gave the opening speeches and expressed their support for the *qigong* cause. On 1 April the medical *qigong* association opened the Hangzhou Qigong Hospital, an addition to the *qigong* therapeutic institutions that already existed in Zhejiang, such as the *qigong* sanatorium and *qigong* clinics.[166] Two weeks later the as-

---

158 DF 30: 41–2.
159 QG 7(4): 164.
160 QG 7(5): 211.
161 QG 8(9): 389.
162 QG 8(10): 481.
163 QG 9(3): 112.
164 QG 9(5): 237; QK 63: inside cover.
165 QG 8(6): 276.
166 QG 8(6): 276.

sociation held its first academic conference, in the city of Wenzhou, where twenty-six papers were presented to seventy participants.[167] On 30 May a *qigong* studies association was founded at Zhejiang University.[168] On 1–2 December the Zhejiang Qigong Science Research Society held a multidisciplinary academic conference in Hangzhou, which was attended by forty researchers.[169] And on 27 December the Qigong, Martial Arts and Sports Academy was established by the Society in Hangzhou, with famous monk Haideng Fashi as its honorary President.[170]

While *qigong* institutions and academic activities developed, the training of *qigong* masters became more systematic and was integrated into state educational structures. Formal training of *qigong* masters resumed in August 1982, organised at Lushan by the Shanghai Institute of Chinese Medicine.[171] A year later the Beidaihe Qigong Sanatorium held its first formal training since the Cultural Revolution.[172] Provincial government funding allowed the sanatorium to expand and regain its position as a major centre for training *qigong* therapists. Over 50,000 persons attended *qigong* trainings at Beidaihe between 1985 and 1996.[173] In 1984 a distance-learning organisation, the China Qigong Academy for Continuing Education (*Zhonghua qigong jinxiu xueyuan*) was jointly established by the CQRS and Guangming University, a prestigious distance-learning institution specialising in Chinese medicine.[174]

A thirty-six-hour compulsory *qigong* course was added to the curriculum of the Beijing Society for Chinese Medicine.[175] Master's degrees in *qigong* were also offered by the China Academy of Chinese Medicine, approved by the State Council's Commission on Diplomas.[176] In 1986 the National Science Commission recognised *qigong* as a scientific discipline within Chinese medicine.[177]

---

167 QG 8(7): 303.
168 QG 9(3): 118.
169 QG 9(3): 118.
170 QG 9(3): 101. Yan Xin was Haideng's most well-known disciple. On Yan Xin, see chapter 5.
171 Li Zhiyong 1988: 422, 426–7.
172 Li Zhiyong 1988: 427.
173 ZG 81: 4.
174 QG 9(9): 392.
175 QG 6(1): 40.
176 QG 9(10): 477.
177 Zhang Honglin 1996: 3.

The State Education Commission also took an interest in *qigong*. After holding a conference on traditional physical education techniques in higher sports education, the Commission organised summer *qigong* workshops for college sports instructors.[178] A *qigong* curriculum for schools was also developed and sent to all provincial and municipal education commissions and institutions of higher learning.

Qigong was recognised as a science by some institutes of higher education, such as Shandong University, which offered an optional course on 'Somatic science—*qigong* and the study of Extraordinary Powers', starting in 1988. The course outline included points accepted as truths in the *qigong* sector:

1. The reality of the Extraordinary Powers of the human body;
2. The use of modern scientific methods in the study of *qigong* functional states and in experiments on external *qi*;
3. Processes of *qigong* functioning;
4. Traditional *qigong*;
5. *Qigong* and ancient Chinese culture;
6. *Qigong* and archaic, ancient, modern and future societies;
7. Why somatic science will probably lead to a scientific and technological revolution that will change the face of the earth.[179]

The organisation of these different training courses by medical and educational institutions had the effect not only of integrating *qigong* into the Chinese educational system, but also of establishing a coherent and standardised 'discipline' presented as having its own history going back to Chinese antiquity, its own theory, its own methodology and its own applications.[180] In 1986 the *Guangming Daily* summarised the achievements of seven years of Extraordinary Powers research: the true existence of Extraordinary Powers had been proven; they were universal and existed in many forms; they induced physiological changes; the miraculous phenomena of samples moved by psychokinesis could be physically observed, and their mechanisms analysed; they were related to *qigong*; and they held the promise of a more systematic vision of the human

---

178 Zhang Zhenhuan 1989: 2–3; QK 58: 4.
179 QG 11(2): 92.
180 For attempts at a comprehensive academic synthesis of the discipline, see Lin Zhongpeng 1988; Hu Chunshen 1989; Xie Huanzhang 1988.

body, with a potentially far-reaching impact on philosophy and on society.[181]

CONCLUSION

Figure 1 shows the networks linking the principal state-sponsored *qigong* associations to political institutions through four key individuals: Qian Xuesen, Wu Shaozu, Lü Bingkui—China's most influential figures in science, sports and Chinese medicine respectively—and Zhang Zhenhuan, who was influential within the military. It is no exaggeration to state that the fate of *qigong* in China was intimately linked to that of these four individuals.[182]

Indeed the controversy between promoters and opponents of Extraordinary Powers research was resolved in the political arena. We have seen how Qian Xuesen used his influence as a great Chinese scientist and key official of China's scientific institutions to encourage the media to publish reports and research on Extraordinary Powers and, later, to directly appeal to the Party leaders to reverse its ban on such publication. As a result, criticism of Extraordinary Powers was banned, while publication of research for 'scientific purposes' was authorised. In practice, the media were free to report any sensational phenomena related to Extraordinary Powers. The political victory of the Extraordinary Powers camp was clear.

At least two of the six members of the Permanent Committee of the 12th Politburo (1982–7)—a directorate which, under Deng Xiaoping's leadership, had absolute political power in China—were known supporters of *qigong* and of Extraordinary Powers: Ye Jianying,[183] who underwent *qigong* treatments at Beidaihe in the

---

181   GM, 29 July 1986: 1.

182   Note that by the mid 1980s the relationship between the health authorities and the COSTIND network seems to have worsened. Qian Xuesen's old age and Zhang Zhenhuan's death made possible the comeback of the anti-*qigong* faction in the media and the scientific community. Wu Shaozu was fired from the Sports Commission after the Falungong affair (Jean-Pierre Cabestan, personal communication, 2001). See chapter 6.

183   A veteran of the Long March, Ye Jianying, who became Minister of Defence in 1975, overthrew the Gang of Four after Mao's death, giving him immense prestige. In 1978 he was elected Chairman of the Permanent Committee of the 5th National People's Congress. He was named Vice-President of the Central Military Commission in 1983. Ye underwent *qigong* treatments at the Beidaihe Sanatorium in the 1950s. (see pp. 36–7).

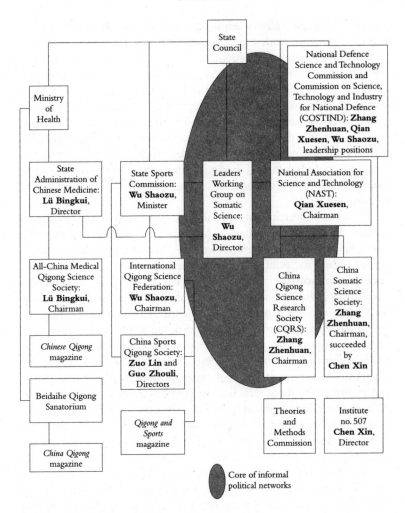

Fig. 1 Qigong political networks

1950s, and was a believer in external *qi* and Extraordinary Powers;[184] and Premier Zhao Ziyang, who, in 1964 as Guangdong provincial Party Secretary, had witnessed an ear-reading child and, consider-

---

184 See p. 53 (support for Gu Hansen's research) and p. 74 (healed by Zhang Baosheng).

ing the potential military applications of the boy's powers, had at the time put him under special and confidential protection,[185] and as Governor of Sichuan province, shortly before his promotion to Premier, was reported to have received Tang Yu.[186] Peng Zhen, one of the most senior members of the Politburo (from 1945 to 1966 and from 1979 to 1987), is also reported to have expressed his sup-. port for *qigong* research in a letter to Health Minister Cui Yueli, warning of the danger of foreign countries surpassing China in Chinese medicine and *qigong*.[187] Other high-level supporters reportedly included Peng Chong, permanent Vice-President of the National People's Congress, and Wang Zhen, Vice-Premier of the State Council.[188]

Three individuals had appealed to the highest leadership to modify Premier Hu Yaobang's decision in *qigong*'s favour in 1982: Qian Xuesen, Zhang Zhenhuan and Wu Shaozu. These three would soon become the political pillars of the *qigong* sector. Qian Xuesen's speeches on 'somatic science' gave *qigong* an ideological underpinning and a prestige that would be invaluable for its legitimation. He also instructed the NAST, and its provincial and municipal branches, which were responsible for scientific education and popularisation, to support and propagate *qigong* and Extraordinary Powers throughout the country.[189] In 1986 Zhang Zhenhuan founded the CQRS, China's main national state-sponsored *qigong* association, under the umbrella of which most *qigong* activity would take place. Wu Shaozu, after becoming Sports Minister in 1988, was placed in charge of the official administration of *qigong*. Qian Xuesen was the chief designer of China's atomic weapons programme; Zhang Zhenhuan and Wu Shaozu were at various times Vice-Chairmen of the China Nuclear Society. Zhang was Brigadier-General in the People's Liberation Army, a rank that was granted to Wu in 1988. Furthermore, the career paths of Qian, Zhang and Wu, reveal that all three were originally colleagues in the COSTIND and its predecessor before 1982, the National Defence Science and Technology

---

185   Li Peicai 1988: 8–9, quoted in Kane 1993: 161.
186   Dong 1984: 87; Liu Huajie 2004: 5. As a leader of the liberal faction of the CCP, Zhao was fired and placed under house arrest after the 1989 Tiananmen student movement.
187   Letter dated 7 March 1983, quoted by Zhang Zhenhuan 1988b: 15.
188   Liu Huajie 2004: 3.
189   Yu Guangyuan 2002: 8.

Commission. Qian Xuesen was Vice-Chairman of its technology commission from 1970 to 1982. Zhang Zhenhuan was Chairman of the same commission until his retirement in 1985. Wu Shaozu was bureau director from 1975 to 1982, then Vice-Minister responsible for COSTIND from 1983 to 1985, and then Political Commissar from 1985. COSTIND was charged with managing the defence industry and the 'Third Line'—large industrial complexes built in remote inland localities for security in case of an enemy attack on the coast. The agency was also responsible for financing military research and production, as well as the space industry and the production of satellites, missiles and nuclear weapons.[190] According to Yeu-Farn Wang, COSTIND was created as a result of lobbying by the Chinese defence establishment to protect its research and development budgets in a period of cuts in defence spending. To do so, it had mobilised the personal networks of its most influential figures, such as Qian Xuesen, with senior political leaders including Deng Xiaoping, overstepping the state bureaucracy.[191] The same individuals who were lobbying for *qigong* were thus lobbying for the defence research establishment; and lobbying the same political leaders, presumably at the same time. The disbanding of COSTIND in 1998 occurs at the same time as the end of political support for *qigong*. Clearly, the *qigong* movement is intricately tied with the COSTIND phase in the history of China's military-industrial complex.

The parallels between this story and the Soviet military's well-known fascination with paranormal research merit further study—a fascination which, according to a scholar of new religious movements in Russia,[192] began in the late 1970s and grew in the early 1980s, at the same time as the *qigong* movement was expanding in China. General-Secretary Leonid Brejnev was reportedly treated by a spiritual healer, and the Soviet Academy of Sciences opened a paranormal research laboratory. But the difference between the Soviet Union and China was that in the latter case, political patronage extended beyond the laboratories and fanned the spread of a mass popular movement.

190 Wortzel 1999: 57–8.
191 Wang, Yeu-Farn 1993: 117.
192 Marat Shterin, personal communication, January 2004.

3

THE GRANDMASTERS

By 1981 the *qigong* sector had taken a definitive form, which would remain basically unchanged until its collapse in 1999: a public and legitimate space opened up by national and local state-sponsored organisations, with the encouragement of senior leaders of the State Council. Within this space a network of scientists tried to establish a new '*qigong* science', while hundreds of masters emerged from obscurity to enter the space and propagate body technologies derived from traditional lineages they claimed to have inherited, or which they had invented themselves.

Indeed *qigong* benefited from influential networks of political supporters, the most significant of which were linked to the defence science establishment, and which acted to stifle criticisms of *qigong* and Extraordinary Powers. A flourishing subculture grew under this protection, with its associations, magazines, conferences, healing and cultural activities. The methods that the various emerging masters taught, in addition to the 'triple discipline' of the body, breath and mind of 1950s *qigong*, often included an assortment of magical practices: healing by external *qi*, 'spontaneous movements',[1] 'information objects',[2] 'cosmic language'[3] etc. *Qigong* masters were federated in state-sponsored associations affiliated to state medical, scientific and sports authorities. A space was thus opened within which traditional masters could practise their healing arts and create charismatic networks under the guise of *qigong*. Millions of adepts congregated in parks and public spaces every morning to practise exercise routines disseminated by the denominations. Throughout the 1980s *qigong* became a legitimised outlet for the resurgence, reconfiguration and 'modernisation' of religious beliefs and prac-

1 See pp. 136–7.
2 See p. 160.
3 See pp. 151–2.

tices. The interplay and interpenetration of these popular networks and official institutions gave form to the *qigong* sector.

In this space, opened by state-sponsored *qigong* associations and magazines, propagated by the state-owned media, deployed in scientific, educational and medical institutions, and made visible in the parks, gardens and public spaces of urban China, masters, adepts and researchers communicated with each other, elaborating *qigong* as a path for the regeneration of the individual, of China and of the world. Different masters and sects contributed to the '*qigong* cause' through their methods, their healings, their laboratory experiments, their conceptual elaborations, their practical innovations and their systems of propagation. State agencies and political leaders contributed by elaborating an ideological framework, by conferring encouragements and permissions, by removing bureaucratic obstacles, by contributing state assets, and by protecting against criticism. *Qigong* prospered by combining the institutional support of the state and the popular dynamism of the masters and their denominations.

This public space of *qigong* found its legitimacy in the unifying and materialist concept of *qigong* created by Liu Guizhen's team in 1949, which had been rehabilitated after the Cultural Revolution. The medical institutions of *qigong* had also been re-established. But if the *qigong* of the 1950s had been confined to a limited number of institutions, the model, pioneered by Guo Lin and imitated by dozens of other masters from 1980 onwards, of national networks of collective practice sites in parks and public spaces, turned *qigong* into a nationwide mass movement. Further, since the 'discovery' of the material basis of external *qi* by Gu Hansen, *qigong* presented itself as a field of research with implications for the totality of science.

Qigong thus brought into its fold masters of different traditions who could, using the materialist and scientific *qigong* label, openly teach and find a large clientele of patients and followers. If Liu Guizhen and Guo Lin had placed their *qigong* methods firmly within the conceptual framework of institutionalised Chinese medicine, and did not identify themselves as '*qigong* masters', others would inscribe their methods in explicitly Taoist, Buddhist or Tantric frames of reference.

The phenomenon of masters who 'came out of the mountains' (*chushan*) to publicly teach techniques derived from folk, Taoist,

Buddhist, martial and medical traditions was unprecedented in China's history. In terms of numbers, traditions which had previously been limited by primitive forms of communication to small networks of disciples were spread to millions of practitioners in the space of a few years. Masters from a diversity of backgrounds could recognise each other for the first time under the common banner of *qigong*, form a 'sector' recognised by the state, and share information through *qigong* conferences, meetings and magazines, an unthinkable possibility in the traditional world of secret and isolated personal lines of transmission.

One of the first masters to 'come out of the mountains' was Yang Meijun, whose 'Great Goose Qigong' became one of the most popular denominations. Yang heralded the appearance of religious and charismatic motifs in *qigong* practice. She was a seventy-seven-year old woman who claimed to have been trained by her grandfather into a Taoist tradition, in which one imitates the movements of the great goose, a symbol of immortality. Yang had participated in the anti-Japanese guerrilla war and had lived in the Communist Party base of Yan'an before the establishment of the People's Republic. She had concealed her knowledge of body technologies until the end of the Cultural Revolution. Her Great Goose Qigong was one of the first methods to claim explicitly a Taoist heritage rather than an affiliation with modernised Chinese medicine.[4] After Liu Guizhen, the cadre and communist clinician, and Guo Lin, the intrepid self-taught anti-cancer combatant, Yang Meijun emerged as the venerable inheritor of a secret lineage and as the possessor of concealed magical powers. Besides teaching her gymnastic exercises, she used her powers to treat the ill by projecting her *qi* onto patients. *Qigong* was no longer exclusively a self-training exercise: by receiving the mysterious *qi* emitted by the master, patients entered into a new type of relationship with her and with the powerful traditions she was perceived to embody.

The following passage, written by members of the prestigious China Academy of Sciences and published in early 1981, foreshadows the beginning of a cult of the charismatic master and of her mystic powers, as well as the fascination of Chinese scientists for the prodigies of *qigong*:

---

[4] See Yang Meijun 1986 for a description of the postures of Great Goose Qigong.

On the foundation of her ancestral method, master Yang learned from reputed masters everywhere, finally reaching a high level of accomplishment. ... Her method is complete; there is no technique that she doesn't master, be it the arts of the still body, the moving body, or swordsmanship, or even sitting, lying or walking *qigong*, light or heavy *qigong*, the emission of *qi*, diagnosing illnesses, or feeling at a distance. To speak only of the emission of *qi* at a distance, children with Extraordinary Powers and those who have a high degree of *qigong* attainment can see a profusion of colours in the *qi* flowing from her hands .... She has used *qigong* methods to discover, preserve and develop the Extraordinary Powers of several children, enabling them to ... acquire new ones ceaselessly. She has also opened our own telepathic abilities to communicate mentally at will with [such] children.

Among the disciples of Yang Meijun, the great majority are scientific researchers; this is the result of the master's arduous efforts. Generally, scientific researchers ... have a special difficulty in learning *qigong*. But master Yang knows full well that for the *qigong* cause to develop, it cannot separate itself from modern scientific technology. If we don't transmit high-level *qigong* virtuosity to people who are capable of leading scientific research, they won't be able to understand the nature of *qigong*, or to accomplish research on *qigong*. ...

Qigong is a precious scientific heritage which has been bequeathed to us by our ancestors. Conserving and transmitting this heritage is a glorious mission conferred on us by history. If the millennial transmission of this exalted and profound virtuosity were to be lost with our generation, such that our descendants would be able to research *qigong* only through archaeology, we would be condemned by history. We take this opportunity to make this call: arise, to preserve and disseminate the grand and profound virtuosity of master Yang and other similar *qigong* figures, so that we can contribute as we should to our country's research on the system of somatic science.[5]

The spread of *qigong* occurred in a context in which Deng Xiaoping's policy of reforms and opening up had created the conditions for a religious revival in the 1980s. In the countryside this revival manifested itself through the rebuilding of temples destroyed during the Cultural Revolution and through the reconstitution of ritual networks.[6] In the cities, however, the renewed interest in religion was more diffuse: books on religious subjects found a large reader-

[5] QG 2(1): 16–17. The authors Zhang Wenjie and Cao Jian were researchers at the Semiconductor Research Institute of the China Academy of Sciences.
[6] See notably Dean 1993; Siu 1990; Aijmer and Ho 2000; Chau 2005; Eng and Lin 2002; Flower 2004; Yang 2000; DuBois 2005.

ship, and television serials on religious themes such as the *Journey to the West* were smash hits. 'Martial arts fever' added to the spiritual ferment. Kung fu novels and films from Hong Kong and Taiwan flooded mainland theatres and bookstalls, fuelling the growth of a burgeoning martial arts subculture. Itinerant martial arts troupes resurfaced and entertained crowds with their exploits. Blockbuster movies such as *Shaolin Temple* triggered a cult following among youth, who flocked to the temples of Shaolin, Wudang and Emei in search of the secret teachings of a master.

These films and novels depict Buddhist monks and Taoist masters who can fly, disappear and reappear, and read people's minds— abilities they are said to have acquired through the mastery of 'inner cultivation' (*neigong*), which involves the body, breath and mind control exercises associated with *qigong*. For thousands of kung fu fans, it thus became apparent that the magical feats of the past and the stunts of pulp films were not fiction: they could be mastered through initiation to a *qigong* master. *Qigong* masters, with their miraculous healing abilities and their Extraordinary Powers, soon came to be seen as living incarnations of the wizards of kung fu culture.

THE LEGEND OF THE GRANDMASTER

Increasingly *qigong* masters were becoming charismatic figures who stole the limelight from the body techniques, which one did not even need to practise: one could be cured directly by the master. The *qigong* master combined in his own body the powers of the magicians of ancient times and the knowledge of a great scientist.

Legends grew around the most famous masters, many of whom were said to have demonstrated miraculous powers from their early childhood in a poor countryside surrounded by mountains, grottoes and temples. *Qigong* literature and the publications of the different denominations are full of biographies which share a mythical structure often containing common themes, and reminiscent of a Chinese tradition of hagiographic literature going back at least as far as the *Biographies of the Immortals* of the first century BC.[7] Typically the

---

[7]   *Liexian zhuan*, Taoist Canon 294, after K. Schipper, 1975, *Concordance du Tao Tsang*, Paris: École Française d'Extrême-Orient. For biographies of *qigong* masters, see for example, on Yan Xin: Zhang Bangshen 1992: 304–6 and Qin Hui 1990; on Chen Linfeng: Chen Linfeng 1993: 254–62; on Zhang Hongbao: Ji Yi 1990a;

future *qigong* master is presented as a country boy or girl who grows up under the harsh peasant living conditions of his or her family, and stands out for his or her unique qualities: intelligence, cunning, filial piety and precocious manifestation of a miraculous power. Yan Xin's story emphasises the magical scenery, the mysterious grottoes and the holy temples of the region surrounding his native village, which he explored from a tender age and which impregnated him with mystical energies.[8] Typically the masters were said to have received initiation from as early as the age of four from a succession of mysterious sages, monks and masters representing all the esoteric traditions of Taoism, Buddhism, Confucianism, Chinese medicine and martial arts. The turning point in the child's life is an encounter with an unknown sage. A mysterious personage whose identity is unknown, lacking a fixed abode and wandering from place to place, sometimes a Buddhist monk or a Taoist hermit, a 'superman' capable of working miracles, an old man seeking a disciple to pass on an ancient, secret teaching, the sage identifies the future disciple who is still in his or her tender childhood years. The sage appears in the child's dreams, watches during his or her games, magically corrects behaviour, initiates him or her into moral and esoteric secrets, and gives a strict training regimen including martial arts, meditation, mantra recitation, healing techniques and the study of scriptures. After a period of incubation, during which the young master conceals his or her abilities, the initiator gives the command to 'go out of the mountains' (*chushan*)—to manifest his or her powers and knowledge to the public, in order to deliver the world from its agony. 'From now on, you can go out of the mountains and found your lineage, in order to save all sentient beings', Chen Linfeng's master told him.[9] Thus the *qigong* master doesn't choose to become a master: he or she is chosen by the sages who transmit the secret teaching. The meeting between the sage and the disciple is often considered to be predestined—the *yuanfen* or fruit of karma. In Li Hongzhi's case, however, it is Li himself who, after reflecting

---

on Li Hongzhi: Li Hongzhi 2000 [1994]: 14–20. Excerpts of these biographies are quoted at length in Palmer 2005a: 186–96. See Penny 2003 for a critical study of the different versions of Li Hongzhi's biography, discussed in the context of the Chinese tradition of hagiographic literature. See also Penny, 'Immortality and Transcendence' in Kohn 2004, pp. 109–33; and Penny 2002c.

8 Zhang Bangshen 1992: 304.

9 Chen Linfeng 1993: 262.

Table 1   QIGONG MASTERS' INITIATION TO BODY
                          TECHNOLOGIES

Period of initiation	No. of masters	%
Republican period: 1911–49	15	6.7
First *qigong wave*: 1950–64	45	20.2
Ban on *qigong*: 1965–78	52	23.3
Second *qigong wave*: 1979–91	111	49.8
Total	223	100.0

Note   Based on answers given by 223 of the total sample of 554 masters
listed in WH. The remaining 331 masters did not specify when they were
first initiated.

on the suffering of the world, gives himself the mission of saving
the world by adapting his esoteric wisdom to the needs of common
people; the sages come back to help him set every movement and
posture of the method, until it 'assembles all the mysterious forces
of the universe and is the quintessence of the entire universe'.[10] Invested with this mission, the master belongs to a different category
from common people. His or her exceptional nature expresses itself
through the ability to transcend physical laws, giving the capacity
to heal incurable diseases. In some cases, the master is depicted
as controlling all the powers of the universe. Zhang Hongbao is
called a 'god'.[11] Yan Xin is compared to an 'Immortal', to a 'Living
Buddha'. Li Hongzhi poses as an omniscient spirit of the universe,
from whom even the 'Buddhas, Taos and Gods' learn the 'Great
Dharma'.[12]

THE ORIGINS OF THE QIGONG MASTERS

Who were these masters? This section, using biographical data,
looks at where they came from, traces how they entered the *qigong*
sector, and identifies their place in society. It then looks at the strategies deployed by entrepreneurial individuals as they strove to be
recognised as masters and to acquire the charisma expected of a
master in the *qigong* sector.

[10]   Li Hongzhi 2000 [1994]: 20.
[11]   Ji Yi 1990a: 66–7.
[12]   Li Hongzhi 1998b: 37.

Table 2   CLAIMED SOURCE OF MASTERS'
TRADITIONAL INITIATION

Tradition	No. of masters	%
Martial (*wu*)	75	47.5
Medical (*yi*)	55	34.8
Buddhist (*fo*)	16	10.2
Taoist (*dao*)	15	9.5
Literati/Confucian (*wen/ru*)	7	4.4
Book of Changes (*zhouyi, yijing*)	4	2.5
Extraordinary Powers (*teyigongneng*)	3	1.9
Muslim (*musilin*)	1	0.6

Note   Based on answers given by 158 masters (28.5 per cent of the sample)
who claimed to have been initiated by family tradition or during their childhood or adolescence. Note, several masters claimed initiation into more than
one tradition, hence the sum of all categories is higher than 158 and percentages
total more than 100.

While modern, institutional and élitist *qigong* had been eradicated during the Cultural Revolution, underground lineages of
traditional body technologies had continued to be transmitted in
the marginalised worlds of martial arts, family healing traditions
and popular religion. Those lineages had in fact continued to exist
since before 1949. Cut off from the popular world, official *qigong*
had co-opted only a minority of popular masters between 1949
and 1965. The rest had had nothing to do with the new *qigong*
institutions. Traditional body technologies had thus been practised
in two distinct worlds: the institutional world of *qigong*, and the
popular world in which, as in previous historical periods, a great
variety of body techniques were transmitted in different isolated
lineages, which lacked a single unifying concept or community of
practitioners transcending the particular traditions.

But the success of Guo Lin's *qigong* method in the late 1970s
triggered a bandwagon effect, with dozens of denominations appearing between 1979 and 1981. Most of the masters who began
to teach their methods openly after 1978 had not been involved in
the medical *qigong* institutions of the 1950s and early 1960s. Rather
they were holders of body technology traditions which had been
transmitted underground since before the Communist regime.

Table 3　INSTITUTIONAL AFFILIATION OF MASTERS

Institutional Affiliation	No. of masters	%
Medical: doctor or nurse in a health care institution; graduate of a medical school.	130	23.5
Educational: teacher in a primary, secondary or tertiary school or college.	73	13.2
Scientific or technical: researcher in a research unit in a recognised discipline; engineer in a technical unit.	52	9.4
Political: secretary-general or deputy secretary of a Party branch; official of a unit.	26	4.7
Martial arts: trainer or member of a martial arts association.	25	4.5
Sports: member of a sports commission or association.	23	4.2
Cultural: writer, journalist, painter, musician, dancer, calligrapher, photographer, member of a literary or artistic association.	21	3.8
Military/police: cadre or trainer in a military or police unit.	20	3.6
Religious: monk in a Buddhist or Taoist monastery.	3	0.5

Note　Percentages of the entire sample of 554 masters. Note that some masters claimed more than one institutional affiliation, while 253 masters (46%) did not mention any institutional affiliation other than *qigong* organizations.

In the new, more open climate following the end of the Cultural Revolution they 'came out of the mountains' and transmitted their techniques under the legitimised name of *qigong*. Traditional lineages were modified to fit with the mass transmission model developed by Guo Lin.

Many of the *qigong* masters of the 1980s claimed to have learned body technologies in traditional lineages in the early days of the Communist regime, without mentioning any contact with the official *qigong* units of that period. It was only in the 1980s that they proclaimed themselves as '*qigong* masters', inscribing the techniques they had inherited into the *qigong* category, and joining the *qigong* sector. But in the 1950s and 1960s they had learned body technologies from relatives or from Taoist, Buddhist or martial arts masters, independently of the development of *qigong* within medical insti-

Table 4   AGE OF QIGONG MASTERS

Year of birth	Age in 1990	Number	%
Not declared	–	68	n/a
1900–9	80–89	4	0.8
1910–19	70–79	7	1.4
1920–9	60–69	41	8.4
1930–9	50–59	119	24.5
1940–9	40–49	120	24.7
1950–9	30–39	105	21.6
1960–9	20–29	80	16.5
1970–9	10–19	9	1.9
1980–9	0–9	1	0.2

Note   Percentages calculated after eliminating masters whose year of birth is unknown.

tutions. Likewise many '*qigong* masters' who appeared in the 1980s had learned traditional body technologies during the Cultural Revolution years. This was notably the case of some of the most famous masters, such as Yan Xin and Li Hongzhi.[13]

Using data in a biographical directory of over 500 *qigong* masters,[14] an impression can be formed of the ways in which body technologies were transmitted during that period. After 1965, although the *qigong* institutions had been shut down, traditional body technologies continued to be transmitted in popular settings, following the traditional pattern: individual and often secret transmission in family, medical, religious or martial arts lineages. In some cases body technologies were learned as a result of the special circumstances of the Cultural Revolution, such as training to be a barefoot doctor or being sent to the countryside. Large numbers of individuals

13   See chapters 5 (for Yan Xin) and 8 (for Li Hongzhi).
14   WH: 500–99. The entries in this directory having been submitted by the masters themselves, the accuracy of the data cannot be verified. We can assume that, in an attempt to present themselves as having inherited ancient traditions, and as having a long experience in *qigong* practice, these aspects of their biographies are exaggerated. Even taking this probable distortion into account, however, the overall data as analysed here still leads to conclusions at variance with the one *qigong* masters typically present of themselves: most masters had in fact only recently learned traditional body technologies.

who had learned body techniques in these settings would proclaim themselves '*qigong* masters' in the 1980s.[15]

According to this directory, we can estimate that a sizable minority of the masters first learned body technologies between 1965 and 1977. It thus appears that there was no 'gap' in the transmission of traditional body technologies during the Cultural Revolution. But most *qigong* masters were only recently initiated to traditional body technologies: out of 223 masters who mentioned the year of their first initiation to body technologies, half claimed to have begun in or after 1979, in the heat of the *qigong* wave (see Table 1).

As a whole, *qigong* masters had few concrete links with the traditional lineages of the past. Almost three quarters of the sample (71.5 per cent) did not claim to be inheritors of a traditional lineage, while only 30 per cent claimed to have been initiated during their childhood or adolescence. Given the tendency of *qigong* masters to fabricate a genealogy of traditional lineages in order to enhance their credibility, we can assume that the true figure would be even lower. Of these, almost half claimed to have learned martial arts, and over a third claimed a traditional medical affiliation (see Table 2). One tenth affirmed having being initiated to Buddhist and Taoist traditions respectively. Finally, other cases also existed: literati (Confucian) tradition; training in the *Book of Changes*, transmission of Extraordinary Powers, Islam. In these traditional lineages, transmission occurred either within the family (by the father, the grandfather, an uncle etc.) or outside the family (by a martial arts master, a monk etc.). According to the sample, the medical and Taoist traditions were mainly transmitted within the family line, while martial arts and Buddhist traditions tended to be transmitted outside the family.

To summarise, the sample shows that the martial and medical traditions predominated among those masters who had been initiated into a traditional lineage. This data suggests that *qigong* has its roots in the popular martial arts and healing milieus. But one enigma remains: how many of these traditional lineages linked to popular sects and redemptive societies, which were so widespread in the decades preceding the CCP regime, used healing arts as recruitment tactics, and played an important role in the diffusion of

---

15 For some specific examples, see Palmer 2005a: 88–91.

traditional body technologies in popular culture?[16] A *qigong* master would naturally never declare such an affiliation, such groups having been ruthlessly suppressed as 'counterrevolutionary secret societies' in the first years of the People's Republic.[17]

As for their current institutional affiliation, half of the masters declared that they belonged to medical, educational, scientific or political institutions: the core of the *qigong* sector was made up of petty intellectuals: among the masters, there were few or no university professors or high-level scientists. Rather, they were medical workers, primary or secondary school teachers, engineers, and technicians. (See Table 3)

Turning to their age, *qigong* masters are products of the Mao generation: barely 10 per cent were old enough to have spent much of their life in the pre-Communist days; less than one sixth was part of the young post-Mao generation.[18] At the peak of '*qigong* fever' in 1990 the majority of *qigong* masters was made up of middle-aged men[19] who had lived most of their lives under Mao (1949–76).

These data indicate that as a whole *qigong* masters formed a new and marginal community, partly derived from popular traditions (principally martial arts and traditional medicine), and at the margins of modern knowledge institutions. They had almost no link with official religious institutions, whether Buddhist or Taoist. As a consequence, they held a precarious position vis-à-vis both orthodox religious traditions and modern institutions.

ELEMENTS OF CHARISMA

By the end of the 1980s, and under the influence of paranormal discourse, miraculous powers had become essential to the role of the master. It was no longer enough to create and to teach a *qigong* method. But, as we have seen, *qigong* masters were a group of middle-aged (principally) men, of ordinary status in society, and marginal vis-à-vis both traditional and modern institutions. The role of *qigong* master, however, required that they be superhumans, holders

16 Naquin 1976: 29–30; Naquin 1985: 282; Zheng Guanglu 1995: 86–94.
17 See Shao 1997; Palmer forthcoming b.
18 Born just before, during or after the Cultural Revolution, this generation has a different mentality from the one that preceded it, which was completely moulded by Maoist culture.
19 According to the data in WH, over 80 per cent of *qigong* masters were men.

of a mystic force inherited from secret traditions going back to high antiquity, and transmitters of a path of salvation for humanity. How could they come to be identified with such an image? The career of the *qigong* master was a process of creating a public personality surrounded by a legend, until coming to be naturally and unconsciously perceived as an incarnation of the archetype. The essential factor in the emergence of the master was public charisma: the identity between the master and the mythical figure had to be convincing and not artificial. The master had to cultivate an image of a 'true' *qigong* master and not of a charlatan, in a context where 'phonies' were increasingly numerous. The status of '*qigong* master' was never objectively acquired or universally recognised: it was the subject of a perpetual struggle.

A master's charisma was composed of four major ingredients: healing powers; virtue; initiation into a tradition; and status as a person of science. First, powers: this was the most important criterion. Since there was no 'orthodox' *qigong* tradition that could separate the 'true' masters from the 'fake' ones, the demonstration of true powers was the only way to prove one's abilities as an authentic master. Thus the public demonstrations of Extraordinary Powers, the *qi*-emission séances, the charismatic lectures and the testimonies of the healed became events contributing to the image of a person endowed with Extraordinary Powers, which could be seen and felt by the average person. When a 'legend' grew around a master, that master quickly took on a superhuman stature.

Second, virtue: this quality was recognised when a master lived a simple life and treated the sick for free. We find here the ancient Chinese notion of virtue as a charismatic force. The criterion of virtue serves to judge the master's intentions: does the master heal for money—which could lead to swindling people—or have a true mission of sacrifice for others?

Third, initiation into a tradition: the master is an initiate, the inheritor of a secret tradition transmitted from antiquity to a tiny number of the elect. This notion created a link between the master and the magical powers of the mythical figures of the past—sages, immortals and awakened ones. The master became an incarnation of those myths, and created a concrete and living link between disciples and the mythical tradition.

At the same time—and this is the fourth ingredient—the master is presented as a person of science, a 'life scientist' who conducted laboratory experiments, embodying in his or her person the powers of science. Thus the master's search for collaborators in the prestigious universities and institutions that could lend their scientific aura.[20]

But the master's credibility was never definitively acquired. Always doubted by part of the public and contested by the anti-*qigong* polemicists, the master's aura rested on weak foundations. The affiliations to traditional lineages were difficult, if not impossible, to prove, and it was well known in the *qigong* milieu that they were often invented. Recognition from official and scientific institutions could be withdrawn as scientific opinion and the political winds changed. And the alleged healing powers and Extraordinary Powers of the masters were the subject of a heated controversy.[21]

In itself, then, the master's charisma was insufficient. To consolidate the support of thousands, if not millions of practitioners, the master had to cultivate two networks: in the direction of official circles, a network of Connections—relationships based on reciprocal obligations[22]—and in the direction of the public, a network for the teaching and transmission of his or her method. A typical master's career would thus go through the following phases:

First, the learning of body technologies—either from a traditional master or *qigong* master, or from self-instruction manuals. Having mastered the basic postures as well as the healing techniques (emission of external *qi*, divination etc.), the would-be master could start healing amongst family members, friends, neighbours and colleagues. A group of patients and students would form, who believed in the Extraordinary Powers and who would then consider the would-be a 'master'.

The next step involved recognition as a master by the *qigong* sector: this was called 'coming out of the mountains' (*chushan*), an expression that evokes the image of a sage who renounces his secluded life as a hermit to save humanity. To create such an event, the would-be master had to create his own *qigong* method, which, at the beginning, could be little more than a name attached to a simple set of postures. He or she also had to cultivate relationships with the leaders of a state-sponsored *qigong* association; give lectures in a university; collaborate with scientists on Extraordinary Powers

20 See chapter 4.
21 See chapter 6.
22 See introduction, pp. 15–17.

research; be hired by a hospital or a clinic; be featured in a newspaper article or a television report. By these means, the master could enter the *qigong* circle and acquire a certain reputation.

The number of practitioners of the would-be master's method would increase, as well as the number of sick people imploring treatment. Local state-sponsored *qigong* associations in other cities and regions of China would proffer invitations to give lectures and workshops. All of this allowed the master to make money and to expand his or her network of students. The master could also accept personal disciples (*tudi*).

At the same time, in order to be able to create a transmission system that would be efficient and replicable on a large scale, the master's method had to be compact, easy to teach, and offer a clear path of progression. It also had to be replicable in writing: the master needed to publish a book on him/herself and his/her method. Most masters were unable to write a book, so they simply edited the transcripts of their lectures, or hired a writer. And from the master's network of political supporters an official would be asked to compose a calligraphic foreword. If the master was able to advance the printing costs of the book, finding a publisher was not a problem.

With the master's method, book and transmission network, the denomination could expand on a large scale. But if the master wanted to rise a notch higher, to become a celebrity, or even the greatest of the *qigong* masters, the support of Officials was essential—to open doors, to strengthen the denomination's legitimacy, and for protection in case of bureaucratic actions against the master or the denomination. The mass media also played a capital role in the 'deification' of certain masters, such as Yan Xin and Zhang Hongbao.[23]

Yan Xin, the most famous of the masters, was an unknown doctor of Chinese medicine until a local newspaper published a report on a miraculous healing attributed to him. He was then invited to Beijing by Zhang Zhenhuan, the *qigong* sector's main political supporter, who introduced him into the *qigong* circuit. He healed and gave lectures in several cities, and collaborated with researchers at Qinghua University in an experiment on external *qi*, which received sensational media coverage.[24] He published his method,

23 See Appendix.
24 See pp. 138–43.

'Yan Xin Qigong', and began a charismatic lecture tour of China. He also created a transmission network, but left China before his organisation was consolidated. As a result, his network was not influential in the *qigong* sector.

The other most reputed grandmaster, Zhang Hongbao, was an unknown student who learned *qigong* by himself and by signing up for various *qigong* training workshops in the Beijing area. He built up an initial core of disciples—who were college professors and classmates—and had himself invited to give a lecture at his university. He founded his method, 'Qigong for Nourishing Life and Increasing Intelligence' and an organisation to propagate it. Invited to give workshops in universities, government agencies and media organs, he quickly entered the capital city's networks of power. Television features made him famous all over China, and a hagiographic bestseller on him by reporter Ji Yi turned him into a national idol. With the help of military and political officials in outlying provinces (Sichuan and Shaanxi), he built his huge transmission organisation, which continued to expand even after Zhang Hongbao's disappearance in 1995.[25]

A master's career thus consisted of cultivating around him/herself a charismatic aura; a network of political relations; and a mass of followers. *Qigong* masters were not modest hermits or secretive sages like those from whom they claimed to inherit their knowledge and power. They were public figures engaged in a perpetual struggle to be recognised and accepted as grandmasters by the public.

---

[25] See p. 218.

4

QIGONG SCIENTISM

In his book *Swirls of Qi in the Celestial Empire*, *qigong* master and popular chronicler Zheng Guanglu describes the impact on the popular imagination of the fusion of Extraordinary Powers and *qigong*:

From the end of the 1970s to the beginning of the 1980s *qigong* was still mainly an effective method of physical culture, prevention and therapy. Later this conception of *qigong* came to be called 'traditional *qigong*'.

Around the middle of the 1980s, ever since Extraordinary Powers were considered as the superior level of *qigong* … the meaning of *qigong* has been greatly enriched and enlarged. The health and therapeutic efficacy of *qigong* is now seen merely as an elementary, even accessory, function of *qigong*. Restricting *qigong* to the field of therapy is seen as a serious obstacle to its development.

Thus a new *qigong* was born.

This new *qigong* is considered an art of physical training, of illness prevention, of therapy, of performance, of combat, of police investigation, of geological prospecting, of intelligence development, of stimulation of functions, of increasing one's powers.

Its advanced level is shown by Extraordinary Powers: penetrating vision, distant vision, distant sensation, the ability to immobilise one's body, to fly miraculously, to cross walls, to soar spiritually, to call the wind and bring the rain, to know the past and the future.

Qigong has become an 'art of the Immortals' for which nothing is impossible.[1]

Paranormal *qigong* triggered great hope and enthusiasm, and became the basis of a discourse which merged the magical imagination of martial arts novels with the futuristic utopia of science fiction, stimulating hope for the resurrection of Chinese civilisation, the salvation of humanity and a paradisiacal future in which nothing would be impossible for man. This discourse, which was

---

[1]   ZGL: 58.

elaborated by scientific and intellectual *qigong* enthusiasts, created a bridge between popular practices and beliefs and intellectual values and ideologies. Scientistic discourse of *qigong* thus played a key role in creating common values for the *qigong* milieu, energising it as a utopian movement, and providing it with political legitimacy. This chapter will examine *qigong*'s attempt to become a science. It begins by looking at the core components of the *qigong* movement's vision of itself as a revolutionary science and knowledge system. It then turns to the practical strategies deployed by the *qigong* sector to be recognised as a science by the scientific community and the general public. Finally, it looks at the dynamics between three groups of people—*qigong* practitioners, Extraordinary Powers researchers, and sceptics—and how the tensions between them shaped the contours of *qigong* discourse.

BASIC DISCOURSES

As they watched a *qigong* master move a cigarette butt with his Extraordinary Powers, journalists Li Jianxin and Zheng Qin had the feeling of witnessing a historic moment, when the magical powers of kung fu heroes manifest themselves before one's very eyes. The scene occurs at a banquet in a Beijing restaurant, in the presence of Zhang Yaoting, office director of the Leaders' Working Group on Somatic Sciences. Without physical contact, *Qigong* master Liu Xinyu has just moved a cigarette butt placed under a parsley leaf and a piece of paper.

[Liu Xinyu] turned to his side, tilted his head, and looked at the objects obliquely. Just when he tilted his head, the cigarette butt moved. Everyone exclaimed and applauded.

The cigarette butt's movement was very strange … as if a formless force connected Liu Xinyu's head to the cigarette butt—he only needed to move his head to make the cigarette butt move.

It was as if the cigarette butt had its own living consciousness, which wanted to come out from under the parsley leaf and the piece of paper that covered [it]. By this turn, the cigarette butt freed itself [from the parsley and the paper] and put itself completely in the open. …

[Then, the cigarette butt rose up, as if to salute Zhang Yaoting].

When Liu had moved the butt the first time, he had already given it a kind of vital force, a kind of soul. From that moment, it was no longer a lifeless cigarette butt, but a little spirit with a soul. Liu Xinyu could communicate with it, ask it to make different movements; when he gave it an order, the butt obeyed—and this without him intensely staring at it. So Liu Xinyu could relax and drink, and the butt continued to nod.

The myriad beings all have a soul.

The myriad beings can communicate spiritually.

Liu Xinyu said: 'I communicate with them, I give them a vital force.'

... Liu Xinyu took [the author's] pen, signed his autograph on the cigarette butt, and wrote the date: 1 November 1994. And he asked Zhang Yaoting to sign the butt as well.

Thus this little cigarette butt became an important souvenir: the trace of an important experiment in somatic science. Its existence ... proves that in our world, there are indeed certain efficient forces, which cannot yet be explained by the forces already known to physics.

Liu Xinyu said: 'This cigarette butt can cure illnesses: for example, in the case of a headache or of pain in some part of the body, you only need to point the cigarette butt towards the affected area for a moment, and you will notice the result.'

Zhang Yaoting asked for a white napkin; he wrapped it around the cigarette butt and placed it into his coat pocket, in order to keep it at home. ...

[Liu Xinyu] uses an inner power.

It is a power out of the ordinary.

Perhaps it is the marvellous power of the heroes of martial arts novels.

... In a small restaurant in Beijing, we witnessed this marvellous power with our own eyes: a power which, in the past, could only be found in the novels of errant knights. But this time, it absolutely and truly appeared under our eyes, emanating from the hand of our own friend.[2]

This story encapsulates many ideas and images common in *qigong* discourse: the animistic cosmology—all creatures have a soul, and *qigong* masters can communicate with them; the association with the imagery of martial arts novels, a popular literary genre which highlights the exploits of *gongfu* masters with magical powers; and the realisation that these powers, still unknown to modern physics, are true and proven by this 'important experiment in somatic science' conducted on a used cigarette butt during a restaurant banquet. The idea that *qigong* was the true manifestation of the magic of popular legends, and thus a great scientific discovery of historical significance, is central to the discourse of the *qigong* movement, which can be summarised as six propositions:

1. *Qigong* practice permits the emergence of Extraordinary Powers;

---

2 QDL: 156–7.

2. External *qi* and Extraordinary Powers are material facts, and the basis of somatic science;
3. *Qigong* is the source and essence of Chinese civilisation;
4. Somatic science will trigger a new scientific revolution;
5. This revolution will allow China to recover its place as a leader among world nations;
6. *Qigong* carries the promise of a radiant future for all humanity.

These propositions are interrelated to form an ideological structure (see Fig. 2).

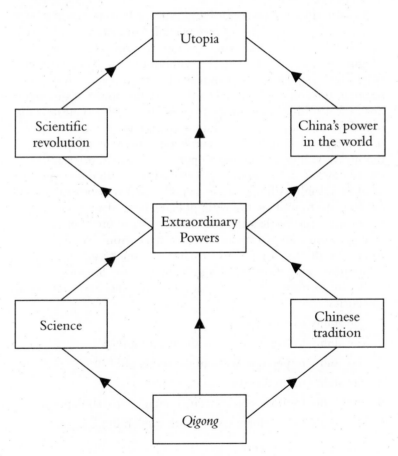

Fig. 2   Ideological structure of *qigong* discourse

EXTRAORDINARY POWERS

Figure 2 illustrates the central location of Extraordinary Powers in *qigong* discourse. Through Extraordinary Powers the *qigong* adept can find deliverance from illness and from the limitations of this world, and through Extraordinary Powers nothing will be impossible for man in the future. Thanks to Extraordinary Powers China has a unique civilisation, and will regain her place as a world leader. Also thanks to Extraordinary Powers, *qigong* is an important subject for science, and it will trigger the new scientific revolution. In *qigong*, then, the ultimate objective became to acquire Extraordinary Powers.

So what does *teyi gongneng* (Extraordinary Powers) actually refer to? According to 'hard *qigong*' master Ding Mingyue, Extraordinary Powers refers to the following abilities: to stop mosquitoes from stinging people; to kick a chicken without making it cluck; to provoke a fight between two inanimate objects; to attract a fish out of water; to turn off a light or light a fire with the power of a thought; not to feel cold in mid-winter; to make an egg fly; to create a fog to hide one's body; to make Chinese characters appear on a surface of water; to make knocking sounds on a door in the middle of the night, without anyone being present; to have a truck roll over one's body and escape injury; to pierce a brick with one's finger; to swallow a drink with one's nose; to pull a car with one's tongue; to swallow fire; to walk on fire without being burned; to swallow glass; to break a wine bottle with one's head; to stand on a light bulb or an egg; to cause an increase or decrease in a person's blood pressure; to change the smell of water; to change a duck egg into a cube without breaking it; and to change a chicken into a parrot.[3]

Writer Ke Yunlu divided Extraordinary Powers into a few main categories:

1. the ability to cure disease;
2. the ability to live normally without eating (*bigu*);
3. the ability to perceive without the senses (ESP);
4. the ability to predict the future;
5. the ability to move objects from a distance (psychokinesis);
6. the ability to transform matter with one's mind.[4]

---

3   Ding Mingyue 1994: 147–9.
4   Ke Yunlu 1994, 1996.

Qigong master Zhang Hongbao, using concepts borrowed from Buddhism, described five ascending levels of Extraordinary Powers. The first, called 'eye of flesh' (*rouyangong*), involves the ability to perceive *qi* and auras emanating from other people or objects, allowing one to diagnose illness through such direct perception. The second, called 'eye of heaven' (*tianyangong*), is the ability to see through or inside one's own body, the body of other people, or other objects, in other words to see through any obstacles to the object of one's gaze. The third, 'eye of wisdom' (*huiyangong*), involves the ability to see through time and bring back messages from the past or future. The fourth, 'eye of Dharma' (*fayangong*), refers to psychokinesis, which can be subdivided into three categories: minor psychokinesis, such as catching a pill in mid-air or making leaves fall off a tree then reattach themselves; intermediate psychokinesis, such as tearing up a business card and restoring it to its original condition; and major psychokinesis, such as moving a mountain, bringing an animal back to life, or reverting from old age to youth. The fifth, 'eye of Buddha' (*foyangong*), is the ability to change the meaning of someone's life, to lead them from ignorance to enlightenment. It is also the ability to open up other people's Extraordinary Powers, and to exert a 'magnetic' attraction on others.[5]

Extraordinary Powers are thus a category which overlaps with that of paranormal phenomena in the West, defined by parapsychologists as 'patterns of organism–environment interaction that appear to be anomalous with respect to known physical laws', also called 'psychic' or 'psi' phenomena, and including psychokinesis and extra-sensory perception such as telepathy, clairvoyance and precognition.[6] The Chinese notion of Extraordinary Powers, however, seems to place a greater emphasis on healing powers than does the category of the paranormal. According to Chinese somatic scientists, all humans possess latent Extraordinary Powers. The only difference between individuals is that each person has a different Extraordinary Powers potential, which most people have never developed.[7] The great discovery is that *qigong* is an effective means to develop the latent Extraordinary Powers of the human body.[8] *Qigong* discourse rests on the premise that *qigong* is much more than

5 Ji Yi 1991: 121–42.
6 Hess 1993: 7.
7 Zhang Hongbao, quoted in Ji Yi 1991: 120.
8 Ke Yunlu 1996: 30.

a simple hygienic or therapeutic technique, and that the magical, mystical and extraordinary dimension, expressed as Extraordinary Powers, is essential to the definition of *qigong*.[9]

At the same time, Extraordinary Powers were conceived as a material reality with an empirical existence. On 23 February 1986 Qian Xuesen elaborated his vision of a 'phenomenological science of *qigong*', based on a concept of man as an open 'megasystem' in intimate relation with his environment. Following a Marxist dialectical logic, the mind is seen as the movement of matter in the brain, which affects the matter of the organs. *Qigong* arranges and orders the pre-existing elements of the human body, producing a healthy functional state that strengthens immunity.

Qian advocated using the methods of systems science to elaborate a strategy for *qigong* research. He proposed three methodological principles:

1. Begin by investigating the experience of *qigong* practitioners, and the objective changes observed during *qigong* therapy;

2. At a higher level, synthesise the experience of *qigong* masters, as a basis for compiling *qigong* teaching manuals;

3. At an even higher level, research and compile *qigong* theoretical texts.

Qian Xuesen considered that such a research programme would lead to the construction of a '*qigong* phenomenology' (*weixiang qigongxue*), which would consist of collecting, classifying and systematising knowledge, data and documents on *qigong*. Then, on the basis of an increasingly coherent synthesis of such elements, it would be possible to elaborate a scientific model for *qigong*, which would conform to Marxist philosophy and systems science. *Qigong* could thus pass from the status of a 'phenomenological' science to that of a 'true' science.[10]

The powers of *qigong* and Extraordinary Powers were not seen as supernatural in the sense that they were expressions of a different ontological reality than that of the material world: rather, they were seen as universal material forces, which are mysterious only

---

9 During the 1990s some individuals in *qigong* circles, such as Zhang Honglin and Sima Nan, contested the link between *qigong* and Extraordinary Powers. Their view was a minority position in the *qigong* milieu, but led to heated controversy. See chapter 6.

10 QG 7(3): 99.

because their mechanisms are for the moment still unknown to science. *Qigong* and Extraordinary Powers could thus be subjects of legitimate scientific research, within the framework of a new discipline called 'somatic science' by Qian Xuesen, the goal of which would be to discover the laws governing such forces in order to allow humanity to master them. The subject matter of somatic science would include the human body, the protection of the body's ordinary functions, and the exploitation of new latent functions of the body.[11] The new discipline's research programme would thus involve conducting empirical research on Extraordinary Powers phenomena; establishing a classification of different types of functions; discovering their physical and physiological mechanisms; and investigating their social and cultural applications.[12]

QIGONG AND CHINESE CIVILISATION

Although somatic researchers studied much the same phenomena as Western parapsychologists, they considered themselves to have a great advantage over their foreign colleagues: through *qigong* they had at their disposal a systematic method for producing such phenomena, tried and tested over more than 5,000 years, the applications of which were already described in a huge corpus of ancient theoretical and technical texts.[13]

Chinese cosmology, in which *qi* is a key concept, provided modern somatic scientists with the basis of a theoretical framework which was lacking in Western parapsychology. Thus Yan Xin presented *qigong* as a renaissance of Chinese civilisation following centuries of decay. According to Yan, Extraordinary Powers had been perfectly mastered by the ancient Chinese, who made use of them to establish civilisation. In ancient China it was common for men to 'see at an infinite distance and hear as far as the wind can blow'.[14] Great figures such as Laozi were accomplished *qigong* masters.

During [its first historical] period, *qigong* was largely used by society in all aspects of human life. It served to preserve health, to prevent and to treat diseases. It was also used for the development of certain Extraordinary Powers such as predicting events (the *Book of Changes* is one example),

11 Qian Xuesen 1998b.
12 Ke Yunlu, quoted in QDL: 67–8; Qian Xuesen 1998a: 2–6.
13 Qian Xuesen 1988: 206–7.
14 Yan Xin 1998: 60.

for social control (politics), war and communication with nature. It was the basis for the development of culture, including the creation of written language, the discovery of herbal medicine and the emergence of various forms of art. And, most important, it laid the foundations on which religions were created.[15]

Qigong is thus the source of Chinese civilisation;[16] at the same time it is a scientific method: the founders of Chinese civilisation possessed a true science—a science which gave them the magical powers described in ancient literature, and which allowed China to enter its Golden Age.

Yan Xin states that during the second period in the history of *qigong*, which lasted from 2,000 years ago until modern times, religions were founded by accomplished *qigong* masters. As religions became more formalised, they gradually replaced the essence of *qigong* with religious dogma, and discouraged the teaching of *qigong*. As a result true *qigong* masters hid in the mountains, and only a very small number of disciples could gain access to their secret teachings.[17] The science of *qigong* was corrupted by religion, feudalism and superstition. Yan Xin states:

Under the influence of feudal consciousness, certain people mystified, impaired and transformed [*qigong*]. During this process, it was wrapped in a false garb, and erroneous contents were added. In order to reinforce their domination, feudal lords added terrible things to *qigong*; and purely religious people, in order to conform to the requirements of feudalism, also added horrible things. Consciously or not, *qigong* was transformed by people, and lost its [original] content from late antiquity.[18]

In Yan Xin's historical schema, the third, contemporary era is characterised by the reappearance of *qigong* and Extraordinary Powers and their widespread recognition. They attain a scientific basis, and are taught at a scale not seen in over a thousand years.[19] The history of *qigong*, identified with the essence of Chinese civilisation, thus passes through stages of original purity, decadence and resurrection.[20]

15 IYXQA 1995: 3–4; see also Qin Hui 1990: 202–3; Yan Xin 1988: 24–7.
16 It was also commonly believed in *qigong* circles that *qigong* is the source of Chinese medicine: see Qian Xuesen 1981b: 219.
17 IYXQA 1995: 4–5; see also Qin Hui 1990: 203; Yan Xin 1988: 27–8.
18 Yan Xin 1998: 60.
19 IYXQA 1995: 5.
20 For similar historical schema by other authors, see Tao Bingfu and Yang Weihe

THE SCIENTIFIC REVOLUTION

Qigong was seen as more than a simple renaissance of ancient traditions. It was also more than the scientific proof and mastery of paranormal force. *Qigong* was seen as opening the possibility of a new holistic cosmology that could encompass the wisdom of the past and the discoveries of the future. For Qian Xuesen, it was a new school of thought based on the idea that 'man is a supersystem in the environment of the megasystem of the universe'.[21] The integration of *qigong*, Chinese medicine and Extraordinary Powers into somatic science would

> ... transform modern science, making science advance one step further. This is the great mission that we must accomplish. As soon as this mission is accomplished, it will inevitably provoke the explosion of a new scientific revolution ... We can all consider that it will be the scientific revolution of the Orient. During this process Marxist philosophy will deepen and develop itself. ... At present, in foreign countries, they all say that technology must be developed. I consider that the highest of high technologies is the scientific technology of *qigong*.[22]

For Qian, *qigong* offered the solution to the renewal of Marxism.[23] He was reported as saying that this would be 'an even greater scientific revolution than quantum mechanics and relativity'.[24] Another author described *qigong* as the key to bridging, with the aid of dialectical philosophy, the opposition between modern science and traditional holism, and thereby between the spiritual and the material, the subjective and the objective, unity and opposition, outward investigation and inner contemplation, and the whole and the part. This would lead to an evolutionary leap, from the 'kingdom of necessity' to the 'kingdom of freedom'.[25]

In line with Chinese totalistic visions of science as an all-encompassing system of knowledge, the truly revolutionary aspect

---

1981: 1–10; Zhang Zhenhuan and Tao Zulai 1989. For an essay arguing that *qigong* is closely linked to the development of traditional Chinese philosophy, religion, non-interventionist political culture and ethics, as well as literary culture, song, opera and painting, see Li Ping 1998.

21   Qian Xuesen 1996: 471. On Qian's promotion of 'cultural systems engineering' for the furtherance of spiritual civilisation, see Bakken 2000: 50–9.

22   Qian Xuesen 1988: 323–4.

23   Qian Xuesen 1988: 138–46.

24   Meeting of the China Somatic Science Society, October 1982, quoted in TJH.

25   Tao Zulai 1990: 359.

of *qigong* was that it not only promised technological progress, but also a new, all-embracing cosmology. With Yan Xin, *qigong* began to acquire an increasingly moral dimension. In one of his 'power-inducing lectures' he describes *qigong* as

... an ideal, all-encompassing form of erudition which includes multiple forms of knowledge, allows mankind to know himself and the universe, has an epistemology and a methodology, and contains a philosophy of life, of the world and of the cosmos ... It is a complete scientific discipline. ... [As a science of the mind, *qigong* requires one] to stay in an enlightened, virtuous and moral state of mind, nourished by a high ideal. The ancient *qigong* masters of high antiquity had already recognised that man, if he wants true happiness, must have a luminous and infinite inner heart, and be benevolent to men and things. ... The Ancients, in high antiquity, according to primary sources on *qigong* from 7,000 years ago ... [emphasised the importance of] 'being rooted in virtue' (*zhongde weiben*). ... Thus the simultaneous training of both spirit and body is the most important characteristic of *qigong*. It is not merely mechanical gestures, nor the arduous but superficial training of ordinary martial arts, but a training of the inner spirit. It involves linking our thoughts to the great common aspiration of the whole world ..., to use our wisdom to harmonise all things in need of harmony. The greater our contribution, the greater our merit, and the higher our benefit; the bodily and spiritual benefit then becomes obvious. Thus the concrete training of the body is of secondary importance.[26]

Indeed, *qigong* can englobe everything: it is a true 'omni-science'. Journalist Ji Yi, author of several books on *qigong*, wrote, 'if we can connect the essences of Eastern and Western civilisations, and integrate ancient and modern culture, a new scientific and technological revolution will erupt [which] will trigger an explosion of human knowledge.'[27] One of the most elaborate syntheses was developed by Zhang Hongbao, master of Zhonggong, whose 'Qilin Culture' aimed to combine all forms of knowledge into a single, integrated system:

During the lectures [at the Beijing Great Hall of Sciences], Mr Zhang solemnly proclaimed to China and the world that the Zhonggong cultural system, which came to him by inspiration, would be formally named Qilin Culture. This creature known to the Chinese nation as a bringer of good fortune, thus found a new lustre. The *qilin* combines in a single body the essence of different species of living beings: the dragon's head,

26   Yan Xin 1996: side B.
27   Ji Yi 1990a: 57–8.

the pig's nose, the serpent's scales, the deer's body, the tiger's back, the bear's thighs, the ox's hooves and the lion's tail. It belongs to none of these species, but combines the powers of each. By thus naming his scientific research system, this symbolises that Qilin Culture is the spark produced by the friction of ancient and modern cultures, and the fruit of the integration of Western and Eastern philosophies. It absorbs the essence of the Chinese nation, and rests on the shoulders of the giants of the history of science. From the heights of cosmology and methodology, and based on the different aspects of philosophy and the natural and social sciences, it explores the different laws of life and movement. It is a deep wisdom with rich contents.

Qilin Culture is the crystallisation of the great inspiration, the great enlightenment and the great wisdom of Master Zhang Hongbao. ... It smelts in a single furnace the Way of Heaven, the Way of Earth, the Way of Man, government, economy, military affairs, art and philosophy. It covers virtue, intelligence and the body; it neglects neither the natural sciences, nor the social sciences, nor the life sciences. ... It rests on the soil of the Realm of Spirit;[28] it is a remarkable contribution of the Chinese nation, to the universe and to the human race.[29]

Zhang Hongbao's Qilin Culture included eight systems:

1. A philosophical system based on the 'Supreme Whirl' (*xuanji*), a modification of the traditional Chinese 'Supreme Ultimate', known as the *taiji* or yin–yang symbol (Fig. 3). While the *taiji* figure looks like two fish, the Supreme Whirl looks like two eagle heads, taking inspiration from Marxist and Maoist dialectics to 'reflect the inevitable struggle in the process of the development of things'.[30] The Supreme Whirl was said to explain the origin of creatures, their functioning and their final destiny.

2. A life sciences system, which was the application of *qilin* philosophy to pierce the secrets of life. The system included two parts: first, a methodology, which included the theories of the biological machine, of the control of the categories of *qi* sensation, of the power of total biological information and of the nature of mental powers; second, a theory of Extraordinary Powers, including the different types of functions, the six ways to make them appear, the methods to refine them, their precise locations in the body and the eight types of superhuman.

---

28 *Shenzhou*: China. Could also be translated as 'Realm of the Gods'.
29 Ji Yi 1991: 155–60.
30 Zhang Hongbao 1993: 151–2.

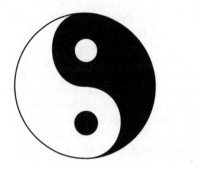

Fig. 3　The Taiji symbol and the Zhonggong Supreme Whirl symbol

3. A system of 'extraordinary medicine' which differed in seven ways from Chinese medicine, Western medicine and *qigong* therapy.

4. A system of art and therapy, including a style of architecture and sculpture, *qigong* dance, *qigong* music, *qigong* painting, martial arts, spontaneous poetry etc.

5. A system of education, including an accelerated method for the improvement of intelligence and for the training of individuals with Extraordinary Powers.

6. A system of industrial and political administration: a science of leadership, management, behaviour and commercial psychology, combining the political and strategic arts of ancient China and of the *Book of Changes* with modern enterprise administration.

7. A system of behaviour: rules for walking, sitting and lying down; a work ethic; a discipline for creating a new man.

8. A system of body practices in eight levels, known as Zhonggong.[31]

Qilin Culture's modern management theory, based on the traditional yin–yang and five-elements cosmology, was the basis for the Zhonggong organisation, and claimed to be applicable to family, business or government. It aimed to synthesise the best aspects of the five phases of human social development: primitive society, slave society, feudal society, capitalist society and communist society.

---

[31]　Ji Yi 1991: 155–60; Liu Zhidong 1993: 219.

This schema accepted the Marxist phases of history, but rejected the notion of a dialectical opposition between phases: 'each type of society had its excellent methods of administration, which one can borrow.' Thus the notion of the collective (*gong*) of the primitive and communist phases were retained, as well as the private interests (*si*) of the slave, feudal and capitalist phases, and their notions of the hierarchy between juniors and seniors and between ministers and the prince. Finally, capitalist management methods were adopted.[32]

Zhonggong's 'interpersonal relations system' was based on the equality and mutual help of primitive society, the paternalistic respect of historical clans and the ritual hierarchy of Confucian culture.

The 'profit sharing system' made profit the sole criterion for revenue distribution. Regardless of if a person worked with dedication all day long, if he didn't make profits, he would earn nothing and would even be punished. Salary included three components: remuneration based on profits earned, a fixed annual salary and a salary based on seniority.

The 'personnel management system' planned for the hiring of staff on fixed-term contracts of six months to one year; after several successive contracts, the employee could be hired indefinitely and be provided with housing, retirement pension and health insurance.

Overall Qilin Culture aimed to meet human needs at three levels. Materially, it would solve concrete problems and advocated the use of market laws, using notions of enterprise, capital, price, profit etc., which were just being introduced to China in the early 1990s. Then at the level of 'spirit' and 'values', it attempted to create different types of 'collective forms' and 'etiquette' that would nurture the values of family, society, and a thirst for perfection which would generate faith aesthetics and morality. The third level involved 'saving and enlightening mankind, healing illness and increasing *gong*': a transcendence that would allow people to experience 'sudden enlightenment', for themselves, and to understand the nature of man and the universe.[33]

As an all-encompassing discourse which touches on everything in the universe, *qigong* united the cosmological tendencies of both sci-

---

32 This system is described in Lü Feng 1993: 221–6.
33 Lü Feng 1993: 223–6.

ence and religion with the evolutionary teleology of Marxism. As a principle of moral conduct, *qigong* united technical—and thus scientific—practice with the moral teachings of traditional religion. *Qigong* aimed to achieve a perfect synthesis between Chinese tradition and the modern cult of scientism. This synthesis, however, through the scientific revolution it aimed to trigger, promised to transcend both current science and past religion.

Indeed, '*qigong* science' claimed to shake the very foundations of modern science. Best-selling novelist Ke Yunlu stated that the question of Extraordinary Powers was of 'world importance', for their scientific proof could be considered as the 'third most important scientific discovery' in human history, after relativity theory and quantum mechanics.[34] Another author, Liu Zhidong, compares the impact of *qigong* theory with Darwin's evolutionary theory, a discovery which could 'shake the world'.[35]

But while the scientific revolutions of the past began in the West, this time it was China which had a great advance over the rest of the world: the new scientific revolution would be the work of Chinese people, and would propel China to the top. Qian Xuesen wrote that once *qigong* became a true science, 'we descendants of the Yellow Emperor will no longer be ashamed of our ancestors, and our reputation will spread to the whole world'.[36] Zhang Yaoting, office director of the Leaders' Working Group on Somatic Science, is reported to have stated that *qigong* would allow China to become an international superpower.[37] Best-selling author Ji Yi claimed, 'scientists predict that the first country to break the secret of Extraordinary Powers will be the first and most powerful state in the new century.'[38] And General Zhang Zhenhuan raised a tantalising possibility: 'Imagine more than a billion people using *qigong* to increase their intelligence: what would be the magnitude of such power when conjoined?'[39]

Such ideas stimulated much enthusiasm. Journalist Sima Nan, a former *qigong* adept who later became a leading anti-*qigong* critic, recalls his first feelings when learning of Extraordinary Powers:

34   Ke Yunlu 1996: 28.
35   Liu Zhidong 1993: 159.
36   Qian Xuesen 1998a: 7–8.
37   Quoted in QDL: 98.
38   Ji Yi 1991: 37.
39   Zhang Zhenhuan 1988a: 19.

At the beginning of the 1980s, when I was a student, I had a powerful experience one day. One Sunday morning ..., having learned in a newspaper article of this 'somatic science' which was going to force the rewriting of all of humanity's scientific knowledge, I wanted to charge ahead with a boundless enthusiasm. Like many people, I dreamed of a wonderful and mysterious 'futuristic world', toward which we were irresistibly drawn.[40]

In this future world, thanks to *qigong*, no material obstacle would be able to block the satisfaction of human desires. *Qigong* apologists Li Jianxin and Zheng Qin wrote that the human body in a *qigong* state 'can produce any kind of result, be it physical, chemical or biological', indeed that 'the *qi* of *qigong* is omnipotent ... it can produce any effect sought by the observer'.[41]

In the same vein, grandmaster Zhang Hongbao described the future paradise which would be brought about by *qigong*:

The world is currently pregnant with the fourth technological revolution (also called the fourth wave). This revolution differs from the three previous ones, in that its central focus will be biological engineering. ... It is not difficult to imagine that in several years, when *qigong* will be practised by the entire population, and when somatic science will have made important breakthroughs, mankind will not only enjoy full health and physical and mental vigour, as well as a superior intelligence, but there will also be innumerable *qigong* grandmasters and persons whose Extraordinary Powers will be triggered by *qigong* .... Such a world may very well become a fairyland [*shenxian leyuan*].[42]

QIGONG UTOPIANISM

An 'archaeology' of *qigong* discourse would reveal that *qigong* is composed of four distinct layers of meaning, allowing the easy passage between seemingly contradictory forms of expression and practice.

The first layer, the most profound and archaic, is an animist substratum. The universe is perceived as imbued with invisible forces, which it is possible to manipulate through the mastery of specific techniques. *Qigong* gymnastics is a kind of dance between the practitioner and invisible force flows. Its meditation techniques allow the adept to act on these forces through the exercise of mental

40 Quoted in Li Liyan 1998: 7–8.
41 QDL: 221–2.
42 Quoted in Ji Yi 1990a: 141.

power. The use of charms, 'information objects' and incantations expresses the idea that certain objects and sounds can be infused with magical powers.

The second layer is an implicit form of messianism. At this level appear the grandmasters, whose power over invisible forces is such that they have the ability to save all of humanity. The grandmasters do more than teach methods for attaining health and healing, promising a return to the original virtue and greatness of Chinese culture. Their ultimate goal is for all mankind to join their practice, triggering a process of collective renewal and ushering in a new area of universal health and bliss. At this level the quest for invisible powers is no longer an individual pursuit like at the first level, but is part of a process of collective renewal, fundamental for the future of the world and of humanity.

The third layer is formed by modernist scientism. In China, scientistic ideology rests on a millenarian eschatology: the old, decadent culture will be destroyed and replaced by a new scientific civilisation which will save humanity. Science can do miracles, it is the key to controlling the invisible forces of the universe. Science will save China; China must accept science; *qigong* is Chinese science.

Finally, a layer of romantic nationalism, a reaction to the Western domination of scientific modernity. Here, the superiority of Chinese civilisation is asserted, arguing that *qigong* is a superior form of science. Thus a return to the traditional wisdom of China will allow China to surpass the science of the West: the science that will save the world will be Chinese science.

It is science itself, in its entirety and down to its foundations, that *qigong* saw as its object. *Qigong* sought not only to 'scientise' itself, adopting the superficial forms of science—research societies, schools, journals, materialist concepts—but, reaching much further, it sought to conquer the fortress of knowledge, to save science itself. With boundless confidence, *qigong*, marrying messianic strains with utopian scientism, saw itself as the very future of science and the key to the wellbeing of mankind.

STRATEGIES OF LEGITIMATION

The *qigong* sector formed itself around this inspiring and legitimising discourse, bringing into its fold an assortment of practices which had long been disdained, excluded or marginalised not only by Western science and medicine, but even by modern Chinese medicine and by its predecessor, literati medicine, for centuries: incantations, divination, magical battles, martial arts, trance, inner alchemy and so on. The rejects of the great official medical institutions, hoping to rid themselves of the odious label of 'superstition', huddled under the banner of *qigong*, which gave them a new identity as 'gems of Chinese civilisation', and which was at the same time a 'cutting-edge scientific discipline'.

The category of Extraordinary Powers includes most phenomena which do not have a place within orthodox science. But the definition of such phenomena as 'extraordinary' rather than 'supernatural' expresses a desire to inscribe them within a single material universe, rather than into a separate ontological reality. Such a conceptual choice was imposed by the materialistic monism of the official ideology, but also reflected the long tradition of cosmic holism in Chinese thought. Practically, this had profound implications: it became necessary to convince the mainstream scientific community to accept the existence and the implications of such phenomena. The relationship between *qigong* and scientific institutions thus became a fundamental issue, as the scientific community became the ultimate judge of *qigong*'s legitimacy.

Atheism and scientism being at the core of the CCP ideology, Chinese scientific institutions can have a significant political influence: as the arbiters and guarantors of scientific truth, they are, *ipso facto*, the defenders of the ideological scientism. In communist China a scientific fact is never neutral: its implications are not merely empirical, but also ideological and political. Conversely, whatever is rejected by the scientific community as false, anti-scientific or pseudo-scientific can be consigned to the categories of political heresy and 'feudal superstition'.

The scientific community's attitude toward *qigong* thus became crucial for the *qigong* sector's survival. Located outside the religious orthodoxy recognised and protected by the state,[43] but containing practices, concepts, symbols and historical roots in popular religion, *qigong* rested on a precarious political and ideological ground. The scientific community's approval was thus a *sine qua non* condition of its legitimate existence. It thus exercised a normative influence on the *qigong* sector, both directly—it was the scientific community,

43 The five official religions of Buddhism, Taoism, Protestantism, Catholicism and Islam, each with its state-supervised associations.

and not the *qigong* sector itself, which had the authority to validate *qigong*'s scientific pretensions—and indirectly—in order to project an image of conformity to official scientism, the *qigong* sector took the scientific community as an institutional and ideological model.

In order to 'solemnly enter the Sanctuary of Science' (*tangtang zhengzhengde mairu kexue shengdian*),[44] the *qigong* milieu adopted two parallel strategies: (1) the strategy of 'proof': produce scientific proofs of *qigong* through laboratory experiments; (2) the strategy of mimicry: adopt the external forms of scientific institutions, going so far as to proclaim *qigong* as a super-science, a synthesis surpassing all conventional scientific disciplines. Some figures in the *qigong* sector summed up the strategy as 'science saves *qigong* and *qigong* saves science'.[45]

The strategy of 'proof' involved establishing research collaborations between *qigong* masters and scientists for laboratory experiments. In a typical set-up, the master would send his *qi* towards a sample—a patient, some mushrooms, a rabbit or a liquid solution—and the researcher would observe and measure any changes in the sample during *qi* emission. Ideally the measurements would be made with an instrument capable of instantly recording quantitative data on the effect of the *qi*.

A more popular derivative of the laboratory experiment was the public Extraordinary Powers demonstration, on stage in front of an audience, or in any setting such as a restaurant, a sitting room etc., with witnesses present. Indeed, the effects perceived or felt by the audience were considered as scientific 'proof': 'seeing is believing'. For much of the public, anything palpable or visible with one's own senses was considered scientifically true.

In all cases the strategy of 'proof' required the production of 'facts' demonstrating the immediate and material effects of *qigong*: It was necessary to prove that *qigong* existed, as if it were a material entity; that Extraordinary Powers existed, that *qi* was a material substance producing effects measurable by an instrument, just like any other physical substance. The 'proof' strategy neglected what practitioners of body technologies in traditions other than *qigong* might have seen as the spiritual, philosophical, moral or metaphysical dimensions of the effects of practice. In the *qigong* milieu the goal was concrete, material, scientific *proof*.

44   ZGL: 119.
45   Yan Xin 1988: 26–7.

This strategy also paid little attention to the long-term material effects of *qigong*: longitudinal studies on the effects of continued *qigong* practice on various aspects of physical or mental health did not have the attraction of revolutionary 'discoveries' such as transforming the molecular structure of water at a distance of 2,000 km. *Qigong* advocates craved to make a sensation: to produce hard science, with clear and instant conclusions, confirming and proving their claims without a doubt.

How could the public and the state, who were for the most part ignorant of the scientific method and of the details of *qigong* 'research' and 'experiments', be convinced that such proofs existed? All that was needed was the public approval of famous scientists, such as Qian Xuesen, from prestigious institutions such as Qinghua University or the China Academy of Science. The fame and prestige of such scientific institutions was a good way to obtain political and ideological protection and public credibility. Whether the 'research' in question was conclusive or not mattered little.

Further, and along the same lines, the second strategy deployed by *qigong* in the face of science was that of mimicry: to organise itself like a scientific community, in order to give the state, the public and itself the image of a scientific discipline, actively contributing to the progress of science. This strategy was expressed thus:

- self-designation as '*qigong* science', 'scientific *qigong*' and 'somatic science';

- self-attribution by *qigong* masters of titles such as 'scientist', or even fraudulent self-attribution of academic titles such as doctor or professor. For example, the book *Grandmaster Yan Xin in North America*[46] contains reproductions and Chinese translations of several certificates of honour and recognition conferred by various American organisations to 'Dr Yan Xin', translated into the Chinese as 'Yan Xin, PhD' (*Yan Xin boshi*)—whereas Yan Xin never obtained a graduate university degree. Zhang Hongbao and Chen Linfeng called themselves 'life science researcher' and the like;

- establishment of semi-official *qigong* organisations as academic societies, often affiliated to semi-official national, provincial or municipal scientific commissions;

[46]   Wu Xutian 1992.

-   affiliation of denominations to the semi-official *qigong* associations, often as 'scientific associations';

-   the frequent organisation of conferences, seminars and symposia ostensibly dedicated to the presentation of research on *qigong* science;

-   the publication of *qigong* 'scientific journals' containing, alongside hagiographic articles on *qigong* masters and didactic presentation of *qigong* techniques, articles and reports on laboratory experiments (these journals were actually popular magazines without a review process);

-   the elaboration of *qigong* as a scientific discipline with its standardised genealogy, its theoretical corpus, its set of concepts, its pedagogical materials and its specialised courses.[47]

QIGONG PRACTITIONERS, RESEARCHERS AND SCEPTICS

By adopting the ideology of scientism, whether by conviction or by opportunism, the *qigong* sector engaged in a new dynamic in its internal and external relations. A new discourse of scientific orthodoxy could be felt, giving materialist interpretations to practices and concepts inherited from Chinese popular traditions. According to the *qigong* historiography described above, superstitions had been mixed into *qigong* owing to past feudal and religious influences, deforming the true nature of *qigong*. The renaissance of *qigong* thus required the elimination of such impurities and the eradication of the superstitions in order to create a scientific *qigong*. But how could the superstitions be identified and eradicated? There was no consensus on this point. Controversies raged on which practices were acceptable and 'scientific', and which were not. Three groups of people played a role in these debates, pulling the definition of orthodoxy in different directions: *qigong* practitioners, somatic scientists and sceptics. Here 'somatic scientists' means those who promoted the project of a somatic science and were actively engaged in the production of a discourse of somatic science: they included Extraordinary Powers researchers, but also key *qigong* masters such as Yan Xin and Zhang Hongbao, who also participated in the elaboration of the discourse. These three groups are analogous to the New Agers,

---

47   See for example Xie Huanzhang 1988.

parapsychologists and sceptics described by anthropologist David Hess, whose interactions and views of each other shape the content and boundaries of paranormal discourse in America.[48]

At stake around *qigong* were different understandings of what science was and meant. Since the end of the Cultural Revolution everybody knew through Party propaganda that science and technology would be the new saviours of the nation and the motors of China's development, and that the people should strengthen its development. But for most people, whose education was rudimentary, science was simply whatever was obviously 'true' and logical: 'seek truth from facts', said Deng Xiaoping.

For the *qigong* practitioner, the 'facts' of science were the immediate and palpable results of *qigong* practice. If it worked to heal illness or improve health, it was obviously scientific. This type of 'science' encouraged practical empiricism. Any type of magical, divinatory or mantric technique could be tried out; if the 'experiment' worked, it was true. If it didn't, further experimentation on other techniques was warranted. For some, the experimentation of inner states through body techniques could also be conceived of as doing science. The inner body became an instrument for observing the cosmos. Contrary to institutionalised science, in which a small number of specialists produce knowledge for passive consumption by everyone else, this was a type of scientific activity that anyone could engage in. Thousands of amateur scholars devoted themselves to studying classical texts on body cultivation and trying out different methods, exchanging observations and commentary in *qigong* journals. This was a conscious project of engaging in the prestigious activity of scientific research. The body became a laboratory. A scientific attitude was seen as necessary to save body technologies from centuries of superstitious dross, but also to enable *qigong* to create a new type of science. For them, scientism was not an abstract ideology, but an embodied practice.

For many intellectual practitioners and advocates of *qigong*, a wide range of magical practices were true, but it was the folk explanations of their effects that were wrong. Thus science simply meant to replace 'superstitious' explanations based on ghosts and demons with more rational-sounding, and thus 'scientific', theories based on the materialist framework of *qigong* science, with its con-

---

48 Hess 1993.

cepts of '*qi*' and 'information'. Yan Xin, for example, explained that the ancient practice of the kowtow, involving prostration before a master, a lord or a divinity in such a manner that the forehead hit the ground, was not a superstition, but a type of *qigong* for exercising the parietal bone, which only appears after birth. 'The ancients discovered that training the parietal bone allows one to verify the effect of *qigong* practice. So they used the method of the kowtow as training.'[49]

Yan Xin also explained that the 'superstitious' practice of burning incense before images or statues of gods was actually a *qigong* method to create an atmosphere conducive for meditation, for stimulating the circulation of *qi* along the meridians, and for measuring the passage of time. The custom of burning 'spirit money' for the dead was originally invented by *qigong* adepts who had visions of ancestors in need. Actually, said Yan, they had misinterpreted the origin of those messages: they did not come from the souls of ancestors asking for money, but were residual 'information' left behind by the ancestors while they were still alive, and detected but misunderstood by *qigong* masters with Extraordinary Powers.[50] Similarly, the powers of shamanistic healers were actually derived from *qigong*. In one hagiographic account of Yan Xin's life, he confronts a female medium, telling her that her powers are just as real without burning incense and paper money, and he orders her to heal the sick without using those 'feudal forms'. When she refuses, he uses his own magical powers to make her collapse on the ground. She finally concedes defeat and agrees to practise healing 'without forms', displaying a miraculous ability to divine and heal the illnesses of people unknown to her. Finally, after admitting to swindling her patients, she promises 'Master Yan, I will never do such a thing again; never will I feign to be possessed by spirits and ghosts. I will abandon all superstitious stories and use only scientific explanations.'[51]

49 Yan Xin, quoted in Qin Hui 1990: 203.
50 Yan Xin 1988: 24–7; Qin Hui 1990: 203–5; Ming Zhen 1988: 38–39.
51 Qin Hui 1990: 206–10. In a similar vein, Falungong practitioners claimed that Falungong cultivation freed them 'from the blind worship of images of supernatural beings in Buddhist monasteries, Taoist temples and Christian churches'; rather than bowing down and burning incense, 'higher-level beings will come to help us if we practise cultivation' (Falungong practitioners, 'A Ten-Thousand-Word Letter to the Party Centre', *Chinese Law and Government*, 32(6): 69–88, p. 82. Translation of Falungong xiulianzhe, 'Zhi dang zhongyang wanyan shu', 27 July 1999, posted

Yan Xin thus affirmed the efficacy of many, if not most, practices considered 'superstitious' in socialist China, while at the same time posing as a hero in the struggle against feudal superstition. The problem was merely their erroneous formulation or interpretation, which could be corrected with *qigong* science, or simply be replaced by more advanced techniques: Yan Xin claimed that today 'forms have changed', and that his own techniques were more efficient than traditional folk practices.[52]

Often, however, the forms didn't change, only their names did; for example, talismanic water (*fushui*) became 'information water' (*xinxi shui*).[53] The miracles and resurrection of Jesus, Indian yoga, Sufism, Chinese geomancy, the auras around the heads of saints in Buddhist and Christian iconography, the exploits of the Monkey King in the *Journey to the West*, indeed all magical and religious phenomena could be recast as not the product of the imagination or the work of gods, but as material facts explainable with *qigong*.[54] Superstition merely consisted in attributing such phenomena to gods rather than to *qi*.

This recasting of old superstitions in a new garb provided somatic scientists with a vast and legitimate field for research. Though few, somatic scientists had the key role of providing laboratory proof of the existence of these phenomena, and reformulating them within a new scientific system.

Such an approach was harshly criticised by a minority of *qigong* researchers and practitioners, such as Zhang Honglin and Sima Nan, as well as polemicists such as Yu Guangyuan and He Zuoxiu, who were willing to admit that *qigong* was a 'gem of Chinese civilisation', but claimed that the category of *qigong* should apply only to body, breath and mind training exercises, the effects of which could be observed and explained with modern scientific concepts. In their eyes, the rest was merely 'pseudo-*qigong*': disguised superstition which had to be eliminated.

In a series of articles published in 1989 Zhang Honglin, Director of the China Academy of Chinese Medicine's Qigong Research

---

on <minghuiwang, http://minghui.ca> (accessed in November 2003) at <http://pkg2.minghui.org/gb/shishi/0899/wanyanshu.html>.

52 Yan Xin, quoted in ZGL: 162–78.

53 Despeux 1997: 276.

54 Xie Huanzhang 1988: 287, quoted in Xu 1999: 977. For a *qigong* interpretation of the Bible and Jesus' miracles, see also Ke Yunlu 1995b: 19–20.

Laboratory, argued that external *qi* was merely the result of psychological suggestion. According to Zhang's clinical research, each time external *qi* is used to treat a sick person, psychological suggestion, through speech, body movement, facial expression or other signs, is always consciously or unconsciously applied. If such techniques are not used or if they are interrupted, the external *qi* has no effect.[55] Therefore, concluded Zhang, external *qi* was 'a kind of psychological suggestion with Chinese characteristics'.[56]

Zhang Honglin also refuted the experiments by Gu Hansen, Feng Lida and Yan Xin, which had supposedly proven the material existence of external *qi*. He claimed the experiments lacked methodological rigour and had never been replicated. He also argued that external *qi* was not mentioned in the classical texts of Chinese medicine, and that there were no 'external *qi* masters' in the traditions *qigong* was derived from. To those who claimed that external *qi* therapy could be learned through *qigong* practice and not by studying hypnosis and suggestion techniques, he answered,

> ... this type of therapy is very simple: one only needs to go to a region where one is unknown, and to make people believe that you are a 'master of external *qi*', thanks to your rhetorical ability or some certificate; better yet, to make people believe that you are the disciple of the nth generation of such-and-such a great master, and to utter 'scientific' truths half incomprehensible to the ordinary person, and you become an 'external *qi*' master in a wink. At that moment, you will only need to stretch out your arm for people to feel your 'external *qi*' or the pathological *qi* of an illness, and [your therapy] will be effective for some people.

Zhang Honglin wrote that there were three types of 'external *qi* masters': the first were those who, owing to a lack of education, sincerely believed in the existence of external *qi*. The second were those who knew that external *qi* was psychological suggestion, which they knew and mastered, but who, for their own interest, deceived the ignorant masses and sheltered themselves behind *qigong* and science to become founders of new religions. These were true 'quacks' and 'sorcerers' who had a bad impact on scientific *qigong*. The third were the small minority who knew that external *qi* was psychological suggestion and who used scientific methods to understand and improve a Chinese-style '*qigong* psychotherapy'.[57]

55   JKB, 1 July 1989: 1.
56   Zhang Honglin 1989a.
57   Zhang Honglin 1989b.

RESPONSES TO POLEMIC

Such arguments were marshalled by sceptics in newspaper articles against 'pseudo-*qigong*' from 1979 to 1982, 1988 to 1990, and again in 1995. Criticism of 'miraculous *qigong*' boiled down to two arguments. A theoretical objection: if Extraordinary Powers existed, the whole edifice of science would crumble. 'There would then be no way to erect fundamental scientific laws. For example, moving a pill through glass: could physics and mechanics then continue to exist?'[58] And an empirical objection: there is no scientific proof of Extraordinary Powers; no demonstration of such powers has ever been reproduced in a controlled experimental setting.

Critics of Extraordinary Powers always stressed that they had no objection to *qigong* exercise in itself, undoubtedly beneficial for health and a valuable cultural heritage. They objected only to Extraordinary Powers and to the amalgam of Extraordinary Powers and *qigong*. Why then did the great majority of *qigong* masters and other major figures insist on such an amalgam in the face of strong ideological pressure and the great difficulty in marshalling convincing scientific proof? Why did they take criticism of Extraordinary Powers as attacks on *qigong* as a whole?

The answer to this question can be situated at the level of the methodology advocated by somatic science. In *qigong* circles it was often repeated that 'with faith, efficacy; without faith, no efficacy' (*xin ze ling, bu xin ze bu ling*).[59] This idiom, which simply means that 'it only works when you believe in it', is erected into a methodological principle to be integrated into experiments on Extraordinary Powers. If individuals with Extraordinary Powers fail in their demonstrations in the presence of sceptics, it is because the latter unconsciously emit 'information' that perturbs the Extraordinary Powers of the subject being observed. For Chen Xin, the 'sarcasm' of the critics 'has an interference effect' on the psychological state of people with Extraordinary Powers, thus harming their concentration.[60] According to Ke Yunlu, Extraordinary Powers are intimately connected to the physiological and psychological state of the subject, who is highly influenced by his or her environment. The experimental set-up must therefore create an environment conducive to the appearance of Extraordinary Powers. A high 'level of

58   ZGL: 240.
59   See Xu 1999: 983.
60   SMK 21: 7.

psychological support' must be ensured through a relaxed, trusting and enthusiastic atmosphere. Indeed, according to quantum mechanics, the observer and the experimental set-up have an impact on the subject of observation. It is thus necessary to use a holistic approach and connect the observer, the observation set-up and the observed.[61] Yan Xin thus insisted that *qigong* masters who are the subjects of experiments must participate fully in the design of the experimental set-up, which must conform to their conditions.

Conventional science sees belief as a factor to eliminate—thus Zhang Honglin concluded that external *qi* was nothing but 'psychological suggestion',[62] while others spoke of the 'placebo effect'.[63] But *qigong* rejected the subject/object dualism of conventional science. *Qigong* science considered belief a variable which produces concrete effects, and which should therefore be manipulated like other variables in order to produce the desired results.

The controversy seems to boil down to the name that should be given to what happens in the interaction between a *qigong* master and his patient or disciple: external *qi* or suggestion? But the choice of names reflects a crucial conflict over the power to define and manipulate the effects at the heart of the dispute. Ke Yunlu claimed that scientists refused to admit the existence of Extraordinary Powers because to do so would entail the end of their authority and of the social position they had built their careers to attain. In like manner, the charisma of the *qigong* masters, on which their celebrity and livelihood depended, would dissipate if their powers were nothing but 'suggestion'. In such a case *qigong* would no longer be a cutting-edge science, but a branch of psychology, involving neither magic, nor scientific discovery, nor a Chinese invention. Suggestion being perceived as a form of illusion, or of inducing of consciousness, *qigong* would involve no esoteric knowledge. The true experts would not be *qigong* masters, but psychologists. For Zhang Honglin,

if psychologists who have systematically mastered the techniques of suggestion and hypnosis practised 'external *qi*' therapy, their therapeutic efficacy would undoubtedly be greater than the masters of external *qi*, because they have a better understanding of the methods of suggestion.[64]

61 Ke Yunlu 1996: 32.
62 Zhang Honglin 1989a, 1989b.
63 Eisenberg 1985.
64 Zhang Honglin 1989a, 1989b.

In such a case, then, the *qigong* masters would have nothing exceptional: they should, to be qualified, take psychology classes! The link with ancient cosmologies of *qi* would no longer be obvious, and the whole mythical, 'extraordinary' dimension would disappear. The entire edifice of *qigong* discourse collapses if external *qi* is defined as psychological suggestion. Furthermore, beyond discourse, the very configuration of the *qigong* milieu would be shaken: almost all the *gongfa* were based on notions of *qi*, of external *qi* and of Extraordinary Powers, all of which were seen as part of an ancient heritage and as scientific breakthroughs. External *qi* healing sessions, power-inducing lectures, the 'fields of *qi*' produced by collective *qigong* practice, the magnetic powers of the grandmasters who could attract audiences in the thousands, the new discipline of somatic science—all the fundamental elements in the configuration and culture of the *qigong* milieu would be reduced to naught.

Qigong advocates were thus vigorous in their defensive polemic. Six main arguments were deployed to respond to the critics.

The modernist argument

Science never stops progressing and replacing old theories with new ones. *Qigong* is an avant-garde science, it is thus natural that scientists are opposed to it, just like Copernicus, Galileo, Darwin and Einstein were targets of opposition in their day.[65] If *qigong* phenomena appear to be contrary to science, it is because modern science has not yet found adequate concepts and methods to observe, define and explain them.[66] In his novel *The Great Qigong Master*, Ke Yunlu describes the reaction of some scientists to a fictional Extraordinary Powers experiment:

The reaction of the scientists [in the audience] was ambivalent. Some cried in excitement and surprise, others raised their eyebrows. Some looked confused, others seemed to be grieved. We can understand this. They have studied physics all their life. The research subjects and theoretical systems that they depend on to survive are in danger of collapse: can a man take such a thing lightly? ...

It is the same for the philosophers. If [the philosopher] is sensible, young and creative, if he can overthrow old authority to create a new thought and a new glory, he will vigorously support research on Extraordinary

---

65 QDL: 252.
66 See Xu 1999: 978.

Powers; if he is slow, old-fashioned and rigid, if he is attached to his own position of authority and to his old theoretical system, he will probably resist instinctively.'[67]

Qigong thus presented itself as a young, avant-garde and revolutionary movement which challenged conventional rigidities, and was not afraid of new ideas and of overthrowing old authority structures.

The nationalist argument

Qigong is a gem of Chinese civilisation, with a rich history of over 5,000 years. To attack *qigong* is to attack this precious legacy of our ancestors and to denigrate Chinese culture. Worse, it is to allow Westerners to overtake China in a field in which the Chinese are the leaders. 'If we do not conduct assiduous research in this field, we will regress', said Zhang Zhenhuan at the inauguration of the China Somatic Science Society,[68] noting that the President of Mexico supported such research on the ancient culture of the Mayas, and that Western countries were already at an advantage when it came to material conditions for research.[69] For Feng Lida, *qigong* risked following the same disastrous course as the other 'four great inventions'[70] of ancient China:

The root is in China, the flowers and fruit are abroad. ... Foreigners, holding the force of modern technology, as soon as they have brought *qigong* back with them, will probably make great breakthroughs, which might even trigger a scientific revolution. In such a case, we will only be powerless spectators.[71]

To underline that China risked losing its opportunity, Ji Yi described the scientific research on the paranormal being carried out in the West and in the Soviet Union for over 100 years.[72] Another author, Xu Dai, asked: 'if American somatic science surpasses China, what will China be able to do?' Quoting a report, he claimed that the CIA had spent US$20 million on paranormal research between 1975 and 1995. As proof of the importance given to Extraordinary

---

67   Ke Yunlu 1989: 122, 127.
68   Official speech by Zhang Zhenhuan, quoted in ZGL: 239.
69   Zhang Zhenhuan 1988c: 173.
70   Paper, the printing press, the compass and gunpowder.
71   Feng Lida radio interview, quoted in QDL: 122–3.
72   Ji Yi 1991: 37–78.

Powers by the Americans, he cites a case in which the CIA supposedly hired a person with Extraordinary Powers to telepathically kill Libyan President Colonel Khadafy in 1986 (the mortal thought-bullets were deflected by 100 female guards surrounding Khadafy's tent).[73]

Here, the *qigong* sector presented itself as the defender of Chinese tradition, and as promoting Chinese strength in its competition with foreign powers.

The argument of popularity

If so many people practise *qigong* and do research on it, it must be true:

So you say that the tens of millions of people who practise *qigong*, the several institutions of higher learning, Jiaotong, Fudan and Qinghua Universities, the numerous research institutes, who all believe in *qigong*, and who devote an immense effort to research, all these people are out of their minds?[74]

The *qigong* sector saw itself not as a marginal movement, but as enjoying the support of both the broad masses and the scientific élite. To attack *qigong* was to attack all of Chinese society.

The esoteric argument

Not everyone is capable of accepting or perceiving Extraordinary Powers. Those who refuse to believe in them are simply at an inferior level. Indeed Extraordinary Powers phenomena go against ordinary experience. It is thus inevitable that they would provoke a strong reaction of denial, which may affect the observer's objectivity.[75] Speaking of external *qi* critic Zhang Honglin, Ji Yi stated,

Qigong cultivation has several levels. If Zhang Honglin says that *qigong* is only *daoyin* gymnastics, he isn't wrong, but in the process of *qigong* cultivation, *daoyin* is a mere passage. It is only after having crossed this passage that one enters the truly marvellous realms. But Zhang Honglin is still blocked in that passage.[76]

---

73 DF 57: 38–9. Similar explanations, attributing the failure of magical offensives to the presence of women on city walls, were common in the Taiping and Boxer rebellions. See Cohen 1997: 119–45.
74 Wang Xiubi, quoted in QDL: 252.
75 Ke Yunlu, quoted in QDL: 54–5.
76 Ji Yi, quoted in QDL: 138.

In the same vein, Yan Xin said that to deny external *qi* would be to deny Chinese medicine and all of science. The controversies around external *qi* are nothing but a debate between 'insiders' (*neihang*) and 'outsiders' (*waihang*).[77] Others went even further, claiming that *qigong* critics were themselves initiates who used their own Extraordinary Powers against *qigong* advocates. Thus it was claimed that the American magician James Randi, who visited China on a CSICOP delegation, used his magical powers to disrupt the Extraordinary Powers of the Chinese masters tested by the delegation.[78] Another claimed that even Marxist theoretician Yu Guangyuan, a key critic of Extraordinary Powers research, had Extraordinary Powers of his own, which made Zhang Baosheng fail each time the two individuals faced off:

Yu Guangyuan is a great scholar, who has many students and a great mass of followers, just like a religious figure. His virtual information field is very powerful, and he occupies an important location in the comprehensive database of the universe. Yu Guangyuan doesn't practise *qigong*, but owing to the effect of his numerous followers, wherever he goes, his body emits a powerful information field. ... When [Zhang Baosheng] is affected by the interference of this powerful information field, he is incapable of reacting, so he fails.[79]

The *qigong* sector thus perceived itself as a circle of initiates, who know and master powers that only other initiates can recognise and defeat.

The argument of fear

Yan Xin used this argument to explain why no American scientific journal has published the articles by his collaborators on his external *qi* experiments: American professors are afraid to reveal that he has succeeded in reviving dead proteins because this would put into question the doctrine that the resurrection of Jesus was the work of God:

---

[77]   Yan Xin 1998: 111.

[78]   The Committee for the Scientific Investigation of Claims of the Paranormal (CSICOP) was founded by American philosopher Paul Kurtz in 1976. Its membership includes North America's leading sceptical figures, including scientists and professional magicians. CSICOP publishes the popular quarterly magazine *Skeptical Inquirer*, which aims to debunk claims of paranormal phenomena. For more on CSICOP, see Hess 1993: 11–12, 87–8.

[79]   Quoted in Yu Guangyuan 1996: 6.

They fear for their brains, as soon as this theological dogma is shaken. There are many universities where theology is taught, many are those who blindly believe in it, ... in addition, they are all armed, ... they can simply eliminate you.

They are also afraid of being assassinated by the food industry: if *bigu* is proven, it will no longer be necessary to eat, and the industry will lose its markets.[80]

Here *qigong* is seen as opening the door to such revolutionary changes that it threatens powerful interests, which would not hesitate to kill to stop its spread.

The argument of counterfeits

Qigong defenders often repeated that if there were so many *qigong* quacks and swindlers, it was because the powers of *qigong* were true, and unscrupulous people wanted to profit from them. For Zhang Yaoting, 'if there is fake Maotai liquor, it is because Maotai is good liquor;[81] if there is fake *qigong*, it is because *qigong* is good.'[82]

In the three latter arguments the failures of *qigong* become proofs of its force: failures occur due to the incomprehension of non-initiates, to the Extraordinary Powers of its critics, to the fear of revealing a revolutionary discovery, and to its benefits which attract swindlers. Overall, the arguments made in *qigong's* defence show that the *qigong* sector saw itself as an avant-garde scientific movement possessing esoteric knowledge, holding the essence of Chinese culture, enjoying the support of the masses and of the élite, and causing fear and envy.

For the *qigong* movement to succeed in China's ideological field, somatic scientists and other *qigong* spokespeople had to win the public debate with the sceptics on the one hand, and convince *qigong* masters and practitioners to accept their scientific formulations and discourse on the other. Producing scientific proofs was the means to defeat the sceptics: the small group of somatic science

---

80 Yan Xin, quoted in QDL: 97–9.
81 Maotai liquor, produced in Guizhou province, is considered to be China's best alcoholic drink.
82 Zhang Yaoting 1998: 24.

researchers thus played a crucial role for the life of the movement. But, while waiting for conclusive and unassailable proofs, the *qigong* sector used simple political means to have its critics muzzled each time the sceptics became too vocal, putting an end to the polemics of 1979–82, 1988–90 and 1995. This could work so long as the *qigong* movement had the right political connections. But by the mid 1990s this would no longer be the case; and the failure to produce scientific proof further strengthened the sceptics' hand.

Lyman Miller, in his study on the relationship between science and politics in the People's Republic of China,[83] has described a conflict between two approaches within the Chinese scientific community: the 'monist' approach, whose chief proponents were Qian Xuesen and He Zuoxiu,[84] defended the need for Party interference in scientific work and the use of Marxist philosophy to guide scientific research; and the 'pluralist' approach, exemplified by Fang Lizhi[85] and Yu Guangyuan, which advocated scientific independence and the freedom of debate. The *Bulletin of Natural Dialectics*, directed by Yu Guangyuan in the 1980s, was a forum on Marxist philosophy in which daring liberal reinterpretations were often discussed. It was attacked by Qian Xuesen as a source of 'spiritual pollution'.[86]

The key figures in this controversy on science and politics played a determining role in the polemics around *qigong*. As we have seen,

[83] Miller 1996.

[84] He Zuoxiu played a leading role in the anti-*qigong* polemic of 1995. His criticism of Falungong in April 1999 triggered the chain of demonstrations in Tianjin and Beijing that led to the repression of Falungong. Born in Shanghai in 1927, he joined the CCP at the age of twenty. After majoring in chemistry and physics at Shanghai Jiaotong University and Qinghua University, he was assigned to the newly-established Central Propaganda Department, and was then transferred to the Atomic Research Institute of the China Academy of Science. He was sent to the Soviet Union to study nuclear physics and cosmology. In the 1960s he took part in the development of China's hydrogen bomb (HX, 29 July 1999: 12). According to Miller, He Zuoxiu was a fierce defender of the role of Marxist philosophy in scientific development, including in debates on the 'Big Bang' and quantum physics. He was involved in the campaign of criticism against Fang Lizhi, the dissident physicist who, after the 1989 Tiananmen student movement, found asylum in the United States. Fang has called He Zuoxiu the 'ideological KGB' of science (Miller 1996: 170, 315).

[85] Fang, who was strongly criticised by He Zuoxiu for his positions on the independence of science, was arrested on 11 June 1989, and took refuge in the American Embassy in Beijing for a year until he was able to leave for the United States.

[86] Miller 1996: 130.

Qian Xuesen used his political influence to block criticism of *qigong* and Extraordinary Powers research, which he wanted to promote in the name of nationalist utopianism, while the chief critic of Extraordinary Powers, Yu Guangyuan, advocated free scientific debate between the promoters and adversaries of paranormal research.[87] But around 1995, as the aging Qian Xuesen's political influence waned, He Zuoxiu took his place as the chief advocate of political control over science: but, contrary to Qian, He Zuoxiu was opposed to Extraordinary Powers research, and played a major role in the politicisation of the anti-*qigong* polemic. The *qigong* movement's use of political means to silence its critics would turn against it by the mid 1990s, when the same politicised means were used to discredit *qigong* science.

---

[87] See Yu Guangyuan 1982.

5

QIGONG FEVER

What had begun as isolated currents in the early 1980s—*qigong*, Extraordinary Powers research, the magical feats of martial arts fiction—began to merge in the popular imagination. *Qigong* was said to develop the Extraordinary Powers latent in everyone's body. Real-life observation and scientific research had proven the existence of the supernatural feats of ancient Chinese popular legends, literature and culture. Chinese *qigong* became the scientifically tested key to breaking the laws of classical physics. The old legends were true, *qigong* would turn them into science, and China would be at the forefront of a new global scientific revolution.

Qigong techniques began to diversify; incorporating practices that increasingly stretched the intended secular content of the *qigong* concept. Liu Guizhen's and Guo Lin's methods had insisted on self-control and on the active aspect of *qigong* exercises, in which the practitioner is the 'commander' in his struggle against illness, contrary to other forms of treatment which turn the patient into a passive recipient of the doctor's cures. But since Gu Hansen's experiments, external *qi* had become central to the concept of *qigong*. By disseminating on a large scale the technique of healing others with external *qi*, Yang Meijun propagated a new type of therapeutic relationship in which the patient doesn't need to practise *qigong* but directly receives the healing force of the master, without the mediation of instruments, medicines or physical contact. From then on learning to emit *qi* would become a component of most *qigong* methods—one practised *qigong* not only to heal oneself, but also to heal others. In addition, Zhao Jinxiang and Liang Shifeng's methods of the 'Flying Crane'[1] and of the 'Spontaneous Five-Animals

---

[1]   On Zhao Jinxiang and this denomination, see Palmer 2005a: 107; Zhao Jinx-iang 1986, 1987, 1993.

Frolic'[2] aimed to trigger a trance, during which the practitioner hits or massages herself, spontaneously carries out kung fu, *taijiquan* or dance movements, or even falls and rolls on the ground. In this type of *qigong*, visions of gods or aliens were frequent. The method led to crowds of practitioners falling in to trance in city parks, many of whom experienced miraculous healings. The beginning of the 1980s saw a wave of 'spontaneous movements *qigong*' spread across China, described by Ots and Micollier as a channel for collective catharsis after the Cultural Revolution.[3] This was far from the self-control of Liu Guizhen's methods.

THE YAN XIN PHENOMENON

Qigong fever was raised to a frenzy in the second half of the 1980s by the young and previously unknown Yan Xin. Adulated like a god by the crowds, he became the incarnation of the image of the *qigong* grandmaster, holder of infinite miraculous powers and herald of the new scientific revolution. Born in 1950 in a peasant family in Fuyan village, in the hills near Jiangyou (Sichuan), Yan Xin had been sent to the countryside as a 'barefoot doctor' after finishing high school. From 1974 to 1977 he studied at the Chengdu Institute of Chinese Medicine, and was then given a teaching position in Mianyang, not far from his hometown. Around that time he became a disciple of the famous Shaolin monk, martial arts master Haideng, whose hometown of Chonghua was in the same area as his own,[4] and who was himself a disciple of the Taoist monk Zhu Zhihan (1873–1973), a native of Shandong known for his exploits during the Boxer rebellion, who had moved to Sichuan after the uprising had been crushed.[5]

In 1981 Yan Xin was transferred to the Chongqing Institute of Chinese Medicine. During the years in Chengdu, Mianyang and

2 On Liang Shifeng and his denomination, see Palmer 2005a: 107–8; QG 2(2): 60–72; Liang Shifeng 1988.

3 Ots 1994; Micollier 1999.

4 Qin Hui 1990: 96–7.

5 Zheng Guanglu, 'Sichuan yihetuan yundong he Emeipai wugong de xingcheng' [The Sichuan Boxer movement and the emergence of the Emei school of martial arts], <http://www.5panda.com/people/2/zhengguanglu_01.htm> (accessed 14 May 2004); Zhang Qin, 'Zhu Zhihan', <http://202.98.123.203:82/gate/big5/ sc2w.scol.com.cn/prog/news_Detail.asp?docid=2336> (accessed 30 March 2006). On the Boxers in Sichuan, see Zheng Guanglu 1995: 70–7.

Chongqing he led an ordinary life, and acquired a reputation for practising *qigong*; but nobody would have guessed that he was about to be propelled to national fame. In Chongqing his work relationships were strained: criticised and punished by his institute for having helped a patient to obtain medicines through the 'back door',[6] and for treating the sick with 'feudal superstitions', he took long-term sick leave in the second half of 1984.[7]

Only a few months later, in the beginning of 1985, the *Sichuan Workers' Newspaper* reported the 'marvellous' therapeutic powers of Yan Xin.[8] The report described the case of worker Jiang Zili, who, struck by a truck, had a crushed vertebra. His doctors had told him he would have to lay on a wooden board for six months, and that he would never recover his full mobility. But thanks to Yan Xin, reported the newspaper, he healed in ten days:

Yan Xin entered the room and glanced at the patient; then he asked everyone present to leave and to wait [outside] and closed the door.

Before an hour had passed the door opened and Jiang Zili stepped out, walking alone, unaided and without crutches. At once he went outside and walked one kilometre. 'He's a miracle doctor!', everyone exclaimed.

How did Dr Yan Xin heal young Jiang's wound? Your reporter went to young Jiang's home. Jiang, his face beaming, explained: 'Dr Yan stood a few centimetres from me and treated me with *qigong*. After half an hour I could get out of bed, bend down, jump and move as I wished. I took no medicines.'

'A miracle doctor! A miracle!' In a month and a half of interviews, all gave the same reaction.

The story was republished by several other newspapers and magazines.[9] Yan Xin was suddenly famous. He started to receive letters from sick people from all over China begging him to heal them. Thus began a period of constant moving around the country. In May 1986 a construction company in Shijiazhuang, in north China invited him to Hebei province to treat one of its employees. He then went from city to city, answering the pleas of the sick. His reputation spread: he was known for his virtue (he refused payment or gifts from patients) and for his healing powers, which could make paraplegics walk.

6   I.e. by short-circuiting normal procedures through Connections. On the 'back door', see Yang 1994.
7   ZGL: 121; Qin Hui 1990: 58, 149–51.
8   SGB, 15 January 1985:4.
9   GM, 18 November 1986: 1; ZGL: 123–4.

Around the summer of 1986 Zhang Zhenhuan, a Vice-President of COSTIND and Chairman of the China Qigong Science Research Society, heard reports of Yan's miraculous healing abilities. At that time famous Chinese atomic scientist Deng Jiaxian, who was terminally ill with cancer, had asked his friend Wan Li (b. 1916), member of the Politburo, to help arrange better treatment for him. Through the Central Military Commission, Wan contacted Zhang Zhenhuan, who suggested *qigong* treatment by Yan Xin. With the agreement of Defence Minister Zhang Aiping,[10] COSTIND obtained Yan Xin's release from his employer, the Chongqing Institute of Chinese Medicine, and summoned him to Beijing. Though he was unable to cure Deng Jiaxian, who died shortly after the *qigong* treatment, he was reported to have considerably alleviated his pain. Through Zhang Zhenhuan's networks in Beijing, he treated several other influential individuals, who all testified to their satisfaction.[11] With the aid of Zhang Zhenhuan's political, military and scientific connections, Yan Xin's reputation skyrocketed. Stories circulated that while on a *qigong* delegation to Japan, without a drop of sweat and without even moving his body, he crushed some of Japan's top martial artists who dared to challenge him.[12] On 18 November 1986 he was consecrated by the *Guangming Daily*, which wrote of him:

Have you ever met a doctor who travels thousands of miles to find the ill? What a coincidence: your journalist just met one. Holding letters and telegrams from the sick in search of a cure, he leaves Chongqing and passes through the cities of Rangfan, Wuchang, Shijiazhuang, Beijing, Tianjin and Miyun ... in each city, he treats the ill, who describe his medical art as sublime and virtuous. ... He combines in a single body Chinese medicine, *qigong*, martial arts and Extraordinary Powers; his treatments often have incredible results.[13]

YAN XIN'S EXPERIMENTS AT QINGHUA UNIVERSITY

The *qigong* research group at Qinghua University became interested in Yan Xin's case and invited him to collaborate in its laboratory studies. The first experiment was held on 22 December 1986.

10 Li Peicai 1988: 246–58, quoted in Kane 1993: 162.
11 ZGL: 124–6; TJH.
12 Qin Hui 1990: 1–6.
13 GM, 18 November 1986: 1.

The miracle master would face the cold and precise instruments of science. What would be the result of the encounter? Li Shengping, one of the researchers, described the scene:

Accompanied by the professors of the research team, Dr Yan Xin entered the laser laboratory of the Science Building. The professors first showed him the usage of the different instruments, and explained how they had previously held experiments on [the effect of external *qi*] on the refraction of liquid crystals. [Yan Xin] was in a good mood; as soon as he entered the room, he emitted Power, without anyone knowing it. When the experiment was about to begin, the professors asked Yan Xin for permission to turn the lights off. Yan Xin, smiling, nodded his approval. But an unexplainable phenomenon happened; no matter how they moved the switch ... the lights wouldn't turn off! Other professors also tried, still to no effect. The atmosphere in the laboratory became tense: if the light couldn't be turned off, the phototube would be unable to function normally. The first day of experiments barely begun, the first experiment could not be accomplished. Everyone looked at each other: there was nothing to be done. At that moment Yan Xin revealed the answer to the riddle, and said, smiling: 'If you hadn't spoken to me about turning the lights out, they could have been turned off; but since you told me they had to be turned off, I was able to stop you from doing so.' And he stepped forward, pressed lightly on the switch, and all the lights went out. ... Suddenly, the atmosphere in the laboratory livened up. Everyone began to feel that the day's experiments might have unimaginable results. But Yan Xin seemed uninterested in the liquid crystal. He walked to the automatic recorder and asked a professor: 'what were the figures from the previous experiment like?' When the professor had finished describing the figure, the transcriptor strangely began to draw a figure like the one from the previous experiment. In an instant, under the effect of Yan Xin's *qigong*, several complete 'experimental figures' were drawn. The professors realised right away that Yan Xin hadn't sent *gong* to the liquid crystal, but that he was [directly] controlling the transcriptor. This thought had barely come to their minds when the transcriptor started to make a strident noise that it normally made only when the signals were too large or too small. But everyone had their eyes fixed on the transcriptor's pen, which didn't move to the sides, but remained stuck in the middle, as [the machine made] mixed noises. None of the professors present had ever seen such a phenomenon. While everyone was still dumbfounded, Yan Xin started his next act. He went into another laboratory more than ten metres away from the transcriptor, emitted his *gong* with a shout, and the transcriptor immediately recorded a pulsation. Another shout, and another, and as many pulsations were recorded. He then approached the transcriptor, and hit his head with his hands—one strike, two strikes, and the pen recorded differently-shaped pulsations. It was simply too miraculous. Everyone looked at his demon-strations in a state of extreme excitement. ...[14]

Yan Xin was then taken to another laboratory, where he was asked to send his *gong* into a test-tube of tap water. Where other mas-ters would put themselves into an appropriate position, wave their hands around the sample or even jump around it, to the point of becoming flushed, Yan Xin, to the amazement of the researchers, nonchalantly told them after a few seconds that his *gong* emission was accomplished. The results of the experiment were miraculous:

The analysis of the Raman effect of the information water[15] was indeed different from that of ordinary water. Good news, this was truly joyous news! One must know that the average person's body is made up of 65 per cent water; the effect of external *qi* on ordinary water and on water in the body follows the same logic. To discover the secret of information water means to discover external *qi*'s power to cure illnesses. This was a result fraught with meaning! Everyone had their eyes riveted to that instrument, which had cost several hundred thousand American dollars. ... The pro-fessors present confirmed [the results], that the experiment was true, that it was not a magic trick, but that it was a miracle produced by man!

On 27 December the experiments were repeated, but this time with Yan Xin emitting his *gong* at a distance of 7 km from the laboratory. In the ensuing month further experiments were conducted, with different samples (0.9 per cent saline, 50 per cent glucose solution, and 1.5 mg/ml medemycene), and at varying distances, up to 2,000 km, with Yan Xin sending *qi* from Guangzhou when prompted by telephone. In each case changes were observed in the samples: The researchers concluded that external *qi* emitted by a *qigong* master could produce an effect on several types of substances found in hu-man body cells, and that this was certainly a major cause of healing by *qigong*. Emission of external *qi* from a distance of 2,000 km could change the molecular structure of water![16]

The inscriptions registered by the laboratory instruments were seen as irrefutable signs of the master's power, turning him into a great scientist. Indeed, thanks to these instruments, the invisible and

14 Originally published in *Zhonghua qigong*, 2 (1987); reproduced in ZGL: 138–41, and Lü Yulan and Cheng Xia 1988. For similar descriptions of the scene, see Qin Hui 1990: 8–12; Ming Zhen 1988: 230–40.

15 *Xinxishui*—water into which a master's *qi* has been emitted.

16 Ming Zhen 1988: 241–2; Qin Hui 1990: 258; ZGL: 142; He Zuoxiu 2002: 40–1.

ineffable *qi* of Chinese tradition left a quantifiable, decodable trace: a fact to be reported in the annals of science.[17] Through *qi*, the master's body communicated with the machine: the marriage between ancient magic and modern science was consummated.

The news was reported in several papers at the end of January 1987, including the *Guangming Daily*[18] and the international edition of the *People's Daily*.[19] The Qinghua University researchers drafted six articles,[20] which received a rave review from Qian Xuesen:

The contents of this paper are a world first, proving beyond a doubt that the human body can influence matter without contact, and change its molecular structure. This type of work has never been seen in the past. It must be published immediately, and without delay proclaim the success of the Chinese to the whole world! ... [This is] a new scientific discovery, heralding a scientific revolution.[21]

The news made a sensation. The scene was captivating; the *qigong* master, in a modern laboratory, surrounded by famous scientists, emits *qi* towards precision instruments that inscribe signs, which are then translated into esoteric scientific jargon. Such a scene would become a central image in the bestselling novel *The Great Qigong Master*, published by famous author Ke Yunlu two years later.[22] One of China's most prestigious scientific institutions had provided irrefutable proof of the extraordinary phenomena of *qigong*, which were the subject of a long religious and martial arts tradition, and of which Yan Xin was the living embodiment. The gates of the imagination could now be opened wide. The 'laboratory miracle' realised the dream of reconciling ancient magic and modern science. Writers and journalists carried the conclusions ever further: a *qigong* master could, by changing the molecular composition of malignant cells, cure cancer and AIDS. He could transform tap water into medicine or into antiviral liquid. He could, by changing

17 On laboratory science as a process of transformation of signs into inscriptions, see Latour and Woolgar 1986.
18 GM, 24 January 1987: 1.
19 HW, 25 January, 1987: 4.
20 ZZ 11(10): 770–5; ZZ 11(9): 647–9, 650–2, 653–5. The series of articles is reproduced in Ming Zhen 1988: 252–309. For an English version of a similar article, see 'The External Qi Experiments from the United States to Beijing, China', translation of article published in *Zhongguo qigong*, 1 (1993): 4–6, <http://www.qigong.net/english/science/experiment/yanus.htm> (accessed January 1999).
21 Qian Xuesen 1987; also quoted in Ming Zhen 1988: 246.
22 Ke Yunlu 1989. See pp. 153–4.

atmospheric pressure, trigger wind and rain. He could even change the direction of laser beams, and intercept enemy nuclear missiles and modify their trajectory, making them explode on enemy territory.[23] The strategic and political genius of Hitler and Mao could now be explained as the expression of their Extraordinary Powers (but Hitler lost them when he took too many stimulant and depressant drugs).[24]

A few months later a huge fire ravaged the forests of Daxing'anling in Liaoning province: the headquarters of the Shenyang Military Area Command invited Yan Xin to conduct an 'experiment' on the powers of external *qi* to extinguish forest fires. The hypothesis was the following: if it was possible to change the molecular structure of the oxygen and hydrogen in the area surrounding the fire, transforming it into carbon dioxide, the fire's range could be controlled. If it was possible to change the molecular structure of water, it would be possible to move clouds from other areas towards the fire zone and induce rain. If it was possible to change the molecular structure of flammable substances, this would help to slow the progression of fire. Changing the atmospheric pressure would also make underground water rise, and so on.[25] Under the cover of 'scientific experimentation', the leaders were calling on Yan Xin as a rainmaking shaman.

He received the authorities' invitation on 15 May 1987. Yan Xin predicted that the 'results' of the 'experiment' would manifest themselves within three days. According to the journalist who followed Yan Xin, on the afternoon of 17 May the sky was clear, without a single cloud, at 4:31 pm. Ten minutes later the sky was completely covered by black clouds. And after a further ten minutes a mighty storm erupted, which lasted 47 minutes. The news spread all over China: with his superhuman powers Yan Xin had put out the Daxing'anling fire![26]

POWER-INDUCING LECTURES

Yan Xin was inundated with mail and invitations from sick people imploring his help. In order to allow greater numbers of people

23 Qin Hui 1990: 258; ZGL: 144; He Zuoxiu 2002: 41.
24 Lü Yulan and Cheng Xia 1988: 4.
25 Qin Hui 1990: 270–1; ZGL: 144.
26 People were still talking about this miracle in Chengdu in the early 1990s.

to benefit from his powers, leaders of the CQRS came up with a new way to propagate *qigong*: the 'Power-inducing scientific *qigong* lecture' (*daigong qigong kexue baogaohui*). These were lectures given by Yan Xin on the scientific aspects of *qigong* and on the methods of *qigong* practice and healing, during which he sent *qi* and used his power to induce the audience members' latent *gong*. In Yan Xin's words, these conferences were 'scientific experiments' on the effects of the emission of *qigong* 'messages' (*xinxi*) on the audience.

Yan Xin's 'lectures' attracted growing crowds. His talks were unusually long, lasting between five and fourteen hours without pause or interruption: but audiences remained attentive to each of his words. No chatting, knitting, newspaper reading or frequent exits to the restrooms could be observed, as is usually the case in meetings and lectures in China: on the contrary, audiences were as hypnotised; many fell into trance states, and it was not uncommon for paraplegics to stand up and walk during the lectures.[27]

Work units, ministries and local governments rushed to invite Yan Xin to give lectures. Between 1987 and 1988 he gave over 200, to a total audience of approximately one million, at venues including the Central Party School, the PLA Political Academy, Beijing University, Qinghua University and sports stadiums in most of China's large cities. Each time, tickets sold out: 7,000 in Shenyang, 8,000 in Guangzhou, with black-market tickets being sold for 100 yuan, a month's wages at the time.[28] In Shanghai 23,000 tickets for two lectures were sold out in half a day.[29]

On 8 October 1987 Yan Xin lit a 40 watt bulb with his hand while lecturing at Beijing University. A professor of electronic engineering ran on stage and cried, 'his body just conducted an electric charge of 220 volts!'[30] Miraculous cures were frequent. There was talk of a girl who after a conference with Yan Xin entered a state of *bigu* fasting and stopped eating for over eight years, without losing any weight;[31] a woman whose kidney stones vanished after going to one of Yan Xin's lectures; a young man who after listening to Yan Xin discovered he could see through objects and practise psychokinesis, moving a telephone and a bicycle with his mind; a

27 Qin Hui 1990: 281; ZGL: 152.
28 QG 60: 17.
29 ZGL: 220.
30 BQB, 12 May 1995: 3.
31 Ke Yunlu 1996: 29. On *bigu*, see p. 151.

deaf man who recovered his hearing; an army doctor whose father's liver stones disappeared after he went to a Yan Xin lecture at Qinghua University, thousands of kilometres away.[32]

PILGRIMAGE TO YAN XIN'S VILLAGE

Yan Xin acquired the stature of a god, a *huofo* or 'living Buddha'. His native village of Dong'an became a pilgrimage site. Thousands of sick people from across China, even from Hong Kong and Taiwan, travelled dozens, hundreds or even thousands of kilometres to approach the grandmaster at his family home. Yan Xin rarely went home, but the pilgrims didn't hesitate to wait for weeks. Others hoped to absorb the special energies of the spot, thanks to its excellent *fengshui*[33] and its 'magnetic field', in order to acquire Extraordinary Powers for themselves. During the 1988 Chinese New Year holidays more than 2,400 people converged on the village, hoping to see the master on his return home for the traditional festival. On his arrival Yan Xin housed some gravely ill people in the family's rear courtyard and treated them, while others cried, shouted, fell into convulsions, and started to send *qi* to heal each other.

Yan Xin refused payment, so the 'pilgrims' spontaneously raised funds to contribute to the cleaning and renovation of Dong'an village. In a day and a half some 560 persons donated over 10,000 yuan,[34] beginning a new tradition. Indeed, a few years later Yan Xin followers in Canada and the United States donated $85,000 to pave the streets and build a parking lot for pilgrims, plant trees, build a dam, and protect the environment.[35]

---

32 Qin Hui 1990: 282–9; ZGL: 156.
33 *Fengshui* is the Chinese art of geomancy, by which the location of a new house is chosen in relation to currents of terrestrial *qi*, the shape of the hills, the pattern of the rivers and the dates of the traditional calendar. On *Fengshui*, see Feuchtwang 2002; Bruun 2003.
34 ZGL: 144–9.
35 'Campaign to Preserve the Natural Beauty of Dr Yan Xin's Home Town in China', <http://www.interlog.com/~pparsons/toronto/dongan.htm> (accessed January 1999); 'Update on the Campaign to Preserve the Natural Beauty of Dr Yan Xin's Home Town in China', <http://www.interlog.com/~pparsons/toronto/engsumm.htm> (accessed January 1999); 'Four Days in Fuyan Village', <http://www-acs.ucsd.edu/~dhu/yxq/papers/4-days.html> (accessed January 1999).

THE RISE OF ZHANG HONGBAO

Shortly after Yan Xin's eruption on to the national scene in 1986 another grandmaster, Zhang Hongbao, 'came out of the mountains' with a strategy to co-opt, organise and systematically conquer the bubbling world of *qigong* and its mass of practitioners. Through his Zhonggong denomination, Zhang Hongbao would attempt to integrate the *qigong* movement into a modern commercial enterprise.

Born in Harbin on 5 January 1954 in to a family of coalminers, Zhang Hongbao spent ten years, from the ages of fourteen to twenty-four, on a farm during the Cultural Revolution. During that time he began to practise martial arts with some youths from Beijing and Shanghai. He also quickly moved up the farm hierarchy: from breaker of stones he was promoted to security guard, then statistician, technician and finally teacher at the farm school. In 1977 he was sent to the Harbin School of Metallurgy, after which he joined the CCP and was appointed as a high school physics teacher in a mining region. He devoted himself to Party work, and rapidly rose up the mine's political hierarchy. He missed no opportunity to continue his studies: cadres' training sessions, night classes, distance learning programme in management psychology. In 1985 he was admitted to the Economic Management programme at the Beijing University of Science and Technology.[36]

In Beijing Zhang Hongbao did not obtain high grades. His thesis on leadership theory was not much appreciated by his professors. However, his interests were many: he took law courses at People's University, studied Chinese and Western medicine, and registered at the Chinese Qigong Further Education Academy. He became a passionate *qigong* practitioner, and took lessons from several masters. Finally, he developed his own method, the 'Chinese Qigong for Nourishing Life and Increasing Intelligence' (*Zhonghua yangsheng yizhi gong*) or Zhonggong—a method characterised by its use of mechanical engineering jargon: it included a 'principal project' and 'auxiliary projects', and drew on the theories of automation, physics, information, relativity, systems and bionics.[37]

Zhang Hongbao's abilities as a seer earned him a reputation that began to spread beyond his campus. Zhang's powers were 'discovered' by one of his roommates, with whom he shared a bunk-bed:

---

36 Ji Yi 1990a: 46–52; Zhang Hongbao 2001: 1–2.
37 Ji Yi 1990a: 57; Zhang Hongbao 2001: 2.

when the roommate's stomach ache suddenly disappeared, he attributed the healing to Zhang's *qigong* practice right above him. After graduating Zhang was hired by the university to conduct research on *qigong*.[38] One spring day in 1987 he was invited to give his first lecture at the university, at which he demonstrated his Extraordinary Powers, by asking volunteers to come on to the stage and meditate, and then by making their bodies shake without touching them.[39]

On an auspicious day, the eighth day of the eighth month of 1987, Zhang Hongbao 'came out of the mountains' for the official launch of his denomination, by founding the Beijing Haidian District Qigong Science Research Institute. During the following year he carried out a strategy to infiltrate systematically the academic, media and legal élites of the capital. After teaching Zhonggong in various schools and universities, he was invited in November 1987 to Beijing University, where he gave two week-long 'accelerated workshops' to over one thousand participants, many of whom were faculty members and researchers from various universities, including the President of Beijing University.[40] After the workshop, many of them could emit, collect and transform *qi*. Several became diehard *qigong* practitioners. The event was reported in the *People's Daily*, giving Zhang Hongbao a national reputation.[41]

Zhang's second target was the heart of the Chinese scientific community: the China Academy of Sciences, the China Academy of Social Sciences and the China Academy of Agricultural Sciences. He gave workshops in each establishment. One of these seminars was the subject of a three-minute report on the national CCTV news programme.[42] In the report Zhang was shown making five or six persons wobble by pointing his finger at them, from a distance of several metres. This made him a celebrity.[43]

Such media attention enabled Zhang to penetrate his third target: Beijing's media élite. On 4 January 1988 he organised a five-day fast-track workshop for members of the media and cultural circles. One hundred and thirty people signed up, including a Deputy

38 ZQB, 2 January 1988: 2.
39 Ji Yi 1990a: 59.
40 Ji Yi 1990a: 61.
41 RR, 10 January 1988: 3.
42 Ji Yi 1990a: 64.
43 BQB, 8 January 1988: 7.

Minister of Culture, leaders of the China Writers' Association and
a famous singer.[44] The *People's Daily* reported that in a few months
over 7,000 persons had attended Zhang Hongbao's trainings, which
had even been held in the *Daily's* own offices.[45] Several other major newspapers ran articles on Zhang Hongbao: the *China Youth
News*,[46] the *Beijing Youth News*,[47] the *China Electronics News*[48] and
others. Thanks to Zhang Hongbao, wrote the *Beijing Youth News*,
intellectuals could take *qigong* seriously. 'His lectures shook the intellectual world. It is obviously not so difficult to open the gate of
qigong.' But as soon as the gate opens, continued the article's author,
one's mental and spiritual abilities are strengthened, and one's illnesses can heal.[49]

Having charmed the media, Zhang Hongbao set his sights on
the centres of political power. On 10 January 1988 he gave a 'power-inducing lecture' at the Central Party School's main auditorium,
which was filled to capacity; hundreds of others had to follow the
event on closed-circuit television in other rooms. Zhang Hongbao
invited the president of the school on to the stage and to send *qi* towards the audience, which was instructed to receive the *qi* with one
hand: only five minutes later audience members were amazed to
discover that the fingers of their 'receiving' hand were now longer
than those of the other hand! A minister claimed that his leg pain
had disappeared.[50] Zhang then gave a one-week workshop at the
Party School.[51]

Then it was the turn of the police and justice ministries to invite Zhang to give workshops. Altogether, from 1987 to 1990 he
held some fifty fast-track workshops in various government agencies in Beijing.[52] People talked of a 'Zhonggong fever' in Beijing.
A personality cult began, fanned by the best-selling hagiographic
novel *The Great Qigong Master Comes out of the Mountains* by Ji Yi,
published in 1990, which told of Zhang's miracles, of Extraordinary
Powers and of the Zhonggong method. The book's total sales were

44 Ji Yi 1990a: 75.
45 RR, 10 January 1988: 3.
46 ZQB, 2 January 1988: 2.
47 BQB, 8 January 1988: 7.
48 ZDB, 22 January 1988: 4.
49 BQB, 8 January 1988: 7.
50 Ji Yi 1990a: 76.
51 ZDB, 22 January 1988: 4.
52 Zhang Hongbao 2001: 3.

estimated to have reached 10 million.[53] The book is full of stories of miraculous phenomena: masters who heal from a thousand miles away, who kill goldfish by their glance, who make tyres pop from their anger. It tells of the weight of the human soul (7.1 g), of the aura around every person's head, of the first human (an Asian woman), of the conquest of the citadel of science by the spirit of *qigong*, of the 'thought war' that will take place in 2020, and of the 'miraculous swirl' of Zhonggong, whose master is described as nothing less than a god:

Three incredible oriental characters are shaking China and the world:
   Zhang Hong Bao!
   Zhang Hongbao, a man tormented by illness.
   Zhang Hongbao, a man with a brilliant official career.
   Zhang Hongbao, a man of mystery and enigmas.
   Zhang Hongbao, a man with unlimited magical powers.
   Is he a man, or a god?
   Where does he come from, and where is he going?
   The power of his thought and concentration, the power of his wisdom and the power of his spirit, the power of his magical technique, his powers of communication and of spiritual transformation .... Has he obtained them from a famous Master? From the Heavenly Way? From a god?
   Who knows? You? Me? Him?
   A heavenly phenomenon? An earthly phenomenon? A human phenomenon?
   The Universe. The Universe. The Universe.
   Transformation. Transformation. Transformation.
   A quest begun during his illness, his eyes opened during his search, a complete and total awakening to all that exists in the universe, he realises his mission to bring good to the people of the three worlds,[54] and to save men and all beings.
   There is no Dharma in the world. ... Total enlightenment is the Dharma.
   Here, then, is Zhang Hongbao. In the darkness, sitting on the ground, he becomes a god. He unites in the palm of his hand all the functions and magical powers transmitted and documented in written and oral history, including the magical techniques of Buddhism, Taoism, Confucianism, therapy, martial arts, popular [magic], as well as Indian Yoga and Western Christianity ...'[55]

---

53   QDL: 132.
54   Reference to the Buddhist *triloka*: the world of sensual desire, the material and sensible world, and the formless world of the spirit.
55   Ji Yi 1990a: 66–7.

Ji Yi would continue to write other books on Zhang Hongbao and on *qigong*, making a career of *qigong* literature, until he founded his own denomination, Great Buddha Qigong, in 1994.[56]

A WAVE OF POWER-INDUCING LECTURES

With the charismatic grandmasters '*qigong* fever' reached its climax. Yan Xin's imitators were legion, and 'power-inducing lectures' became a regular fixture of the *qigong* milieu: any *qigong* master with a claim to public recognition had to be able to produce healings or Extraordinary Powers phenomena during his lectures. Audiences were easily charmed: merely giving the title of 'power-inducing lecture' to a basic lecture on *qigong* theory was sufficient to make audience members fall into trance.[57]

To meet the demand for *qigong* lectures, work units organised public screenings of video and audiotapes of Yan Xin's talks. Since external *qi* was considered to be a form of 'information' or 'message', the efficacy of the recorded lectures was said to be as great as the Master's presence.

The Central People's Radio invited Yan Xin to give a 'power-inducing lecture' on the national airwaves. China Central Television (CCTV) invited Zhang Hongbao and another master, Zhang Jialing, to perform *qigong* demonstrations during the Chinese New Year special programme: the most watched television show in China. Zhang Hongbao fried a fish in his hand with 'electric *qigong*'. Famous comedians Ma Ji and Hou Yuewen ate the fish skewers on the live broadcast. Zhang Jialing, an adept at 'light *qigong*', stood on a balloon and on a sheet of paper suspended between two wooden ladders.

Zhang Jialing became a new *qigong* celebrity. The CCTV president, full of enthusiasm, invited him back to the following year's show. Journalists flocked to his martial arts academy and described his ability to walk on water. The 'light *gong*' airborne acrobatics of kung fu novels and movies were true![58]

---

56   See Ji Yi 1990a and b. On Great Buddha Qigong, see chapter 7, figure 4.

57   ZGL: 200 mentions a *qigong* master who chided his audience, several of whom were in trance, saying that he had *not* emitted any *gong*. A similar case is also mentioned in Ji Yi 1993.

58   ZGL: 254–5.

THE BIGU WAVE

At Yan Xin's lectures, many people entered a state of fasting, ceasing to eat or drink for days or weeks, and even, it was claimed in some cases, for over a year. This phenomenon, called *bigu*,[59] became a new fad in the *qigong* milieu. *Bigu* could be practised at different degrees of intensity. Partial fasting involved taking only small quantities of water, fruits or other foods, while total fasting required abstention from any liquids or solids for a defined period: days, weeks, months or until (unintentional) death. *Bigu* practitioners considered that they 'ingested' *qi* through *qigong*, and tried to keep fit during the period of fasting: they worked, studied or even climbed mountains with as much or more energy than those who continued to eat.

In June 1988 *Qigong* magazine published the results of a *bigu* experiment on master Zhang Rongtang of Zhejiang, the founder of 'gyrating *qigong*', who claimed to be able to spin his body 1,700 rotations in twenty minutes without getting dizzy. In the *bigu* experiment the master's daily intake was limited to 100 ml of honey, 200 ml of saline solution and 700 ml of boiled water. He fasted for nine days under constant hospital surveillance, all the while continuing to give *qigong* lessons, and even climbing Yuhuang Mountain. His health was reported to be perfectly normal at the end of the fast.[60] Later that year thirteen of Zhang Rongtang's disciples, after practising 'gyrating *qigong*' for twenty days, started a three-day *bigu* fast, during which they climbed a mountain near Hangzhou, arriving at the summit, without fatigue and full of vigour, on the morning of the third day.

These reports stimulated an explosion of interest in *bigu*. Some imagined the applications of *bigu* in aeronautics, in medicine and so on: 'If astronauts had powers of *bigu*, it would be possible to design manned spacecraft to fly farther and with a larger crew.'[61]

ZHANG XIANGYU AND 'COSMIC LANGUAGE'

Another widespread phenomenon during the *qigong* wave was glossolalia or 'cosmic language', a condition analogous to 'speaking in

59 The literal meaning of *bigu* is 'to abstain from grains', a term with its origins in Taoist dietetics. But in the *qigong* milieu, *bigu* became a vague designation for any type of fast or dietary abstention. On Taoist *bigu*, see Schipper 1993: 167–70.
60 QG 9(6): 243–5. See also ZGL: 289.
61 QG 10(6): 285.

tongues'. The most notorious promoter of this was Zhang Xiangyu, an actress from the windswept province of Qinghai, north of Tibet, who claimed to have been pushed by a puff of *qi* to run without stopping for days and nights on end in August 1985.[62] A hundred days later she played host in her kitchen to the Jade Emperor, the Queen Mother, Guanyin, Sakyamuni, the Venerable Lord Lao and other popular divinities, to whom she offered grapes and apples. 'Great ones and lesser ones, they all came', she said.[63] She then heard a voice in 'cosmic language' tell her that she could treat the sick. She quit her acting job to devote herself to her new calling as a healer, and moved to Beijing in 1986, where she entered the *qigong* sector. The next year she was invited to demonstrate her healing powers to the CQRS; the experiments proved inconclusive.[64] One day, as she wondered how to transmit her power to others,

> ... the familiar voice suddenly spoke from the darkness: 'this *gong* is called Nature's Centre Gong (*Daziran zhongxin gong*); it hasn't been passed down in a long time. Your mission is to propagate this denomination, and to save humanity.'[65]

She proclaimed herself a '*qigong* grandmaster' and claimed to be in direct communication with the universe, whose messages she transmitted through revelations of 'cosmic language' (*yuzhou yu*) and 'cosmic songs' (*yuzhou ge*). She taught her method in several provinces and in 1989 established the Nature's Centre Qigong Research Society in Beijing. The *gongfa* attracted tens of thousands of followers. A tree in the Temple of Heaven Park, said to be infused with her *qi* after she had emerged victorious from a struggle with a demon at that spot, became a magnet for followers who would speak 'cosmic tongues' and fall into spontaneous movements around the tree.[66] Li Peicai, who worked for the COSTIND propaganda department, wrote a bestselling book, *The Soul of Nature*, which described Zhang Xiangyu's miraculous exploits, her struggles against sick people's ancestors' souls and her messianic mission:

---

[62] Born in Beijing in 1944, Zhang Xiangyu had dropped out of school after primary school. In 1959 she started work for a camera factory, then in 1964 passed auditions to join the Datong (Shanxi) theatre troupe. In 1969 she was transferred to the Zhangjiakou theatre troupe, and in 1972 to the Qinghai troupe.

[63] Li Peicai 1989: 7.

[64] ZGL: 328.

[65] Li Peicai 1989: 28.

[66] Chen 2003b: 73.

This *gong* will spread to the world; only this *gong* can save humanity. Without this *gong* a great calamity will be inevitable. This *gongfa* must be propagated urgently in China and throughout the world; we must absolutely not hesitate. The year 2000 is approaching—the twenty-first century will see changes that will overturn the heavens and the earth. What to do? This *gong* must absolutely be propagated as fast as possible ... Courageously lead people to Nature: such is the best method of salvation. Without it you face extinction and death.[67]

QIGONG BESTSELLERS

Hagiographic books on *qigong* masters became a new form of popular literature. Besides the book on Zhang Hongbao mentioned earlier, the top-selling work in this genre was *The Great Qigong Master*, a novel by the famous writer Ke Yunlu. Published in October 1989, it sold 700,000 copies.[68] The novel describes one man's quest to uncover the mysteries of *qigong*, Extraordinary Powers, the *Book of Changes*, the *Laozi*, *yin* and *yang*, Chinese medicine, physiognomy, geomancy, Chinese characters, oriental mysticism, UFOs etc. In his search for answers, the protagonist becomes friends with a *qigong* grandmaster—who resembles Yan Xin in all respects—and confronts a sceptical bureaucrat who refuses to believe in the master's miraculous feats, even after seeing them with his own eyes. The story tells of a struggle against superficiality and ignorance, in a search for the true meaning of life. Thus the author in his preface entitled 'Human self-transcendence: somato-cosmology' fully encapsulates the utopian vision of *qigong*:

Young people, you tell me: our greatest anguish is that we can't find the meaning of life!

I understand. ...

In writing *The Great Qigong Master*, I don't treat *qigong* as a method to attain longevity—although it does effectively bring long life.

Even less as a refuge or a shield against the different conflicts and crises of the modern world.

Qigong is a high level technique, but it is more than that. Great *qigong* should have a noble spirit. Let's rather say that we want to discover a noble spirit in *qigong*.

At present, man needs a new spirit.

Our era needs to find a new meaning. ...

67   Li Peicai 1989: 417.
68   QDL: 33.

We will awake to a higher human and cosmic truth.

This will trigger a great leap forward for humanity.

This cannot be called a 'fourth wave' or a 'second renaissance'. The significance is even greater.

If we can say that fire and human work created man, the truth unveiled by 'somato-cosmology' will lead man to a level of wisdom comparable to [that which led to] the mastery of fire, but at a much higher level. It will make mankind evolve to a higher stage of life. ...

We will become a humanity more capable of conversing with the superior intelligence of the universe.

We will turn our backs to today's closed-mindedness, superficiality and stupidity.

We will be more open, more direct, more sincere, more altruistic, more tolerant, more artistic, more relaxed, more natural, more able to put into practice our historic cooperation and our mission in life.

We will be like a golden baby.

We will be like the dawn sun.

We will be positive, transcendental and radiant.

We will enlighten the world.[69]

CONCLUSION: QIGONG BECOMES AN OUTLET FOR MASS RELIGIOSITY

The number of *qigong* practitioners is difficult to assess; estimates vary from 10 million to over 100 million—8 per cent of the Chinese population and over 20 per cent of its urban inhabitants—depending on the period and on whether one counts only regular practitioners or those who have occasionally practised at some point or another. As an example, the number of regular practitioners in Beijing in 1985, before the *qigong* craze had reached its peak, was estimated by the Beijing Qigong Research Society to be 300,000,[70] of whom about half practised *qigong* at the seventy-seven practice points led by different denominations registered with the BQRS, and the others at practice points managed by trade unions, youth associations or women's federations.[71]

Ke Yunlu's idealism addresses one end of the spectrum of people's interest in *qigong*, which ranged from the down-to-earth need for healing and health, to a mystic search for ultimate meaning and

69   Ke Yunlu 1989: 26–8.
70   ZGL: 12.
71   ZGL: 12.

transcendence. The spread of *qigong* was stimulated by the growing numbers of practitioners and of sick people who had been cured by *qigong*, who became passionate promoters of this miraculous path of healing. The minority core of the practitioners was made up of the 'disciples' (*dizi*) of a single master, who were the key links in the denomination's transmission chains: as 'assistants' (*fudaoyuan*), they were in charge of the 'practice points' (*liangongdian*) of each method in the parks, leading the group practice. The floating mass of ordinary practitioners, on the other hand, easily moved from one method to another.

The majority of practitioners did so to improve their health and live a longer life. They were mostly retired people: *qigong* practice helped them to come out of their solitude. Another group were sick people, who practised *qigong* with the hope of healing. Some did heal, and others failed. Those who did heal became fervent believers, practitioners and defenders of *qigong*. The pioneers of modern *qigong*, such as Liu Guizhen, Wang Juemin and Guo Lin, were of this category. Others were curious, learning *qigong* with the hope of discovering, through personal experience, the mysterious phenomena attributed to *qigong*. Finally, some were motivated by a spiritual search, seeing in *qigong* a means to enter the world of Chinese mysticism. They were often intellectuals trained with a scientific and materialist worldview, whose involvement in *qigong* led them to a greater interest in religion.

Many practitioners, who began *qigong* for health, healing or out of curiosity, were drawn through *qigong* into a spiritual quest. Indeed *qigong* is what Hervieu-Léger calls a 'converter', which makes it possible to move easily 'from one type of experience to another and from one symbolic universe to another'.[72] The denominations have the religious characteristics of 'chains of memory' as defined by Hervieu-Léger, in that they can trigger, by transforming the practitioner's relationship to his or her body, a recomposition of his or her mental and somatic world around a tradition shaped by the master's *gongfa*. But such a religious orientation is not inevitable: a large number, if not the majority, of practitioners never went beyond the original goal of health or healing.

Qigong was taught in primary schools to increase pupils' intelligence, was used in professional sports and military training, and

---

[72] Hervieu-Léger 2001: 136.

qigong masters with Extraordinary Powers were employed by the geological prospection bureau to detect underground mineral deposits. The *qigong* grandmaster became a charismatic idol, crystallising the evolution of *qigong* towards mass religiosity. Combining in a single figure the legendary immortal superman and the modern image of the scientific technician, integrating traditional religion and the faith in modern science. He or she incarnated both remembrance of the past and the cult of modernity. All of the contradictions of modern China seemed to resolve themselves in the powers of the master's own body.

We have seen how *qigong* took on an ever-expanding scope and resonance. A form of therapy and health discipline in the 1950s, *qigong* became a method for acquiring Extraordinary Powers at the end of the 1970s, then heralded a new scientific revolution in the mid 1980s. With the moral teachings of Yan Xin and the charismatic grandmasters, *qigong* became an 'omni-science' connecting all aspects of human knowledge and culture, and acquired an ethical dimension which transcended body practice. *Qigong* touched on all themes: hygiene, aesthetics, medicine, education, science, traditional philosophy, religion—fields which took on a new meaning in the light of *qigong*, and which where, through *qigong*, integrated into a whole.

The sets of body and breathing exercises, such as those introduced by Liu Guizhen, remained as the foundation of *qigong* practice, but were relegated to a secondary position in charismatic *qigong* which consisted in the sick person or the audience member receiving the *gong* of the grandmaster. Such transmission of *gong* no longer required the adoption of specific body postures, or the circulation of perceptible *qi* between master and patient: the master's *gong* acted instantaneously, from any distance. Its only container, if it had one, was the master's utterance: Yan Xin's healing method consisted of 'casual chat' with the patient. His lectures were an endless flow of words. Body techniques were almost forgotten, as adepts plunged into the master's field of *gong*.

From secret teaching in traditional lineages before 1949, transmission changed into public but individual coaching in the 1950s. Then, in the 1970s transmission became collective in the parks. To the wave of 'spontaneous movement' trances of the early 1980s[73]

---

[73] For further discussion of spontaneous movements in *qigong*, see Ots 1994.

Yan Xin added the formula of the 'power-inducing lecture' for audiences of thousands of people, leading the mass *qigong* phenomenon to its climax.

By the second half of the 1980s religious practices and concepts had thus become integral to the originally secular concept of *qigong*, expressing a faith in the efficacy of a reconstituted tradition as well as in the promise of a utopian future, which practitioners could feel intimately in the depth of their body and consciousness. Through *qigong* practice they could mentally and physiologically enter the world of ancient legends, of hermits, immortals and sages, of mythical animals and supermen, seen as the sources of Chinese civilisation and which, through *qigong*, were resuscitated. The deep mental states that could be triggered by the effects of practice, and the phenomena perceived by the practitioner, could give the sensation of participating in avant-garde scientific research and in the transformation of oneself and of the world.

6

CONTROVERSY AND CRISIS

The second World Qigong Congress, held in Xi'an from 10 to 14 September 1989, was planned as an occasion to celebrate the victories of the *qigong* movement over the previous decade. Over 500 delegates attended, coming from China and other East and Southeast Asian countries as well as from North America, the Soviet Union and Togo. Thousands of *qigong* fans and sick people congregated outside the conference hall, hoping to receive the *qi* of some great master. The masters who converged on Xi'an from all parts of China to attend the congress were solicited by various units in the ancient capital to give power-inducing lectures.[1] But despite the crowds and the excited atmosphere of the congress, the delegates agreed that the *qigong* sector was in a state of crisis. Quackery and deviations were tarnishing the image of *qigong*. The anti-*qigong* polemic was reviving after seven years of silence. And, with the general tightening of government control of popular groups following the 4 June student movement, the state was preparing to regulate *qigong*.

With such large numbers of *qigong* practitioners, the syndrome of *zouhuo rumo* started to become an issue. *Zouhuo rumo* is a state in which *qigong* practice triggers uncontrollable effects, either physiological, as in 'becoming inflamed'—headaches, nausea or pain in various parts of the body, disrupted circulation of *qi*, increased blood pressure, uncontrolled body movements etc.—or mental, as in 'falling into a spell'—delirium, paranoia, hallucinations, passivity, loss of mental faculties, incoherent speech, severe emotional distress or behaviour harmful to oneself or others. *Zouhuo rumo* first caught the public's attention in the early 1980s when practitioners of Flying Crane Qigong who had entered the state of 'spontaneous movements *qigong*', were unable to come out of it.[2]

---

1 ZGL: 340–7; Ji Yi 1993. For the conference papers, see Guo Zhouli 1989.
2 See Miura 1989: 353.

Victims of *zouhuo rumo* were often taken by their families to the outpatient clinics of psychiatric hospitals, some of which opened special clinics for treating what Chinese psychiatrists called '*qigong* deviation' (*qigong piancha*). A minority were diagnosed with schizophrenia or other psychotic disorders, and admitted to inpatient wards.[3] These included patients who refused to eat or drink, who had delusions of grandeur, who thought themselves invisible and omniscient, or the reincarnations of the Jade Emperor etc.[4] Zhang Tongling, a psychiatrist at the Beijing University of Medical Sciences, opened a clinic for *qigong* deviation in 1989 where, over the next six years, she treated about four hundred patients. In her analysis of the cases[5] she concluded that *qigong* could either exacerbate pre-existing mental disorders or trigger psychotic symptoms for the first time among vulnerable individuals with an obsessive interest in *qigong*. Psychiatric research on *qigong* deviation led to the creation of a new category of mental illness, '*qigong* psychotic reaction', classified as a 'culture-bound syndrome' in the *Diagnostic and Statistical Manual of Mental Disorders*, the main reference for the international psychiatric profession, which defined the disorder as 'an acute, time-limited episode characterised by dissociative, paranoid, or other psychotic or non-psychotic symptoms that may occur after participation in the Chinese folk health enhancing practice of *qigong* ('exercise of vital energy'). Especially vulnerable are individuals who become overly involved in this practice.'[6] Other cases of *qigong* deviation were fatal. These included individuals who starved to death while practicing *bigu*, those who committed suicide in order to 'ascend to heaven', and those who died while committing dangerous acts out of delusions of omnipotence, such as jumping from a building with the intention of flying. These cases caused concern among the public and in state health authorities. They would also be taken up by anti-*qigong* polemicists as ammunition against the *qigong* sector.[7]

3   Chen 2003b: 93.
4   For descriptions of cases of *qigong* deviation, see ZGL: 276–92; Chen 2003b: 77–106; Xu Shenghan 1994; Shan 2000; Lee 2000; Leung et al. 2001.
5   GR, 16 August 1995: 5; KX 1996(39): 19–22.
6   DSM-IV 1994: 847.
7   The cases of 'victims' of Falungong reported in the Chinese media in 1999–2000, if true, appear like typical examples of *qigong* deviation, rather than being specifically linked to Falungong as distinct from other, legal *qigong* methods.

QUACKERY

The other problem was quackery. Power-inducing lectures and video screenings and the sale of *qi*-filled objects were becoming lucrative lines of business. With the growth of a market for *qigong*-related events and products, *qigong* was becoming commodified. Self-proclaimed grandmasters were legion, claiming the ability to heal any type of illness and often charging high fees for their therapies, lectures and objects onto which they had emitted their *qi*, such as 'information tea' and 'information paintings' said to contain invisible messages that could cure myopia, high blood pressure or cancer. Masters with self-proclaimed 'divine' and 'miraculous' powers, who professed to possess 'secret techniques' asserted their ability to cure any illness, even AIDS. Chiromancers and fortune-tellers offered their divination services under the *qigong* label. It was not unusual for masters to charge 100 or 200 yuan, or ten times as much for clients from Hong Kong, for their 'information diagnosis' or to 'see through' the patient's body. Some used their Extraordinary Powers to 'diagnose' illnesses that the client didn't suffer from, only to charge exorbitant amounts to 'cure' them.[8] One master went so far as to claim that during a 44-day-long 'scientific experiment', he had managed, by sending his *qi*, to cause 90 per cent of the world's mosquitoes to mutate so that they would no longer sting humans but instead stick their probosces in tree leaves, weeds and fleas.[9] Such stories began seriously to tarnish the image of *qigong* masters.

RENEWED POLEMICS

A small but increasingly active group of sceptics, who had been silenced since the 1982 no-criticism policy, became more vocal. Already in March 1988 a delegation of the Committee for the Scientific Investigation of Claims of the Paranormal (CSICOP), an American association of sceptical scientists and professional magicians dedicated to debunking paranormal claims, had been invited to China by the *Science and Technology Daily* to investigate Extraordinary Powers claims, offering a reward of $10,000 to whoever could prove the existence of Extraordinary Powers. A handful of *qigong* masters and Extraordinary Powers children responded to the

8   QK 110: 26.
9   ZGL: 344; Ji Yi 1993: 513.

challenge, but were unable to demonstrate their alleged powers to the foreign delegates.[10] The Chinese hosts of the delegation were strongly criticised by Extraordinary Powers advocates for lacking patriotism, for having invited a 'foreign gunmen's brigade' (*yangqiangdui*)—an expression previously used during the Boxer rebellion of 1900 to describe the foreign armies that brought to naught the magical powers of the rebels' body technologies—to come and destroy China's cultural heritage and hamper the development of Extraordinary Powers research. Since the political influence wielded by these advocates was evident to the *Science and Technology Daily*, its coverage described the visit only as 'academic exchange' and included some translated articles by CSICOP members criticising the paranormal in general terms, but made no mention of the embarrassing failure of the Chinese *qigong* masters,[11] which was only reported seven years later.[12]

A few months later Chen Xin, the director of the 507 Institute of the COSTIND, invited the Leaders' Working Group on Somatic Science to observe a demonstration of Zhang Baosheng's fabled powers; and for added legitimacy, invited He Zuoxiu and other sceptical scientists, as well as some professional magicians. This time, under controlled experimental conditions, the abilities which Zhang had so often displayed to hundreds of audiences, completely vanished. After three hours and many attempts to divert the audience's attention, Zhang was unable to remove a pill from a sealed bottle, or to 'read with his ears' a poem placed in a sealed envelope. The organisers admitted the failure of the experiment, and that Zhang Baosheng cheated sometimes, but maintained that *sometimes* his powers *were* real. Others said that He Zuoxiu had Extraordinary Powers himself, with which he had neutralised Zhang Baosheng.[13] As in the case of the CSICOP visit, this incident was not publicly reported until 1995, while a hagiographic bestseller on Zhang Baosheng's miracles[14] was released only six months after he failed this crucial test.

10 Kurtz, Paul, 'The China Syndrome: Further Reflections on the State of Paranormal Belief in China', *Skeptical Inquirer*, 13 (autumn 1988): 46–9; ZGL: 267–71.
11 KR, 19 July 1988: 4.
12 See pp. 170–1.
13 BQB, 26 May 1995: 1; He Zuoxiu 1996a: 8–9; He Zuoxiu 2002: 32–6; QDL: 96, 230.
14 Song Shaoming 1988.

Around the same time so-called 'light *qigong*' and 'electric *qigong*' were revealed to be mere stunts that could be learned by anyone without practising *qigong*.[15] In April 1989 Qinghua University declared in the newspaper *Health* that Yan Xin's famous experiments had nothing to do with the university, and were not conclusive.[16] Doubting Yan Xin's abilities, some professors at Beijing University invited him to an experiment on the treatment of kidney stones. When Yan arrived at the laboratory the professors handed him a kidney stone and asked him to break it with his *qi*. But Yan claimed he broke kidney stones only when they were in a patient's body.[17] This seemed to confirm the claim of a leading *qigong* researcher, Zhang Honglin, who wrote in several articles in 1989 that so-called external *qi* did not exist, and that according to his experiments, external *qi* didn't work in the absence of psychological suggestion.[18]

NEW QIGONG REGULATIONS

These *qigong* controversies came to the attention of the state health authorities in a climate of stricter government control over society following the 1989 Tiananmen student movement. In the autumn of 1989 the Ministry of Civil Affairs ordered denominations to re-register with the authorities,[19] and the Tax Bureau started to levy taxes on *qigong* activities. These two measures caused the closing of several *qigong* groups.

On 19 October 1989 the Ministry of Health issued new 'Regulations to reinforce the administration of *qigong* therapy', which stipulated that *qigong* masters who engaged in therapy were required to have medical qualifications and to obtain a '*qigong* therapy licence', and that organisations that offered *qigong* therapy would have to obtain the authorisation of local health authorities. This policy marked the first attempt by a state organ to regulate *qigong* directly.

According to a spokesperson of the State Administration of Chinese Medicine, the policy meant that 'from now on, titles commonly used by medical practitioners and others, such as "*qigong*

15 ZTB, 19 March 1989: 1, 8; JKB, 30 April 1989: 1.
16 JKB, 13 April 1989: 1.
17 GR, 26 July 1994: 1.
18 JKB, 1 July 1989: 1; Zhang Honglin 1989a.
19 Ji Yi 1990a: 104.

master", "*qigong* grandmaster", "great *qigong* master", "international *qigong* master" and so on, are invalid and are not recognised by the State Administration'.[20] The new policy was estimated to threaten the status and jobs of at least half the *qigong* masters on the market.[21] But could it be applied? The health ministry's intervention was an attempt to establish its authority over a movement it had helped to create but had now lost control of. It reflected dissensions within the government and within the *qigong* sector itself over how to deal with the *qigong* wave and the problems it created.

Hu Ximing, the new director of the State Administration of Chinese Medicine and a Deputy Minister of Health, explained the new policy in a press conference in Beijing in October 1989.[22] His speech betrays nostalgia for the 1950s, when *qigong* remained strictly confined within state medical institutions. Hu questioned the existence of external *qi* and advocated a return to *qigong* as a form of self-training. Without mentioning names, he criticised Yan Xin's 'experiments', charismatic lectures and alleged ability to cure illnesses from a distance of thousands of kilometres. In a veiled attack on Zhang Zhenhuan, president and promoter of several state-sponsored *qigong* associations and protector of Yan Xin, he blamed the *qigong* 'research societies' and 'associations' for creating 'chaos' in the *qigong* sector by allowing therapeutic *qigong* activities. Hu's speech signalled the end of the state medical authorities' active support for *qigong*. From then on they would act as sceptical regulators, rather than promoters of *qigong*.

Whereas, under Lü Bingkui's leadership, the State Administration of Chinese Medicine had actively encouraged *qigong*'s development, under Hu Ximing, it would now concentrate on its regulation and control. The enthusiasm of the 1980s had clearly faded, and sceptics now had the upper hand in the medical bureaucracy. Breaking with the attitude of the 1950s and the early 1980s, the institutions of Chinese medicine ceased to be the locomotives of the *qigong* movement. But Zhang Zhenhuan had a different idea: that the State Council create a new administrative body in charge of the planning, organisation and coordination of 'somatic science', which, by Qian Xuesen's definition, included *qigong*, Chinese med-

---

20 Xing Sishao, interview published in QK 3 (1991), translated in Zhu and Penny 1994: 21–5.
21 ZGL: 354; Ji Yi 1990a: 104.
22 This speech is reproduced in ZGL: 347–53.

icine and Extraordinary Powers. Under such a setup, *qigong* would not be subordinated to Chinese medicine, but would have equal status with it. The CQRS submitted a proposal to this effect to the National People's Congress and to the State Council.[23] However, Zhang's plan was never adopted. But Hu Ximing's project also hit obstacles. Shortly after Hu's regulations were promulgated, Zhang Zhenhuan, who had the greatest political influence on the *qigong* sector, gave a cool response to the new policy, expressing his reservations about its implementation:

Now that a government organ has stepped forward to manage *qigong*, that is a good thing, and we will actively support the application [of the new regulations]. But we consider that the successful application of this document will require much work: it is not with simple directives on paper that all problems can be solved. We hope that the administrative authorities ... will make a complete investigation, and will be truly attentive to the masses' opinion, to the research societies, and others, in order to establish a regulatory framework that will be complete, rigorous, and reasonable, and not to cut everything with a single strike of the knife. We propose that a system of professional qualification be established for *qigong* masters who are not authorised to practise medicine, in order to allow those who are particularly accomplished to treat patients after obtaining this qualification. The masses as a whole need [this], we cannot fail to consider [this idea].[24]

The other authorities (in science, education, sports etc.), which were not involved in the policy's elaboration and promulgation, did not cooperate in the application of the new rules. This reflected a problem that would persistently plague Chinese bureaucracies in their attempts to regulate *qigong*: it could not be neatly pigeonholed under a single department's jurisdiction. This allowed *qigong* to continue flourishing within the cracks of the system, and to exploit the notorious lack of cooperation between bureaucracies. Furthermore, the vagueness of the conditions for accrediting masters and denominations, as well as the absence of standard national criteria, made the granting of *qigong* licenses on the basis of personal connections rather than on objective norms inevitable.

---

23 ZGL: 356–7.
24 Quoted in ZGL: 358.

ZHANG XIANGYU'S ARREST AND YAN XIN'S EXILE

The new policy turn caused a cold wind to blow over the *qigong* milieu from 1989 to 1991. Some of the most visible and controversial figures in the *qigong* movement fell by the wayside. Zhang Xiangyu was arrested in May 1990 for quackery and illegal medical practice, after she had held a series of mass healing lectures which, at a cost of 35 yuan per person—a week's wage for the average person—netted her over 1 million yuan. Scores of attendees started speaking 'cosmic language' or having visions of gods. Official reports claim that local residents, fed up with the thousands of followers who overran their neighbourhood for several days, complained to the police; that hospital outpatient wards suddenly received an influx of cases of '*qigong* deviation' among people who, after attending the events, suffered from hallucinations or disruptive behaviour; and that several of her followers died shortly after receiving her treatment. Finally, the Beijing municipal government had Zhang charged with practising medicine without a permit; teaching *qigong* without the authorisation of the health authorities; and organising a large public gathering without police permission. Her arrest and sentencing to seven years' imprisonment, widely reported in the press—which called her a 'witch' and a 'swindler'—had a chilling effect on the *qigong* movement.[25]

At the same time, Yan Xin's career as a grandmaster in China was coming to an end. His two last power-inducing lectures, held in the Shanghai Stadium before a combined audience of 23,000, were failures. This time the listeners weren't swayed by his charisma: only a small number felt Yan's *qi*. Worse, a man died during the lecture. Sick with chronic heart disease, he fell into spontaneous movements, jumping and gesticulating, then collapsed, foam dripping from his mouth. The people around him, thinking he was simply in trance, saw nothing unusual—until later it was discovered that he had stopped breathing.[26]

On June 20 Yan Xin left China for the United States, ostensibly to present the results of his research to an international conference on *qigong* and Chinese medicine at Berkeley.[27] The delegation

---

25 BR, 14 April 1990: 2; Zhang Minghui and Zhang Yang, 'Zhang Xiangyu: The Circumstances Surrounding Her Arrest' in Zhu and Penny 1994: 27–32, originally published in BWB, 13 January 1991; ZGL: 330.

26 ZGL: 222–3.

27 IYXQA 1995.

was organised by Zhang Zhenhuan: but, while the other delegates were given business passports valid for only one trip, Yan Xin was provided with a personal passport valid for five years and renewable. The plan was for Yan Xin to stay in the United States, thereby avoiding the fate of Zhang Xiangyu. In Yan's words, 'old Zhang [Zhenhuan] meant by [the personal passport] that I should prepare myself for a long stay, that I shouldn't be in a hurry to come back.'[28] Zhang Zhenhuan was reported to have told Yan Xin that this move abroad was a necessary precaution, some people having accused *qigong* of contributing to the 1989 student movement.[29] He also encouraged Yan Xin to promote *qigong* in the West, where he could continue his research using advanced Western methods, and increase the material resources of the *qigong* movement. Thus Yan Xin, whose uncontrolled charisma was becoming a liability for the *qigong* movement in China, was discreetly removed from the stage.

For a year or so no large-scale power-inducing lectures were held. Denominations were required to register for practice points in parks, where the large *qigong* practice groups dwindled to scattered pockets of individuals.

CONTINUED ACTIVITY

The new regulations and the arrest of Zhang Xiangyu emboldened the critics of the *qigong* movement, who became more outspoken and started to organise themselves into a network to campaign against the 'pseudo-*qigong*' (*wei qigong*) linked to Extraordinary Powers, which had strayed from the classical self-discipline of body, breath and mind of Liu Guizhen's original *qigong*.[30] In July 1990,

28   QDL: 87–8.
29   If such accusations were in fact made, they had little effect. State intervention in the *qigong* milieu after 1989 was the result of a general tightening after the Tiananmen events, as well as a reaction to the 'chaos' in the *qigong* circles. So far I have found no evidence that the *qigong* movement played a role in the 1989 student movement, or that it was accused of playing such a role afterwards. The situation changed after 2000, when some of the most noted *qigong* masters exiled in the United States joined forces with the political dissident movement: Zhang Hongbao participated in a short-lived 'shadow government' (<http://www.tangben.com/message/message.cfm?ID=23788> [accessed 2 January 2005]), while the *Epoch Times* overseas Chinese newspaper, founded and staffed by Falungong practitioners, ran a series of anti-CCP editorials in November 2004 (Epoch Group 2005).
30   See chapter 1.

feeling attacked, the Leaders' Working Group on Somatic Science wrote to the central government, seeking its support. In response, the CCP Central Committee and the State Council decided that Extraordinary Powers research could continue. As in 1982, the highest levels of the state intervened to impose a truce between the promoters and adversaries of *qigong*. Li Tieying, a former Minister of Electronic Industry who had been a strong supporter of the crackdown on the 1989 student movement, was put in charge of the *qigong* dossier. At a meeting of the Leaders' Working Group on 12 December 1990 he announced the official policy of the Five Principles for Work in Somatic Sciences—principles which essentially repeated the line decided in 1982, after Qian Xuesen's intervention:[31]

1. No criticism;

2. No promotion;

3. No polemics;

4. Organise solid scientific research;

5. Forbid any use of the terms '*qigong*' and 'Extraordinary Powers' in all cases where they merely mask feudal superstition and quackery.[32]

Sports minister Wu Shaozu, a strong supporter of the *qigong* movement and Extraordinary Powers research,[33] was appointed President of the Leaders' Working Group, which was expanded to six members. The Group's mandate was defined as leading the management and research on *qigong* and Extraordinary Powers, by facilitating communication and coordination between the various ministries involved with *qigong*. The Group was not, as Zhang Zhenhuan would have hoped, an administrative authority. Its offices were established within the Martial Arts Research Institute of the State Sports Commission.[34]

As in 1982, the policy had the concrete effect once again of silencing *qigong*'s critics, while the *qigong* milieu could continue to expand. For example, journalist Sima Nan—whose anti-*qigong* polemics will be described below—had in 1990 produced a video

---

31 See pp. 71–2.
32 QDL: 202.
33 See pp. 71–2.
34 JG.

which exposed the Extraordinary Powers of *qigong* masters as conjuring tricks. No publisher dared to release the video until 1995, and no television network was willing to air it. The embarrassing failure of Extraordinary Powers masters to convince the CSICOP delegation in 1988, and of Zhang Baosheng to demonstrate his powers to He Zuoxiu and the Leaders' Working Group representatives, were similarly not reported until 1995. On the other hand, hagiographic books extolling the miraculous powers of *qigong* masters such as Yan Xin, Zhang Hongbao and Li Hongzhi were published freely during this period and often became bestsellers.[35] The political influence of the *qigong* networks was demonstrated once again. If the medical institutions had now taken their distance from the *qigong* sector, the three other chief political proponents of *qigong*: Qian Xuesen, Zhang Zhenhuan and Wu Shaozu, all of whom had links with COSTIND, did not temper their pro-*qigong* enthusiasm.

Zhang Zhenhuan and his networks remained active through the CQRS, the Ministry of Education and somatic science circles. In 1990, together with Qian Xuesen and Zhu Runlong, editor-in-chief of *Ziran* magazine, he called the first meeting of the board of directors of the China Somatic Science Society, which decided to launch a new magazine titled *Chinese Somatic Science* (*Zhongguo renti kexue*). In July 1991 the society also organised a national conference on developing human Extraordinary Powers potential.[36] Within the educational system, Zhang was also involved in organising a conference on the applications of *qigong* in primary and secondary education, held on 22–25 August 1991, to discuss a report of the National Education Commission proposing to expand the use of *qigong* in schools. The report cited the benefits of such a plan: increasing pupils' intelligence and academic performance, preventing and curing myopia, and improving students' health.[37]

Qigong sports networks, with Wu Shaozu at their core, played a growing role in the *qigong* sector, where they dominated international exchanges through the International Qigong Science Federation. A Russian edition of their magazine, *Qigong and Sports*, was

---

[35] See for example the following mass-circulation *qigong* books published between 1989 and 1995: Ji Yi 1990a, 1990b, 1991, 1993; Ke Yunlu 1989, 1993, 1994, 1995a, 1995b; Chen Linfeng 1993; Li Hongzhi 1993, 1994, 1995a, 1995b; Li Lun 1989.

[36] QK 102: 39.

[37] QG 13(5): 238; QK 102: 39.

launched at the end of 1991, with a circulation of 80,000.[38] In 1992 the Wuhan Sports Academy enrolled its first undergraduate class specialised in *qigong*.[39] In 1993 Wu Shaozu presided over the first World Taiji Cultivation Congress, which featured *qigong*, *taijiquan* and massage.[40] In November of the same year, at the third National Conference on Sports Qigong held in Shanghai, a deputy director of the National Sports Commission announced that *qigong* would be given an important place in the new National Plan of Physical Fitness for All Citizens. The *qigong* sector greeted this news with enthusiasm, hoping to use the plan for fresh legitimacy. As the general social atmosphere started to relax following Deng Xiaoping's south China tour in early 1992, giving a fresh start to China's reform policy, it seemed that the post-Tiananmen 'cold spell' was over, and that the winds were once again blowing in *qigong*'s favour.

The regulations on *qigong* now created opportunities for the state-sponsored *qigong* associations, which attempted to profit from the requirement that *qigong* masters register with them. Before the Falungong crackdown in 1999, attempts to regulate *qigong* by the state-sponsored associations were in good part motivated by a desire to obtain a share of the booming profits to be gained from *qigong*'s commercialisation. The semi-official associations were clearly into the *qigong* business and were not interested in suppressing *qigong*; rather, they wanted to control the movement and partake of its financial benefits. Recognition and membership in a national semi-official association implied legality and legitimacy, but it also carried the cost of disbursing a significant proportion of revenues to the semi-official association. In actual practice, the main criterion for acceptance into a semi-official association was often the amount of income the master was able to generate in his activities and turn over to the association.

THE DEATH OF ZHANG ZHENHUAN

But the *qigong* movement's prospects darkened again with the death of Zhang Zhenhuan on 23 March 1994. *Qigong* masters, including Yan Xin, converged on Beijing from China and abroad to attend his funeral. Nicknamed the 'father of *qigong*' and the 'guardian spirit

---

38 TY 36: 47; QDL: 6.
39 TY 36: 16.
40 QDL: 192.

of *qigong*', Zhang had played a pivotal role in the political defence of *qigong*. Anxiety now spread in the *qigong* sector: who would now protect *qigong* against its enemies? Only days before passing away Zhang had written letters to the principal figures of the *qigong* circle, warning that the opposition was preparing to go on the offensive. And he was reported to have told his old friend Qian Xuesen that he had struggled for many causes in his life, including the fight for the hydrogen bomb in the 1960s, and for the super-computer in the 1970s. 'Each time, I conquered the fortress. In my aging days I will have struggled for somatic science, but this time, it seems that victory has not been attained.'[41]

A few months after the general's death, the opposing camp went on the offensive. On 11 October 1994 the International Qigong Science Federation was dissolved by order of the Ministry of Civil Affairs, on the grounds that it had not registered with the ministry, was thus illegal, and had a 'negative influence on society'.[42] The federation's offices in Xi'an were sealed by the police, who also searched the home of the organisation's Secretary-General, Guo Zhouli. News of this action, which was reported on national radio, had the effect of a bomb on the *qigong* sector. That day was called the 'Xi'an incident' of the *qigong* movement.[43] Indeed, the International Qigong Science Federation, whose Chairman was none other than Sports Minister Wu Shaozu, was a central node in the *qigong* political network. Soon afterwards the State Council issued a circular on 'scientific popularisation work' that signalled the beginning of a campaign against 'pseudo-science' (*wei kexue*) and a green light for the public criticism of 'pseudo-*qigong*'.[44]

POLEMICS IN 1995

Throughout 1995 journalist and former *qigong* master Sima Nan waged a heated polemic against 'pseudo-*qigong*' in a series of television and radio interviews and newspaper articles. Sima Nan claimed

[41]   Quoted in QDL: 1, 2.

[42]   RR, 13 October 1994: 2.

[43]   QDL: 3, 7. In Chinese history the expression 'Xi'an incident' (*Xi'an shijian*) refers to the kidnapping in Xi'an of the Chinese President, General Chiang Kai-shek, by general Zhang Xueliang in December 1936, forcing him to negotiate a truce with the CCP.

[44]   BQB, 14 April 1995: 1; He Zuoxiu 2002: 12.

to have been a *qigong* disciple and to have learned all the conjuring tricks of the *qigong* masters. On his televised appearances he would first perform the tricks, then reveal the sleight-of-hand. Anti-*qigong* articles appeared in the press all through 1995. The results of the CSICOP delegation and of Zhang Baosheng's failed demonstration were finally reported.[45] The Chairman of the China Academy of Sciences and several other influential Chinese scientists spoke or wrote against *qigong*, calling it pseudo-science, superstition, quackery and a dangerous cult similar to the Aum Shinrikyo sect of Japan. This polemic turned the scientific community against *qigong* and Extraordinary Powers, and shattered *qigong's* ideological and political legitimacy. In a controversial book entitled *The Inside Story on Miraculous Qigong*,[46] Sima Nan accused a number of masters (without naming them, but obviously referring to Zhang Hongbao of Zhonggong, among others) of harbouring political ambitions, and questioned their recruitment of Party leaders as disciples and their holding workshops at the Party Central School and other influential units.[47] In an eerily prophetic passage he warned:

If grandmasters start playing politics, it will be like a naughty boy playing with fire: either they will burn themselves, or they will do a great wrong to the people. For a stable society governed by the rule of law, these gangster-style grandmasters, who try to penetrate people's hearts by means of religious consciousness, are great political enemies ... In a time when reforms are deepening and society undergoes deep changes, people's interests and relationships are being modified, and some members of society are feeling cast aside and disoriented, an uprising of this type of dissident force (an extremely rapid and massive uprising) would certainly not be auspicious. As soon as social chaos prevails, the influence of these people should not be underestimated, because they will have a social base. The lessons of history are already too numerous![48]

Even Qian Xuesen's support for *qigong* was for the first time publicly criticised in the press, by his long-time colleague He Zuoxiu: 'to call experiments that are wholly contrary to scientific methods a "new scientific discovery", "a sign of an impending scientific revolution", "a high-level experiment" is not science, it's a joke!'[49]

45   BQB, 26 May 1995: 1; NF, 30 June 1995: 1.
46   Sima Nan 1995.
47   Sima Nan 1995: 660, quoted in QDL: 23.
48   Sima Nan 1995: 356, quoted in QDL: 22.
49   GR, 26 July 1994: 1.

Four overseas Chinese Nobel Prize winners publicly declared their support for He Zuoxiu's attacks on pseudo-science.[50] A flood of anti-*qigong* articles appeared in several major newspapers, indicating the existence of an organised campaign,[51] spearheaded by the China Society for Natural Dialectics, and counting Yu Guangyuan, Sima Nan, He Zuoxiu and Guo Zhengyi as its key spokesmen. In September 1995 this network of opponents issued a 'Proposal' aimed at all the powerful sectors of society which had aided the spread of *qigong*: scientists were called on to respect scientific principles; government officials were reminded to stick to atheism and materialism, and to remove any obstacles to the struggle against pseudo-science; the media were entreated to stop propagating superstition; and the judiciary was told to apply the law in dissolving any superstitious activities and organisations.[52]

Wu Shaozu nonetheless continued to promote *qigong*. On 16 August 1995 he responded to the controversy in an interview with the *China Youth Daily*, in which he declared that the wrong tendencies in *qigong* had to be opposed, but that research had to be conducted on what was true; *qigong* should not be radically rejected in its entirety.[53] A few weeks later, during a meeting of the China Sports Research Society, he maintained that the popular practice of *qigong* was a good thing, that research on *qigong* and Extraordinary Powers were highly significant, and that somatic sciences couldn't be accused of 'pseudo-science' on the basis of a few failed experiments.[54]

Wu then appealed to the central leadership to put an end to the anti-*qigong* polemic. In response to his efforts, the State Council issued a circular to the country's central press organs, reaffirming the 'five principles for work in somatic sciences', promulgated in 1990, which banned criticism of somatic science in the media. The

50 GR, 21 August 1995: 1.
51 See for example GR, 26 July 1995: 1; GR, 3 August 1995: 1; GR, 9 August 1995: 1; GR, 11 August 1995: 1; GR, 16 August 1995: 1, 5; GR, 18 August 1995: 1; GR, 23 August 1995: 1, 5; GR, 30 August 1995: 5; GR, 3 August 1995: 1; GR, 9 August 1995: 1, 5; GR, 21 August 1995: 1; GR, 16 August 1995: 5; GR, 20 August 1995: 1; GR, 6 September 1995: 5; GR, 13 September 1995: 5; GR, 20 September 1995: 5; GR, 22 September 1995: 1; GR, 22 September 1995: 3. Many of these articles are reproduced in He Zuoxiu 1996b.
52 Gong Yuzhi 2002: 2.
53 ZQB, 16 August 1995.
54 QDL: 188.

circular stated that experience had shown that this policy was a
good one.[55] Thanks to this new intervention by the State Council,
the anti-*qigong* camp was once again silenced, much to the dis-
may of the polemists, who petitioned to the higher authorities to
complain that the policy was an obstacle to the struggle against
pseudo-science.[56]

In the autumn of 1995 *qigong* advocates once again took the
offensive. The Leaders'Working Group on Somatic Science wrote
to the State Council, asserting that Extraordinary Powers were true,
and attacking He Zuoxiu and Sima Nan for violating the 'Triple
No' directive.[57] Chen Xin, the new President of the China Somatic Science Society, published an open letter responding to the
criticisms which had been levelled against *qigong*. He stressed that
the exceptional powers of Zhang Baosheng had been proven to
renowned scientists under rigorous experimental conditions; that
somatic science research had always benefited from the Party's support and had always followed the official line of 'no promotion and
no criticism'; that it had always respected the scientific method; and
that the virulence of the criticism had a negative emotional impact
on individuals with Extraordinary Powers, harming their powers
during experiments.[58] *China Somatic Science* magazine published
an 'open letter to Zhang Baosheng' calling on him to stop giving
public performances, on the grounds that Extraordinary Powers
were not a 'show' to be turned on or off at will like a television set,
merely giving fodder to critics.[59]

On 1 September Ke Yunlu published an open letter to the four
Chinese Nobel Prize winners who had attacked Extraordinary
Powers research, in which he invited them to train their own children in *qigong* methods, so as to develop their latent Extraordinary Powers. Two months later Ke launched a campaign to collect
thousands of case histories of illnesses cured by *qigong*. The purpose
was to legitimise *qigong* and somatic science by creating a massive
database of healing cases. Thirty-five denominations participated
in the campaign, in which all people who had recovered their
health thanks to *qigong* were asked to support the *qigong* cause by

55   QDL: 202.
56   TJH: III.
57   He Zuoxiu 2002: 36.
58   SMK 21: 7.
59   Reproduced in He Zuoxiu 2002: 61–4.

sending their case histories and medical dossiers to the campaign headquarters.[60]

The autumn of 1995 was also marked by the return of Yan Xin to China for a few months, helping to boost the morale of the *qigong* milieu. On 20 October he briefly appeared at opening ceremonies of the World Taiji Cultivation Congress. Although he didn't speak, his mere presence caused a sensation: Yan Xin was back! The next day, he was received by Zhang Yaoting, the office director of the Leaders' Working Group on Somatic Sciences. This meeting, which was also attended by Guo Zhouli of the reconstituted International Qigong Science Federation, signified an official recognition for Yan Xin and his activities in North America. But Zhang Yaoting warned him not to act like a god, not to make exaggerated statements, and to struggle for *qigong*'s rightful place in the history of science.[61]

During his stay in Beijing Yan remained in hiding and changed accommodation several times; despite such precautions, he was followed everywhere by fans and curious onlookers.[62] A week later he was invited to Xi'an to meet with the editorial staff of the *International Qigong News*, on the occasion of the celebration of its one hundredth issue. Although his trip had been kept confidential, news of his arrival spread, and hundreds of people massed around the site of the meeting. In order to satisfy so many fans, a power-inducing lecture was improvised on the spot. A few months later, on his return to his native village, a power-inducing lecture was held in the city of Mianyang (Sichuan), for an audience of several thousand people.[63]

Millions continued to practise *qigong*, but the *qigong* world was now definitely consigned to the margins of the mainstream culture it had so hopefully tried to enter and transform a few years earlier. Practitioners continued to gather in the parks every morning, a few new schools were founded, the International Qigong Science Federation sent a large delegation to the fourth World Qigong Congress, held in April 1995 in Vancouver, and *qigong* continued to spread in the West. But in China, the *qigong* movement had clearly lost its steam. After 1995 the number of new books published on *qigong* diminished rapidly, and many *qigong* organisations shrank or folded.

60 QDL: 68.
61 Quoted in QDL: 105–6.
62 QDL: 100.
63 QDL: 101.

DEBATES WITHIN THE QIGONG SECTOR

After Zhang Zhenhuan's death, and under the pressure of the anti-*qigong* campaign, the *qigong* sector entered a phase of soul-searching. Debate on the causes of the crisis and the ways to overcome it dominated the agendas of the national and regional state-sponsored *qigong* associations throughout 1995. A consensus emerged that too many *qigong* masters had a low level of education and thus of 'moral quality' (*suzhi*), leading them excessively to seek fame and fortune.[64] There was also too much swindling and quackery going on in the name of *qigong*, with people using bogus *qigong* healing, training and *qi*-filled objects as sources of quick profits.[65] The issue of greedy, unethical swindlers making money with 'fake' *qigong* reflected a general social preoccupation in 1990s China as, in the wake of economic liberalisation and the growth of free enterprise, the market in general was flooded with poor-quality goods and fake imitations pushed by unscrupulous entrepreneurs out to make a killing.

The need to impose some form of 'orthodoxy' in the *qigong* sector was also stressed by several association leaders and *qigong* masters, who called for an end to the deification of masters and the tendency to mix *qigong* and religion. Pang Heming, founder of Zhinenggong, for instance, suggested separating denominations based strictly on body cultivation from those which claimed an affiliation to Buddhism or Taoism, which should be managed by the religious affairs authorities.[66] Xu Yixing, a leader of the Beijing Qigong Research Society, attacked the tendency of some masters to proclaim themselves living Buddhas or descendants of Bodhisattvas, and stressed that *qigong* groups could not be transformed into religious organisations.[67] Related to the lack of orthodoxy in the *qigong* milieu was the absence of a single authority in charge of *qigong*. There were several national state-sponsored *qigong* associations, but no cooperation between them: the CQRS, the China Qigong Sports Society, the China Medical Qigong Science Society, the International Qigong Science Federation, the China Somatic Science Research Society etc. Thus for *qigong* groups to expand unchecked in the large gaps between these organisations was relatively easy.[68]

64 DF 53: 2–3; ZG 64: 2–4.
65 DF 53: 2–3.
66 DF 45: 2.
67 DF 51: 3.
68 ZG 64: 2–4; QDL: 272–3.

Following these debates the main state-sponsored *qigong* associations took measures to strengthen their authority and control within the *qigong* sector. In December 1995 a new leadership was named for the CQRS, with Huang Jingbo, a former Governor and Party Secretary of Qinghai province, as the new General Director, and Liu Ji, a Vice-Director of the National Sports Commission, as his deputy. Almost three hundred directors were appointed, including retired officials loyal to the Party, officials from the government ministries and departments of sports, education, science and health, reputable *qigong* masters and leaders of provincial state-sponsored *qigong* associations.[69] At the first meeting of the new board, Liu Ji read a speech by Wu Shaozu, which laid down his directives for the *qigong* sector's development. The directives merely reiterated the government's general policy towards *qigong* since 1979: a relatively 'democratic' attitude that encouraged the flourishing of different denominations as long as they professed their loyalty to the Party and proclaimed the importance of science and of fighting superstition. On 19 and 29 January 1996 Wu Shaozu called a national meeting on somatic science at which he confirmed to the main figures in the *qigong* sector the Party's and the government's support for somatic sciences. The effect of *qigong* on the health of the masses was stressed: the number of regular *qigong* practitioners was estimated at 60 million, more than any other sport. Despite the offensive of the anti-*qigong* polemic, then, the 'sports' networks of *qigong*, centred on Wu Shaozu, kept their course.

THE MEDICAL AUTHORITIES' POSITION

However, the medical authorities did not take such a lenient approach. Tension continued between the encouragement of the sports authorities and the tightened control advocated by medical institutions. In December 1995 Zhu Guoben, Deputy Director of the State Administration of Chinese Medicine, noted that *qigong* did not enjoy the recognition of Chinese medicine circles, and was developing slowly within their institutions, compared to the flourishing of *qigong* among the masses. Chinese doctors, he said, were ashamed to learn *qigong*. He compared *qigong* to acupuncture, which, after having been abolished as a recognised discipline by

69 DF 55: 34.

the Qing dynasty court in 1822, had been fully resurrected and returned to the mainstream since the 1950s. '*Qigong* fever', on the other hand, was essentially a popular phenomenon, still marginal in medical institutions. *Qigong*'s situation was the same as that of Chinese medicine in the 1930s and 1940s, when it had been looked down on by Western medicine in China. 'People worry: if we open this specialty [*qigong*], won't hospitals of Chinese medicine become places for monsters and demons?'[70] Such attitudes reproduced the tendency of the Chinese tradition of literati medicine, which was contemptuous of popular thaumaturgic healing.[71] Some of the leading figures in medical *qigong* denied the existence of external *qi*, claiming it had nothing to do with the internal *qi* of Chinese medicine. Chinese medicine circles, eager to gain respectability vis-à-vis Western medicine, did not want to be associated with the charlatans and superstitions of the external *qi* healers.

The State Administration of Chinese Medicine condemned the interference of other government departments that authorised *qigong* therapeutic activities. It left the question of external *qi* open for research, but did not encourage its use in therapy. And it insisted that *qigong* be confined to the framework of 'therapy, prevention and hygiene' of Chinese medicine.[72] The magazine *China Qigong*, which was run under the auspices of the Health Department, changed its editor and announced a new editorial policy, promising to 'return to the purity of [*qigong*'s] roots, clear out chaos and return to order', and to follow the guidance of the health authorities, which forbade the deification of masters and the propagation of religious content under the label of *qigong*.[73] Modern *qigong*, which owed its birth and its initial growth to China's medical institutions, had since the 1980s developed almost entirely outside of them.

THE GOVERNMENT DECLARES ITS POLICY

In the middle of 1996, after the Leaders' Working Group on Somatic Science sent a report on the *qigong* situation to the Party Central Committee and the State Council,[74] the government issued

---

70 ZG 70: 6.
71 See Fang Ling 2002.
72 ZG 70: 7.
73 ZG 70: 1.
74 JG.

a new policy on *qigong*, which tried to divide responsibility between the medical and sports bureaucracies. The 'Notice on strengthening the management of social *qigong*' defined two categories of *qigong*: 'Hygienic *qigong*' (*jianshen qigong*) referring to body cultivation for health improvement, was assigned to the sports authorities, while '*qigong* therapy' (*qigong yiliao*), involving the teaching or practice of *qigong* as treatment for illness, came under the medical authorities. The document also outlined the responsibilities of other departments: Civil Affairs, for the registration of *qigong* groups; Industry and Commerce, for commercial matters; Public Security, for keeping order; Central Propaganda, for information control. The harmonisation of the various departments' actions was assigned to the Sports Commission, i.e. Wu Shaozu.

The new policy also required *qigong* groups to obtain permits from the 'relevant authorities' before organising large scale activities, practising in public spaces, disseminating information, engaging in commerce, or conducting any activity touching on politics, public order or international relations. Mass *qigong* activities would have to be positive and scientific, and avoid false exaggerations. The illegal practice of medicine, spreading superstitions, and fraud would be punished. *Qigong* associations were to 'respect the law' and obey the relevant authorities.[75]

The new policy was little more than a vague declaration of principles, but it expressed a hardening of the state's attitude towards *qigong*. Excesses would be tolerated less than before, submission to the Party line more closely monitored. But the most significant element of the 'Notice' was the leading role given to Wu Shaozu. At the beginning of the 1980s two political networks had supported and encouraged *qigong*'s development: Lü Bingkui's Chinese medicine networks, and the military-scientific networks of Qian Xuesen, Zhang Zhenhuan and Wu Shaozu. Since the medical authorities' position shift in 1989, Zhang Zhenhuan's death in 1994 and the advanced age of Qian Xuesen, Wu Shaozu was now the only high-ranking leader to mediate between the government and the *qigong* sector. As a *qigong* enthusiast, Wu Shaozu would continue to try to protect the *qigong* sector in an increasingly unfavourable political environment.

75   ZG 80: 1.

THE RECTIFICATION CAMPAIGN

Under its new director, Huang Jingbo, the CQRS began a 'rectification' campaign in 1996. On 17 April Zhang Xiaoping, a *qigong*
master famous for his claim to be a Bodhisattva with higher powers
than all other masters, was arrested and accused of hiring an author to write miraculous fables about him, of illegally giving public
courses of his *gongfa*,[76] of swindling great sums of money from his
disciples, and of seducing his female followers.[77]

But the rectification campaign was not easy. After five months of
discussions, no consensus had been reached on criteria for the accreditation of masters and denominations.[78] Huang Jingbo wanted
to incorporate all the state-sponsored *qigong* associations into a single structure controlling all denominations. He aimed to central-
ise all denominations' revenues under the CQRS and ordered all
denominations to open a CCP branch committee.[79] These measures were not well received within the *qigong* circles. By May 1996
Huang Jingbo admitted that few provinces had accomplished the
centralisation and consolidation work. Among the obstacles was the
fear experienced by several local state-sponsored *qigong* associations
of lawsuits from 'defrocked' *qigong* masters. For instance, a master
from Zhejiang, Chen Letian, sued the provincial *qigong* society after
its newsletter accused him of 'political errors' and swindling. He
hired a lawyer to seek 300,000 yuan in damages. Chen Letian's
complaint was published by *Qigong and Sports* magazine, indicating
the *qigong* sports network support for Chen against the Zhejiang
qigong society.[80]

Huang Jingbo stressed the simmering conflicts in the *qigong* sector thus:

On the surface, the *qigong* sector is calm. But the comrades must know that
this struggle is not simple, to the point where blood might be spilled. For
instance, these illegal *qigong* masters who have been unmasked, and who
have lost all their money and their reputation, do not easily accept their
fate and may seek revenge.[81]

76   See Zhang Xiaoping 1993.
77   DF 58: 26–7.
78   DF 56: 8.
79   YPFX: 8.
80   TY 58: 40.
81   DF 56: 8.

Huang also attempted to impose political orthodoxy on *qigong*: 'How to unite? Not around Buddha, or around the Dao, but unite under the direction of the proletariat, unite under the direction of the Communist Party, unite under the Party's policy and laws.'[82] At the end of 1996 he summoned three hundred *qigong* masters and researchers from north China to a political study conference, where they discussed the resolutions of the sixth National People's Congress, with the purpose of making the *qigong* sector accept the 'absolute' authority of the Party and government on the *qigong* cause.[83]

In a show of loyalty, Pang Heming, master of Zhinenggong, organised a conference on the theme 'How to use Marxist philosophy to guide the development of *qigong*'. For almost two days 218 Zhinenggong delegates listened to academics and officials lecture them about materialism *vs* idealism, socialism *vs* theology, and science *vs* superstition. This was the first such political meeting to be organised by a *qigong* denomination. It demonstrates the CCP's determination to impose a hard ideological line on the *qigong* sector, but also Pang Heming's desire to be seen as 'loyal' in order to protect his denomination's interests.[84]

Not all denominations were so enthusiastic. Li Hongzhi, who refused to pay Falungong's revenues to the CQRS or to establish a CCP branch within his association, withdrew from the Society.[85] But in any case, the CQRS had become redundant: once the government transferred the responsibility for *qigong* to the state sports and medical authorities, the CQRS lost any real authority. NAST ceased to recognise it,[86] and it was placed under the Sports Commission. For all practical purposes, the CQRS ceased to function after 1996.

That same year the publication of Li Hongzhi's books was banned, and Li moved to the United States. Despite no longer being registered with the CQRS, and thus without any legal status, Falungong continued to grow rapidly, and, after a brief hiatus, Li Hongzhi's books continued to be published by the millions. Clearly, the new policy was not being enforced.

82 DF 56: 7.
83 DF 60: 40.
84 DF 62: 2–4; DF 62: 8; DF 63: 14–17.
85 YPFX: 8.
86 YPFX: 8.

On 25 January 1998 two members of the State Council called a meeting of the Leaders'Working Group on Somatic Science, stressing that serious problems continued to exist in the *qigong* sector since the 1996 policy had been announced: some denominations continued to establish organisations without permission, even setting up commercial businesses as fronts for their denomination.[87] Some denominations continued to mislead the people by holding excessively expensive training workshops, and the publication of *qigong* books and magazines was not being controlled. The meeting decided to discourage the 'social applications' of somatic sciences such as public demonstrations of *qigong* and Extraordinary Powers, *qigong* therapy and *qigong* training workshops.[88] Shortly afterwards the Leaders' Working Group on Somatic Science was disbanded: the *qigong* movement thus lost its institutional lobby at the centre of the government.[89]

One month later the State Sports Commission released the official procedure for the accreditation of masters and denominations. Masters were required to apply in person at the provincial sports commission, where they would fill out a form on the origins, history and content of their method; provide copies of the main books, tapes and materials of the denomination, and 'scientific proof' of its health benefits (in the form of at least thirty medical case histories). The materials would be examined by a panel of representatives from the police, civil administration, education, propaganda and industry and commerce departments, as well as experts in medicine, religion, philosophy, psychology, sports etc. The panel's recommendations would be submitted to the provincial sports commission, which would send its opinion to the State Sports Commission, where a national panel would again examine the applications and make its recommendations to the Martial Arts Research Institute, which would make the final decision. The applicant was required to meet the panel in person—a provision which excluded masters who were in exile (Li Hongzhi) or in hiding (Zhang Hongbao). Panels would vote on their *gongfa* by secret ballot, based on the clarity of the method and its origins, its conformity with 'socialist spiritual civilisation' and its proven effectiveness for the health of the masses. Some of the better known denominations, such as

87 Notably Zhonggong.
88 ZM 54: 1.
89 Liu Huajie 2004: 198.

Zhinenggong, Yan Xin Qigong,[90] Great Goose Qigong, Ma Litang Qigong, and Guo Lin Qigong, as well as some more obscure methods, were accredited through this procedure.[91] But neither Zhonggong nor Falungong, which were the denominations with by far the largest numbers of practitioners, were accredited—threatening to consign the whole regulatory process to irrelevance.

[90] Although Yan Xin had emigrated to the United States, he remained on good terms with the Chinese authorities and returned to China frequently.
[91] ZM 61: 1.

7
CONTROL AND RATIONALISATION

With its tens of millions of practitioners, *qigong* had become, by the end of the 1980s, a movement of significant size and influence. Its potential for mass mobilisation did not fail to be noticed by certain masters and political leaders. But the movement was still poorly organised. The question of control began to be felt. The 1990s were characterised by attempts on the part of both state organs and mass denominations to unify, to regulate, to manage, and to co-opt *qigong* practitioners, masters and groups. While political enthusiasm for *qigong* diminished, and the state attempted to impose increasingly strict regulations on the *qigong* sector, certain mass denominations became more sophisticated and better organised. Expansion and control became the new trend. Certain state agencies, the state-sponsored *qigong* associations and the *qigong* masters' organisations sought to exploit the vast profits that could be generated by *qigong*-related activities and products. A new generation of denominations appeared, with a more structured organisation, a more elaborate ideology, a more varied range of activities and a more systematic expansion strategy than the first generation of methods that had appeared in the 1980s. Some of them, such as Zhonggong and Falungong, had the ambition of becoming more than just one denomination among others, but to dominate the entire *qigong* sector and to have a deep influence on Chinese society. Basing themselves on the *qigong* transmission model in parks and public spaces, they put in place strategies for systematic, large-scale expansion, concentrating powerful human, symbolic and financial resources. Such goals put these two denominations in tension with the state-sponsored *qigong* associations, which were attempting to establish their authority, and with the CCP, which has always been suspicious of large popular organisations. Both the state and these organisations tried to impose more stable forms of authority on the *qigong* movement. But the mass organisations created by Zhang Hongbao and Li Hongzhi, and the invisible political networks they cultivated within the Party and the administration, were practically impossible to control by official and state-sponsored agencies.

CRISIS IN THE QIGONG SECTOR

So far we have looked at how, in response to controversies, the state attempted to dampen the *qigong* craze through increased regulation. Until the Falungong crisis in 1999, however, the state paid little attention to the *organised* dimension of denominations. Indeed, its main concern after 1989 was the 'chaos' or apparent *disorganisation* of the *qigong* movement, which it attempted to solve through new regulations and 'rectification' campaigns. Until the repression of Falungong, government attempts to 'strengthen the administration' of *qigong* mostly aimed at setting norms for the behaviour of *qigong* masters and criteria for the official recognition of denominations. How these norms and criteria were to be enforced, however, was not a simple matter of issuing regulations and using coercion to force the *qigong* sector to follow them. The main state organs in charge of *qigong*—medical and sports authorities—had few resources to enforce new policies, which were not always clear to begin with, and lack of coordination between bureaucracies added to the 'chaos'. Just as political support for *qigong* was built up in the 1980s through complex webs of relationships between masters, officials, scientists, media, bureaucracies and legitimating institutions, applying the 'spirit' of new state policies was done through similar mixtures of formal and informal channels, characterised by constant give-and-take between the *qigong* milieu and state actors. This chapter will begin by analysing the normative mechanisms of official authority in relation to which the *qigong* sector had to define itself.

It will then look at the distribution of authority within denominations. Just as, throughout the 1990s the state attempted to strengthen its 'management' of the *qigong* sector, denominations also tried to develop more efficient operational systems for their networks of, in some cases, millions of practitioners spanning dozens of provinces and even extending internationally. A rationalising trend became apparent in several denominations, as procedures were put in place to maximise efficiency by developing (1) body technologies that could produce *qi*, health and Extraordinary Powers as rapidly as possible among practitioners; (2) commodified training packages and healing products that could maximise profitability; (3) promotion and transmission systems that could reach the largest number of people in the shortest period of time; and (4) procedures of internal management and control that aimed to retain the loyalty of practitioners and prevent them from switching to other *gongfa*, while keeping them from siphoning off profits and charismatic influence. Various denominations attempted different strategies of rationalisation, with varying degrees of success. This chapter will present the standard model of transmission, followed by the examples of two denominations, Zangmigong and Zhonggong. The former illustrates how a denomination interacted with the state to protect its interests, while the latter represents an attempt to turn a denomination into a large commercial corporation.

MECHANISMS OF STATE NORMATIVE CONTROL

Formal speeches at the meetings of state-sponsored *qigong* associations, as well as editorials in the *qigong* magazines, invariably stressed that the Party and the government could be thanked for the historically unprecedented development of *qigong* during the 1980s:

Qigong has a long history of several millennia on the great soil of China. Born in primitive society, it went through slave society, feudal society, semi-colonial and semi-feudal society, and socialist society. It has an immense dynamism that has allowed it to pass through each historical phase without weakening. But in Chinese history ... *qigong* has been officially and openly approved, supported, directed and managed by only one party and one government: The Chinese Communist Party and the Chinese People's Government.[1]

The story of *qigong* since the founding of the communist regime shows that there is truth to such a judgement. We have already seen the role of certain CCP and government leaders, first in the 'invention' of modern *qigong*, and then at each stage of the movement's development. Here, we take a brief look at the normative structures within which *qigong* groups interacted with state and Party power.

In People's China, theoretically, ideological power is held by the CCP, while material power is in the hands of the People's govern-

[1] Che Guocheng and Ke Yuwen 1997: 21.

ment. In practice, boundaries between the Party and the state are difficult to draw. The Party's ideological control applied, in principle, to the *qigong* sector just as it did to all other sectors of Chinese society. The Party line towards *qigong* can be summarised by the following points:

1. Submission to the CCP and recognition of its leading and irreplaceable role in the development of China and of *qigong*—in other terms, no organisation was to attempt to replace the CCP, to compete with it, or to intervene in the country's political affairs. This principle was fundamental: the history of *qigong* since 1949 shows that if the Party was remarkably tolerant towards the non-respect of other aspects of its policy towards *qigong*, actions interpreted as political, such as Falungong's demonstrations, were ruthlessly suppressed.

2. Acceptance and application of Marxist philosophy, dialectical materialism and historical materialism as a guiding ideology—ontological idealism, theism and religious doctrines were to be struggled against. An editorial in the magazine *Oriental Science Qigong* thus insisted:

   The world is material, matter is in motion, matter and spirit can transform into each other. This is the fundamental principle of Marxism-Leninism, and it is also the only correct method for the knowledge and improvement of the world by men. This dialectical materialist perspective is also the only correct guiding ideology of *qigong*. ... In *qigong* practice all schools seek after spirit, mind and consciousness: this can lead some people to a false conception of *qigong* as idealist or immaterial, and contrary to Marxist-Leninist dialectical materialism. ... In fact, this is a prejudice and an error about *qigong*. Let us stress that the spirit, mind and consciousness which *qigong* practice pursues are essentially different from the pure empty mind of idealism. [The effects of *qigong* are produced by] a particular reaction in the human brain of objectively existing matter which, through a particular type of material movement, acts on matter.[2]

3. Protect and propagate science; 'scientise' (*kexuehua*) *qigong*—reject and struggle against 'feudal superstitions'.

4. Contribute to the 'construction of material civilisation': improve the population's health through the mass practice of hygienic and therapeutic *qigong*; contribute to economic development

2 DF 64: 2.

by using *qigong* to increase production or by establishing *qigong* commercial enterprises.

5. Contribute to the 'construction of spiritual civilisation': promote good moral behaviour through *qigong* practice; develop the population's intelligence through *qigong* practice; protect and renew the 'gems of Chinese civilisation'.

6. Unite the different components of society and of the *qigong* sector under the Party banner; promote the free flourishing of *qigong* schools and denominations and avoid sectarianism within the *qigong* sector—the Party would not support one denomination over another, nor would it allow one denomination to attempt to exclude or to harm another.[3]

The creation and promotion of modern *qigong* by Party leaders and state organs played an important role in the implementation of this policy. Indeed *qigong*, as a new category, transcended the myriad of divided and dispersed groups and sectarian traditions of the pre-communist period, most of which were more or less embedded in some form of religious practice. From this amorphous milieu the Party line sought to create a new community—a social 'sector' (*jie*) that would be united, conscious of itself and tributary to its leadership.

The Party's strategy was to neutralise the potential political threat posed by the largest mass denominations; to separate the *qigong* sector from religious circles; to ensure the *qigong* sector's submission to scientism and materialism; to promote public forms of practice rather than secret transmission along traditional lines; and to orient *qigong*'s development towards national policy goals in the fields of health, sports, education, science and defence.

Official institutions were the external instruments through which the CCP imposed its ideological control on the *qigong* milieu. Indeed registering denominations as legal associations, holding public events, obtaining media coverage, using public spaces for collective practice almost always required the approval of the 'relevant authorities' (*youguan bumen*).

What were the 'relevant authorities'? The answer to this was often unclear. Until the second half of the 1990s the NAST, the State Sports Commission, the Ministry of Health and its State Ad-

---

3   DF 53: 12–15; DF 53: 9–11; DF 51: 3; DF 56: 2–9.

ministration of Chinese Medicine, as well as parts of COSTIND, each played an active role in the *qigong* sector by directly or indirectly sponsoring their own official *qigong* associations. *Qigong* also touched on the jurisdictions of other ministries and state agencies which, at various times, intervened in its development: the Central Propaganda Bureau, the State Education Commission, the Ministry of Civil Affairs, the Ministry of Public Security, and the State Administration for Industry and Commerce. The government tried to coordinate the *qigong* policies and actions of the different state organs starting in 1986, when it created the interministerial Leaders' Working Group on Somatic Science.[4]

Coordination between the local, provincial and national levels was even more complex than between the different national ministries. As a result, by the early 1990s the overall structure of the *qigong* sector could be compared to a Christmas tree, various associations and organisations hanging like so many balls from different branches of the state tree, various networks linking up different branches like streamers, winding their way around the tree without being formally attached to each other through a single administration in charge of *qigong*. Table 5, which compiles data gleaned from seventy-six organisations listed in Wu Hao's *qigong* directory, shows the diversity of institutional affiliations of *qigong* associations.[5]

Denominations had two options vis-à-vis the state: the first was to avoid official control completely by not seeking the approval of 'relevant authorities' for their activities. In such a case the group would be, if not illegal, at least outside the law. This approach was followed by most of the smaller groups, whose members were unaware of regulations and, like most Chinese, avoided contact with the bureaucracy in order to avoid complications. Generally if the group members didn't carry out large-scale public activities, caused no trouble, and didn't attract the attention of the authorities, they could act without much interference. Being outside state control, nothing could force them to conform to the Party ideology: such small, unofficial groups were free in terms of belief and ideology.

The other option was to seek the approval of the 'relevant authorities'. The larger the organisation, the more it would be compelled to follow this path, not only to stay out of trouble, but also in order

4   See p. 78
5   WH.

Table 5   OFFICIAL AFFILIATIONS OF QIGONG
ASSOCIATIONS

Sponsoring institution or association	*Number*
State-sponsored *qigong* association	39
NAST or provincial/municipal science and technology associations (*kexie*)	36
Sports commission (*tiwei*)	14
Medical institution or organisation	9
Civil affairs administration (*minzhengju*)	4
Education commission (*jiaowei*)	3
Academic association	2
Martial arts association	2
Taoist association (*daojiao xiehui*)	1
Municipal park	1
Youth league (*qingnian lianhehui*)	1
Taijiquan association	1

to establish its credibility with the public, which was suspicious of the quacks and swindlers who claimed to be *qigong* masters.

At the local level, however, it was often hard to know who the 'relevant authorities' were; furthermore, directly approaching a bureaucracy is rarely a fruitful undertaking in China. A *qigong* master seeking legitimation had to cultivate connections with local leaders, often by using his healing abilities to treat sick officials, or by sharing profits with them. Through the contacts made in such a manner, he could then obtain a certificate issued by some authority—the science and technology committee of the municipal government, for example, or a state-sponsored *qigong* association, or a factory trade union. Indeed some units were easier to approach than others. The crucial point was that the approving unit be affiliated to a higher-level administration, the chain of legitimation thus rising upwards from one unit to another, up to the central authorities in Beijing. In theory the state-sponsored *qigong* associations, which were themselves affiliated to state organs, were the 'relevant authority' with which any *qigong* organisation had to register. But in practice the state-sponsored associations had great difficulties in imposing their authority: they could easily be circumvented.

The role of officials in the propagation of *qigong* is illustrated by the case of Shijiazhuang, where a journalist from the newspaper *Health* described how, in the headquarters of the municipal Party Committee, he was able to locate three persons engaged in healing others through *qigong*, including one of the city's highest officials, who acted as a part-time *qigong* master in the evenings. Among the city's six deputy mayors, five practised *qigong*, as well as over one third of the forty-two members of the municipal Party committee. With such a large number of *qigong* supporters among the municipal leadership, it was no surprise that the local government encouraged the propagation of *qigong*.[6]

The personal help of officials, obtained through the cultivation of Connections, was key in obtaining official approval. The Connections system, although it subverted official lines of authority, did not prevent ideological conformity, defensive and superficial as it may have been. Indeed by encouraging and legitimising the activities of a denomination, the official exposed himself to attacks from his rivals if the *qigong* group got into trouble. The more a denomination appeared to conform to ideological orthodoxy in its public discourse and activities, the less risk it posed to a potential official supporter. Denominations that cultivated an image of ideological orthodoxy would find it easier to cultivate the public support of officials than denominations with a heterodox image. Conformity to Party ideology was thus achieved in a subtle and indirect manner, through the official who supported the activities of a denomination. In places far from the power centre of Beijing, ideological orthodoxy was less crucial as a determining factor in the legitimation of denominations. Thus the state-sponsored *qigong* associations based in the capital stayed closer to the 'hard' Party line than the associations based in provincial cities.

Conforming to the Party line was thus 'voluntary', i.e. to impose it by force was usually not necessary, contrary to the way one might believe based on a stereotyped image of a communist regime. Rather, conformity was accomplished through personal reciprocal ties between masters and officials. But in the case of serious mischief, other government organs could intervene to put an end to the abuses. In this case, if the influence of the master's political protector was not strong enough, or if the protector opportunisti-

6 Report published in *Health* on 5 June 1988, quoted in Wang Jisheng 1989: 316–17.

cally decided to let go of the master, the latter or his network risked becoming the target of punitive measures.

The example of master Chen Linfeng is a case in point.[7] Through his connections in the Ministry of Aerospace Industry, Chen was invited to use his Extraordinary Powers to forecast the result of the launching of the Aoxing B1 rocket.[8] Chen claimed he telepathically 'saw' errors in the rocket's launching programme, which, if they had not been detected, would have caused an accident with damages of one billion yuan. After the programme was corrected and the rocket successfully launched, the Ministry of Aeronautical Industry reportedly paid Chen Linfeng a reward of 200,000 yuan (approximately US$ 30,000).

The *Workers' Daily* revealed the machinations behind the reward in a front page story on 23 September 1995: after the satellite launch a Hong Kong business and the World Association of Chinese People, also based in Hong Kong, donated 400,000 yuan to the Rocket Research Institute, to congratulate the scientists involved in the successful launch. But a condition was attached to the donation: half of the amount was to be awarded to Chen Linfeng as a prize to thank him for using his Extraordinary Powers to save the rocket. As it were, several members of the Rocket Research Institute were disciples of Chen Linfeng, who was the founder and Vice-President of the World Association of Chinese People. Thus, through organisations that he controlled, Chen Linfeng himself was behind the donation to the Institute and, through the Institute, back to himself as a reward. The other beneficiaries of this operation were the members of the Rocket Institute, who were, in effect, given a 200,000 yuan payoff by Chen Linfeng in exchange for lending the prestige of their institute to the claim that his powers had rescued the satellite.

After the affair was revealed, the General Aeronautics Corporation, which was in charge of the Institute, released a circular banning all staff members from communicating with Chen Linfeng, and declared that the master had never been involved in the rocket launching preparations.[9]

We will see later how support within the government allowed Falungong to expand openly between 1996 and 1999, even though

7 On Chen Linfeng's denomination, see Chen Linfeng 1988, 1993.
8 RR, 12 April 1999: 11.
9 GR, 23 August 1995: 1.

it was already technically illegal and several repressive measures had been decided. It was only when the Zhongnanhai demonstration triggered the personal ire of Jiang Zemin that Falungong's official supporters could no longer do anything to stop the massive repression campaign launched against it. Falungong is the exception that proves the rule, the other denominations having for the most part always assumed a posture of obedience to the authorities.

The subtle process of 'voluntary' submission to CCP norms required that all parties be aware of the official line. The propaganda system here played a key role in the *qigong* sector. Party directives were transmitted to Party members—especially officials—during study meetings where they listened to speeches from higher-ranked officials and read political documents. The directors of the state-sponsored *qigong* associations, who were often retired officials and Party members, took part in such study meetings. They, or other officials, then transmitted the Party line to the *qigong* sector through their opening and closing speeches at the meetings and conferences promoted by the state-sponsored *qigong* associations.

These speeches were sometimes published in *qigong* magazines, allowing the broad membership of the *qigong* sector to become aware of official policy. Theoretically, the *qigong* press was required to conform to Party orthodoxy; in practice, this was hardly the case. *Oriental Science Qigong* (*Dongfang qigong*), published by the Beijing Qigong Research Society, was the only *qigong* magazine to regularly publish political articles, editorials and speeches, and to offer a content relatively compatible with Party ideology.

Also in theory, the denominations were required to retransmit political guidance to their volunteers and practitioners during study sessions. In practice, only a handful of groups, such as Zangmigong and Zhineng Gong, regularly conducted political indoctrination activities.[10]

To conclude, the CCP had little *direct* influence on the grassroots of the *qigong* milieu and on the practices of the followers. However, through networks of political patronage mobilised in the legitimisation process for denominations, it played an essential role in the general configuration of the *qigong* sector. As long as the denominations 'played the game' of conforming to the Party, they were relatively free in their activities. But if an organisation, such

10   See p. 202.

as Falungong, refused to play the game, the state would intervene to suppress it.

State control on the *qigong* sector thus operated through two modalities: an increasingly rationalised regulatory framework, which was still only partially effective, and more personalistic loyalties based on connections.

THE MASS DENOMINATIONS

We now turn to the ways in which denominations established and rationalised the relationship between *qigong* masters and practitioners. The *gongfa* was a transforming link, infinitely replicable, and operational in the absence of personal contact between the master and the practitioners. Transmission could thus occur on a massive scale. Where, through direct oral teaching, the traditional master could only transmit to a handful of persons during his lifetime, the *qigong* master could, through the *gongfa*, simultaneously reach millions of followers in all parts of China and even of the world. The mass denomination, the model of which had been developed by Guo Lin, was usually made of the following elements:

- a master, founder or inheritor and transmitter of the *gongfa*;
- the method, the name of which is also the name of the denomination, made up of two parts: a technical part (*gongfa*) and a theoretical part (*gongli*);
- a range of transmission media: books, audio and videotapes, which exalt the master and explain the method;
- a transmission network, linking the master to the grassroots of practitioners throughout China and abroad, made up of practice centre leaders in parks and public spaces;
- a network of associations, schools, clinics etc., often registered with government agencies or affiliated to state-sponsored *qigong* associations.

The organised aspect of the *qigong* milieu remained largely unnoticed by both practitioners and observers until the 1999 Falungong protests and crackdown. In fact, the denominations were transmission tools which had the effect of enlarging the network of practitioners and of leading to the practitioners' affiliation to the denomination.

The number of denominations is difficult to estimate, and the number of practitioners of a single method could vary between a handful of disciples to tens of millions of followers. It was common in *qigong* circles to speak of over 3,000 denominations. The life-span of a denomination was often short, some of them going through periods of effervescence and phenomenal expansion, followed by a quick fall into obscurity. Their practitioners would then drift to other methods.

The thousands of denominations followed a relatively homogeneous model of organisation and transmission. *Qigong* organisations aimed to structure the floating mass of practitioners into centralised networks. The denomination was an integrated network linking the master and his core disciples to the mass of practitioners throughout the country and abroad. At each level of organisation, 'trainers' or 'assistants' propagated the method within a specific geographic area. Each level of training in the method corresponded to a hierarchical level in the denomination. Anyone could freely learn the basic postures of the method by joining a practice point in a park or public space, and by imitating the assistant and the experienced practitioners. For a fee, one could then sign up for beginner or intermediate training workshops lasting one or two weeks, organised by general training stations. Capable and enthusiastic participants in these workshops would then be chosen to lead practice points and teach the basic postures of the method.

Higher level training was normally provided only by the master in person. At this level the 'cadres' (*gugan*) were recruited to lead the general training stations and the central organisation. At this stage advanced training often covered the denomination's organisational methods. Progression to a higher level in the training system was thus linked to a deeper involvement in the denomination. Denominations that were capable of leading their disciples along the whole process, from the basic body movements to integration into an organisational structure, were most successful in retaining their followers and in expanding over a long period. Many denominations, however, unable to accompany practitioners along such a path, produced a floating mass of practitioners who wandered from one denomination to another, until a better organised denomination was able to retain them. Denominations such as Zhonggong and Falungong were thus able to recoup large numbers of practitioners of other denominations.

The transmission system of a method can be illustrated by placing the practitioners in concentric circles around the master, according to their level of progression and their degree of involvement in the work of transmission. This is illustrated in Figure 4, using the example of 'Great Buddha Qigong' (*Dafo gong*), founded by writer Ji Yi in 1995.

Denominations were the instrument for the transmission of the master's method, all the while creating a hierarchy of disciples. The typical denomination included the levels of organisation indicated in Figure 5, which illustrates the case of Falungong. The master controlled his central organisation, either officially as president, or behind the scenes, with close disciples acting as officers. Organisations were usually affiliated to a state-sponsored *qigong* association. They directed the overall expansion of the denomination and represented it vis-à-vis national state-sponsored associations and state bureaucracies.

Local branches ('training stations'), active at the regional, municipal or neighbourhood level, were led by practitioners who, depending on the denomination, were volunteers or paid. They were the link between the central node and the grassroots practice sites. They represented the denomination to local state-sponsored associations and government agencies. These local branches ensured the smooth running of practice points within a specified jurisdiction and organised beginner and intermediate training workshops.

Local practice points were located at specific spots in parks and public spaces, where free daily exercise sessions were led by volunteers in the mornings and evenings. The volunteers would often hang a banner with the denomination's name and general information on nearby trees or walls, and would bring a portable cassette-player to play the accompanying music for the exercises and meditations. It was common to find practice points of different methods at various locations in the same park.

A denomination could function with virtually no material investment or support. Most public activity took place in parks and public spaces, which could be used for free. Training workshops could be held in rooms rented for a small cost in schools or other institutions—or even for free, with the host unit receiving a commission on revenues from the workshop registrations.

Denominations were 'virtual' organisations able to mobilise thousands, even tens of millions of followers throughout China,

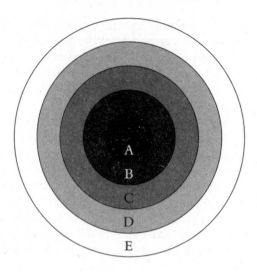

Fig. 4 Levels of involvement in a denomination:

A. The master (Ji Yi), President of the Dafogong General Association

B. Personal disciples and initiates, Vice-Presidents of the Dafogong General Association: Yin Ai, Chief Transmitter of the Dharma (*shouxi chuanfashi*) and Li Shun, Great Master of Extraordinary Healing, authorised to give public lectures on 'Dafogong Life and Health Science' throughout China.

C. Active members of the denomination, involved in its hierarchy and in the transmission of the method:
  - 'High-level masters' (*gaoji fashi*);
  - 'Transmitter' (*chuanren*): at this level, one could become a chairman, vice-chairman or secretary-general of a local Dafogong association affiliated to the area's state-sponsored *qigong* association, as well as coach at a training station (*fudaozhan zhanzhang*);
  - 'Master of Health' (*jiankang fashi*): after taking this 300-yuan course, one could become a member of the Dafogong General Association and establish training stations.

D. Practitioners devoted to the serious practice of one denomination. After following a 100-yuan correspondence course, including illustrated guidebooks, power-inducing audiotapes and 'great Buddha magical cards' (*dafo tongling ka*), one could obtain the Family Health Master Certificate (*jiating baojianshi jieye zheng*).

E. Occasional and short-term practitioners, who readily switch from one denomination to another.

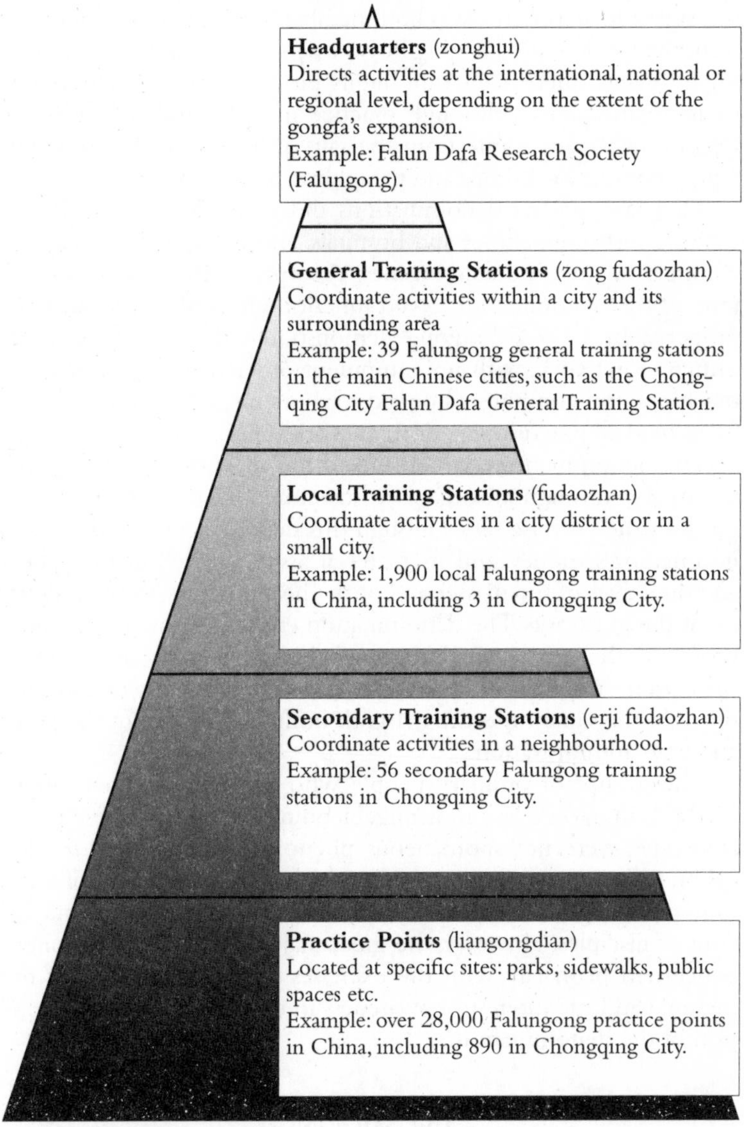

Headquarters (zonghui)
Directs activities at the international, national or regional level, depending on the extent of the gongfa's expansion.
Example: Falun Dafa Research Society (Falungong).

General Training Stations (zong fudaozhan)
Coordinate activities within a city and its surrounding area
Example: 39 Falungong general training stations in the main Chinese cities, such as the Chongqing City Falun Dafa General Training Station.

Local Training Stations (fudaozhan)
Coordinate activities in a city district or in a small city.
Example: 1,900 local Falungong training stations in China, including 3 in Chongqing City.

Secondary Training Stations (erji fudaozhan)
Coordinate activities in a neighbourhood.
Example: 56 secondary Falungong training stations in Chongqing City.

Practice Points (liangongdian)
Located at specific sites: parks, sidewalks, public spaces etc.
Example: over 28,000 Falungong practice points in China, including 890 in Chongqing City.

Fig. 5 Typical organisational structure of a denomination

Source Kwang 1999. This is a schematic representation which does not take into account regional variations. For a more detailed study of Falungong's structure, see Tong 2002a.

through a structure that was both flexible and hierarchical, and free
from the burden of managing heavy assets. *Qigong* activities, requiring little investment, were thus highly profitable for the masters and
their organisations—although practice in parks and at home was
free, profit streams came from the sale of books, audio and video
tapes, training workshops and paraphernalia.

That said, several denominations did own hard assets, such as
training institutes, clinics and hospitals, and even, as in the case of
Zhonggong, incorporated business enterprises. But the 'nerve system' of the denomination could function efficiently without such
property. In 1999 Falungong demonstrated the efficiency of its
immense network, with no equipment other than telephones, fax
machines and computers hooked to modems, which were owned
by individual practitioners or their work unit.

The denominations, which linked the mass of practitioners to
the master through an organised structure, did more than merely
transmit the exercise sets. Through this network circulated the denomination's money and its material assets, as well as the orders
and directives of the master and of the headquarters, to the followers at the grassroots. The denomination ensured its own expansion,
protected the master, and mobilised the followers at the order of
the master or of the headquarters—as in the Falungong demonstrations. At the same time, the network infiltrated itself into the Party
and state administration.

The groups of ordinary people who practised different *qigong*
methods in parks every morning, blending into the Chinese urban
landscape, were not spontaneous phenomena: they were the local branches of the denomination which, through a chain of local,
municipal, regional and national links, led to the master and his
core of disciples. However, the great majority of the practitioners,
concerned primarily with the exercises and the teachings of the
master, had little interest or awareness in the organisational dimension of the denomination.

ZANGMIGONG[11]

Zangmigong was an 'ideal' example of a denomination: directly and
explicitly derived from Tibetan Buddhism, it defined its method

11 This section is based on data collected from the 1997–9 issues of Zangmi
Gong's internal newsletter, *Zangmi Qigong Information*. Each issue of the newslet-

as a science, and scrupulously attempted to respect CCP directives and policies. A small denomination, its transmission system
followed the same model as that of the larger *qigong* organisations.
Furthermore, Zangmigong was a successful example of the integration of a denomination into state institutional networks.

Zangmigong was directed by the Tantric Qigong Specialised
Commission (TQSC—*Zangmi qigong zhuanye weiyuanhui*), founded
in 1990 by Liu Shanglin, who called himself a '*qigong* trainer' (*qigong
jiaolianyuan*) rather than 'master'. He claimed to be a disciple of
Fahai, a fortieth-generation Tibetan lama of the Gelugpa sect of
Tibetan Buddhism. Zangmigong or 'Tantric Qigong', based on the
Tibetan Buddhist practices and texts passed down to Liu Shanglin,
consisted of sitting meditation, the recitation of incantations and
study of the *Diamond Sutra*. The method stressed the cultivation of
virtue, which was supposed to take up 70 per cent of the practitioner's effort, the body exercises taking up the remaining 30 per
cent.

The TQSC, based in Tieli, a secondary city in the Manchurian
province of Heilongjiang, ran a network of nine training stations
which coordinated Zangmigong activities in each part of the province. Workshops were the organisation's chief source of revenues.
Denomination activities were limited to Heilongjiang province and
a few other cities in north-east China. Active in local community
life, the association participated in Party events and commemo-
rations, and organised fundraising campaigns for flood victims.
It acquired a five-storey headquarters in Tieli in 1994. A crèche
was set up in the building to look after the children of workshop
participants.

The TQSC was affiliated to the Heilongjiang Qigong Committee, a branch of the Provincial Sports Commission. It was also a
member of the state-sponsored Heilongjiang Qigong Science Research Society, the provincial affiliate of the CQRS.

Propagation methods

Zangmigong's propagation strategy aimed to open new areas to the
denomination, and to revitalise areas where it was already established. As long as the local authorities didn't intervene, promotional

---

ter consisted of one photocopied double-sided A3 sheet of paper and contained
detailed information on the association's activities and organisation.

activities could be held in any public space: parks, riverbanks, side-walks and residential compounds, where volunteers would hang banners and posters and play taped music. In virgin areas promotion began with the teaching of the basic techniques (mantra recitation and gymnastic *qigong*) to a small group of new practitioners. Followers would take the initiative to chat with curious onlookers, to teach them the method, and to send them *qi* to treat their illnesses. Practitioners were encouraged to promote Zangmigong to their family members, their friends and their neighbours, and to take advantage of social activities and meetings to talk about the *gongfa*. In presenting Zangmigong, followers would share their own personal experiences of healing and wellness from practice, and would stress the method's legitimacy by raising the following points: (1) Zangmigong was accredited by the provincial and national (state-sponsored) organisations responsible for *qigong*; (2) the method conformed to the State Sports Commission's criteria for *qigong*: it was clear, complete, scientific, and was expanding in a healthy manner; (3) the founder, Liu Shanglin, was a man of high virtue, and the method's miraculous effects were proven; (4) the denomination possessed its own building in Tieli.

'Power-inducing lectures' by Liu Shanglin were used as major promotional events. In one instance a hundred volunteers cruised the parks and sidewalks to promote the lecture, which was attended by 3,000 people; this led to 750 workshop registrations. The enthusiasm generated by the event motivated volunteers to disperse to outlying towns and factories, where they gave workshops for 1,400 people.[12]

The effectiveness of the propagation effort was seen to depend on the spirit of devotion and gratitude of the practitioners, who were exhorted to tell themselves:

I am a beneficiary of Zangmigong, I must think of the source of my happiness, and not forget the blessings I have received from Zangmigong. I can express my gratitude by enthusiastically propagating the method. My numerous illnesses have been eradicated thanks to Zangmigong. Those who [have been] sick better understand the suffering of the sick. I am now in good health, but I cannot forget that multitudes of sick people are still suffering. I must share my experience with them, and proclaim the miraculous effect of Zangmigong: such is my sacred duty.[13]

12 ZM 6: 2.
13 ZM 47: 1–2.

Aside from volunteer promotion of the *gongfa*, a practitioner's devotion could be expressed through financial sacrifice: often, members of teaching teams paid their travelling expenses to other cities. Practitioners sometimes pooled contributions to cover workshop fees for low-income participants.[14]

Regular '*gong* assemblies' were held in several cities to bring practitioners together to learn and share experiences. The agenda for such meetings would typically include collective meditation with recitation of the *Diamond Sutra*, speeches by TQSC leaders, and testimony by miraculously cured practitioners. '*Gong* assemblies' were sometimes combined with outings to scenic spots outside the city. Groups of volunteers occasionally visited retirement homes or orphanages to teach *qigong* to the residents and encourage them.[15]

Liu Shanglin devoted much of his time to giving workshops.[16] Themes included *qigong* and *bigu* for treatment of chronic and gynaecological illnesses; the *Diamond Sutra*, said by Liu to describe the highest level of tantric cultivation, 'transcending all religion' and 'containing all religion'; health, hygiene and *qigong* for seniors; and advanced workshops for practice-point trainers. Most workshops lasted two weeks. Almost 7,000 people attended TQSC workshops in 1998.[17]

Workshops were integrated into a systematic programme of research and publication on the results of Zangmigong practice. Workshop participants were tested for various biological indicators. Some of the research was funded by the Heilongjiang Institute of Chinese Medicine and by the provincial government. Results were presented at Zangmigong and *qigong* conferences, and published in edited Zangmigong volumes.[18]

The TQSC was active in international exchanges. Liu Shanglin cultivated relationships with Finland, not only for teaching Zangmigong, but also to establish Sino-Finnish economic cooperation for exploiting forestry resources in the Tieli area. Liu Shanglin presented papers at a conference on holistic medicine held at the University of Southern California. But exchanges were most developed

14 ZM 61: 2.
15 ZM 47: 2; ZM 56: 2.
16 ZM 64: 1–2.
17 ZM 64: 1–2; ZM 41: 1; ZM 42: 1–2.
18 Cf. Liu Shanglin 1999.

with Japan: the TQSC organised two international conferences on Zangmigong jointly with a Japanese *qigong* association.

Zangmigong was also involved in community events. The denomination joined an anti-smoking campaign and declared its headquarters a 'smoke-free building'.[19] The TQSC worked with the education authorities to train teachers in a method for primary and secondary school pupils to exercise their eyes and their concentration.[20] Practitioners were invited by the Sports Commission to participate in a public performance of various *qigong*, dance and sports groups. After the floods of the summer of 1998 the TQSC launched a fundraising campaign through its network of practice sites. A circular was sent to all general and local training centres, asking them to devote all their energies to raising funds and donations in kind for the flood victims. Over 43,000 yuan, 3,000 items of clothing and 128 pairs of shoes were collected, earning Liu Shanglin an interview on national television.[21]

Integration to state institutions

Liu Shanglin was a Party member, and the TQSC had its own CCP branch committee. The association's integration to state structures was regularly affirmed through the attendance of its leaders at official meetings called to transmit central government directives, and through the holding of meetings of TQSC meetings for the same purpose. This process is illustrated by a series of meetings held in 1998.

At the time the government's chief preoccupation was to 'rectify' the *qigong* sector and to establish a uniform administrative structure for *qigong*, in response to the 'chaos' that was seen to prevail in *qigong* circles.[22] The new policy had been promulgated in a circular issued jointly by seven central government ministries.[23]

At a meeting of the TQSC on 19 January 1997 some fifty delegates from twenty-one training stations were told that the implementation of the seven ministries' document had been the main issue during the year.[24]

19   ZM 55: 1.
20   ZM 57: 1.
21   ZM 59: 1; ZM 60: 1.
22   See pp. 181–2.
23   See pp. 176–7.
24   ZM 40: 3.

At the next meeting, held half a year later, Vice-Director Tian Yugeng reported on two important meetings that he had attended. First, a meeting of the Heilongjiang Qigong Science Research Society, which was told of CQRS's decision to finish the 'rectification' in the autumn, and that all *qigong* groups would have to re-register at that time. Second, a meeting called by the Provincial Sports Commission, where representatives of *qigong* associations were told of the results of a meeting of the State Sports Commission which had studied a speech by Sports Minister Wu Shaozu concerning the administration of *qigong*.

Another series of meetings was held in the autumn. In September Tian Yugeng reported to the TQSC about a meeting of the Provincial Sports Commission, which had been called to discuss how to apply new directives of the State Sports Commission.

These events show how a local denomination, in this case the TQSC, called meetings to transmit the directives of meetings of the provincial-level sports commission and state-sponsored *qigong* association, which had themselves been held to relay policies announced at meetings of the State Sports Commission and the CQRS. The state attempted to control denominations through the state-sponsored associations that linked the popular *qigong* milieu to official bureaucracies: the state-sponsored associations functioned as official organs, and their leadership was appointed by their tutelary government departments, but their members included representatives of the denominations. The state tried to influence the denominations by involving their leaders in the transmission of its policies through cascading series of meetings from the summit to the base.

At the same time the denomination took advantage of its integration in the bureaucratic structure to defend its interests and expand its influence. This dynamic of interpenetration of state and denomination influences can be seen in the Provincial Work Meeting on the Administration of Hygienic Qigong, held at Harbin on 22–23 July 1998.

The meeting was called by the provincial Physical Education and Sports Association, a state-sponsored association affiliated to the Provincial Sports Commission. Delegates of the different denominations registered with the Sports Commission and with the Heilongjiang Qigong Science Research Society, as well as representatives of six provincial departments, were summoned to the meeting. The principal officials present were a Deputy Director of the Sports Commission and two former Vice-Presidents of the Provincial People's Congress. Altogether twenty delegates and seventeen observers were present.

The officials began the meeting with speeches stressing the guidelines promulgated at a national meeting on the administration of *qigong*, summarising speeches by Wu Shaozu and other national officials on the subject, and exhorting the participants to 'raise the banners of science, law, unity and civilisation'.

After these speeches the delegates divided into two groups to discuss the problem of the management of the *qigong* sector, and to make recommendations. The Zangmigong delegate took advantage of the group discussions to promote Zangmigong, to give an image of Zangmigong as a 'loyal subject', and to make his own suggestions. He stated that his purpose in going to the meeting was to study the spirit of the new policy; that Zangmigong had been developing very well in the previous nine years by applying the national health policy; but that the work was complicated by the existence of two state-sponsored *qigong* associations in charge of *qigong* in different parts of the province and affiliated to two different government departments. 'Our talk had the effect of publicising Zangmigong, and of creating positive feelings toward Zangmigong on the part of the delegates present, who expressed their support for the future work.'[25]

The meeting was concluded by an official, who summarised the delegates' concerns: the co-existence of two provincial state-sponsored *qigong* associations had to end; the problem of Falungong's expansion[26] and the strong opposition to it from various quarters; the problem of *qigong* masters from outside the province coming to give lectures and workshops, i.e. Li Hongzhi; and the problem of *qigong* masters' accreditation.[27]

This type of meeting shows how the state tried to unite the different actors of the *qigong* sector into a single community under its direction. The participation of officials signified both the state's willingness to legitimise *qigong*, as well as its intention to control it. The state imposed the agenda, devoted to transmitting the 'spirit' of national-level meetings and speeches, and to its local application.

---

25 ZM 58: 1–2.
26 Falungong's name isn't explicitly mentioned in the article, which refers to 'a certain *gongfa*'.
27 ZM 58: 1–2.

The representatives of the denominations, such as Zangmigong, by attending and participating in the discussions, associated themselves with this process and displayed an image of conforming to the 'spirit' of the central government.

At the same time Zangmigong played its own game, which was to protect its own interests by presenting itself as having always been faithful to the Party's policy, and by seeking support from the officials present at the meeting. By entering the state's sphere of influence, Zangmigong hoped to expand its own networks of influence within state structures.

Political activities

The TQSC's Party branch regularly organised activities for major political events. For example, the staff and all workshop participants present at the headquarters were summoned to watch Deng Xiaoping's funeral on television on 25 February 1997.[28] On the occasion of Hong Kong's retrocession to the PRC a few months later, the TQSC organised several events. In Harbin the local leader of the Zangmigong training station organised a series of exhibits, healing activities, information stands and Zangmigong teaching events, as part of celebrations sponsored by the municipal state-sponsored *qigong* association on 21 June. Similar events were held in other cities. In Qiqihar the local Zangmigong branch held a song and dance show. One of the acts was entitled 'Trusting the Great Helmsman', which, according to the association's Vice-President, 'expressed the practitioners' determination to develop the cause of *qigong*, to struggle in unison, ... to move forward on the path of socialism with Chinese characteristics, under the leadership of the central core of the Party formed by comrade Jiang Zemin.'[29]

In September 1997 the leaders of the TQSC and the members of its Party branch watched the 15th Party Congress on television, then met to study its 'spirit'. Liu Shanglin raised the issue of problems related to the organisation of workshops in different cities, and the association's financial deficit. 'We must, through study, increase our moral qualities and make a breakthrough in the spirit of the 15th Congress, in order to free ourselves from difficulties and to

28 ZM 41: 1.
29 ZM 45: 1.

pull ourselves out of this low point: all of us must reflect on the ways of giving a new momentum to the cause of Zangmigong, and to find solutions.'[30]

During the meeting they discussed such questions as the relationship between Deng Xiaoping theory, Marxism–Leninism and Mao Zedong thought; the principles of the reform of state institutions; the concept of socialism with Chinese characteristics; the significance of Jiang Zemin's closing speech, and how to use the spirit of the 15th Congress to guide the work of Zangmigong. To the last question, the participants responded with the following injunctions: reinforce the teaching of Zangmigong; broaden the appeal of Zangmigong; advance scientific research to enable Zangmigong to contribute further to the people's health; and discover new forms of treatment for chronic illnesses. Finally, they resolved to build spiritual civilisation, improve moral quality, and make an immense effort for the construction of the pyramid-shaped buildings for the association's planned meditation centre.[31]

Through its political activities, the TQSC thus became a conduit for Party discourse and propaganda. But at the same time, the denomination used its participation in political meetings and events to convey an image of loyalty in order to obtain political support for its activities and promote itself to the public. The political activities never went deeper than diffusing Party discourse, the modalities of the application of which were never specified. The vagueness of the directives in terms of implementation allowed local organisations to draw on Party propaganda to legitimise activities which they had been planning anyway, as shown by the following passage:

The main tasks for 1998 are the following:

Vigorously apply the spirit of the seven national ministries' document and understand that the propagation of *qigong* activities is essential for the policy of health for the whole people, and that the spirit of the 15th Party Congress, concerning the stimulation of all forces in the service of socialism with Chinese characteristics, creates an excellent opportunity for the development of *qigong*. This opportunity must be seized fully through ardent effort.

Understand that Tantric Qigong is an important component of traditional Chinese culture. Studying the relevant Buddhist theories is necessary to improve one's level of practice, as well as to build the culture

30   ZM 48: 1a.
31   ZM 49: 1.

of socialism with Chinese characteristics in the spirit of the 15th Party Congress ...[32]

Conclusion: the dynamic of interpenetration

More than many denominations, Zangmigong was able to balance the contradictory forces pulling on the *qigong* milieu. On the one hand the practices transmitted by Zangmigong were directly derived from Tibetan religion: meditation techniques, collective recitation of scriptures, *guanding* initiation[33] and mantras were religious practices that Zangmigong, as a mass denomination, taught openly to thousands of people—a form of proselytism that official religious organisations were strictly forbidden from engaging in outside of temple or church premises.

On the other hand the association was an obedient subject of the Party, with its own active CCP branch, which supported the government during political rituals, and endeavoured to stay within the limits of government regulations and to follow state policies. The scope of the association's activities was regional, and the number of practitioners not too high: the TQSC could not be seen as a political threat. It tried to conduct scientific research, and it participated in the region's economic development through the construction of a meditation retreat and by facilitating the introduction of Finnish forestry companies. Zangmigong had found a niche in the local community. Instead of stressing the quest for Extraordinary Powers that could be criticised as 'pseudo-science', the *gongfa* equated Buddhist compassion and detachment with the Communist spirit of service to society. Zangmigong was one of the few denominations not to be dismantled by the state following the anti-Falungong repression campaign in 1999.[34] This illustrates the unspoken agreement which governed the *qigong* sector until 1999: as long as denominations overtly submitted to the Party, were seen to contribute to social and economic development, and presented no political threat, they were relatively free to act and expand as they wished.

---

[32] ZM 53: 1.

[33] A tantric initiation ritual in which the master sprinkles water on to the top of the disciple's head.

[34] Nonetheless, it did virtually cease its activities after 2000, following the implementation of the new, extremely restrictive, state policy on *qigong* (see p. 280).

ZHONGGONG

Zhonggong carried to the extreme a logic of commercialisation that was becoming increasingly pronounced in the *qigong* sector in the 1990s, in line with the overall tendency of Chinese society with the introduction of the market economy. We have already seen how Zhang Hongbao, in the wake of Yan Xin's popularity, became a famous master at the end of the 1980s, and how he penetrated Beijing's academic, scientific, media and political circles.[35] Contrary to Yan Xin, who was in a sense carried away by a wave he had helped to amplify, Zhang Hongbao had a fine understanding of the dynamics of the *qigong* milieu and of the profits he could make from it. Zhonggong's expansion followed a calculated and targeted strategy. The ambition wasn't only to rationalise *qigong* in order to commodify it: Zhang Hongbao aimed to create his own cultural system based on *qigong*, and to build a national commercial organisation to promote and manage it.

The training system

More than any other denomination, Zhonggong proposed a systematic training structure—in eight ascending levels—giving the practitioner a clear path of progression, which could stimulate the individual to advance. While other denominations proposed different workshops to learn different types of techniques, such as sitting meditation, gymnastics, inner alchemy etc., Zhonggong workshops were each geared to the acquisition of specific *skills* which the participant could master with satisfaction at the end of a few days of training. In addition, the workshops trained participants in Zhonggong organisational and managerial techniques as early as the second level, allowing them to integrate with the denomination structure and giving them the skills to set up what could be called their own local Zhonggong franchises.

Stage one included basic techniques and postures; manipulation of *qi* (collecting, emitting, receiving and exchanging *qi*); meditation on the 'microscopic orbit'; Zhonggong diagnostic and therapy techniques etc.

Stage two covered methods for the organisation and control of collective sessions; *qigong* performance arts (walking on a sheet of paper suspended in the air, standing on a light bulb, changing the

---

[35] See pp. 146–50.

alcohol content of wine etc.); correction of eight types of *qigong* deviation; the 'secrets of secrets' of Buddhist and Taoist techniques; specific types of therapy for over thirty diseases etc.

Stage three consisted of still meditation and visualisation methods; *qigong* hypnosis; spontaneous motion *qigong* (dance, music, poetry and spontaneous boxing); additional healing techniques etc.

Stage four included electric *qigong*; hard *qigong*; Extraordinary Powers: telepathy, distant vision, predicting the future.

Stage five covered concepts and methods for the creation of living space (Chinese geomancy); arts of the bedchamber (sexual techniques); dietetics—the art of regaining one's youth; massage techniques; regulation of the emotions; debunking of the eight 'evil arts': the demon who knocks on the door; piercing one's cheeks with nails; the egg that walks; swallowing fire etc.[36]

The contents of the sixth, seventh and eighth levels were not publicly disclosed. They involved training in the higher-level management of Zhonggong organisations. Each level corresponded to a one- or two-week workshop. Stages one and two were taught at local training stations or at centres such as Qingchengshan, which also offered stages three, four and five. The price of room, board and tuition for residential workshops was 144 yuan per week in 1994, equivalent to approximately one week's wages for the average Chinese at the time.[37]

It was a standardised training model, with its set curriculum and manuals, replicable in thousands of stations and centres across China. The stress was on productivity, with quantified targets for the sale of workshops. Workshops had a highly structured organisation of time, in which each task, as well as the moment of its execution, was clearly assigned in written procedural manuals. Trainers were to induce systematically participants into a state of suggestibility, which was presented as a method for entering a '*gong* reception state'. The training regimen focused on the transmission of concepts by means of body techniques. For instance, a technique in which one lengthens one's finger by a few millimetres through mental effort is used as the support for teaching the 'mental force theory',

---

[36] Qingchengshan renti kexue peixun xuexiao, 2004, 'Changnian juban Zhang Hongbao "Zhonggong" babu gaoji gongfa yi, er, san, si bu gong shucheng ban' [Levels 1, 2, 3 and 4 of the advanced eight-level Zhonggong accelerated workshops offered year round], advertising flyer.

[37] Ibid.

one of the elements of Zhonggong ideology. The participant, able visibly to lengthen his or her finger, believed he or she was already in possession of a minor Extraordinary Power; the individual could now believe in all Extraordinary Powers phenomena, for which Zhonggong theory provided a conceptual framework. The idea that persistence in practising Zhonggong would allow the participant to acquire even more Extraordinary Powers would provide motivation to continue the training and practise with enthusiasm.[38]

Trainers were given their own systematic training. The insistence was on loyalty toward the master and Zhonggong: 'become a model of respect for the master and love for the cause; make group interest one's first criteria, be loyal to the cause of Qilin Culture, have the courage to sacrifice ....'[39] Workshops were highly structured and standardised. Trainers' responsibilities were spelled out in detail in their training manuals. Among their duties, they had to ensure doctrinal purity and orthopraxis: transmit the methods by following the correct organisation of time, content, method and order of presentation, without errors and without straying from the instructional materials; without teaching elements from a higher-level workshop; without mixing in elements from other *qigong* methods; and to explain Extraordinary Powers phenomena in a scientific manner, without using superstitious or mystical terms. Each trainer was given numerical sales targets. They were required to teach stage one to a minimum of 600 persons per year, from among whom a minimum target of 50 per cent were to sign up for a stage two workshop; and a target of 60 per cent of stage two students were to progress to stage three. For the sale of books and tapes, the target was 100 per cent of stage one and 85 per cent of stage two participants; for the sale of souvenirs, the target was 40 per cent of stage one and 60 per cent of stage two participants (100 per cent in the more affluent Special Economic Zones—Shenzhen, Zhuhai, Xiamen and Hainan).

Trainers were also to identify and recruit human resources from among workshop participants, including persons with Extraordinary Powers and individuals with teaching and management abili-

---

[38] Qingchengshan renti kexue peixun xuexiao, 1997, *Zhonghua yangsheng yizhi gong yibu gong jiaoshi xuexi ziliao* [Study manual for trainers of level 1 of the Chinese Qigong for Nourishing Life and Increasing Intelligence], Dujiangyan, internal publication, pp. 13–14.

[39] Ibid., p. 16.

ties. At least 50 per cent of stage one participants and 20 per cent of stage two participants were to be recorded as having experienced extraordinary healing during training.[40]

There are many similarities between this marketing structure and the direct sales and pyramid schemes which were popular in China in the 1990s (and which were banned around 1997). This is an area which remains to be investigated, but it is significant that Zhonggong rapidly adopted some of the most 'cutting-edge' sales and management techniques at a time, in the early 1990s, when they were still quite a novelty in China.

The expansion strategy

Zhang Hongbao had begun by establishing his organisation in the capital and cultivated his ties with the centres of power, as described in chapter 5. In July 1989 he founded one of the first incorporated *qigong* enterprises, a Sino-American joint venture.[41] Then, from 3 to 6 November 1990, in a series of lectures on 'The Science of Life and the Order of the Great Tao' at the Beijing Great Hall of Sciences, he officially launched his new ideological system, Qilin Culture.[42] The list of audience members read like a roster of the capital's political élite: the Secretary-General of the Central Propaganda Department, a Vice-President of the Party Central School, a Vice-President of the Military Sciences Academy, several retired provincial governors and military commanders etc.

The grandmaster then moved to expand in the provinces. Using his ties with regional political and military leaders, Sichuan, Shaanxi and Tianjin became the key bases of his empire. On 4 June 1989—date of the Tiananmen crackdown—Zhang Hongbao left Beijing for Sichuan, where he established the Zhonggong headquarters in a converted army barracks at Mt Qingcheng, known as the birthplace of Taoism. The Qingcheng barracks were refurbished as a retreat for Zhonggong workshops, and as a post-secondary

---

40 Qingchengshan renti kexue peixun xuexiao, 1997, *Zhonghua yangsheng yizhi gong erbu gong jiaoshi xuexi ziliao* [Study manual for trainers of level 2 of the Chinese Qigong for Nourishing Life and Increasing Intelligence], Dujiangyan, internal publication, p. 16.

41 WH: 556.

42 The *qi* and the *lin* are respectively the male and female of the Chinese mythological unicorn. Its appearance presages the coming of a great sage. On modern Confucian interpretations of the *qilin*, see Chen 1999: 247–69.

Extraordinary Powers college.[43] In December 1990 Zhang Hong-bao also established a management training institute in Chongqing, for the training of cadres for the Zhonggong organisation. For the first intake of students he chose a group of devoted and talented disciples, who learned the Zhonggong management system with him. This group of disciples then became the core managers of the growing number of Zhonggong provincial branches and commercial enterprises.[44] In April 1991 he established the Qilin Culture University in Xi'an,[45] which offered programmes in tourism, hotel management, economics, commerce, finance, traditional healing, public relations, educational management, martial arts and marketing. The university's mission was to raise human resources for the expanding number of Zhonggong training centres and enterprises. Distance learning courses were also provided, in association with Zhonggong branches in Hong Kong and Australia.[46] Also in Shaanxi province, Zhang Hongbao founded the Centre for Reincarnation Research[47] and the Centre for Extraordinary Medicine Research[48] based in a sanatorium reserved for provincial government leaders.[49]

The management system

A national Zhonggong organisation, integrating the various organs and branches throughout China, was established in 1994, through a business enterprise owned by Zhang Hongbao: the Taiweike Nourishing Life Services Co. However, for reasons that are not clear, this company was dissolved by the Beijing municipal government after a few months of existence, around the same time that it tried to arrest Zhang Hongbao. In April 1995 the Mt Qingcheng and Chongqing institutes then united to establish, with the approval of the State Economic Reforms Commission, the Qilin Group, a business conglomerate based in Tianjin, under which the three 'systems' of Zhonggong were integrated: training institutes, affiliated products (medicines, teas, liqueurs etc.) and real estate. In total, the

43 QL 1: 55; QL 1: 59.
44 Zhang Hongbao 2001: 2; QL 1: 53.
45 WH: 556.
46 QL 1: 54.
47 SMK 20: 9.
48 'Extraordinary medicine' was Zhonggong's therapeutic system.
49 QL 1: 32.

Qilin Group claimed to manage over 3,000 Zhonggong branches, thirty properties, over 100,000 *qigong* practice points and as many employees.[50]

In the summer of 1995 Zhang Hongbao declared the end of Zhonggong's initial phase of growth, and decided to enter an 'adjustment period' of three years, with the purpose of consolidating the millions of practitioners, the thousands of practice sites and the dozens of branches, organs and businesses into a well-managed, profitable enterprise. Zhang Hongbao asked his provincial and national cadres to study business administration, using Harvard Business School materials, with the goal of reaching an MBA level within three years.[51]

Zhonggong's systematic organisation allowed it to draw into its orbit a large number of practitioners of other, less well organised denominations: by 1995 Zhonggong claimed to have 30 million practitioners—a figure that is certainly exaggerated, although an estimate of at least several million would not be unreasonable. If Zhonggong was able to expand so massively, it was largely thanks to its comprehensive management and transmission system.

At the base level, training stations were places where practitioners could meet and socialise as well as practise *qigong*. They were also enterprises offering a range of Zhonggong products, healing services and basic training courses. For example, the no. 9251 training station in Chengdu was located in a converted old temple building on Dragon King Temple Street. A gathering of followers was held every Saturday evening. In a large room decorated with portraits of the master, men and women of all ages sat on benches against the walls to meditate, while others, in the middle of the room, practised fluid and spontaneous-movement '*qigong* dance' to the rhythms of traditional Chinese music played on a cassette player. After the dance a leader of the station led a group meditation session.

Also anyone could go to the station at any time to practice the method. In the daytime retired people came to meditate in a small side room in which incense sticks burned in front of a portrait of Zhang Hongbao and Zhonggong symbols, and where Zhonggong music tapes were played.

The station offered first- and second-stage Zhonggong workshops, treatment of illnesses by Extraordinary Powers therapists,

50 Zhang Hongbao 2001: 4, 5; SMK 21: 16–17.
51 Zhang Hongbao 2001: 5.

distance diagnosis and therapy (with *gong*-filled prescriptions sent by post and long-distance emission of *gong*), Extraordinary Powers divination, and assistance in making travel arrangements for persons coming from afar. Station personnel included Zhonggong disciples who had completed stage four of the eight Zhonggong training levels, some of whom claimed to be able to see auras or to see through the human body.[52]

The local station's activities were primarily social and therapeutic. At the grassroots Zhonggong, through providing healing and friendship, could transmit its method to the population and integrate practitioners into its training system. At the national and international levels the denomination's activities were directed by the International Zhonggong General Assembly. Regional organisations based in Beijing, Xi'an, Chengdu etc. coordinated the network's expansion in districts covering several provinces. The Chengdu district, for instance, covered Sichuan, Yunnan, Guizhou, Hubei, Guangxi and Tibet. General training stations and/or 'life science schools', based in major cities, coordinated networks of local training stations. Each local organisation was, in theory, registered with the local authorities.[53]

Besides this basic structure, Zhonggong had its central training and marketing organs in Beijing, Xi'an, Sichuan and Hong Kong. Leading cadres were trained in Zhonggong management at the Chongqing International University of Life Sciences and Technology. The Xi'an Qilin Culture University taught Zhonggong ideology and methods. The Mt Qingcheng institutes organised research, publication and workshop activities, and trained people with Extraordinary Powers to master and increase their powers. The Qilin Group, based in Tianjin, as well as several subsidiaries and other companies, marketed books, audiovisual products, '*qigong* holiday retreats', 'information tea' etc. From Hong Kong Zhonggong products and services were promoted toward overseas Chinese communities.[54]

---

[52] Zhonggong Chengdu Longwangmiao Zhengjie 9251 Fudaozhan [No. 9251 Zhonggong training station, Dragon King Temple St, Chengdu] 'Jianjie' [Brief introduction], advertising flyer, Chengdu.
[53] When the local centre was registered with the Industrial and Commercial Bureau, it was called 'practice station'; but if it was registered with the Education Commission, it was called 'school'.
[54] WH: 556.

At the summit of the Zhonggong hierarchy were the master's personal disciples, who led a career within the organisation. They accumulated functions, progressed from one organ to another, and founded new branches or enterprises. The central core was made up of about ten individuals, who were members of the Zhonggong International General Assembly. Prior to joining Zhonggong, most of them had come from three different circles: academia, media and the Chengdu branch of the People's Liberation Army.[55]

The higher echelons of the Zhonggong organisation were modelled on the structure of the Communist Unit system. Organisational culture had the same emphasis on ideology and boilerplate propaganda, the same bureaucratic hierarchy of units, the same domination by a core of cadres who were the protégés of the master, the same style of meetings and speeches, the same inflamed rhetoric against the outside enemies of the denomination and against 'erroneous' thoughts and behaviours within the denomination.[56]

The central leadership directed an internal supervisory system to ensure that Zhonggong cadres followed denomination rules: 'The state has its laws, the lineage has its rules' (*guo you guofa, men you mengui*), said one leader. Three methods, based on CCP disciplinary procedures, were used to punish the wayward: self-criticism; loss of titles and functions; expulsion.[57] In one case Zhang Hongbao published a circular distributed to all trainers, expelling from Zhonggong a local station leader who had made apocalyptic prophecies and proclaimed himself Zhang's successor and Amitabha Buddha.[58]

For external protection Zhonggong didn't hesitate to launch lawsuits against critics. For instance, journalist Lu Shangde was sued for denouncing a Zhonggong demonstration as a fraud in an article

55 For biographic details on the Zhonggong leadership, see Palmer 2002b: 456–8.
56 'Guanyu guoji Zhonggong zonghui 1994 nian gongzuo huiyi jingshen de chuanda baogao' [Report on the transmission of the spirit of the 1994 working meeting of the International Zhonggong Council]; 'Zongjie jiwang, kaituo fenjin – Zhonggong Chengdu zhidaoqu gongzuo baogao' [Summarising the errors of the past and marching forward. Zhonggong Chengdu management district work report] in *Shengming Kexue Daobao* [Guidance for life science], March 1994, pp. 2, 3.
57 Ibid., p. 3.
58 Qingchengshan renti kexue peixun xuexiao, 1997, *Zhonghua yangsheng yizhi gong erbu gong jiaoshi xuexi ziliao* [Study manual for trainers of level 2 of the Chinese Qigong for Nourishing Life and Increasing Intelligence], Dujiangyan, internal publication, p. 39.

published in several newspapers in March 1993. The court ruled in Zhonggong's favour. An internal document states: 'We are in a socialist country, where one should not engage in the "freedom of the press" of the capitalist class—to use the special influence of the press to harm an adversary is an immoral conduct.'[59] Elsewhere, senior Zhonggong cadre Huang Guojun claimed, 'in the socialist market economy ... it is perfectly normal for different groups and enterprises to protect their interests against competition.'[60]

Finances

Zhonggong activities were highly profitable. This raised the issue of the management and distribution of revenues in such a vast organisation. Zhang Hongbao framed the issue with his 'theory of invisible capital'. He explained that Zhonggong was based on the invisible capital made up by his own 'field of *qi*', thanks to which economic and social benefits could be generated and transformed into material capital. The 'invisible capital' was also made up of the patents, intellectual property, trademarks, copyright, marketing rights etc.—which were exclusively owned by Zhang Hongbao and ceded for operational purposes to the Zhonggong central organs.[61]

Local training stations were treated as separate enterprises responsible for all material investments. Zhang Hongbao's invisible capital was considered to make up 70 per cent of the investment of each enterprise, which was thus, in theory, required to pay 70 per cent of its revenue to the central organisation. In practice, the proportion required by the latter was more in the range of 20–30 per cent.

But it was difficult to control revenues. Local training stations were tempted not to report all of their income, in order to avoid paying their dues, or to sell illegal copies of books, tapes and materials without paying royalties to the central organisation. Some

---

59 Ibid., p. 21.

60 'Guanyu guoji Zhonggong zonghui 1994 nian gongzuo huiyi jingshen de chuanda baogao' [Report on the transmission of the spirit of the 1994 working meeting of the International Zhonggong Council], *Shengming Kexue Daobao* [Guidance for life science], March 1994, p. 3.

61 Qingchengshan renti kexue peixun xuexiao, 1997, *Zhonghua yangsheng yizhi gong erbu gong jiaoshi xuexi ziliao* [Study manual for trainers of level 2 of the Chinese Qigong for Nourishing Life and Increasing Intelligence], Dujiangyan, internal publication, pp. 26–8.

trainers went so far as to create their own denomination, teaching the Zhonggong techniques under a new name. Profit drains seem to have been a major problem in Zhonggong, such that discussion of the issue was part of the training curriculum as early as stage two workshops. Course materials stressed that far from requiring disciples to pay important sums of money to the central organs, it was Zhang Hongbao who was sacrificing more than half of the 70 per cent of profits due to him, in order to help local training centres to develop and make money.[62] The problem of financial discipline was often mentioned by Zhonggong officials in their speeches, and I was told of a problem of 'embezzlement' at the Mt Qingcheng base, where local Zhonggong cadres were allegedly keeping revenues for themselves.

CONCLUSION

Yan Xin had symbolised the phenomenon of the grandmaster's charisma. To this charismatic dimension, Zhang Hongbao added a national organisation with its own system of human resource training, permitting to consolidate and deepen the practitioner's commitment and transform the human energy released by *qigong* into financial profits. While other *qigong* masters had created their own transmission networks covering all of China, with national, regional and local training stations, none had gone as far as Zhang Hongbao in a strategy of expansion, commercialisation and management. Zhonggong can be described as a commercial-bureaucratic organisation modelled on the CCP and managing a vast economic enterprise. Its chief activity was the sale of *qigong* workshops. This system of administration, partly inspired by Western commercial management theories, was elaborated at the beginning of the 1990s, when such notions were just beginning to appear in China.

In this chapter, we have seen the complex strategies deployed by denominations, building relations of patronage with officials and mutual cooptation with bureaucracies, all the while complementing the charismatic authority of the master with rationalised systems of propagation, training, sales and control. In the example of Zangmigong these strategies seemed to have worked fairly well—but this may be because of the relatively small size and influ-

---

62 Ibid., p. 24.

ence of Liu Shanglin's denomination. In the case of Zhonggong the
strategies were at first amazingly effective: Zhonggong became the
largest mass organisation in China outside the Communist Party.
In fact the name Zhonggong itself is a homophone of the abbreviated name of the CCP, Zhonggong. Indeed, rumours circulated
that Zhang Hongbao was trying to co-opt the *qigong* movement
to build a popular movement capable of transforming itself into a
political party.

However, an organisation as large as Zhonggong could not, of
course, avoid attracting the suspicion and opposition of certain
officials. As early as March 1994 Beijing municipal authorities
closed Zhang Hongbao's International Qigong Service Co., and
the local police received the order to arrest him. The reasons for
this arrest warrant are not clear. Zhang fled and continued to lead
his movement in hiding. But his organisation continued to exist
in other parts of China, indicating that the Beijing incident was
only the result of a local government decision. From 1995 to 1998
many Zhonggong organisations were investigated by the police.
But there was no general crackdown or ban on Zhonggong, and
Zhang Hongbao remained missing. According to Zhang, the authorities began planning a crackdown at the end of 1998—but the
Falungong crisis, which erupted after the April 1999 Zhongnanhai
protest, diverted the government's energies away from Zhonggong
for a few extra months.[63]

---

[63]   Zhang Hongbao 2001: 4–7.

8

MILITANT QIGONG: THE EMERGENCE OF FALUNGONG

Zhonggong was soon eclipsed by Falungong as the most popular denomination in China. During the period 1996–9, while Zhonggong rapidly declined, Falungong, although it had been founded only a few years earlier, experienced stunning growth. Like Zhonggong, Falungong was not recognised by the state-sponsored *qigong* associations after 1996, and was under police pressure. Falungong's success compared to Zhonggong in a context of official hostility can be attributed to two factors: first, while Zhonggong had created a heavy bureaucratic-style administration, with cadres, buildings and business dealings, which could easily attract official attention and which were difficult to maintain in an unfavourable environment, Falungong had perfected a light and flexible model of *qigong* transmission networks through free practice groups in parks and public spaces. Secondly, while Zhonggong, as a commercial organisation, was based on the profit motive, using bonuses and commissions to encourage its cadres—a method which was difficult to sustain at a period when the *qigong* boom was clearly in decline, Falungong crystallised, reinforced and radicalised notions of selfless discipline and sacrifice, triggering a strong force for individual and collective mobilisation.

Indeed, '*qigong* science', unable to produce replicable experimental proof of its claims, had sunken into ridicule, and had failed to achieve the eagerly-desired union with science. The first years of Falungong coincide with a period of confusion and exhaustion in *qigong* circles as they bore the brunt of the media campaign against pseudo-science. In this context, Li Hongzhi, founder of Falungong or 'Dharma-Wheel Qigong', redefined his method as having entirely different objectives from *qigong*: the purpose of practice should be neither physical health nor the development of Extraordinary Powers, but to purify one's heart and attain spiritual salvation.

While public opinion turned against the greed and quackery of many masters, Li Hongzhi condemned the commercialisation of *qigong*. Falungong linked the body technologies of *qigong* to a moralistic, messianic and apocalyptic doctrine. This approach allowed the method to spread rapidly, attracting millions of *qigong* adepts, retired people and marginalised intellectuals. Indeed, by the mid 1990s the Unit system of life-long security, which had structured the lives of urban Chinese for almost fifty years, was beginning to unravel under market-oriented reforms and an ever-deeper corruption. This was not a time for flights of free subjectivity in an over-structured environment, like the *qigong* of the 1980s, but for finding certainty in a disintegrating social world. Exploiting nostalgia for the altruism of the Maoist days, Falungong organised a movement of resistance against the growing social, moral and spiritual dissolution.[1]

Around 1994 Li Hongzhi began to teach that the purpose of body technologies was not good health, but spiritual salvation: a goal that must pass through the physical and social suffering that can result from practising the fundamental virtues of truth, compassion and forbearance. Falling ill, or suffering the abuse of colleagues, bosses or the police become salutary trials through which the practitioner could reimburse his karmic debts. Falungong no longer presented itself as a *qigong* method but as the Great Law or Dharma (*Fa*) of the universe, a doctrine with its own sacred scripture, *Zhuan Falun* ('Turning the Dharma-Wheel'),[2] which transcends all forms of material organisation, is superior to all philosophies, laws, teachings, religions and body cultivation methods in the history of humanity, and offers the only path of salvation from the apocalyptic end of the *kalpa* or universal cycle, in which the universe is destroyed.

THE LAUNCH OF FALUNGONG, 1992–4

Li Hongzhi, originally named Li Lai, was born in 1951 or 1952[3] in Gongzhulin, a small agricultural town on the Manchurian plains of

---

1 For a sociological analysis of Falungong, see Madsen 2000.

2 For an online edition of *Zhuan Falun*, see the Falungong website: <www.falundafa.org>.

3 According to his original birth records and identification documents, Li Hongzhi was born on 27 July 1952. On 24 September 1994 he had his birthday changed to 13 May 1951, which corresponds to Buddha's birthday by the tradi-

Jilin province. Li Hongzhi's birth was difficult; mother and baby almost died.[4] At the age of two his parents, petty functionaries, moved with him to the provincial capital, Changchun, a large industrial city, where he went to primary and middle school. He was shy and thoughtful; his grades were average, and his only known distinction was his skill at the trumpet.[5] He spent eight years as a trumpet player in the army and in a forest rangers brigade. His workmates remember him as introverted. At this time, during the 1970s, according to his hagiography, Li Hongzhi was initiated by several Buddhist and Taoist masters.[6]

After the end of the Cultural Revolution he was promoted to the position of attendant at a forest ranger's guesthouse, then in 1982, at the age of thirty, he returned to Changchun as a clerk in the security office of the municipal grain ration distribution centre. He soon began his involvement in the *qigong* milieu.[7] He took workshops given by the masters of the 'Esoteric Chan Qigong' and of the 'Qigong of the Nine Palaces and Eight Trigrams', read books on Buddhism, Taoism, pyramids and the Bermuda Triangle, and, first in secret then with a handful of disciples, elaborated his own *gongfa*. In 1991 he travelled to Thailand to visit his mother and sister, who had emigrated there.[8] It was also around that time that he took unpaid leave from work, in order to devote himself entirely to *qigong*.[9]

On 13–22 May 1992 Li Hongzhi rented the auditorium of a Changchun high school for his 'coming out of the mountains'. Over three hundred and fifty people signed up for the first two workshops on Falungong, sponsored by the Changchun City Somatic Science Research Society.[10] At 30 yuan per person the workshop netted over 10,000 yuan (over $1,000), a considerable sum at the time. Shortly afterwards he organised 800-person workshops at

---

tional calendar (Research Office of the Ministry of Public Security, 'Li Hongzhi: The Man and His Deeds', *Chinese Law and Government*, 32(5): 56–64. Translation of 'Li Hongzhi, qiren qishi' in HW, 23 July 1999: 2).

4 Hua and Han 1999: 139.
5 Hua and Han 1999: 139, 172; Zhang and Qiao 1999: 41.
6 Li Hongzhi 2000 [1994].
7 YPFX: 1.
8 Zhang and Qiao 1999: 41, 58.
9 Research Office of the Ministry of Public Security, 'Li Hongzhi: The Man and His Deeds', *Chinese Law and Government*, 32(5): 56–64. Translation of 'Li Hongzhi, qiren qishi' in HW, 23 July 1999: 2.
10 CME.

the Changchun Army Club and at the Provincial Party Commission.[11] Falungong's launch was a success, and among Li Hongzhi's first generation of disciples he could count members of the city's military and political élite, who would give him useful support. He founded the Falungong Research Society, and named four CCP members as Vice-Presidents, including a leader of the local police and a university professor.[12] Groups of practitioners started to form each morning in the parks of Changchun.

Encouraged by his success in Changchun Li Hongzhi headed for Beijing. From June 1992 to March 1993 he gave nine workshops sponsored by the CQRS, at venues including the Second Artillery Auditorium, the Nuclear Equipment Factory Auditorium and the Great Hall of the Air Missiles Bureau: in all approximately 9,000 people attended.[13] As described by one observer,

… as though drawn by Li's personal 'magnetism', hundreds of Pekingites turned up recently for an afternoon of holy rolling, trance dancing, faith healing and speaking in tongues. They presented a fair cross-section of the city: crew-cut teenagers in cryptically emblazoned T-shirts, older matrons in floral print suits, bespectacled bureaucrats, bandy-legged farmers from the kerbside vegetable markets, daisy-fresh co-eds in cotton frocks.[14]

From then on Li Hongzhi would easily attract more than one thousand participants per workshop. At the Oriental Health Expo Li Hongzhi rented a stand and healed the sick and the curious. Under the effect of his *qi*, paraplegics cast aside their crutches and their wheelchairs: the public mobbed his stand, snapped up the Falungong pamphlets, crowded around the master for his autograph, seen as possibly imbued with magical power, and hoped for the healing of some real or imaginary illness. The Expo organisers invited Li Hongzhi to come back the following year, this time as an advisor to the Board of Directors. At the 1993 edition he treated thousands of people, gave three packed lectures, and won the top prizes offered by the Expo organisers: the 'Greatest Contributor to Progress in Cutting-Edge Science' award and the 'Most Popular Master' award.[15]

11   Zhang and Qiao 1999: 70.
12   Zhang and Qiao 1999: 70.
13   Zhang and Qiao 1999: 74; CME.
14   Kaye, Lincoln, 'Traveler's Tales', *Far Eastern Economic Review*, 23 July 1992: 24, quoted in Porter 2003: 117.
15   Zhang and Qiao 1999: 76–7; CME.

Li Hongzhi donated the proceeds from his second lecture to a foundation for policemen injured while in pursuit of criminals.[16] He had already treated such wounded policemen at a ceremony organised by the Central Propaganda Department and the Public Security Ministry, and promised free treatment for all the 'heroes' recognised by the foundation.[17] In 1994, to raise funds for the foundation, he gave two mass lectures at the Public Security University, which brought in over 50,000 yuan. Through such philanthropic activity Li Hongzhi made many friends in the state police system, obtained favourable coverage in the *People's Security* newspaper, and increased his influence in the CQRS.

Indeed the CQRS and its regional affiliates, which collected 40 per cent of the revenues of the thirty or so denominations which it recognised,[18] was only too glad to afford its protection and recognition to a *qigong* master like Li Hongzhi, whose lectures and workshops were so profitable.

Li Hongzhi thus found himself a place in the national *qigong* sector. He established the Great Law of the Dharma Wheel (Falun Dafa) Research Society, affiliated to the CQRS which, through its networks in the *qigong* sector, helped organise lectures and workshops for Li Hongzhi in many large cities in 1993 and 1994. His first book, *China Falungong*,[19] was published in 1993 by the Military Affairs Friendship and Culture Publishing Co. In the spring of 1995 he made his first international tour, giving lectures and workshops in France, Germany and Sweden.[20] Thousands joined his workshops and the number of Falungong practitioners rose exponentially, reaching the millions within three years.

THE TRANSFORMATION OF FALUNGONG

In short, Li Hongzhi followed the typical career of a successful *qigong* master, who played his role well, made his way into the *qigong* circles, cultivated relations with Officials, and met the expectations

16   Zhang and Qiao 1999: 77.
17   CME; YPFX 1999: 5.
18   Zhang and Qiao 1999: 77; 'The Truth about whether Falungong has an Organization', *Chinese Law and Government*, 32(6): 62–8, p. 63. Translation of 'Youguan falungong shifou you zuzhi de zhenxiang', 31 July 1999, document posted on <www.chinesenewsnet.com, duowei xinwenwang>.
19   ZFG.
20   CME.

of the public. His Falungong appeared a denomination with a Buddhist theme, just as other denominations claimed Taoist, martial arts or tantric origins.

His lectures were dominated by moral, esoteric, demonological, apocalyptic, messianic and sectarian themes. In itself, this was not atypical for a *qigong* master: others, including Yang Meijun, Yan Xin, Zhang Xiangyu and Zhang Xiaoping, had also touched on such themes with varying degrees of emphasis. But around the end of 1994 and beginning of 1995 Li Hongzhi introduced new elements which would subtly but profoundly change the nature of Falungong, until ideology replaced body training as its chief object.

In the autumn of 1994 he began to stress that Falungong was not a form of *qigong* but a higher universal Dharma or *Fa*. He compared the leaders of practice sites to temple abbots, whose role was to guide adepts to salvation.[21] He forbade practitioners from healing others.[22] He changed his birthday registration to 13 May 1951, which in that year was the 8th day of the 4th lunar month, traditionally celebrated as the birthday of Sakyamuni Buddha.[23] And he decided to withdraw Falungong's membership from the CQRS, on the grounds that 'all the *qigong* society did is try to make money off the *qigong* masters, and they didn't do any research on *qigong*'.[24]

In his book *Turning the Dharma Wheel (Zhuan Falun)*,[25] first published in early 1995, as well as in his later writings, Li Hongzhi clearly spells out his rejection of key points of *qigong* discourse, which he replaces with a more clearly millenarian structure. Extraordinary Powers are relegated to lower forms of *qigong*, the object of Falungong practice being one's 'spiritual nature' (*xinxing*) and salvation from the demonic world of 'ordinary people'. The vision of a radiant future of *qigong* supermen is replaced by a dark

[21] Li Hongzhi, Changchun: 1–2.
[22] Li Hongzhi, Changchun: 2.
[23] According to Li Hongzhi, this is purely coincidental; the change was merely to correct an error in his birth registration (Li Hongzhi 1999e). The fact that he changed his birthday registration during the period when he began to claim Falungong as a higher universal Dharma may be significant, or may also be a coincidence. In support of Li's claim, the fact that Li Hongzhi's 'corrected' birthday corresponds with that of Sakyamuni has never, to my knowledge, been used in Falungong sources to elevate Li Hongzhi's status (see Porter 2003: 73). On the iconography of Li Hongzhi as Buddha, see Penny 2002a: 2–5.
[24] Quoted in Schechter 2000: 66.
[25] ZFL.

vision of apocalypse. The ideal of a transcendent renewal of science and tradition remains, but associated with a paranoid fundamentalism: the religions and traditions of the past are, in the present 'period of the end of the Dharma', possessed by demons, and modern science is an extra-terrestrial plot: both should be avoided and the practitioner should be devoted exclusively to the much higher Dharma of Falungong. All other spiritual, philosophical and religious or books are forbidden. In Falungong, body and meditation exercises are vehicles for the transmission of doctrine: 'learning the Great Dharma and reading the Book must be taken as an obligatory daily training.'[26] *Zhuan Falun* is not a technical or theoretical work like most of the popular *qigong* literature: it is sacred scripture; as one adept told me, the 'Bible' of Falungong. A series of other sacred writings would follow, elaborating a doctrine and cosmology that went much further than anything ever published by other *qigong* masters.

LI HONGZHI'S DOCTRINE[27]

Four main themes dominate the master's early writings:[28] (1) an *apocalyptic theme*, stressing the moral decadence of humanity and the omnipresence of the forces of evil. Extra-terrestrials are infiltrating themselves in the body of humanity through modern science, the great enemy of virtue; the Buddhist prophecy of the imminent destruction of the world and inauguration of a new universal cycle is close to being fulfilled. (2) An exhortation to *rigorous spiritual discipline*, calling on followers to purify their hearts of all attachment to the things of this world. The gods have abandoned the orthodox religions of the past, which have already lost completely the spirit of the true Dharma. (3) A *messianic theme*: Li Hongzhi is the omniscient and omnipotent saviour of the entire universe. He has revealed, for the first time in history, the fundamental Law of the universe, which is the only protection against the apocalypse. (4) A

---

26 Li Hongzhi 1996a: 31.

27 This section is a revised version of Palmer 2001b.

28 The analysis that follows is based on the works of Li Hongzhi that circulated in China prior to the 1999 Falungong repression. The quotations given are my own translations from the Chinese original. After 1999 there appear to be some changes in the focus, and in some cases in the content, of Li Hongzhi's teachings. The evolution of Falungong doctrine awaits further research.

sectarian practice: Li Hongzhi's adepts must concentrate exclusively on Falungong; it is forbidden to read or even think about any other religion, philosophy or school of thought or of *qigong*. They must devote themselves heart and soul to Falungong's psycho-physiological discipline; the perceptions and visions triggered by this practice are attributed to Li Hongzhi's supernatural power.

This doctrine is elaborated in the writings of Li Hongzhi, which are considered by adepts as sacred writings (*jing*), and the reading of which constitute an essential component of daily practice. The writings are for the most part comprised of edited transcriptions of Li Hongzhi's sermons given at 'Dharma assemblies' (*fahui*) held during tours around China in 1994 and in Western countries beginning in 1996, and of the Master's answers to disciples' questions during these assemblies. The first of these works, *Zhuan Falun* (Turning the Dharma-Wheel), is considered by many adepts to contain the Law of the universe in its entirety, and in relation to which the other writings only bring clarifications and explanations.

THE APOCALYPTIC THEME

Li Hongzhi, like the sectarian masters of China's past, proclaims that we have now reached the 'age of the end of the Dharma' prophesied by Sakyamuni Buddha—a period which would be marked by unprecedented moral degeneration. 'At present, the universe is undergoing momentous transformation. Each time this transformation occurs, all life in the universe finds itself in a state of extinction … all characteristics and matter which existed in the universe explode, and most are exterminated …. A new universe is then created by the Great Awakened Ones of an extremely high level ….'[29] These extinctions are a cyclical phenomenon which occurs each time civilisation's scientific development outstrips its moral attainment. Hundreds of thousands and even millions of years ago civilisations existed which had reached extremely high levels of material, technological and artistic progress. These civilisations built the moon and the pyramids, which had nothing to do with Egypt. But they had abandoned their morals, and so the Awakened Ones exterminated them.[30] 'In fact, these prehistoric civilisations sunk to the bottom of the sea. Later many changes occurred on Earth and

29   Li Hongzhi, ZFL: 165.
30   Li Hongzhi, Sydney: 23.

(the pyramids) rose back to the surface.'[31] During the apocalypse all science and technology disappears, and the handful of survivors has to start again at the Stone Age.[32] Earth has already undergone eighty-one such mass exterminations.

A small number of living beings, including humans and others, are nonetheless saved from the apocalypse and sent to other planets. These extra-terrestrials now want to return to Earth.[33] Their weapon is modern science, which they use as a tool to infiltrate themselves in the minds of humans. 'I tell you, the development of present-day society is entirely produced and controlled by aliens.'[34] Science is actually a religion with its own clergy of bachelors, masters, doctors, research fellows and professors. But contrary to the divinely-transmitted religions, science is spread by aliens in order to control humans.[35] The aliens, in order to conduct experiments on humans, abduct them and use them as pets on their planet. They have discovered that humans have a perfect body, and want to take possession of it. By using science to infiltrate themselves in human bodies, they aim to substitute men with themselves. They inject their 'things' into human molecules and cells, turning them into slaves of computers and machines, until they can be replaced by the aliens. 'Why are computers developing so rapidly? Why is the human brain suddenly so active? This is the result of the manipulation of the human mind by extra-terrestrials. They have assigned a serial number to each human capable of using a computer.'[36]

Modern science is the greatest enemy of morality. 'As soon as we speak of morals and of the distinction between good and evil, such non-scientific subjects are seen as superstitions. But isn't that using the bludgeon of science to beat away at the essential dimension of man—human virtues?'[37] For science cannot confirm the existence of gods or of virtue; it is ignorant of the moral retribution of karmic causality.[38]

The tyranny of amoral science is symptomatic of the moral decline of contemporary society and of the end of the universal cycle.

31 ZFL II: 13–14.
32 ZFL II: 38–40.
33 Li Hongzhi, Europe: 70–1.
34 Li Hongzhi, North America: 4.
35 Li Hongzhi, Europe: 28.
36 Li Hongzhi, Europe: 70–1.
37 Li Hongzhi, Sydney: 21.
38 Li Hongzhi, Europe: 29.

In ancient China those who pursued a spiritual calling were admired by others. But today such persons are objects of derision. 'In mainland China the Cultural Revolution has eliminated people's so-called old ideas, forbidding them from believing in the sayings of Confucius. People no longer have self-mastery, they have no norms, and they no longer believe in religion. They no longer believe that they will be punished for their evil deeds.'[39] Since the opening-up and reform policy the economy has livened up, but negative things are also penetrating the country.[40] Although the older generation continues to cherish its values, ensuring the preservation of the social order, Chinese youth does not have the slightest inkling of morality.[41] 'Today, when people study Lei Feng,[42] they say that he was crazy. But in the 1950s and 1960s who would have said that he was crazy? The moral level of humanity is sliding deeper and deeper. People's sole ambition is personal profit; they hurt others for their own interest, they struggle and scheme against each other without an afterthought.'[43]

'Today', says Li Hongzhi, 'beauty is valued less than ugliness, goodness less than evil and a well-groomed appearance less than shabby attire.'[44] In the past singers were trained in the art of music; today any ugly and uncouth good-for-nothing can climb onto the stage, cry out at the top of his voice, and become an instant celebrity. Elegant halls are filled with the noise of 'disco' and 'rock'. In the past art sought after beauty; today it erupts with demonic tendencies—a consequence of the sexual promiscuity of artists. Prostitution, fashion and football riots are all signs of demonic power.[45] 'As for the toys sold in shops, in the past dolls were a pleasure to look at. Nowadays the uglier they are the better they sell. Skulls, monsters, there are even toys shaped like faeces: the more horrible they are the higher the sales!'[46] 'People recognise only money and not people. There is no feeling, human relationships have become

---

39　ZFL II: 123–4.
40　ZFL: 310.
41　Li Hongzhi, Explanations: 3.
42　A People's Liberation Army soldier in the 1960s, Lei Feng was elevated to the status of national hero and role-model by state propaganda for his self-sacrifice and devotion to serving the people.
43　ZFL: 13.
44　ZFL II: 126–7.
45　ZFL II: 126; Li Hongzhi, Explanations: 89–90.
46　ZFL II: 129.

commercialised.' People don't hesitate to offend the cosmic order for money: products, magazines and films promoting sexual license are to be seen everywhere; drugs are manufactured and sold; drug addicts don't hesitate to cheat and rob others to pay for their fix; things have reached the point where 'people practice intergenerational incest'; 'the abomination of homosexuality reflects the hideous psychological perversion and loss of wisdom of our era.' Underground criminal organisations have infiltrated all sectors of society; their leaders have become the idols of the youth, who scramble to be their followers.[47] If society continues to change this way, in what state can we expect to end up?[48]

'Men wear long hair and women cut theirs short: *yin* is asserting itself while *yang* is weakened, the roles of *yin* and *yang* have been inverted.'[49] For Li Hongzhi, women's liberation destabilises the cosmic balance. In the natural order woman should be *yin* and soft, while man should be *yang* and hard. In the past men knew how to love and protect their wives, and women knew how to take care of their husbands. But since women's liberation we see only divorce, conflicts and abandoned children.[50] Moreover, the world is saturated with the black karmic matter produced by the evil deeds of men. Even stones, bricks, plants, trees and animals are full of impure karmic matter—so much so that medicines can no longer cure diseases, and ever stranger new illnesses keep appearing.[51] The 'creditors' of our karmic debts are coming back to us with misfortune.[52]

Li Hongzhi describes a world full of demons and possessed bodies. Animals, anxious to escape the apocalypse, have begun spiritual cultivation. But, lacking human qualities, they can only progress to the level of demon, from which they try to possess human bodies.[53] These animal demons have already possessed the bodies of Taiwanese monks, Indian gurus, Japanese cult leaders and *qigong* masters and adepts.[54] Even the tablets on altars for ancestor worship are low-level demons.[55] Buddhist icons in temples are possessed by

---

47   ZFL II: 141–2.
48   ZFL II: 131.
49   ZFL II: 139.
50   Li Hongzhi, Explanations: 104–5.
51   ZFL: 257; ZFL II: 45–6.
52   ZFL: 195.
53   ZFL: 102.
54   ZFL II: 131–2, 138; Li Hongzhi, Explanations: 118, 218, 245; ZFL: 183–96, 250.
55   Li Hongzhi, Explanations: 238.

the evil spirits of foxes, snakes and yellow weasels. If you have an impure desire, for example to get rich, the statue will grant your wish, but only in exchange for possessing your body without you knowing it.[56] And so Li Hongzhi concludes: 'The Earth is the trash can of the universe ... the evil men of the universe fall downwards, until they reach its centre: Earth.'[57]

THE MESSIANIC THEME

Li Hongzhi is different from the thousands of *qigong* masters who were active in China in the 1980s and 1990s. According to his early hagiography, Li Hongzhi was initiated into the Great Buddhist Law at the age of four by the Master of Complete Enlightenment; by the age of eight he already possessed immense supernatural powers. During his adolescence he learned Taoist martial arts from the True Man of the Eight Extremes, as well as from as the Master of the True Way who planted esoteric teachings into his mind while he was sleeping. Later came a female Buddhist master, followed by a succession of over twenty masters, who made him undergo unimaginable trials.[58]

As his capacities increased, Li Hongzhi gained a deeper understanding of the state of humanity. 'Mankind should live in superb conditions, but his spiritual confusion leads him into a state in which the soul and body are gnawed away and tortured .... Conscious of his duty, [he] was determined to do everything he could to bring health back to the people and to build a paradise for noble souls. To this end, he decided to create a method of the Great Dharma which could be practised by common people, based on his own Great Dharma which had been transmitted to him alone, and which he had been practising secretly for many years.' All of his masters aided him in this task, so that 'Falungong assimilated not only the distinctive qualities of Li Hongzhi, or merely the best of one, two or several schools, but indeed it integrates all types of prodigious powers of the universe, that is to say its essence, which is now crystallised in Li Hongzhi alone.'[59]

56   ZFL II: 121–2.
57   ZFL II: 43–5.
58   Li Hongzhi 2000 [1994]. This account is no longer available on Falungong websites. See Penny 2003.
59   Li Hongzhi 2000 [1994].

'I only appear to be a man', says the Master.[60] 'The difference between me and you is that my brain is completely open, but not yours.'[61] Li Hongzhi has uncountable 'Dharma-bodies' (*fashen*) which accompany his disciples, protect them and heal them,[62] on the condition that they keep their hearts pure of any selfish desire to be cured.[63] The true disciple is indeed he who practises spiritual discipline with an absolutely pure and devoted heart. If he has the slightest personal desire, he is not a true disciple and Li Hongzhi will do nothing for him, even if he practises all the external forms of Falungong. The 'Dharma-bodies' of Li Hongzhi know all that goes through the minds of his followers.[64]

He has already exorcised the demons and impurities from the bodies of his true disciples, as well as an enormous quantity of their bad karma. But he has not eliminated all of it, in order that they may undergo the trials and suffering which must result from their karmic debts. These trials are necessary for spiritual progress.[65]

In a single training workshop Li Hongzhi claims to eliminate the illnesses of 80 to 90 per cent of the participants and to give them paranormal powers that a whole lifetime of spiritual practise would be unable to achieve.[66] Indeed Falungong allows one to surpass in a short period of time the level of spiritual accomplishment of cave hermits who have been practising spiritual refinement for centuries.[67] For it is not the adept who cultivates himself through his practise, but the Dharma-Wheel (Buddhist swastika) planted by Li Hongzhi in the lower abdomen of each follower, which refines him and increases his psychic powers. The swastika never stops turning and releasing powers, even while the adept is not practising the Falungong exercises.[68]

Li Hongzhi has appeared not only to save humanity, but to 'rectify' all forms of life and matter in the universe. '[I have already]

---

60 Li Hongzhi, North America: 45.
61 Li Hongzhi, Sydney: 20.
62 Li Hongzhi, Explanations: 61; ZFL: 111. On Li Hongzhi's Dharma-bodies, see Penny 2002a.
63 ZFL: 114–15.
64 ZFL: 148–9.
65 ZFL: 113, 131–2.
66 ZFL: 221.
67 Li Hongzhi, Explanations: 110.
68 ZFL: 270. On Li Hongzhi's purification of practitioners' bodies, see Penny 2002a: 6–9.

essentially rectified the universe. All that remains is humanity, that most superficial layer of matter, but this is also on the verge of being accomplished. My *gong* is entirely capable of stopping this material layer from breaking up, exploding or whatever, entirely capable of stopping it (applause). Thus these phenomena which were prophesied in history will simply not occur.'[69] Before Li Hongzhi accomplished his mission the universe had no future. Indeed, after speaking in 1994 of the imminent explosion of the universe, he declared in 1997 that he had already prevented its destruction.[70]

Li Hongzhi's *gong* is transmitted through his 'omnipotent'[71] book, *Zhuan Falun*, every single word of which contains a multitude of Buddhas, Taos, Gods and Dharma-bodies which bring enlightenment to the reader. Each time the adept reads the book, his level of understanding rises to a superior level, and he discovers truths that he had missed the previous time[72]—insights which yet are only a small fraction of the Master's wisdom.[73] The book explains mysteries never before revealed to humanity.[74] '*Zhuan Falun* has shaken strongly the world scientific community!'[75] The highest gods say: 'you have given men a ladder to heaven—*Zhuan Falun*.'[76]

Zhuan Falun explains the Great Law of the universe, which Li Hongzhi reveals to humanity for the first time in the history of our civilisation (it was, however, transmitted on a large scale in a previous universal cycle, hundreds of millions of years ago).[77] This Dharma goes beyond anything that any religion or philosophy has ever taught. All religious teachings and forms of spiritual practice of the past are but low-level forms of this Great Dharma.[78] The teachings of Laozi and Sakyamuni, founders of Taoism and Buddhism, apply only to the Milky Way, while Falungong applies to the whole universe.[79] 'The doctrines of the Buddhist religion cover only the

69   Li Hongzhi, North America: 46.
70   Li Hongzhi, North America: 94.
71   Li Hongzhi, North America: 122.
72   Li Hongzhi, Sydney: 10.
73   Li Hongzhi, Explanations: 106.
74   Li Hongzhi, Sydney: 4.
75   Li Hongzhi, Europe: 18–19.
76   Li Hongzhi, Europe: 16.
77   ZFL: 33.
78   Li Hongzhi, North America: 7.
79   ZFL: 35.

tiniest part of the Buddhist Dharma.'[80] As for Christianity, to compare it with Falungong would be like comparing a ramshackle hut with a magnificent palace.[81]

Orthodox religions, i.e. Taoism and Buddhism (for Li Hongzhi, Christianity is a form of Buddhism[82]), have long been in decline and today practise only external forms. They are now incapable of bringing salvation to humanity. Buddhas and gods no longer pay attention to these religions;[83] rather, they are now studying Falungong by the myriads.[84] For Buddhas and gods only recognise people's hearts and not external religious forms.[85] This is why religious devotees' prayers are never answered nowadays.[86] Li Hongzhi thus rejects most ritualised forms: to become his disciple, it is not necessary to kowtow before the master, one should merely have a pure heart.

'Presently I am the only one in the whole world who is teaching the orthodox Dharma (*zhengfa*). What I am doing has never been done before. I have opened a great gate in this period of the end of the Dharma. In fact this doesn't happen once in a thousand or even ten thousand years ....'[87] To become a Falungong disciple is an opportunity one should not pass by: Li Hongzhi will stop his teaching in the near future. 'I say, time is running out ... I am not only saving humans. When you will have reached enlightenment, I will have other things to do, I won't be able to teach you anymore. I will not be transmitting the Dharma among humans for long .... There will be a day when spiritual practice will come to an end. Everything will stop in a flash, then it won't be easy to practise spiritual discipline ....'[88] At that moment all traces of Falungong will disappear. The ink will vanish from Li Hongzhi's books, which will turn into mere blank pages.[89]

---

80 ZFL II: 146.
81 Li Hongzhi, Europe: 57.
82 ZFL: 159.
83 Li Hongzhi, Europe: 31.
84 Li Hongzhi, Explanations: 37.
85 Li Hongzhi, North America: 59.
86 Li Hongzhi, Sydney: 17.
87 ZFL: 90.
88 Li Hongzhi, North America: 92.
89 Li Hongzhi, North America: 131.

SPIRITUAL TRAINING

'He who wishes to heal his illnesses, cast off misfortune, and eliminate bad karma must practise spiritual discipline (*xiulian*), and return to his authentic root', to his benevolent human nature. '... Such is the true purpose of being human', says Li Hongzhi. 'What should we do? We must purify the body [of the disciple], and make him capable of exercising himself until he reaches a higher level. He must purify his mind of all evil ideas, of the karmic field around his body, and of the factors harming bodily health.'[90]

In this process of purification through spiritual discipline the substance of the body, down to its tiniest particles, is gradually replaced by an energetic matter one hundred million times denser than a molecule of water.[91] But in order to achieve this, one must look inwards, purify one's heart, abandon one's desires, passions and sentiments, cultivate the virtues of patience, understanding and detachment, and conform to the fundamental qualities of the universe which are Truth, Benevolence and Forbearance (*zhen shan ren*).[92]

Virtue or Merit (*de*), according to Li Hongzhi, is a form of white matter which enters our body each time we do a good deed or are victimised by others. Bad karma, on the other hand, is a kind of black matter which penetrates us when we commit an evil deed. Thus if someone insults you, the aggressor's white matter will pass from his body into yours, while your black matter will be absorbed by his body. Therefore, even though you may appear humiliated, the real loser is the aggressor, because he took your black matter and gave you his white matter.[93]

There is a reason for all the ills that afflict society: people must repay the karmic debts they have contracted through their evil deeds in past lives. But at the same time our suffering propels us to seek a way out and to rise to a higher level. If life were pleasant and painless, would there be any reason to strive for anything better?[94] The misfortunes of life put our attachments to the test and give us an opportunity to increase our heart's purity. The transformation of black matter into white matter is an extremely painful process.[95]

90   ZFL: 4–5.
91   ZFL: 6, 66.
92   ZFL: 25–6.
93   ZFL: 28.
94   ZFL: 62.
95   ZFL: 129.

If one's spiritual discipline is successful, one may realise one's Buddha-nature, attain illumination, and enter paradise. If one fails, on the other hand, the merit accumulated by our efforts will only allow us rebirth as a rich or powerful person.[96] The essence of successful spiritual discipline is to recognise that all the benefits of one's discipline come from the master, not from oneself: 'practice comes from the disciple, while *gong* comes from the Master.'[97] Indeed spiritual discipline is a complex process by which the body is transformed in multiple spaces. 'Can you achieve that alone? No, you can't. These things are arranged by the Master ....'[98]

EXCLUSIVE PRACTICE

How does one become a Falungong disciple? One must keep a pure heart, and commit oneself to a path of mental and bodily discipline. This implies the regular study of *Zhuan Falun* which one should first read from cover to cover in a single shot,[99] then reread regularly,[100] and as often as possible.[101] Some practitioners go so far as to commit the entire book to memory. One must also practise five daily series of slow-motion gymnastic and meditation exercises. Falungong gymnastic forms are simpler and easier to learn than many other *qigong* methods, but they must be followed rigorously: even children must not be lax in practising the body postures exactly as prescribed by Li Hongzhi.[102] One must practise as much as possible, even five hours a day if one has the time, but always remembering to give the highest priority to studying Li Hongzhi's writings.[103] Falungong must be practised within society: although some disciples practise spiritual discipline to the exclusion of all other activity, Li Hongzhi does not encourage monasticism. One must undergo the trials of this degenerate world in order to progress along the path.

A cardinal rule of Falungong is that practice must be exclusive. Nobody is forced to practise Falungong, but having choosen to

96 Li Hongzhi, Explanations: 72.
97 ZFL: 29.
98 ZFL: 48.
99 Li Hongzhi, North America: 19.
100 ZFL II: 155.
101 Li Hongzhi, USA: 154.
102 Li Hongzhi, Explanations: 87.
103 Li Hongzhi, 1999d: 72.

follow Li Hongzhi's Law one must devote oneself to it exclusively. Li Hongzhi does not stop anybody from choosing another path, but 'today nobody else can, like me, truly raise [you] to a superior level.'[104] The notion of exclusive practice is common in meditation traditions, which emphasise concentration and the avoidance of mental dispersion. Following this logic, Falungong disciples must focus exclusively on Li Hongzhi's exercises and writings.[105] But this rule is carried to the extreme: even though he draws heavily on the concepts of various Buddhist, Taoist and Christian traditions, Li Hongzhi claims the mixing of traditions is the worst problem in this age of the end of the Dharma.[106] 'It is forbidden to mix even the slightest thought of another *qigong* method' with Falungong practice.[107] To think of another method could deform the rotating swastika planted by Li Hongzhi in the adept's lower abdomen, which could have dangerous consequences.[108] One should not read, or even glance at the books of other *qigong* masters, for they are filled with the spirits of snakes, foxes and weasels. 'A small thought appears in your brain: oh yes, this sentence makes sense. As soon as this thought lights up, the possessor demons [in the book] will emerge.'[109] Li Hongzhi even suggests burning such books, which prevent his Dharma-bodies from protecting his disciples.[110] Most *qigong* masters are swindlers, who are hundreds of times more numerous than authentic masters,[111] 'and you are unable to distinguish them.'[112] Likewise, it is 'absolutely forbidden'[113] to read religious and medical classics such as the *Taoist Canon*, the *Inner Book of the Yellow Emperor*, the *Book of Mountains and Seas*, the *Book of Changes* or Buddhist sutras.[114] 'What do you want to read these books for? They do not deal with practising the Great Dharma, what good is there in reading them? What can you get from them?'[115]

104   ZFL: 40.
105   ZFL: 88–9.
106   ZFL II: 56.
107   ZFL: 90.
108   ZFL: 108.
109   ZFL: 150; Li Hongzhi, Explanations: 279.
110   ZFL: 215.
111   Li Hongzhi, Explanations: 204.
112   ZFL: 107.
113   Li Hongzhi, Explanations: 125.
114   ZFL: 217.
115   Li Hongzhi, Explanations: 82, 139.

The practice of *Taijiquan* is also forbidden,[116] as are martial arts which include a practice of inner discipline.[117] Also forbidden are massage,[118] talismans sold in temples,[119] the recitation of incantations,[120] donating money for the construction of temples,[121] ancestor worship,[122] and even raising pets, for these could become demons after coming into contact with the spiritual energies of the adept.[123] On the other hand, Li Hongzhi discourages, but does not oppose, some disciples' practice of burning incense or making offerings of fruit before his portrait.[124]

Li Hongzhi's obsession with purity applies to human races as well. 'Mixing the races of the world is not allowed. Now that the races are mixed, this has created an extremely grave problem.' For each race has its own celestial world: the white race has its Heaven, which occupies a tiny part of the universe; the yellow race has its Buddha-world and Tao-world, which fill up almost the whole universe. Children born of mixed marriages are not linked to any celestial world, 'they have lost their root'.[125] Cosmic law forbids cultural and racial mixing—this is why, claims Li Hongzhi, Jesus did not allow his disciples to teach their faith in the Orient. It is also why East and West were originally separated by impassable deserts, a barrier which has been destroyed by modern technology. 'As a result of racial mixing ... the body and intelligence of the child are unhealthy .... Modern science knows well that each generation is inferior to the preceding one ....'[126]

The true disciple of Li Hongzhi must not take medicines in case of illness. Therapeutic care only changes the outward form of illness,[127] which actually grows out of a subtle body in a deep space which is untouched by treatment.[128] Illness is a means of repaying

116 Li Hongzhi, Explanations: 161.
117 Li Hongzhi, Explanations: 324.
118 Li Hongzhi, Explanations: 198.
119 Li Hongzhi, Explanations: 175.
120 Li Hongzhi, Explanations: 85.
121 Li Hongzhi, Explanations: 234.
122 Li Hongzhi, Explanations: 270.
123 Li Hongzhi, Explanations: 117–18.
124 Li Hongzhi, Explanations: 89; Li Hongzhi, North America: 115.
125 Li Hongzhi, Sydney: 110–11.
126 Li Hongzhi, Sydney: 112–13.
127 ZFL: 63.
128 ZFL: 251.

one's karmic debt: one must thus let it follow its natural course, unless Li Hongzhi intervenes personally to eradicate it. If common people may take medicines, the spiritual practitioner must abstain if he wishes to eliminate his bad karma.[129]

It is also forbidden to give therapy to others with Falungong. This rule sets Falungong apart from other *qigong* schools, which teach their adepts how to heal the sick by emitting *qi*. According to Li Hongzhi, the practitioner who treats others by *qigong* merely absorbs the morbid energies of the patient into his own body.[130] Thus the bodies of those who attempt to heal others are possessed.[131]

THE BREAK WITH QIGONG

Indeed, centred on the study of scripture, Falungong brings a radical change to the structure of *qigong* practice. Most Falungong followers began learning Falungong like any other *qigong* method, seeking health and healing. But in his writings Li Hongzhi insists that the goal of Falungong is not therapy but spiritual accomplishment (*yuanman*), to detach oneself from the world of ordinary people and to rise in the mystical hierarchy of the *arhats*, bodhisattvas, Buddhas and gods. Illness, as a way to pay back karmic debts accumulated in past lives, should be allowed to run its course. Only illumination through the discipline of Falungong can erase karmic debts completely. Li Hongzhi shows strong contempt for those who remain attached to the desire to heal. To please the master and rise in the spiritual hierarchy, one must follow the Great Dharma of Falungong and forget one's personal problems. Thus Falungong moves from a discourse of illness and healing to a broader one of suffering and salvation. Li Hongzhi can then motivate followers to commit

---

[129] Li Hongzhi, USA, 1997: 17. This aspect of Falungong teachings has been the subject of much controversy. For a thorough discussion of Li Hongzhi's teachings on taking medicine, and how such teachings are put into practice by practitioners in North America, see Porter 2003: 155–77. Porter observes that practitioners have a range of attitudes, but in general initially tend to try to abstain from medical care, but if illness persists or becomes unbearable they do tend to resort to conventional treatments. He concludes that 'the accusation that Li Hongzhi forbids the use of medicine is untrue, but there does seem to be credible evidence that critics … are correct in stating that Falungong creates an environment that encourages practitioners not to use medical care' (p. 172).

[130] ZFL: 74.

[131] ZFL: 250.

themselves to a path that extends far beyond simple concerns of health and therapy: to attain salvation one has the duty to 'propagate the Dharma' (*hongfa*) and 'defend the Dharma' (*hufa*).

Li Hongzhi's doctrine breaks with *qigong*'s ideal of reconciliation. If *qigong* could be described in terms of optimism and fusion, Falungong's outlook is one of pessimism and separation. Here, let us briefly compare the ideological elements of *qigong* and Falungong.

Both have a millenarian structure and an ideal of universal bliss or salvation. But while *qigong* foresees a blissful future for humanity in this world, Li Hongzhi predicted the apocalyptic end of the universe and situated salvation in another dimension.

Both are rooted in body technologies. But where, for *qigong*, the path of accomplishment is based on paranormal powers, in Falungong, the way to salvation is opened by moral and spiritual discipline.

Both recognise the limits of traditional culture and of modern science. However, while *qigong* sought to trigger a revolution and a renaissance by fusing the two, and saw itself as the key to such a union, Falungong uses terms from both traditional religion and modern science but warns against the 'demons' and extra-terrestrials which lurk behind decadent religions and amoral science. It presents itself as a higher law which needs neither the former nor the latter. Where *qigong* is an eclectic brew into which anything can be thrown, Falungong stresses its transcendence and purity from all other forms of knowledge and tradition.

A few mutations—replacing Extraordinary Powers with 'spiritual nature', this-worldly utopia with other-worldly paradise, fusion with transcendence—produced an entirely new doctrine. We can thus begin to understand why so many *qigong* practitioners switched from *qigong* to Falungong after 1995. With so many quacks and swindlers posing as '*qigong* masters', practitioners didn't know who to believe in. Opponents of *qigong* were waging a harsh polemic in the press, and it had become difficult to answer back in the name of '*qigong* science'. *Qigong* schools and lineages had multiplied, but the subculture still lacked a satisfactory conceptual system that could give meaning to the practice, the phenomena and the abuses linked to *qigong*. At such a juncture Li Hongzhi's doctrine was not only able to give explanations, but also to lead *qigong* practitioners to a new level which transcended the old scientific and ethical problems of *qigong*: those of moral struggle and apocalyptic religiosity.

In Falungong, *qigong* exercises are but adjuncts to a clearly elaborated doctrine of salvation. Practitioners are reminded of their spiritual essence and led to a path to transcendence, in which one abandons selfish desires and attachments in order to 'return to one's original nature'. Stressing the moral corruption of contemporary society, Falungong advocates the rejection of common social norms based on money and competition, which should be substituted by a transcendent ideal of conformity to the universal attributes of 'Truth, Benevolence and Forbearance'. Its doctrine gives meaning to suffering, which it explains both as a karmic consequence of one's own sins, and as a necessary test on the path of spiritual progress. It places the current state of humankind within the cyclical phases of the origin, development and decadence of humanity during each cosmic era. Furthermore, it offers a clear and simple path of liberation from the sufferings of this world: a single master, a single book and a single practice.

9
FALUNGONG CHALLENGES THE CCP

In its relations with the *qigong* sector Falungong clearly became increasingly sectarian as it claimed to teach the only path to salvation and strongly warned its practitioners against association with other forms of *qigong* or even other religions. Falungong's ideological totalism had its counterpart in the organisation of its network, which centralised all authority in the person of Li Hongzhi. After breaking with *qigong*, Falungong would soon enter into a collision course with the CCP. This chapter will begin with an outline of the economy of authority in Falungong, then describe how, in the second half of the 1990s Falungong's increasingly militant attitude toward media and government agencies led to heightened tensions, culminating in the 1999 demonstrations and crackdown.

CENTRALISATION OF AUTHORITY

Zhonggong had based its organisation on the rationalised distribution of healing, profits, titles and organisational positions through a complex method administered by a bureaucratic enterprise. In contrast, Falungong relied on the simplicity of its method and the commitment of its followers to ensure its rapid propagation. Li Hongzhi followed the typical *qigong* transmission model for the dissemination of *gongfa*: a national network of local practice points, municipal and regional training stations and a national organisation affiliated until 1996 to the CQRS.[1] Similar to other denominations, the Falun Dafa Research Society, presided over by Li Hongzhi, included as its leading members retired political and military leaders, acting municipal officials and a philosophy professor at the Central Party School.[2]

---

[1] See Tong 2002a.
[2] Deng and Fang Shimin 2000.

Daily practice sessions were the principal vector for Falungong transmission. For example, at the Yulin stadium practice point in Chengdu practice sessions began at 7 pm and were divided into three hour-long segments: (1) practice of Falungong gymnastics; (2) practice of Falungong sitting meditation; (3) recitation of Li Hongzhi's writings. Other sessions were held in the mornings. Assistants also organised Li Hongzhi video screening sessions in their homes, as well as occasional 'experience-sharing assemblies' at which practitioners spoke in turn, witnessing to how Falungong had changed their lives.

The key links in the transmission chain were the practice point 'assistants', who connected the denomination network to the mass of practitioners. Whereas the role of typical denomination assistants was limited to organising and promoting practice point activities and teaching correct postures to the practitioners, Falungong assistants were given a sacred role:

Frankly, practice point coordinators are like monks or abbots of a temple. I am only making an analogy; no one has even promised you an official post. ... Leading a group of practitioners is an act of inestimable merit.[3]

In addition to correcting the new practitioners' wrong postures, the assistants also had to answer questions on *Dafa* doctrine: therefore, they had to study assiduously the master's writings, and listen to his tapes over and over again in order to have a better comprehension than the average practitioner:

The assistants ... must assume their responsibilities. It is not enough merely to lead the body movements. You must clearly understand the *Dafa*, and truly master it ... The new students must be guided. When they ask questions, you must answer with patience. All practice point assistants have this responsibility, to bring salvation to all beings. What is the salvation of all beings? The true salvation of all beings is to attain the *Fa* [Dharma].[4]

Assistants thus had to work for the universal salvation of beings by propagating Falungong. But their role was strictly limited to being transmitters of the master's law:

Recently, when followers propagate the *Dafa*, and attract people who are predisposed to receive the *Fa* and choose the way of cultivation, [many] say that they have saved these people. They say: today I saved so many

3   Li Hongzhi, Changchun: 1–2.
4   Li Hongzhi, Changchun: 1.

people, how many have you saved etc. Actually, it is the *Fa* which saves people, only the Master can do so.[5]

Li Hongzhi insists on this point: assistants must absolutely not see themselves as masters, or harbour the slightest illusion of personal authority: 'You may not represent the master.'[6] Following this logic, disciples are forbidden from giving lectures or talks on Falungong, but instead should meet in groups to read the master's writings or to listen to his audio casettes: 'it is not permissible to transmit the *Fa* like me in big auditoriums. None other than me is capable of speaking of the *Dafa*, of understanding the true meaning of *Fa* at my level.'[7]

Li Hongzhi's attitude was illustrated by the case of Jing Zhan-yi, a disciple who claimed to have observed the formation of new chemical compositions created by his 'primary consciousness' through Falungong practice, and applied for a patent for his new method of observation. In 1995 and 1996 he became a favourite example cited by Falungong followers to prove the scientific value of the *Dafa*.[8] But Li Hongzhi allowed Jing Zhanyi to give talks only to scientists who were not Falungong practitioners, in order to promote Falungong. Practitioners themselves were not to listen to such talks: according to the master, they were of 'no use' to them and could disturb the normal practice.[9]

Assistants, as mentioned earlier, were also barred from providing *qigong* therapy to heal practitioners—this could lead to their acquiring a certain personal influence or charisma.

If someone treats other people's illnesses or invites others to come to our practice point to be treated, this is a violation of *Dafa*. The problem is serious: no one has the right to do so. If such a thing happens, that person is not my disciple. If an assistant does such a thing, replace him right away. These two phenomena must be resolutely eliminated.[10]

Furthermore, assistants were strongly warned against collecting money during Falungong activities: organising workshops and charging registration fees like the master did was strictly forbidden:

5 Li Hongzhi, Essential Points: 38.
6 Li Hongzhi 1998c: 22.
7 Li Hongzhi 1996a: 32.
8 Deng and Fang Shimin 2000: 30.
9 Li Hongzhi, Essential Points: 45.
10 Li Hongzhi, Changchun: 6.

You will not organise fee-charging workshops like me. ... The first requirement is not to ask for money. If we gave you so much, it is not so that you could seek celebrity, but to save you, so that you would cultivate. If you collect fees, my dharma-bodies[11] will take away everything that you have, so that you will no longer belong to our Falun Dafa, and what you teach will not be our Falun Dafa.[12]

When an assistant asked him if it was permissible to reproduce photographs of the master and sell them to practitioners without making a profit, Li Hongzhi answered that the sale of materials, including photographs, will be centralised by the Falun Dafa Research Society.

The general training stations, the secondary training stations and the practice points do not have permission to use money. All these things are controlled by the Falun Dafa Cultivation Research Society, which does nothing without my permission. Any personal action for whatever pretext is unacceptable, it is a violation of rights and forbidden by the laws of society.[13]

All revenues from the sale of books, tapes and Falungong paraphernalia thus went directly to Li Hongzhi. The denomination's branches and links had no financial resources. They were not to accept donations: if businessmen wanted to contribute funds, the practice point or training station was forbidden from accepting the donation, but was required to refer the donor to the Falun Dafa Research Society.[14]

Falungong thus maintained an absolute centralisation of thought, healing and money. These measures demonstrate a further rationalisation of *gongfa* organisation, which also exemplified Falungong's moral rigour, in a *qigong* milieu rife with swindlers and quacks. Li Hongzhi could thus prevent the emergence in his denomination of autonomous centres of power, whether through the vehicle of personal charisma or the accumulation of profits.[15] All forms of power were to flow directly to and from the master, whose author-

---

11   Li Hongzhi claimed to have myriads of Dharma-bodies (*fashen*) which could watch over, protect and give power to each individual practitioner, but could also, as in this example, remove that power.
12   ZFL: 165.
13   Li Hongzhi, Changchun: 24.
14   Li Hongzhi, Changchun: 57–8.
15   On the dispersion of charisma in practice-based movements, see Wallis 1979, discussed in Lu 2005: 181–2.

ity was strictly moral and ideological. Li Hongzhi often insisted on the 'formless' nature of the Falun Dafa network, which does not manage money, does not distribute titles or administrative functions, has no buildings or offices, and whose disciples and assistants must remain in this world to practise cultivation. This centralisation increased the egalitarianism among practitioners, who directly related to the master through studying his books, doing his exercises, and deciding, as individuals and informal networks, how to put his teachings and suggestions into practice.

As we have seen, assistants were compared to monks—but were not to abandon ordinary social life; the master repeated that Falungong was not a religion, and that the external forms of religion were of no importance for cultivation. In spite of this, many followers had a tendency to incorporate popular religious practices into Falungong. This is a recurrent theme in published question-and-answer sessions with practitioners. In most cases, when the practitioner asks for Li's advice on a certain custom, such as reciting mantras or making offerings in temples, the master categorically forbids such practices.[16] In one instance a group of followers from Shandong proposed building a Falungong temple, and started fundraising to that end. Li Hongzhi, in a statement dated 3 March 1999, firmly rejected such an initiative.[17] On the other hand he did consider the possible future establishment of a Falungong monastic community:

You have all seen this photo of me wearing a monk's robe. It was taken for those who, in the future, will be disciples exclusively devoted to cultivation. But the fact that I transmit the Dharma in a Western suit is unprecedented in the history of the world. This has never happened before.[18]

Elsewhere he states, 'there will be disciples specialised in Falun Dafa cultivation in the future, but we have not yet reached such a stage.'[19]

Falungong practice, then, is based on the abnegation of self: one should not expect healing; one should not have the slightest ambition or seek influence or reputation, but humbly serve the Great Dharma. This radically religious dimension of Falungong would

16 See above, p. 236.
17 Li Hongzhi, Essential Points: 88.
18 Li Hongzhi, USA: 30.
19 Li Hongzhi, Changchun: 35.

later become the source of its strength in the face of repression. Compare with Zhonggong: as soon as Zhang Hongbao's organisation had difficulties in distributing material and social benefits, it was unable to motivate its followers, and its organisation withered in the second half of the 1990s, after the master's disappearance and the cooling down of '*qigong* fever'. Falungong, on the other hand, tends to make the disciple insensitive to such factors: when sick, he is paying his karmic debts; rejected by society, he is coming closer to enlightenment. What is seen in the world of 'ordinary people' as a physical or social failure is transformed by Falungong into a victory, and becomes a source of power against demonic forces.

INTERNAL DISSIDENCE AND ITS CONSEQUENCES

Some of Li Hongzhi's earliest disciples, who had been running the Changchun general training station since 1992, apparently did not accept Falungong's new orientation. After the launch of the *gongfa* the master had taught them to use *qigong* to heal illnesses and to offer Falungong workshops and lectures on their own. But since the end of 1994 such activities were strictly forbidden by Li Hongzhi. The Changchun group had acquired a certain influence among local practitioners and was planning to open a Falungong clinic. Li Hongzhi opposed the project, suspecting the group's desire to make money by commercialising Falungong. The individuals in question were criticised several times by Li Hongzhi, until they lost their enthusiasm and had their positions in the denomination revoked.[20]

Out of spite, the dissident faction wrote a long report against Li Hongzhi, which it sent to several central government ministries at the end of 1994.[21] The three-volume report contained several accusations against the master: Li Hongzhi had intentionally changed his birth date to make it coincide with Sakyamuni Buddha's; he had no Extraordinary Powers; he claimed the earth would explode; he had created a new religious sect; he had not paid income tax on fees collected from his workshops; he had kept for himself almost all the income from Falungong workshops; he was unable to cure illnesses; Falungong posters contained superstitious images; his mother claimed he had no special powers; and before 'coming out of the mountains' he had gone to workshops given by other masters.

20   YPFX: 1–2.
21   YPFX: 1–3.

On 2 February 1995 Falungong sent a document to the CQRS, giving a detailed rebuttal of each of the accusations, which was then forwarded to the ministries which had received the anti-Falungong report.[22] Although no action was taken against Falungong at the time, the accusatory report continued to circulate, and the anti-Falungong propaganda campaign of 1999 would recycle the accusations, almost point by point.

The evolution of the relationship between Li Hongzhi and the CQRS in 1995 and 1996 is not clear. According to a Falungong document, the CQRS, the State Sports Commission and the Ministry of Public Security, full of praise for Falungong, asked Li Hongzhi to formalise and reinforce his organisation in order to meet the administrative needs of such a large denomination. But Li Hongzhi rejected this suggestion: on the pretext that he had finished teaching Falungong, he reiterated his intention to withdraw Falungong's affiliation to the CQRS, and in March 1996 sent Ye Hao and Wang Zhiwen, two of his chief disciples, to negotiate with the state-sponsored association.[23]

Let us not forget that the *qigong* sector was the target of a hostile press polemic in 1995.[24] Although the number of Falungong practitioners continued to rise, the *qigong* sector as a whole was on the defensive. Therefore, we cannot exclude the hypothesis that Li Hongzhi's decision to leave the CQRS was motivated by the desire to jump ship. Furthermore, he did not accept the policy of the new director of the CQRS, Huang Jingbo, to collect all revenues of denominations and requiring them to establish a Party branch.[25]

Based on the document just cited, the CQRS officials tried to convince Li Hongzhi's representatives to change his mind on dis-

---

22 YPFX: 3–7. The rebuttal claims that the common birthday is a pure coincidence; that Li Hongzhi refuses to display his Extraordinary Powers as a matter of principle; that Li Hongzhi has never spoken of a future explosion of the world; that Falungong is a cultivation method and not a religion; that the state-sponsored *qigong* associations which had sponsored Li Hongzhi's workshops had taken care of the relevant taxes; that he had given great sums of money to charities; that he had demonstrated his healing abilities at the Oriental Health Expo in 1992 and 1993; that the auras on the master's portraits were true phenomena perceived by practitioners; that Li Hongzhi had secretly practised spiritual cultivation since his early childhood without his mother noticing; and that he had gone to other masters' workshops out of humility, in order to learn how to run a workshop.

23 YPFX: 7.

24 See chapter 6.

25 YPFX: 8.

affiliation. They were reported to have said that at the very time when *qigong* was the target of attacks and calumnies, Falungong, which was growing so rapidly, should rise to defend the *qigong* cause rather than withdraw from the association. Li Hongzhi's representatives replied that the master was now devoting himself exclusively to Buddhist studies and was no longer interested in the matters of this world.

On the other hand the same document claims that the Falungong representatives applied to register a new Falungong Cultivators' Research Society with the CQRS—an association that would represent practitioners, but not the master himself. The CQRS leaders reportedly did not support this initiative, and referred the applicants to the Ministry of Civil Affairs. Falungong sources state that the representatives also applied to the Minority Nationalities Affairs Commission of the National People's Congress to establish a 'non-religious Falungong academic mass association'.[26] This was rejected and they were referred to the China Buddhist Association, where they applied to form a 'non-religious' Buddhist cultural group. Here too they were unsuccessful, so they then applied to the United Front Department of the CCP Central Committee, which also rejected their application to establish a 'non-religious academic association'.[27] At the end of 1997 Falungong representatives officially reported to the Civil Administration and Public Security ministries that in the face of repeated refusals, they would no longer apply to register a formal association.[28] However, the Falun Dafa Research Society continued to issue notices and circulars to the training stations until the end of July 1999.[29]

The reasons for this application to form a new society, and its cool reception by the CQRS, are not clear; but they may well have been related to financial issues: an association of 'cultivators' that

---

26 According to Tong (2002a: 64 n.35), quoting a Falungong source, the decision to approach this Committee was based on personal connections with some of its leaders.

27 CME; Tong 2002a: 641; 'The Truth about whether Falungong has an Organization', *Chinese Law and Government*, 32(6): 62–8, p. 64. Translation of 'Youguan falungong shifou you zuzhi de zhenxiang', 31 July 1999, document posted on <www.chinesenewsnet.com, duowei xinwenwang>.

28 CME; Tong 2002a: 641.

29 This goes against Porter's contention that the society had disbanded after 1997 (Porter 2003: 182–4). Some of these notices can be consulted online at <http://faluncanada.net/fldfbb/> accessed 3 June 2005).

did not include the master would obviously, following Li Hongzhi's principles, not handle the funds from the sale of Falungong books and materials; and thus would not be able to disburse Falungong revenues to the CQRS. The new structure proposed by Li Hongzhi's representatives may have been an attempt to remove the master and his profit streams from CQRS control, while retaining the legitimacy of an officially registered 'cultivators' association.

FIRST MEASURES AGAINST FALUNGONG

On 8 June 1996 the *Beijing Daily* listed *Zhuan Falun* volume II as the no. 10 bestseller for April at the Beijing Wholesale Book Market.[30] But a few days later, on June 17, Falungong was criticised in the influential *Guangming Daily*, in an article that called *Zhuan Falun* a 'pseudo-scientific book propagating feudal superstitions'. The article's author ridiculed the book's contents and worried that the book was being published legally. He wrote that the history of humanity 'is the history of the struggle between science and superstition, between true science and pseudo-science', and that the case of *Zhuan Falun* showed that the struggle would be long and arduous. The article called on publishers to raise their level of scientific culture and social responsibility, and to refuse to publish the 'pseudo-scientific books of swindlers'.[31]

The *Guangming Daily* article triggered a wave of press criticisms. Some twenty major newspapers followed suit with articles criticising Falungong. The press campaign was then followed by a directive from the Central Propaganda Department on 24 July 1996, banning the publication of Falungong books.[32]

Thousands of Falungong followers wrote to the *Guangming Daily* and to the CQRS to complain against these measures, claiming that they violated Hu Yaobang's 1982 'Triple No' directive. Li Hongzhi encouraged such action in a sermon on 28 August, in which he blasted the practitioners and assistants who did nothing to respond

---

30 ZFL II; BR, 8 June 1996: 4.
31 GM, 17 June 1996: 4.
32 Chen Xingqiao 1998: 146. This directive was only respected for a short time. In 1996 and 1997 Li Hongzhi's books were published in Hong Kong, but from 1998 to 1999 mainland publishers, such as the Inner Mongolia Culture Press, the Guangxi Nationalities Press and the Qinghai People's Press, resumed the mass publication and distribution of Li Hongzhi's works.

to the attacks. He stressed that activism to defend Falungong is an essential aspect of *Dafa* cultivation, and declared that this turn of events against Falungong was a test, which would separate the false disciples from the true ones:

At present a large number of disciples have attained, or are on the point of attaining, enlightenment. When a man has attained enlightenment it is an extremely serious thing, there is nothing more glorious, more majestic in the universe. That being the case, during cultivation, strict requirements must be imposed on each practitioner, and to advance to a higher level they must fully meet these requirements. As a whole the *Dafa* disciples are up to the mark, but some people still have attachment in their hearts, who, in appearance, say that the *Dafa* is good, but actually don't cultivate. And especially in an environment in which ... everyone, from the highest ranks to the popular masses, says that it is good, even in the government they say it is good, but who is sincere? Who is merely following? Who has praise on their lips, but in reality is causing harm? So we change the trends of ordinary people's society, we make the winds turn, to see who will continue to say that *Dafa* is good, and who changes their attitude: suddenly, all has become clear as crystal.

From the *Guangming Daily* incident until now, each *Dafa* disciple has played a role: some have persisted in their cultivation; to defend the reputation of *Dafa* they have written to the higher authorities and do not tolerate this irresponsible article. But others, in this difficult conjuncture, didn't practise inner cultivation, but spread dissension, making things even more complicated. Others, fearing that their reputation or their personal interest would be affected, abandoned practice, and still others, indifferent to the peace of *Dafa*, spread baseless rumours, aggravating the factors destabilising *Dafa*. ...

Is this affair not a test for the spiritual nature of the *Dafa* disciples?[33]

The state-sponsored *qigong* associations of Changchun city and Jilin province defended Falungong against the criticism. But the CQRS, which, under Huang Jingbo, was in the midst of its 'rectification' campaign, joined the anti-Falungong attacks. On 12 September it issued a report on Falungong in which Li Hongzhi was accused of deifying himself, propagating superstitions, and spreading political calumnies. The report noted that Li Hongzhi had proclaimed several times that he was no longer teaching *qigong*, that his *gongfa* had cut its links with the CQRS, and therefore, that Li Hongzhi was no longer fulfilling his duties as Falungong's legal representative. If

---

33 Li Hongzhi, Essential Points: 50–1.

Falungong wanted to continue existing, the report said, it should submit a new application to the relevant authorities. The report suggested that a campaign to analyse and criticise Falungong be launched, to 'clean up the errors in the propagation of *qigong* and return to the original image of *qigong* science'.[34] On 28 November the CQRS informed the authorities of its decision to expel Falungong from its membership on the grounds that it had failed to attend the association's 'rectification' meetings, its activities violated CQRS regulations, and it refused to mend its ways.[35] To justify its decision, the association submitted the anti-Li Hongzhi report of the Changchun dissident faction. This decision to 'expel' Falungong retroactively, when Falungong had already severed its links with the CQRS, was obviously motivated by the CQRS's desire to protect itself against any allegations of association with Falungong, and to demonstrate its loyalty to the government at a time when *qigong's* legitimacy as a whole was being questioned.

At around the same time Li Hongzhi started spending most of his time abroad, giving lectures and workshops in the United States, Europe, Australia, Thailand, Singapore and Taiwan. In the autumn of 1996 he toured several American cities, many of which gave him the title of 'honorary citizen' (a title that municipal governments routinely confer on guests on request). He applied for investor immigrant status and definitively settled with his wife and daughter on Long Island, NY in 1998.[36]

FALUNGONG MILITANCY

From 1996 onwards, then, Falungong no longer had a legal existence in China, but the denomination continued to function and expand. Li Hongzhi directed the network from abroad, by telephone, fax and e-mail. Online bulletin boards became one of the preferred methods of communication between the master, the central *gongfa* headquarters in Beijing, the regional training stations and the local practice points.[37] A notice issued by the Falungong Foreign Liaison

34 Quoted in Chen Xingqiao 1998: 186.
35 Chen Xingqiao 1998: 186.
36 Kang Xiaoguang 2000: 81; Tong 2002a: 21.
37 See Porter 2003: 207–21 for an analysis of the use of the internet by Falungong. See also O'Leary 2001; Bell and Boas 2003. On general trends in Chinese religion on the internet, see Palmer 2004.

Group in June 1997 stressed that no unauthorised material on Li Hongzhi or Falungong should be posted on the internet, so as to avoid misrepresentation.[38] An official Falun Dafa Bulletin Board was established in Canada in 1998.[39] Indeed, Falungong cultivation no longer involved the mere repetitive practice of exercises and meditations, but now also involved the militant 'defence of the *Fa*' through letter-writing campaigns and demonstrations, which required a discreet, rapid and efficient communication network.

The network of practice site supervisors was activated to mobilise the practitioners to react against any criticism through public actions directed at media and government offices. The resistance, anchored in public displays of bodies in movement, was spectacular. Thousands of disciplined adepts appeared at strategic times and places, 'clarifying the facts' and demanding apologies, rectifications and the withdrawal of offending newspapers from circulation. Such had never been seen in Communist China: a network of millions of potential militants from all social strata and geographic areas, which did not hesitate to display its power on the public square and confront the media. On 24 May 1998 the Beijing Television Station aired a programme on Falungong which, in addition to showing followers practising the exercises and testifying to its health benefits, also contained an interview with physicist and Marxist ideologue He Zuoxiu,[40] who called the group an 'evil cult' that propagated dangerous and unscientific practices and ideas. Falungong responded vigorously to the attacks: five days later more than a thousand practitioners demonstrated in front of the television studio, until its director apologised, aired another report favourable to Falungong, and fired Li Bo, the journalist who had interviewed He Zuoxiu.[41]

Contrary to most other denominations, Falungong did not keep a low profile in the face of public criticism and police investigations.[42] Militancy became an integral part of spiritual cultivation:

---

[38]   Foreign Liaison Group of Falun Dafa Research Society, 'Falun Dafa's Transmission on Internet Notice', <http://faluncanada.net/fldfbb/gonggao970615. htm>, June 15 1997 (accessed 3 June 2005).

[39]   Falun Dafa Research Society, 'Notice on the Setting Up of "Falun Dafa Bulletin Board"', <http://faluncanada.net/fldfbb/setup.htm>, 8 August 1998 (accessed 3 June 2005).

[40]   See p. 134.

[41]   Vermander 2001: 12; Deng and Fang Shimin 2000: 92; CME.

[42]   One other case of militant defence was that of Shen Chang, a master who sued the *Beijing Workers' Daily* after it ridiculed his 'information tea', and who organised

disciples were told to display their allegiance to Falungong openly, even when it was the target of criticism or repressive measures:

There are also many new practitioners who practise in hiding at home, afraid of being discovered by others. Just think: what type of heart is that? ... Cultivation is a serious matter ... There are also [practitioners] who are officials, who are embarrassed to go out and cultivate. If they can't even overcome this little fear, what will they be able to accomplish?[43]

As with other denominations, Falungong practice points were made visible with posters and banners. But beyond such conventional promotional devices the public practice of Falungong aimed to display the *Fa*'s power of attraction. Practitioners often congregated to meditate or recite *Zhuan Falun* on noisy and crowded downtown sidewalks, or at the entrance of parks rather than inside them. Propagating Falungong was a 'duty' of the practitioner. 'You must talk about *Dafa* and spread it', said the master, even if such an obligation wasn't imposed.[44] Beyond proselytising the practitioner was also enjoined to engage himself in the defence of *Dafa*, which became an essential aspect of cultivation:

Q: 'In incidents like that of Beijing [the demonstration at the Beijing TV station in May 1998], what of those practitioners who persist in cultivating?'
A.: 'What do you mean, persist in cultivating? As if no one understood ... that you didn't join [the demonstration] because you were 'persisting in cultivating'! Isn't that what you mean? In your words, you are looking for an excuse for having lost that chance to attain spiritual accomplishment [*yuanman*], and you come and find me. I have already explained as clearly as can be. Each time there is an incident, a major incident like that one, it is the best stage for disciples to pass a test in order to attain accomplishment, it is their best chance. Among us, there are some who are capable of making that step, but there are some who, while they cultivate, just stay put. They have a chance to reach accomplishment, but they don't even move: whatever you do, you don't even deserve accomplishment. To stay at home to cultivate, and for what? ... Actually, you're only looking for an excuse.'[45]

---

a demonstration of 1,000 followers outside the court on the first day of the lawsuit in October 1996, leading the court to delay delivering its verdict (GR, 26 January 1996: 3; Yu Guangyuan 2002: 3; Sima Nan 2002: 8–9, 146–64).
43 Li Hongzhi, Essential Points: 76.
44 ZFL: 294; Li Hongzhi, North America: 72, 85.
45 Li Hongzhi 1998b: 19.

In keeping with such a spirit, Li Hongzhi dismissed the chief assistant of the Beijing Falungong General Training Station for having
stayed at home rather than taking part in a demonstration.[46] Attacks
on Falungong were described by Li Hongzhi as trials that would
test the sincerity of his followers.[47] Indeed salvation was not given
to all; while some would progress to enlightenment, others would
be cast aside:

People talk about the universal salvation of all beings, and Sakyamuni even
included animals. Sakyamuni spoke about the universal salvation of all
beings, he could save all beings and have compassion for all forms of life.
Why don't we do that today? Why do we have to select those who will be
saved? Why are there conditions to take part in our workshops? Because
things are not the same as before. There are extremely evil people, they
have to be purged.[48]

Practitioners were thus faced with a sacred choice: were they ready
to endure trials to advance to a higher level, or would they remain
at the level of the ordinary man?

Cultivation is the most important thing in the universe; thanks to it, man
can rise to the level of the Arhat, the Bodhisattvas, the Buddhas, the Taos
and the Gods. When a person full of karmic force wants to become a god,
is that not a serious matter? Shouldn't one have extremely strict requirements and measure oneself against high standards and correct thoughts?
If you continue to use the concepts of ordinary people to deal with this
problem, aren't you still ordinary people? Such a serious matter ... we tell
you to become a Buddha and you act like a human, you still want to use
human reasoning to measure these things, it's unacceptable, it's not serious,
you cannot practise like that![49]

Falungong thus systematically held peaceful demonstrations against
newspapers and government offices that 'attacked' Falungong and
'hurt the feelings' of its followers, claiming that they had violated
the 'Triple No' policy. Table 6 contains a partial list of demonstrations—many of which drew over 1,000 participants—held between
April 1998 and July 1999.

   In spite of such boldness—after all, Chinese media are, at least
in theory, mouthpieces of the CCP—the authorities were hesitant
to intervene. A large number of Communist Party members were

46 Deng and Fang Shimin 2000: 38.
47 Li Hongzhi, Explanations: 18.
48 Li Hongzhi, Changchun: 3.
49 Li Hongzhi, USA: 3.

Table 6   FALUNGONG DEMONSTRATIONS IN 1998–9

Date	City	Target
Apr. 1998	Jinan	*Jilu Evening News (Jilu wanbao)*
Apr. 1998	Guangzhou	*Southern Daily (Nanfang ribao)*
Apr. 1998	Kunming	*East Road Times (Donglu shibao)*
Apr. 1998	Chaoyang	Chaoyang People's Government and Party Committee
May 1998	Beijing	*Health (Jiankang bao)*
May 1998	Beijing	*China Youth (Zhongguo qingnian bao)*
May 1998	Beijing	Beijing Television
Jun. 1998	Jinan	*Masses' Daily (Dazhong ribao)*
Jul. 1998	Chengdu	*West China Metropolis (Huaxi dushi bao)*
Jul. 1998	Beijing	*Life Magazine (Shenghuo zazhi)*
Sep. 1998	Cangzhou (Hebei)	*Cangzhou Daily (Cangzhou ribao)*
Sep. 1998	Xiamen	*Xiamen Daily (Xiamen ribao)*
Oct. 1998	Chongqing	*Chongqing Daily (Chongqing ribao)*
Nov. 1998	Harbin	*Harbin Daily (Haerbin ribao)*
Dec. 1998	Qianjiang (Zhejiang)	*Qianjiang Evening News (Qianjiang wanbao)*
Dec. 1998	Shenyang	Liaoning Provincial Government and Provincial Party Committee
Jan. 1999	Shenyang	Shenyang Television (*Shenyang dianshitai*)
Mar. 1999	Changzhou (Jiangsu)	*Wujin Daily (Wujin ribao)*
Apr. 1999	Tianjin	Tianjin University; Tianjin City Government
Apr. 1999	Beijing	Zhongnanhai (CCP supreme leaders' compound)
Jul. 1999	Beijing	China Central Television

Sources NF, 30 July 1999: 2; HX, 23 July 1999: 3; Kang Xiaoguang 2000: 102, 103; Sima Nan 2002: 246; CME.

Falungong adepts or sympathisers; some leaders considered Falungong's daily gymnastics a harmless and economical way to keep the masses of Chinese seniors occupied. Others feared the true influence of Falungong and the risk of alienating Li Hongzhi's tens of millions of disciples.

The newspapers and government offices targeted by Falungong demonstrators typically agreed to Falungong demands and issued apologies. A former journalist at the *China Youth Daily* told me that the newspaper's editor-in-chief ordered the paper to publish apologies after consulting his superiors in the Central Propaganda Department. The fact that Falungong successfully pressured a major television station to have a sceptical journalist fired, clearly demonstrates the social influence it was seen to possess, as well its strong backing in the Propaganda Department—or, lacking such backing, the fear the department had of offending Li Hongzhi's followers.

THE FALUNGONG PRACTITIONERS

Indeed, despite the lack of legal status and increasing police harassment beginning in 1996, Li Hongzhi's movement continued to expand, and in spite of the official ban on publishing Falungong books, several government publishing houses were churning out Li Hongzhi's works by the millions. The Wuhan training station, as the national distribution centre for Falungong books and materials, 'distributed 510 containers of publications as container cargo, through vehicles or the postal system, to twenty-three provinces and cities from 1997 to 1999'.[50] Entrepreneurs began to sell pirated editions of Li Hongzhi's books, tapes, videos and portraits to the millions of practitioners willing to purchase copies for themselves and their friends. Key-chains with Li Hongzhi's portraits and Falungong swastikas were even produced and sold as lucky charms to non-practitioners. In an attempt to stop this phenomenon the Falun Dafa Research Society issued two notices in March and April 1998 condemning the use of such charms, ordering practitioners to stop purchasing these pirated books and products, and banning their production by practitioners, trainers and training stations. Those who persisted in such practices should be told to stay away from Falungong followers and not be recognised as disciples of the Dafa.[51]

50   Tong 2002a: 645–6.
51   Falun dafa yanjiuhui, 'Guanyu zhizuo luanjia fashu de gonggao [Notice on the production of phoney Dharma books], <http://faluncanada.net/fldfbb/notice_book.gif>, 28 March 1998 (accessed 3 June 2005); 'Jinzhi zhizuo gouxiao falunzhang yu dafa yinxiang ziliao de tongzhi (ben tongzhi yinfa gei dafa dizi zhouzhi)' [Notice banning the production and sale of Falun emblems and Dafa audiovisual materials (notice published for distribution to all Dafa disciples)], <http://faluncanada.net/fldfbb/tongzhi1c.html>, 1 April 1998 (accessed 3 June 2005).

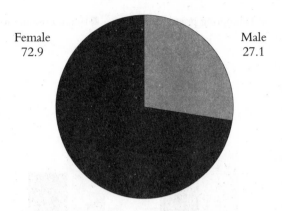

Female
72.9

Male
27.1

Fig. 6   Gender of Falungong Practitioners

Based on the combined results of five health surveys of practitioners conducted in 1998 by Falungong training stations in Guangdong, Beijing, Dalian and Wuhan; total number of respondents: 34 351.

Source   PureInsight.org 2002. For a compilation and analysis of all available surveys of Falungong practitioners in China and North America, see Porter 2003: 113–29.

In another notice the Society condemned the circulation of privately made tapes and transcriptions of Li Hongzhi's lectures, as well as poor quality reproductions of the master's portrait. Only portraits and images approved by the Society were to circulate, and all others were to be destroyed.[52]

On 13 April 1996 a new type of event was launched in Guangzhou: the 'Experience Sharing Assembly', where disciples of all ages and social classes took turns on the stage of a sports stadium to witness to how they had attained the Great *Fa* and how Falungong had changed their life. Falungong practice points multiplied and the number of practitioners grew exponentially. Falungong penetrated the army and the police. The Air Force was said to have 4,000 Falungong practitioners among its ranks, or 20 per cent of the whole contingent.[53] Growing numbers of scientists, university

52   Dafa xuehui, 'Guanyu yange qingli sizi liuchuan fei dafa ziliao de tongzhi' [Notice on the strict elimination of non-Dafa private materials in circulation], <http://faluncanada.net/fldfbb/note990331.htm>, 30 March 1999 (accessed 3 June 2005).

53   Murphy, David, 'Losing Battle: A showdown between Beijing and Falungong so far has no winners – least of all Liu Siying', *Far Eastern Economic Review*, 15 February 2001: 24–5, quoted in Vermander 2001: 9.

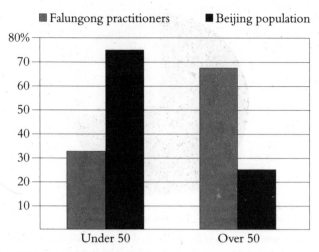

Fig. 7   Percentage of Falungong practitioners *vs* percentage of general population under and over 50 years of age in Beijing

Based on a survey of 12,731 practitioners conducted in Beijing in 1998.[1] The proportion of practitioners over fifty years of age (67%) is in inverse proportion to that in the general population (25% of Beijing residents).[2]

Sources
1   PureInsight.org 2002.
2   Beijing shi tongjiju 2000: 70.

professors and retired officials joined the ranks of Falungong, which became the largest denomination. While '*qigong* fever' had clearly run out of steam and the *qigong* sector was torn and weakened by the anti-pseudo-science and 'rectification' campaigns, Falungong recruited the mass of disoriented *qigong* practitioners.

According to Falungong sources based on surveys of practitioners made in various cities in 1998, almost three quarters of practitioners were women (see Fig. 6) and almost two thirds were over fifty years of age (see Fig. 7): proportions which correspond to my own observation of *qigong* practitioners in general, and which also correspond to overall patterns of traditional religious practice in China: older women are typically the most frequent temple worshippers, as well as the most attentive to health concerns. However, over one fifth (two fifths in Beijing) of practitioners were college graduates, a significantly higher proportion than the national average, and unlike the typical temple-going population.

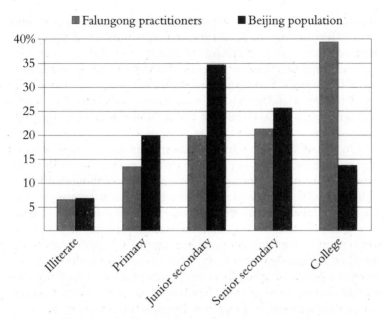

Fig. 8   Educational level: percentage of Falungong practitioners
vs percentage of general population in Beijing

Based on a survey of 584 Falungong practitioners conducted in Zizhu Park, Beijing in 1998.[1]
The proportion (39%) of college-educated practitioners (with a 2-year degree or higher) is
significantly higher than for the general population of Beijing.[2] However, these figures may
be distorted by the higher likeliness of college graduates responding to the survey.

Sources
1   PureInsight.org 2002.
2   Total population aged six and over of 12, 264 million. Guojia tongjiju 1998: 114.

In 1997 Li Hongzhi claimed to have 100 million followers, including 20 million regular practitioners.[54] Later Falungong sources
have repeatedly claimed that Falungong has 100 million followers.
If the gender breakdown given above is accurate, there would thus
be over 72 million female practitioners. Bearing in mind that Falungong was a primarily urban phenomenon, if we assume that 80
per cent of them lived in cities, the number of female urban practitioners would total 57.6 million: one third of all urban women.[55]
Then, taking into account the disproportionately high number of

54   Li Hongzhi, USA: 122.
55   Based on the total number of urban females in 1997: 181,246,100.

practitioners over fifty, we would have a figure of well over 100 per cent of urban women aged fifty or more. Similarly, if we assume that over 20 per cent of Falungong practitioners had a college edu-cation,[56] then two thirds of China's 31.3 million college graduates[57] would have been Falungong practitioners. Clearly, as anyone who lived in China and interacted with those categories of people at the time can attest, the claim of 100 million practitioners is grossly exaggerated.

On the other hand, Chinese government sources have claimed the number of Falungong followers was 2 million. To estimate the true number of practitioners is not easy; and compounded by the difficulty of defining a 'practitioner', given that Falungong has no formal membership and that individuals could join or leave prac-tice groups as they wished, or even practise privately at home.[58] In the vicinity of my residence in the city of Chengdu during the peak of Falungong's growth in 1998–9 there were three practice points: a group of around twenty practitioners in a working-class neighbourhood with perhaps 5,000 residents in the immediate sur-roundings; a group of about one hundred practitioners in a mid-dle-class neighbourhood of approximately 20,000 inhabitants; a group of roughly forty practitioners in a university campus with a student and staff population of approximately 30,000. If, to allow for irregular and at-home practitioners, we multiply these figures by five, we have a total of between 0.7 and 2.5 per cent of the local population practising Falungong. Finally, if we account for the cities, especially in the north-east, that apparently had higher numbers of practitioners (and other cities may have had fewer), and thus estimate that 0.7–5.0 per cent of the urban population was practising Falungong, and then add a much smaller proportion of rural residents, we may very roughly and tentatively estimate that the total number of practitioners was, at its peak, between 3 and 20 million. The higher of the two figures would suggest one seventh of China's college graduates and one third of urban women over fifty years old were practitioners. Again I feel that such estimates are still

56   The 39 per cent for Beijing may be higher than the national average: in a survey of 2005 Falungong practitioners in Wuhan, 22.7 per cent were college graduates. The breakdown of other educational levels was: illiterate, 1.7%; primary, 10%; junior secondary, 18%; senior secondary, 21%.
57   Guojia tongjiju 1998: 115.
58   See Porter 2003: 126–8 for a discussion of this issue.

too high based on my personal experience interacting extensively with college graduates in China during that period. Therefore, a mid-range estimate of 10 million would appear, to me, more reasonable—still a very high number, meaning that one out of every fourteen college graduates and one of every six women aged fifty or more practised Falungong.

Regardless of what the numbers really were, Falungong was a highly visible movement that did not fail to impress the broader society. Mass gatherings of practitioners in public places caused a sensation. In cities such as Leshan (Sichuan) and Wuhan thousands of followers in stadiums formed swastika figures and the Chinese characters for 'truth, goodness and compassion'—spectacular displays of collective unity that easily rivalled the mass choreographies of Party-sponsored rallies.[59] In October 1998 five thousand practitioners congregated at the entrance of the Guangzhou Memorial Park, causing shockwaves to pass through the city, demonstrating the movement's power.[60] All over China the same scene could be observed at dawn: hundreds of people in the parks and on the sidewalks, practising the slow-motion Falungong exercises to the rhythm of taped music, as yellow and red *Fa* banners hanging from trees presented the method and its principles. In the evenings practitioners would often meet in a disciple's home to read *Zhuan Falun*, discuss its teachings, and exchange cultivation experiences.

Other *qigong* masters and denominations were taken aback by Falungong's stunning growth. For instance, resisting Falungong was one of the main objectives of Zangmigong in 1998.[61] The Zangmigong association decided to organise visits to former practitioners who had fallen into the 'trap' of Falungong, and to try to convince them to quit the *Dafa* by explaining the *qigong* rectification campaign and the ban on Falungong books.[62]

---

59 For images of Falungong rallies in Wuhan, see <http://www.faluninfo.net/gallery/default.asp>; in Leshan, see <http://photo.minghui.org/photo/images/fahui/E_china_before1999_7_1.htm> (sites accessed 25 January 2005).
60 Deng and Fang Shimin 2000: 103.
61 See p. 204.
62 ZM 53: 2. The article talks of 'xx gong', but it is clear from the context that it refers to Falungong.

BUDDHIST OPPOSITION TO FALUNGONG

Buddhists were also concerned by Falungong's expansion. Starting in 1996 several Buddhist journals and magazines published articles deploring the fact that this 'heretical sect' (*xiejiao*)—the Buddhists were the first to use this label against Falungong—was turning Buddhists away from the orthodox religion.[63] The official China Buddhist Association held a meeting on 13 January 1998 to discuss how to react to Falungong.[64] Delegates wondered why so many lay Buddhists were turning to Falungong, which was expanding so much faster than Buddhism.[65] One suggestion put forward was that the China Buddhist Association approach the government to draw a clear line between Buddhism and Falungong, in order to stop Li Hongzhi's sect from harming the reputation and interests of Buddhism.[66] But at the same time the China Buddhist Association did not want to alienate Falungong believers by attacking it too harshly.[67]

In March 1998 China's main Buddhist journal, *Fayin*, which until then had refrained from criticising Falungong out of fear of offending the millions of Falungong disciples, published a piece denouncing Falungong as a heretical popular religion entirely foreign to Buddhism, which merely used Buddhist terms and symbols as an outer vestment.[68] The article began by claiming that Falungong was not a form of *qigong* and that its content was quasi-religious. The author then stressed that Li Hongzhi's doctrines were contrary to Buddhism, that Falungong denigrates the Buddhist clergy, and that Li Hongzhi was a 'demon's head who destroys Buddhism and extinguishes the Dharma':

Since the appearance of Falungong, many lay Buddhists who used to recite the name of Buddha for years no longer utter his name; people who had just begun studying Buddhism no longer read the sutras; in order to express their devotion to learning Falungong, they completely clear their homes of Buddhist icons, writings and amulets! Huge posters of Li Hongzhi take the place of the Buddhas, and Li Hongzhi's voice replaces the great six-character name *Namo Amitofo* ... Even worse, Falungong

---

63 Some of these articles are reprinted in Chen Xingqiao 1998.
64 Chen Xingqiao 1998: 5.
65 Chen Xingqiao 1998: 95–6.
66 Chen Xingqiao 1998: 150.
67 Chen Xingqiao 1998: 156.
68 *Fayin* 163 (March 1998): 21–8, reproduced in Chen Xingqiao 1998.

disciples wander in the four directions, seduce well-meaning hearts, and convince people to abandon Buddhism to study Falungong.[69]

The article continued by comparing Falungong to sectarian movements in Chinese popular religion, such as the White Lotus, Patriarch Luo, Yellow Heaven and Unity sects. For the author, Falungong was a 'heretical sect', 'dangerous for *qigong*, dangerous for religion, dangerous for the state and dangerous for society'.[70] Nonetheless, he recognised that some of Li Hongzhi's criticisms of Buddhism were fair, and that Buddhists should reflect on them.

In response, Falungong followers wrote to Li Ruihuan, Chairman of the People's Political Consultative Conference, asserting that the China Buddhist Association's open attacks on Falungong were threatening social stability, demanding that the culprits be held accountable, and that the issue be treated with the utmost seriousness.[71] There was at least one open confrontation with Buddhists: in March 1999 the abbot of the Ciyun monastery in Chongqing called on the police to expel Falungong practitioners who had unfurled banners at the temple's gate and refused to move.[72]

THE HESITATION OF GOVERNMENT AGENCIES

In May 1998 the Sports Commission, noting the growing influence of Falungong, sponsored an investigation into the effects of Falungong, led by a team of medical experts. However, the chief investigator, a professor at the Guangzhou No. 1 Army Medical College, was himself a disciple of Li Hongzhi.[73] More than 12,000 practitioners from Guangdong province were asked about their previous medical history and whether they felt better after practising Falungong. 97.9 per cent of the respondents claimed their health had improved after practising Falungong. The investigation report concluded that such health benefits represented average savings to the state of 1,700 yuan per person per year—a total of 12 million yuan.[74]

69 Chen Xingqiao 1998: 120–1.
70 Chen Xingqiao 1998: 144.
71 ET, 27 April 2005, <www.epochtimes.com/gb/5/4/27/n902043.htm> (accessed 19 May 2005).
72 Hua and Zhong 1999: 113.
73 Deng and Fang Shimin 2000.
74 LH: 2; CME.

The State Sports Commission thus decided that given the high number of Falungong practitioners and the purported health benefits, it would be wise not to attack Falungong directly. As a provincial sports official explained,

Given the large number of practitioners, we cannot use official power to restrict [Falungong]. Three separations must be made: separate the founder and his *gongfa*; separate the effects of the *gongfa* and the deviations of some people who practise it inappropriately; separate the mass of practitioners and the founder.[75]

The Sports Commission's attitude, then, was that despite the reservations one may have had about Li Hongzhi, the 'mass of practitioners' were to be respected, and the positive effects of Falungong were to be recognised. Followers who became ill or died after Falungong practice had only themselves to blame, since they were considered to have practised Falungong incorrectly.[76] An employee of the Martial Arts Research Institute, through which the Sports Commission oversaw the *qigong* sector, was quoted by an American newspaper as saying, 'today, no one dares criticise' Falungong.[77] The person in charge of the Falungong files in the institute was himself a follower of Li Hongzhi.[78]

The State Sports Commission thus maintained a relatively tolerant attitude towards Falungong. This kindled the hopes of Li Hongzhi's disciples to obtain official recognition of Falungong, but not as a *qigong* method. Falungong representatives approached the Sports Commission to that end. Li Hongzhi gave them the following directives:

1. Falungong is not a form of hygienic *qigong*, but a cultivation method that brings health and healing to practitioners as a side effect.

2. Falungong has no organisation, but follows the formless nature of the Great Tao: it has no money, material possessions, official titles or administrative positions. Followers are forbidden from registering with state-sponsored *qigong* associations and from participating in joint activities with hygienic *qigong* or 'fake' *qigong* groups.

75   ZM, 59: 2.
76   The opposite line has been used since the 1999 anti-Falungong crackdown: such cases are presented as proof of the dangerous and evil nature of Falungong.
77   Smith, Craig, 'Sects and Politics: Followed by Millions, Chinese Mystic Rattles Communist Leadership', *Wall Street Journal*, 26 April 1999, p. A1.
78   Ibid., p. A6.

3. The representatives could explain to the Sports Commission that Falungong had withdrawn from the CQRS in order to separate itself from other *qigong* groups, which were only interested in swindling people. Falungong also rejects the procedures for licensing *qigong* masters: one becomes a true master only after decades of cultivation, and not by presenting oneself to an evaluation committee. This procedure encourages selfish attachments, so Falungong would not associate with such people.[79]

Li Hongzhi encouraged Falungong's registration with the government as a single nationwide organisation. But regional Falungong branches were not to register with provincial governments, and Falungong was not to be registered as a *qigong* group or associated with *qigong*. Ultimately, however, Falungong's application to register with the Sports Commission was not approved.[80]

In January and July 1997 the Ministry of Public Security ordered two national investigations to verify accusations that Falungong was engaged in 'illegal religious activities'. The two investigations concluded that 'no problem has been discovered'.[81] A year later, on 21 July 1998, the ministry once again launched an investigation, this time declaring Falungong to be a 'heretical cult' (*xiejiao*), and ordering police stations to collect intelligence on the Falungong network and gather criminal proof against it.[82]

The fact that several investigations were launched in succession by the Public Security department may indicate that it was torn by an internal struggle between supporters and adversaries of Falungong. According to Falungong sources, a group of retired national officials led by Qiao Shi, former Chairman of the National People's Congress, investigated Falungong and reported to the Party's Central Committee's Political and Legislative Affairs Bureau that 'Falungong brings countless benefits to the nation and its people, and not a trace of harm'.[83] Certainly it is known that Li Hongzhi had cultivated excellent relations with the Ministry of Public Security since his arrival in Beijing in 1992. However, if repeated investigations were initiated, it may well have been because

79 Li Hongzhi, Essential Points: 83.
80 'The Truth about whether Falungong has an Organization', *Chinese Law and Government*, 32(6): 62–8, p. 66. Translation of 'Youguan falungong shifou you zuzhi de zhenxiang', 31 July 1999, document posted on <www.chinesenewsnet.com, duowei xinwenwang>.
81 YPFX: 9; CME.
82 LH: 4; CME.
83 CME.

other factions in the ministry, led notably by Luo Gan, were hostile to Falungong.

Following the directives of the July 1998 notice police detectives infiltrated Falungong practice groups, taking advantage of the *gongfa's* principle of openness to any person willing to practise the exercises. In some localities police stations detained practitioners, confiscated their Falungong literature and VCRs, fined them, and forbade them from practising the *gongfa*. In response, thousands of disciples wrote to the Public Security department and even to the central government to express their indignation at this police harassment.[84]

THE ZHONGNANHAI DEMONSTRATION

The network of anti-'pseudo-*qigong*' polemicists raised the alarm about Falungong in 1998 when He Zuoxiu and others issued a report on the sit-ins at media offices, entitled 'The furious Falungong'.[85] On 20 April 1999, at a meeting held to celebrate the May Fourth Movement, Yu Guangyuan warned that groups such as Falungong could attempt to create a disturbance to display their power. He implicitly criticised China's health, religious, educational, media and scientific institutions, and even the CCP itself, for allowing the spread of 'evil activities', and called on them to reflect on their 'grave responsibility' in the spread of 'evil power'.[86]

A week earlier an article by He Zuoxiu had appeared in an obscure student magazine of Tianjin Normal University in which he attacked Li Hongzhi and compared Falungong to the Boxer rebellion, which could bring ruin to the country. He criticised the recruitment of children in primary school playgrounds by Falungong practitioners, and claimed that the mental states provoked by Falungong meditation could cause psychiatric illness.[87] Within hours of the magazine's release more than a hundred messages were

84 LH: 5; Falungong Practitioners, 'A Ten-Thousand-Word Letter to the Party Centre', *Chinese Law and Government*, 32(6): 69–88, pp. 74–5. Translation of Falungong xiulianzhe, 'Zhi dang zhongyang wanyan shu', 27 July 1999, posted on <minghuiwang, http://minghui.ca> (accessed November 2003 at <http://pkg2.minghui.org/gb/shishi/0899/wanyanshu.html>).

85 Gong Yuzhi 2002: 3.

86 Speech reproduced in Yu Guangyuan 2002: 123–30. According to the author, the text was completed on 22 April 1999.

87 He Zuoxiu 1999.

posted about it on a Falungong online bulletin board service, discussing how to respond.[88] The article was seen as highly offensive by Falungong practitioners, who gathered to protest in meditation posture around the university administrative building. According to Falungong sources, the magazine editors initially agreed to publish a correction, but then suddenly changed their attitude and refused to do so.[89] The number of demonstrators grew day by day, as the magazine editor refused to comply with their demand to recall the magazine from circulation, to publish official apologies, and to ban any reproduction of the article by others.[90]

On 22 April at 5:10 pm Li Hongzhi arrived in Beijing on a flight from New York. By 23 April the number of protestors in Tianjin had grown to 6,000.[91] Three hundred riot police were dispatched to disperse the demonstration. Some Falungong followers were beaten, and forty-five were arrested. Hundreds then marched to the municipal government to demand their liberation.[92] But the government claimed the police action had been carried out on orders of the Ministry of Public Security: without further instructions from Beijing, the prisoners would not be freed.

The demonstrators thus decided to head for Beijing to demand justice, while Li Hongzhi flew from Beijing to Hong Kong. According to Kang Xiaoguang, a researcher in the Chinese intelligence agency, whose sources are not specified and cannot be verified, Li Hongzhi had been given a full report of the Tianjin developments upon his arrival in Beijing. According to this account, in the evening of 23 April Li Hongzhi and the key Falungong organisers in China—Li Chang and Ji Liewu—decided to move the demonstration to Beijing, stressing that the numbers would have to be higher than at the Beijing TV Station demonstration of 1998. On the morning of 24 April the following steps were taken to organise the demonstration: each practice station would designate a volunteer to ensure security, order and cleanliness; there would be no slogans, no banners, no tracts, no aggressive language and no mention of the Falun Dafa Research Society or of specific practice

88   Powers and Lee 2002: 265.
89   Longquan Muoke, 'Reflecting on the Historic April 25 Appeal', <www.clearwisdom.net/emh/articles/2005/5/4/60289p.html> (accessed 14 May 2005).
90   Hua and Zhong 1999: 86.
91   HX, 29 July 1999: 12.
92   Kang Xiaoguang 2000: 104.

stations; practitioners would be called on to demonstrate as a form of protection and propagation of the *Fa* on the path to consummation, but participation would be a personal and voluntary choice. Li Hongzhi then flew to Hong Kong at 1:30 pm on 24 April.[93] Statements by Li Hongzhi confirm that he was in Beijing, but he claimed, 'I was changing flights at Beijing on my way to Australia at the time, and I left Beijing without knowing anything about what was going on there.'[94] This statement, posted as a 'scripture' on Falungong websites at the time, was removed sometime in 2004.

By dawn of 25 April the demonstrators' numbers had grown to 10,000, as busloads of Falungong followers from neighbouring cities and provinces converged on the Letters and Petitions Office, located next to Zhongnanhai, the closed compound of the country's leaders, itself a stone's throw from Tiananmen. The demonstrators waited patiently outside the compound, forming three or four rows on the sidewalk. Some stood, others sat down, some read. The crowd remained silent, there were no shouts or slogans.

In China anyone theoretically has the right to appeal to the higher authorities to seek justice. According to Falungong representatives, each protestor thus came as an individual, representing only him or herself, to complain of the 'hurt feelings' and other damages caused by criticism of Falungong and restrictions on fellow Falungong practitioners.[95] According to Kang Xiaoguang, the demonstrators had a variety of motives: there were true believers animated by a spirit of sacrifice and martyrdom, who clearly knew the consequences of their actions; there were naive and goodhearted people without political experience who believed that the Chinese government had nothing against Falungong but that some officials were prejudiced against it, so that it would suffice to 'clarify the facts' to them and they would mend their errors; there were followers who thought Li Hongzhi had sent his *gong* to Zhongnanhai and wanted to absorb it; and there were those who saw this as the last chance for spiritual consummation.[96]

Throughout the day negotiations took place between the Petitions Office and representatives of the protesters. Accounts differ as

---

93　Kang Xiaoguang 2000: 115–16.
94　Li Hongzhi 1999e: 27.
95　See LH: 7.
96　Kang Xiaoguang 2000: 156. Kang's sources are not stated but he seems to rely on internal intelligence reports of the Public Security Department.

to what was involved in these negotiations. According to several Falungong sources, Premier Zhu Rongji emerged from Zhongnanhai sometime between 8:30 and 10:00 am to enquire of the purpose of the stand-in, and assured the protesters that he had already approved of their demands. Zhu assigned the Deputy Director of the Petitions Office to handle the matter. According to Kang Xiaoguang, the Petitions Office met with several groups of protesters, who were unable to give a clear explanation, until Li Chang and Wang Zhiwen, leaders of the Falungong Research Society—who had not taken part in the demonstration—were contacted and came to the guardhouse to negotiate and present their demands:

1. Release the Falungong practitioners detained in Tianjin;

2. Provide a fair and legal environment for Falungong cultivation;

3. Legalise the publication of Falungong books.[97]

The talks lasted all day until, in the evening, the Falungong representatives emerged, telling the demonstrators that the authorities had promised that the State Council would handle the requests, that they could appeal at local complaints offices, and that the prisoners in Tianjin would be released;[98] so they could now go home. According to Kang Xiaoguang's version, Li Chang had been unable to meet with any CCP leaders, which made Li Hongzhi—who was in constant telephone contact with Li Chang from Hong Kong—furious that the demonstration had not continued until the following day. The next day Li Chang and the other Falungong organisers regretted having allowed the demonstration to disperse without accomplishing anything. Ji Liewu then flew to Hong Kong to report to Li Hongzhi, who then took a Cathay Pacific flight to Sydney.[99] According to Falungong sources, the next day an official from the Petitions Office told a *Xinhua* journalist that he had assured the Falungong representatives not to believe in rumours of an imminent suppression of Falungong, stressing that *qigong* had never been banned by any government department and that dif-

---

97 LH: 7; Kang Xiaoguang 2000: 118–20; CME; Longquan Muoke, 'Reflecting on the Historic April 25 Appeal', <www.clearwisdom.net/emh/articles/2005/5/4/60289p.html> (accessed on 14 May 2005).
98 CME; Longquan Muoke, 'Reflecting on the Historic April 25 Appeal', <www.clearwisdom.net/emh/articles/2005/5/4/60289p.html> (accessed 14 May 2005).
99 Kang Xiaoguang 2000: 120–2.

ferent opinions and perspectives on *qigong* were permitted. These assurances encouraged Li Hongzhi's disciples, who believed they would be allowed to practise Falungong freely.[100]

The international media have reported that the Zhongnanhai demonstration caught the Chinese authorities completely by surprise. On the other hand, according to rumours reported in the overseas Chinese press,[101] and later elaborated by Falungong sources, especially from 2005, the demonstrators had had no intention of surrounding Zhongnanhai but merely followed police who led them there, in a deliberate plot hatched by Luo Gan of the Ministry of Public Security.[102] In a conspiracy theory propagated on Falungong websites since 2005 the entire incident, from the Tianjin demonstration to Beijing, was a plot or a trap, cooked up by the Ministry of Public Security under the direct instructions of Luo Gan and Jiang Zemin: He Zuoxiu's deliberately provocative article, the unusually uncompromising attitude of the Tianjin college magazine editors and the violence of the Tianjin police were all deliberately calculated to increase tensions; the demonstrators were then allegedly advised to go to Beijing by the Tianjin police itself; no attempt was made to stop them from converging on Beijing; the police did not act against the protesters and allegedly even led them to line up around Zhongnanhai; Zhu Rongji's approval of their demands was 'blocked' by hostile figures in high positions—all of this could only be a plot to instigate a showdown and justify a final crackdown on Falungong.[103] However, this version does not match with earlier Falungong sources.[104] Earlier Falungong statements from the period following the demonstration clearly indicate that the protestors went to Zhongnanhai, without making a distinction between the Petitions Office and Zhongnanhai, and do not claim that they had no intention to protest there. A notice published by the Falun Dafa online bulletin board on 2 June states that the demonstrators 'were fully aware that there could be danger and they could be subjected to attack and per-

100 LH: 7; Hua and Zhong 1999: 128.
101 *World Journal*, American edition, 20 June 1999, quoted in Ching 2001.
102 ET, 25 April 2005, <www.epochtimes.com/gb/4/4/25/n520034.htm> (accessed 19 May 2005).
103 ET, 25 April 2005, <www.epochtimes.com/gb/4/4/25/n520034.htm> (accessed 19 May 2005).
104 See ET, <www.dajiyuan.com/bg/4/12/15/n467333.htm> (accessed 19 May 2005).

secution. Some people even had their wills written before going to Zhongnanhai to express peacefully their opinions.'[105] Another statement issued three days later explains, 'as a last resort, 10,000 Falun Dafa practitioners gathered peacefully at Zhongnanhai to present facts to the Chinese leaders ... the presenting of facts to the government was settled in peace and with mutual understanding.'[106] In an open letter to Jiang Zemin and Zhu Rongji published in August 1999, Falungong practitioners state that 'disciples went to Zhongnanhai' and go on to justify their reasons.[107] In another Falungong account the subsequent crackdown is explained by Jiang Zemin's jealousy after Zhu Rongji had so successfully handled the incident, resolving it through peaceful dialogue and earning international praise for the Chinese authorities.[108] Furthermore, the fact that Li Hongzhi flew to China in the days immediately preceding the demonstration suggests that he knew what was happening, in spite of his subsequent denials. All of these facts and statements lead me to conclude that the Zhongnanhai demonstration was not an unintentional act on the part of Falungong. However, the prevalence of Byzantine machinations between leaders and factions in the CCP and the Chinese government, and the fact that it is highly implausible for Chinese intelligence services to have been taken by surprise, especially after the Tianjin incident only a few days earlier, makes it likely that inside knowledge of the demonstration plan had indeed been acquired. But by whom and for what purposes? If it can be claimed that Luo Gan of the Ministry of Public Security, an inveterate enemy of Falungong, was aware of the demonstration and may have had a hand in how it proceeded, it can just as easily be argued that Falungong's supporters within the highest levels of the CCP were also informed and involved.

105 'Falun Dafa gonggaolan bianjibu tongzhi' [Notice by the Falun Dafa Bulletin Board Editorial Office], <http://faluncanada.net/fldfbb/notice990603.doc>, 2 June 1999 (accessed 3 June 2005).
106 'Falun Dafa gonggaolan pinglun' [Commentary on the Falun Dafa Bulletin Board], <http://faluncanada.net/fldfbb/comments990605.doc>, 5 June 1999 (accessed 3 June 2005).
107 Falungong Practitioners, 'A Ten-Thousand-Word Letter to the Party Centre', *Chinese Law and Government*, 32(6): 69–88, pp. 75, 77. Translation of Falungong xiulianzhe, 'Zhi dang zhongyang wanyan shu', 27 July 1999, posted on <minghuiwang, http://minghui.ca> (accessed November 2003 at <http://pkg2.minghui.org/gb/shishi/0899/wanyanshu.html>).
108 Longquan Muoke, 'Reflecting on the Historic April 25 Appeal', <www.clearwisdom.net/emh/articles/2005/5/4/60289p.html> (accessed 14 May 2005).

THE CRACKDOWN

Immediately after the Zhongnanhai incident CCP Chairman Jiang Zemin reportedly wrote a letter to the leaders of the Party declaring, 'If the CCP cannot defeat Falungong, it will be the biggest joke on Earth.'[109] This letter gave the green light to repressive measures. A day later the PLA political office issued a circular forbidding members of the armed forces from practising Falungong. On 29 May the neighbourhood committees of Beijing and its suburbs, as well as the city's major units, were instructed to draw up lists of individuals who had participated in the Zhongnanhai demonstration.[110]

Expecting repression, according to Kang Xiaoguang, Falungong activists in several cities appointed 'second' and 'third' lines of substitute training centre coaches, who would step into their functions as soon as the first line was eliminated. These replacements were chosen on the basis of their anonymity, loyalty and organisational ability.[111]

Li Hongzhi started issuing threatening statements. In a 'scripture' (*jingwen*) released on the internet on 2 June he wrote that the 10,000 Zhongnanhai demonstrators were nothing compared to the 100 million Falungong cultivators. Hinting that this great mass of followers might rise up, he declared:

The most frightening thing is to lose the people's hearts. To speak frankly, Falungong practitioners are still in a process of cultivation, they still have a human heart [they are not yet completely detached from this world]. In the face of such unjust treatment, I don't know how long they will be able to bear. That's what I am most worried about.[112]

Similarly, the Falungong online bulletin board, making reference to the allegation that the Zhongnanhai demonstration had been deliberately planned to take place shortly before the anniversary of the 4 June 1989 Tiananmen incident, warned, 'the authorities should quickly sober up to avoid an even more severe consequence … Isn't the act of imperiously pushing one hundred million good people to the opposite side itself producing another "June 4th" incident?'[113]

109   LH: 8; CME.
110   LH: 8.
111   Kang Xiaoguang 2000: 51–3.
112   Li Hongzhi, Essential Points: 89–90.
113   'Falun Dafa gonggaolan bianjibu tongzhi' [Notice by the Falun Dafa Bulle-

On 6 June government agents disrupted Falungong practice sessions in Beijing. In Guangzhou Falungong practitioners were arrested and required by the police to write reports on the denomination's activities. Rumours started to circulate about an emergency meeting of the CCP leadership, which was preparing to label Falungong as an 'evil cult' and to promise a reward of $500 million to whoever brought Li Hongzhi back to China.[114] At the meeting Jiang Zemin was reported to have declared that the Falungong issue was the most serious political conflict since the 1989 Tiananmen student movement.[115] On 10 June the '610 Office', led by Luo Gan, was created to spearhead the struggle against Falungong. At the same time the Xinhua news agency published a dispatch denying rumours that Falungong would be suppressed and that Falungong practitioners would be expelled from the CCP and from public employment, stressing that 'any person may participate in all types of *qigong*-practice and health-building activities, but it is absolutely forbidden to spread superstition or rumours for the purpose of incitement or to conduct activities such as large-scale gatherings that disturb social order and adversely affect social stability in the name of "popularising the Dharma".'[116]

The Falun Dafa Bulletin Board suggested to all practitioners to continue going out to practise Falungong, regardless of any interference they might encounter from various government departments.[117] On 13 June Li Hongzhi authorised his followers to use legitimate means to claim justice.[118] One thousand followers from Benxi (Liaoning) set off for Beijing on 18 June and, despite several police blockades, 500 of them managed to break through and to demonstrate outside the Petitions department beside Zhongnan-

---

tin Board Editorial Office], <http://faluncanada.net/fldfbb/notice990603.doc>, 2 June 1999 (accessed 3 June 2005).

114 LH: 8.

115 CME.

116 Xinhua News Agency, 'Main Points of the Talk Given by Person in Charge of Bureaus of Letters and Petitions of the General Secretariat of the Chinese Communist Party (CCP) Central Committee and of the General Secretariat of the State Council when Receiving a Number of Falungong Appellants', *Chinese Law and Government*, 32(5): 19–21, September–October 1999, p. 20. Translation of original published on <www.peopledaily.com.cn>.

117 'Xiang dalu dafa xiulianzhe jianyi' [Suggestion for cultivators of the Great Fa in mainland China], <http://faluncanada.net/fldfbb/suggestion0608.doc>, 8 June 1999 (accessed 4 June 2005).

118 Li Hongzhi, Essential Points: 91.

hai.[119] A few days later a petition signed by 13,000 Falungong cultivators was sent to Jiang Zemin and Zhu Rongji, demanding that the public practice of Falungong be officially authorised.[120]

When a Falungong bulletin board posting warned that China Central Television was planning to air an anti-Falungong documentary, over 500 practitioners from Tianjin, Hebei and north-east China converged on the station's offices, warning that if the programme was aired it would trigger an even larger influx of protesters, and succeeded in having the programme removed from the station's schedule.[121] In Henan, when the Tangyin county tourism bureau removed a stele commemorating Li Hongzhi from a village temple, 300 practitioners protested at local government and CCP offices, warning that if the stele was not returned, the conflict would deepen and that they would write an open letter to the whole nation.[122]

By the end of June various CCP and government organs let it be understood that their senior leaders considered Falungong an illegal sect that needed to be eliminated. In Beijing the Public Security Bureau identified, followed and monitored the leaders of the training stations and practice points, and went door-to-door to draw up a list of Falungong practitioners. Police were also dispatched to monitor the practice points.[123]

On 26 June 3,000 police were sent to 'clean up' the thirteen Falungong practice points along Chang'an Avenue. Practitioners who refused to leave were taken away by the police. The Shandong provincial Party Secretary declared the need to eradicate Falungong within two or three years, before it could spread in the countryside. In Liaoning province Party cadres were forbidden from practising Falungong, at the risk of being expelled from the Party if they persisted. Falungong books and materials were confiscated. In Jiangxi province colleges and universities received the order to forbid the practice of Falungong on their campuses; a circular stipulated that any meeting of more than three Falungong practitioners would be considered an illegal gathering. In Hubei province police offic-

119 CME.
120 LH: 8.
121 Kang Xiaoguang 2000: 102.
122 Kang Xiaoguang 2000: 104. It was a temple to Yue Fei, located in Caiyuan *xiang*, Chenggang *cun*.
123 LH: 8.

ers disrupted practice sites, dispersed the followers, and confiscated their books. In Guangdong, under the pressure of government officials, some businesses fired employees who were Falungong disciples.[124] On 30 June the Falun Dafa Research Society issued a notice encouraging practitioners to react with calm to this harassment, and to present written reports to local authorities and government departments containing testimonies of the benefits of Falungong to the health of individuals and to the stability of society. Throughout this period Falungong notices stressed that any actions taken against it were the work of individual officials who were violating government laws and policy.[125]

These repressive measures remained local and regional in scope. The national anti-Falungong crackdown only began on 19 July, when a front-page editorial in the *People's Daily*, without mentioning Falungong by name, condemned the laxity of the CCP's base organisations, which tolerated the participation of Party members in 'foolish superstitious activities'.[126] The next day a massive anti-Falungong propaganda campaign was launched on all media—television, radio and press—reminiscent of Cultural Revolution-era struggles. All day long the television networks broadcast documentaries on Falungong followers who were alleged to have died, committed suicide, fallen gravely ill, become mentally deranged, or provoked the breaking up of families. Unit leaders summoned their employees to watch these programmes, which were reproduced in the press, and depicted Falungong as an organisation that was fooling the masses to cover a political agenda.

At dawn on the same day a wave of arrests led to the imprisonment of most key Falungong leaders and assistants in Beijing and the main provincial cities. By evening thousands of Falungong disciples were protesting the arrests in Beijing, Dalian, Guangzhou, Shenzhen and Taiyuan. Police violently dispersed the protesters or arrested demonstrators; in Beijing 2,000 were arrested near Tiananmen Square and locked in a stadium west of the city.[127]

124 LH: 8–9.
125 Falun dafa xuehui, 'Falun dafa gonggaolan tongzhi' [Notice of the Falun Dafa Bulletin Board], <http://faluncanada.net/fldfbb/notice990630.doc>, 30 June 1999 (accessed 4 June 2005).
126 RR, 19 July 1999: 1.
127 *The Guardian*, <www.guardianunlimited.co.uk/Archive/Article/0,4273, 3885367,00.htm>; LH: 11; CME.

On 21 July the Falun Dafa Bulletin Board, warning that 10,000 Beijing policemen were being armed and deployed against Falungong, called on practitioners to 'arise urgently to defend the *Fa*',

... practitioners from all over China can spontaneously organise, breaking through all difficulties and acting swiftly, to take the initiative to present the facts on Falungong to the relevant officials, to the [CCP] Central [Committee] as well as to the provincial and municipal Party Committees, and demand the release of arrested Falungong practitioners, to clear the reputation of Falungong, and to return our normal cultivation environment. [And] also demand that the Party Central [Committee] and the state deal severely with the instigators of these incidents harming Falungong, in the interests of national prosperity and social stability.[128]

On the same day the CCP Central Committee declared Falungong an illegal organisation and banned Party members from participating in its activities.[129] Falungong internet sites were blocked. On 22 July the Department of Civil Affairs declared Falungong an illegal organisation, and banned the public posting of Falungong images, posters or symbols; the distribution of Falungong books, tapes or other materials;[130] the organisation of Falungong teaching and experience-sharing activities; the holding of demonstrations and appeals to government offices etc.[131] The Personnel Department likewise banned all state employees from practising Falungong.[132] One by one, Party organs and government departments issued regulations banning any aspect of Falungong touching on their sphere of jurisdiction.

The same day Li Hongzhi issued a call to governments, international organisations and 'good people' from around the world to support Falungong and to contribute to solving the 'crisis'. He also called on the Chinese government to resolve the issue through

---

128 Dafa xuehui, 'Jinji xingdongqilai hufa' [Urgently arise to defend the Fa], <http://faluncanada.net/fldfbb/notice990720.doc>, 21 July 1999 (accessed 4 June 2005).

129 HW, 23 July 1999: 1, translation published in *Chinese Law and Government*, 32(5): 14–18.

130 HW, 24 July 1999: 3, translation published in *Chinese Law and Government*, 32(5): 29–30.

131 HW, 23 July 1999: 1, translation published in *Chinese Law and Government*, 32(5): 31–2.

132 HW, 24 July 1999: 3, translation published in *Chinese Law and Government*, 32(5): 26–8.

'peaceful dialogue',[133] and 'not to treat the Falungong masses like enemies. Whatever one may say, the people of China understand Falungong very well. The result will be that the people will lose their trust in the government and the leaders of China.'[134] Several dozen demonstrations took place throughout China during the summer, drawing hundreds and sometimes thousands of followers.[135]

133 'News(990727)', <http://faluncanada.net/fldfbb/news990727.doc>, 27 July 1999 (accessed 4 June 2005).
134 Li Hongzhi, Essential Points: 93.
135 Kang Xiaoguang 2000: 53; CME.

EPILOGUE

THE COLLAPSE OF THE QIGONG MOVEMENT

The unfolding of the anti-Falungong repression since 1999 has been widely reported in the media and described in academic literature.[1] At the time of writing, five years of a costly suppression campaign had succeeded in largely, but by no means completely, eliminating Falungong within China, while Li Hongzhi's disciples, now campaigning against the repression from their base in the United States, were behind an increasingly explicit campaign to discredit and topple the CCP.[2]

However, a detailed analysis of these issues is beyond the scope of this book. Here, we look at the impact of the anti-Falungong campaign on the *qigong* sector. In the first days of the repression campaign, the directors of the major state-sponsored *qigong* associations and the masters of the recognised *gongfa*, as well as Yan Xin, were summoned to a meeting at the Martial Arts Research Institute to criticise Li Hongzhi and support the crackdown on Falungong. During the summer of 1999 the CQRS and other *qigong* associations and magazines also organised anti-Falungong events.[3]

State propaganda stressed that *qigong* was not a target of the campaign, which was aimed only at Falungong. Nevertheless, since Falungong had emerged out of the *qigong* sector, all *gongfa*, with their centralised grassroots networks covering China's territory, were now seen as potential political threats. Wu Shaozu, who had done so much to encourage and protect the *qigong* movement,

---

1 See notably, Chang 2004.

2 This campaign has been spearheaded by the media outlets managed and staffed by Falungong activists, notably the overseas Chinese newspaper *Epoch Times*, which has widely distributed a series of anti-CCP tracts and launched a movement to encourage mass defections from the CCP membership. See Epoch Group 2005; <www.theepochtimes.com>, <tuidang.dajiyuan.com>.

3 <http://www.chinaqigong.net/dongtai/6.html> (now dead; accessed March 2001).

and had done nothing to stop Falungong's expansion, was fired from his position as Sports Minister. In September the State Sports Administration, the Ministry of Civil Affairs and the Ministry of Public Security issued a regulation banning *gongfa* associations and allowing the registration of only those local *qigong* associations that were not affiliated to a particular *gongfa*, had no hierarchical ties to other associations in other localities and were registered with the authorities.[4] On 30 October the Standing Committee of the National People's Congress passed a resolution banning 'evil cults (*xiejiao*) which act under the cover of religion, of *qigong* or other illicit forms', stipulating the persecution of cult leaders who 'organise mass demonstrations to disturb the public order and mislead the public, provoke deaths, rape women, swindle people for their money and their possessions, or commit other crimes of superstition and heresy'.[5] This resolution was designed to provide a legal basis for the repression of Falungong, but could also be used to shut down other *qigong* groups.

On 13 December the central authorities decided to suppress Zhonggong.[6] Investigations were opened on three cases of rape allegedly committed by Zhang Hongbao in 1990, 1991 and 1994, and on false documents used by him in 1993. Zhonggong offices and properties were sealed. Zhang Hongbao, who had disappeared in 1995, resurfaced on the American Pacific island of Guam in February 2000. After six months of detention on the island, his request for asylum was rejected, but he was given temporary permission to remain in the United States, where he settled in Washington.[7]

Other *gongfa* masters were also struck down. In Sichuan, for example, Qu Changchun, master of the 'Three-Three-Nine Qigong for Attaining the Origin' (*Sansanjiu chengyuan gong*), and his former disciple Liu Jineng, master of the 'China Natural Extraordinary Qigong' (*Zhongguo ziran teyi gong*) were sentenced respectively to twenty and to fifteen years in prison for swindling and for producing illegal publications.

---

4 <http://www.my169.com~qigong/jingzhi.htm> (now dead; accessed March 2001).
5 'Decision of the Standing Committee of the National People's Congress on Banning Heretical Cult Organisations, and Preventing and Punishing Cult Activities', published in *Beijing Review*, 42 (November 1999): 45.
6 Zhang Hongbao 2001: 7.
7 'China Demands that US Hand Over Qigong Guru', Reuters, <http://dailynews.yahoo.com/h/nm/200000924/wl/religion_china_dc_1.html>.

The state took measures to enforce strict control on public *qigong* practice. According to new regulations issued in 2000, hygienic *qigong* training was a direct responsibility of the state sports authorities, which set up a new Qigong Administration Centre to control all *qigong* activities.[8] Only persons trained and certified by the sports authorities would be allowed to lead practice sessions in parks. Only four standardised methods could be practised, all forms of *daoyin* taken from the classical medical tradition: the Eight Pieces of Brocade (*baduanjin*), the Six-Character Formula (*liuzijue*), the Five-Animal Frolic (*wuqinxi*) and the Muscles and Tendons Training (*yijinjing*).

The state appeared to have succeeded in imposing its control on *qigong*. *Qigong* was reduced to a physical fitness method which could be practised in parks alongside other methods now also encouraged as substitutes to *qigong*: *Taijiquan*, senior's disco dancing and free exercise machines set up in public spaces all over the country. In bookstores books on *qigong* could no longer be found, while yoga manuals and DVDs entered the market, offering an alternative type of traditional body technology.

Most masters stopped their activities, took a low profile, went underground, or emigrated to the West, contributing to the growing popularity of *qigong* within the worlds of alternative medicine and spirituality.[9] Many of the '*qigong* science' scholars and intellectuals shifted their energies to the growing field of Taoist studies. These trends had actually already begun in the 1990s as part of a gradual shift away from scientism to more explicit forms of religion. State promotion of traditional body technologies continued, but with the focus shifting to the martial arts and *taijiquan*. Among upwardly-mobile urbanites yoga seemed to have displaced *qigong* as a more cosmopolitan form of traditional body cultivation better adapted to the commodification of health practices. After the Falungong crackdown *qigong* techniques could still be practised in China, but the *qigong* sector ceased to exist as a vibrant social space.

---

8   'Shanxi sheng jiang qingli zhengdun qigonglei jigou deng minjian zuzhi' [Shanxi province will purge qigong and other popular organisations], <www.qg100.com/news>, 2001 (accessed July 2001).
9   See Komjathy 1996; Siegler 2006.

CONCLUSION

With the Zhongnanhai incident of 25 April 1999, and the anti-Falungong repression that followed it, the story of *qigong* leads us to the centre of the Chinese and international political stage. After those events China experts were left scrambling to find explanations for what had been a completely unexpected development. However, the history of *qigong* shows that the incident represents a dramatic turn in a story that had been unfolding since the first days of the People's Republic—a story that had been intertwined with politics at every stage. *Qigong* could no longer be seen as little more than a passing fad in Chinese pop culture or a failed experiment in fringe science.

Since then the Falungong issue has become a component of the general discourse criticising human rights violations in China. Falungong appears as one of the best-organised and persistent oppositional movements in China, far surpassing democratic dissidents in its organisational and mobilisational capacity, both in China and abroad. The confrontation has had repercussions for non-governmental religious and social groups in general, which were subject to tighter controls in the years immediately following the 1999 crackdown. In the Falungong case the Western human-rights paradigm of a popular movement struggling for its rights in the face of repression intersects the Chinese historical paradigm of a conflict between sectarian rebellion and the imperial state. One of the oddest aspects of the Falungong affair is how it appears as the re-enactment, at the dawn of the twenty-first century, of a historical scenario that has played itself out dozens of times since the suppression of the Yellow Turban movement by the Eastern Han dynasty.[1]

This conclusion will question the state–sect scenario of polarisation and its implications for understanding the dynamics of so-

---

[1] On the history of sectarian rebellion and repression by the Chinese state, see Seiwert 2003 and ter Haar 1992.

cio-religious movements in contemporary China. Indeed, if this type of scenario repeats itself so often in Chinese history, and if a group like Falungong could grow so fast and have such a significant political impact, one might conclude that the Falungong case reveals some deeply engrained patterns of thought and action on the part of both popular movements and the Chinese state, which are as resilient as ever after a full century of modernisation and revolutions.

But framing the story in such a way—be it in terms of a struggle for spiritual freedom against dictatorship, or of sectarian rebellion versus the state—begs another question: if the state is so repressive and body technologies open a space of resistance, why did it tolerate, encourage and even protect the growth of such a space for so long? Given that *qigong* was openly spreading practices, ideas and social organisations sometimes clearly at odds with Marxist ideology, why did repression come so late? What change occurred to make Falungong the specific target of such a harsh crackdown?

When we look back at the two decades preceding the 1999 suppression of Falungong, we find that the *qigong* movement, out of which Falungong was born, enjoyed an unparalleled degree of high-level political support—arguably more than any other non-governmental social or religious group or movement in socialist China—which made possible the explosion of *qigong* in the post-Mao period as the largest expression of mass religiosity in urban China, and indeed one of the most significant cultural phenomena of that period. Understanding this turn of events thus requires that we look back at the entire story of the *qigong* movement, which began with the invention of modern *qigong* within state health institutions in the 1950s, re-emerged in the 1980s as the catalyst of a wave of popular religiosity associated with an ideology of a new scientific revolution with millenarian and utopian overtones, and declined in the 1990s, while Falungong expanded first within the *qigong* movement, and then against it, culminating in its clash with the state in 1999.

Here, I will try to situate the *qigong* movement within a broader social and historical context, proposing hypotheses which in many cases, I admit, are highly speculative. I hope these ideas may stimulate reflection and debate on the broader religious and social transformations of which *qigong* and Falungong are the manifestations in contemporary China.

FROM HEALING TO RELIGIOSITY

The initial project of *qigong* was to integrate traditional body technologies into the process of medical institutionalisation through which traditional Chinese medicine came to occupy a recognised and legitimate place in the Chinese medical system, with its own hospitals, universities and professional practitioners. But modernised Chinese medicine, which gave *qigong* its first institutional identity, later relegated *qigong* to a marginal status, at a time when popular *gongfa* proliferated in society.[2] Why did *qigong* develop outside of the medical institutions, and become a conduit for the expression of popular religiosity?

Qigong, from the moment it moved beyond being a psychocorporal training and began to include the idea of the therapeutic efficacy of the circulation of *qi* between the master's body and other bodies and objects, became an essentially personalistic and charismatic form of healing which could not be institutionalised. As such, it brought into play the healer's paranormal healing powers, the receptivity of the patient and the setting which shaped the relationship between the two actors: as a master told me, for healing to occur there must be both an 'emitting antenna' and a 'receiving antenna'. *Qigong* thus became a setup for facilitating the appearance of the emission and reception of healing powers. The master's charismatic power became his or her chief source of authority. Anyone could aspire to acquire such powers after a short period of practice.

There was no place for such a proliferation of charisma in state institutions, in which the rationalised economy of knowledge and power precludes the personalised ties of charismatic relationships. Institutionalisation would necessitate eliminating the charismatic dimension of *qigong*. Such was indeed what Zhang Honglin proposed when he claimed that external *qi* did not exist, and advocated a return to the 'true' *qigong* as a form of self-training, justified by a historical genealogy of *qigong* in which there is no mention of healing through external *qi*.[3] In a similar vein, Li Hongzhi, referring to the Buddhist tradition of selfless virtue, forbade his disciples from emitting external *qi* through healing others or giving lectures, thus eliminating the possibility of the appearance of charisma among

---

2 See pp. 176–7.
3 See p. 162.

his followers and centralising all charisma around his own person. But in doing so he based his *gongfa* on a source of legitimacy other than that of medical institutions, and indeed strongly discouraged his disciples from seeking medical treatment.[4]

Even in a context of purely individualised self-training, *qigong* practice tends to produce a rupture with the rationality of modern-style institutions. Indeed it is not uncommon for *qigong* practice to trigger mental states and experiences which are difficult or even impossible to explain satisfactorily with materialist theories.[5] The meaning of such experiences must thus be sought elsewhere: either through metaphysical concepts derived from religious traditions, or through new theories, such as those of 'Extraordinary Powers' or 'somatic science', which attempt to transcend the limitations of mechanical materialism. Either way *qigong* draws the practitioner away from the conventional discourses of institutional rationality.

Even in the absence of such intense experiences, *qigong* practice reinforces the tendency, already strong in Chinese culture, to experience the corporal, the emotional, the social and the spiritual as a single undifferentiated whole. One passes easily from physical sensations to social suffering and from there to moral reflection or questioning on the meaning of life or the nature of the universe. The practitioner is thus led to seek a globalising explanatory model, incompatible with the reductionist and analytical categories of medical science.

Whether at the level of social relations founded on charisma or of explanatory models for subjective experience, *qigong* thus propels the practitioner towards worlds which cannot be integrated by modern institutions. The only way to give a coherent form to the experience of *qigong* is to call on the masters and 'witnesses of the past',[6] figures of tradition, to follow their example and their teachings. From health technique, then, *qigong* leads inevitably to chains of belief; its organisation builds itself outside of medical institutions to take on an increasingly religious form.

The passage to religiosity was facilitated by the dense Taoist and Buddhist symbolism associated with traditional body technologies.

---

4   See pp. 237–8.
5   These experiences notably include the sensation of flows of *qi* in the body, the sensation of receiving or emitting *qi* between persons, and visions and insights that can only be labelled 'hallucinations' in biomedical terminology.
6   Hervieu-Léger 1993: 118.

Attempts to secularise the techniques could not obliterate a millennia-long history of their embeddedness in religion. The lineages of which many masters were the inheritors, the religious symbolism of the classical texts describing the techniques, and the magical content of the *gongfu* films and novels which permeated pop culture, all conspired to make the religious roots of *qigong* resurface. *Qigong* became a point of easy access to a tradition which was otherwise distant and closed to the common person, but which could now be embodied through daily practice.[7]

The 'bio-social charisma' of *qigong* adepts, as defined in the introduction to this book, can thus be contrasted to the notion of 'bio-power' used by Foucault to describe the modern state's project of controlling bodies through the positive production and nurturing of the health of populations.[8] The Chinese state's project of a secularised *qigong* can be seen as an attempt to inscribe within the technologies of bio-power China's traditions of cultivating health, which, with their focus on the nurturing of the life of the individual body, appeared to be eminently suited for such a purpose. But ultimately the powers of *qigong* proved to be elusive to such a project, and found their fullest expression in the effervescence of charismatic relationships.

QIGONG AND THE CHINESE SECTARIAN MILIEU

If, by the very nature of the experiences it produces and by the access to traditional symbols it provides, *qigong* is a gateway to religiosity, we might then ask ourselves about the place of the organisations which propagate and structure such experiences within the overall Chinese religious system. The *qigong* milieu was distinct from both the established religions and the temple cults of the communal religion.[9] The structure, practices and discourses of *qigong* groups beg comparison with the nameless nebula of groups collectively

---

7   A comparable phenomenon is described by Jordan and Overmyer in their study of sectarianism in Taiwan (1986: 10).

8   Foucault 1988b: 140.

9   Authoritative works on these traditions in contemporary China are: Dean 1993 on Taoism; Chau 2005 on popular religion; Chen and Deng 2000 on Buddhism; Madsen 1998 on Catholicism; Hunter and Chan 1993 on Protestantism; and Gladney 1991 on Islam. See also Goossaert 2000 on the pivotal role of temples in Chinese religion.

called the 'sectarian milieu'[10] by Western historians of Chinese religion, which has existed since the Han dynasty, and which has spawned hundreds of groups over the centuries.[11] It was a milieu in which a great variety of practices, symbols and types of organisation circulated. These elements could manifest themselves in different configurations in each group, but a number of common traits can be identified: healing and body cultivation technologies which are often gateways to adhesion to the sect; active recruitment of new followers; voluntary rather than ascribed or hereditary membership, which was usually open to anyone, without regard for social status, age or sex; easy access to knowledge of the 'great tradition' which orthodox institutions normally restricted to a small number of religious professionals;[12] a salvational doctrine based on moral transformation; the millenarian promise of a future world of bliss, to be ushered in by a messianic figure often identified as Li Hong, Prince Moonlight or Maitreya; and a dichotomy between the followers of the True Way, who will be saved, and the others, who will be abandoned to their miseries.[13]

10　On the notion of the Chinese 'sectarian milieu', see Seiwert 2003: 365–6. Following the conventions of Sinologists, I use the term 'sect' and 'sectarian' to describe groups characterised by their location outside the institutional structure of Chinese religion with its imperial cult, its state-controlled religious authorities, its monastic institutions, and its communal religion rooted in kinship, locality and profession. Thus, whereas Western sociologists of religion studying Christian societies, beginning with Weber and Troeltsch, offered a sociological definition of the 'sect' with its exclusive, voluntary membership of the spiritually committed, in opposition to the 'Church' which accommodated itself with the wider society (Troeltsch 1960: 331–43), in the Chinese case, in the absence of a dominant 'Church', we can speak of 'sects' located outside the ritual order of the politico-religious state.

11　The most thorough treatment in English of the history of Chinese sectarianism is Seiwert 2003. An even more comprehensive study is Ma Xisha and Han Bingfang 1992. For an earlier introduction, see Overmyer 1976. See also ter Haar 1992 on the 'White Lotus' label often used to designate a wide range of heterodox sects. For a study of the *baojuan* genre of sectarian scripture, see Overmyer 1999. Susan Naquin's work (1976, 1981 and 1985) is especially valuable for its sociological insights. For a comparison of twentieth-century Taiwanese sects with earlier sectarian traditions, see Jordan and Overmyer 1986. Ownby 2003a looks at the Falungong issue with reference to sectarianism and popular religion since the Ming. Liu and Shek 2004 contains several valuable essays covering the range of Chinese sectarian groups and traditions up to the late nineteenth century.

12　Jordan and Overmyer 1986: 10.

13　Seiwert 2003: 47–52; Naquin 1976: 38–41.

A sectarian lineage was centred on the person of a single master, who held the charisma of the lineage. All masters were the inheritors, founders or disciples of a lineage: sectarian masters were not mere healers, philosophers or magicians who practised outside of any structure. Horizontally, in relation to other lineages, there was a process of differentiation, as each sect tried to distinguish itself from others, on the basis of a pool of practices and organisational models common to the milieu. Differentiation was marked by the name of the method, the image of the master, the combination of techniques and the details of doctrine. In some cases, comparable to Falungong, one also finds an exclusivism which tried to cut the disciple's communication with other lineages, by forbidding the use of other sects' books and techniques.[14]

Although body cultivation and healing techniques were an important component of sectarian practice, they were not an end in themselves, but were used for forming and expanding the lineage network.[15] The immediate benefits of the techniques could attract people who did not necessarily have an interest in the religious teachings.[16] The transmission of the techniques created master/student and healer/patient relationships, which became the links in the sectarian chain. The practice of the techniques gave birth to a subculture of adepts who shared a common master, practice and symbols. The simplicity of the techniques,[17] the ease of their rapid and secret transmission and of their discrete and individual practice, without heavy structures such as temples or clerical institutions, allowed a great mobility[18] and was well-adapted to the periodic repression of unorthodox religious groups. The body became the 'temple' of the sectarian adept, who carried it in all his movements, without others knowing. The incorporation of body and healing techniques to sectarian practices could thus facilitate the recruitment and the forming of flexible, underground chains of transmission in a context of repression.

The body technologies common in the *qigong* milieu were similar to those that circulated in the pre-communist sectarian milieu. The relative importance of different techniques did change, with

14   Overmyer 1999: 112–22.
15   Naquin 1976: 29–32; Naquin 1985: 282.
16   Naquin 1985: 282.
17   Naquin 1985: 285–6.
18   Naquin 1976: 41; Naquin 1985: 281.

the gymnastic forms of the medical tradition now taking the dominant position, and the martial arts of invincibility, so central to the Boxer movement and to the Republican-era Red Spears, for example, now relegated to theatrical performance acts. Adaptation to the anti-religious context of socialist China went even further: the secular, hygienic and therapeutic aspect of the techniques was advanced, making possible a public, open and legal expansion, while dissimulating the religious dimension which could be experienced in the intimacy of meditations and of master–disciple relationships. In Falungong, however, the typical sectarian repertoire once again appeared in broad daylight.

The sectarian and *qigong* milieus were thus a world of fluid networks. Although the basic organisational unit was the denomination, called *jiao* or *gong*, with its name and its master, the segmentation of denominations, and the founding and the extinction of groups occurred constantly and easily.[19] Individuals circulated from one group to another, taking on a succession of masters, practising a series of methods, creating their own networks and, occasionally, their own denominations. Thus, while there was no fixed structure uniting all practitioners, masters and groups, all of these interlocking and dynamic networks formed a milieu within which people circulated, a subculture with its common references and well-known figures, and shared norms and values.

The sectarian milieu is thus rooted in underground networks made up of chains of masters and disciples, going back in time and perpetuating themselves in the future. Out of these underground networks emerge public organisations, at different times and places, when repression slackens and circumstances permit it. When public lineages are suppressed or controlled, the networks contract and continue to be transmitted secretly. The *qigong* world is a product of one of these periods of efflorescence, during which a degree of official recognition allowed masters to 'come out of the mountains' and to disseminate techniques to the broader public which were adapted to the political and material realities of contemporary China. The tightening of controls begun in the late 1990s, on the other hand, forced the milieu once again to move underground.

The sectarian milieu could expand or shrink depending on the period and the place, based on two seemingly opposite factors: the

19   Naquin 1976: 7.

first, and obvious one, was the severity of the repression of hetero-dox groups. On the other hand, state restriction of *orthodox* religion could also open the religious field for the expansion of sectarian-ism, which, with its more flexible organisation, is more adapted to repression.

Since the Tang and especially the Song dynasty (960–1279) the imperial state increasingly attempted to tighten control over reli-gion. The revival of Confucianism as a politico-religious ideology was accompanied by a policy restricting the expansion of Buddhism and Taoism. A consequence of this policy was gradually to weaken the 'orthodox' religious institutions, creating the conditions for the flourishing of popular religion and sectarianism.[20] The propagation of sectarianism was facilitated by the wide diffusion of their sacred texts, the *baojuan*.[21] A galaxy of groups appeared, such as the White Lotus, Patriarch Luo, Yellow Heaven, Complete Illumination and Eight Trigram sects. Founded by charismatic masters, most of these groups fissured into multiple branches after a few generations or fused with other networks.[22]

At the end of the Qing and during the republican period (1911–49) popular sects spread rapidly and grew in influence, filling the social void left by the destruction of traditional social structures and temple-based communal religion,[23] and even dominating en-tire villages and regions. For example, in the republican era the Red Spears converted entire villages in north China with the support of local élites, who found in sectarian practices and networks a meth-od of resistance against banditry and looting.[24] In the cities groups such as the Way of Pervasive Unity (Yiguandao)[25] and the Society United in Goodness (Tongshanshe) flourished.[26] As soon as it took power in 1949 the CCP launched a harsh repression against these 'reactionary' societies, leading to the near complete eradication of the sectarian world.[27] At the same time, however, the creation of

20 Ownby 2003a.
21 See Overmyer 1999.
22 Naquin 1985; Seiwert 2003: 365–437.
23 On the destruction of temple-based communal religion, see Schipper 1997; Duara 1995: 85–110; and Nedostup 2001.
24 On the Red Spears, see Perry 1980: 186–207; Tai 1985.
25 On the Yiguandao, see Jordan and Overmyer 1986: 211–49; Ma Xisha and Han Bingfang 1992: 1092–167.
26 On the Tongshanshe, see Wang Chien-ch'uan 1995.
27 See Shao 1997: 452–504.

the new category of *qigong* opened a space within which the body techniques could be legitimately practised, providing an opening for the reappearance of sectarianism in the 1980s and 1990s. We have seen that Yan Xin's genealogy of masters can be traced to a Taoist monk active in the Boxer rebellion,[28] and a leading disciple of the Heavenly Virtue sect played an important role in establishing external *qi* as a field of scientific research [29] Further research is needed to identity more specific links between earlier sectarian groups and *qigong* networks, and to compare their practices and teachings.[30] But from a sociological perspective, in terms of its inner dynamics and its place within the overall contemporary Chinese religious system, *qigong* can justifiably be compared with the earlier sectarian milieu.

INTERPENETRATION AND POLARISATION

Each component of sectarian teachings and practices was potentially destabilising to social and even political order. Charismatic healings put masters in a position of authority over a large number of disciples, which could be converted into political or military uses. The authority of sacred scriptures could challenge the dominant position of the Confucian or Marxist canon, the ideological foundation of the state. The doctrine of moral salvation could point to the moral decadence of the rulers as the source of the disasters, famines and corruption from which the people suffered. Voluntary adhesion and the dichotomy between the saved and the damned undermined the traditional social hierarchies on which the political system rested. And apocalyptic prophecies could spur followers to act against the regime to precipitate the coming of the millennium. Voluntary sects crossed social, geographic and even gender boundaries, and did not fit into the nested hierarchy of the state/communal/kinship religious structure. Nor did they fit into the monastic institutions of Buddhism or Taoism. Thus they were often the sub-

---

28   See p. 137.

29   See pp. 50–1.

30   For example, many of the most characteristic doctrines and teachings of the late Qing and Republican-era urban redemptive societies, such as the Unborn Mother mythology and the doctrine of the unity of the five teachings (Confucianism, Buddhism, Taoism, Christianity and Islam), seem to have been absent in the *qigong* milieu.

ject of state repression, which varied in intensity at different places and periods, largely in response to perceived threats: low, when sects kept a discrete profile, blended in with local life, and escaped the attention of central authorities; high, when charismatic episodes activated latent millenarian or apocalyptic doctrines and spurred active rebellion; and severe, when a sect not only confronted the state but also revealed, in its own doctrine and organisational capability, a potential alternative cosmopolitical order.[31]

However, prior to the Falungong incident these inherent tensions seemed to have been resolved, or at least diffused, in the *qigong* movement. The *qigong* sector was able to establish itself in an intermediary space between state institutions and popular groups. In this space—opened by semi-official *qigong* associations and magazines, propagated by the official media, deployed in scientific, educational and medical institutions, and manifested in the parks, gardens, squares and public spaces of urban China—*qigong* masters, practitioners and researchers communicated with each other and formed an interconnected milieu, united through the *qigong* cause of personal and collective regeneration. Masters and groups contributed their methods, their healings, their laboratory experiments, their conceptual explanations, their practical innovations and their propagation models to this cause. Official institutions and political leaders contributed an ideological framework, encouragement, permissions and protection, removed administrative obstacles, and provided state resources.

The *qigong* episode thus forces us to abandon a conflictual model that places state authority in opposition to the autonomy of individuals and popular groups. It reveals a movement that developed through the interpenetration of networks, groups, institutions, practices and conceptual systems in which it is impossible to separate fully the state and popular groups as distinct entities. An image of the state as a monolithic entity makes way for a landscape of interconnected persons, networks and institutions that advance, retreat,

---

31 Notable rebellions linked to heterodox religious networks were the rebellions of the Yellow Turbans (184), Sun En (399), Faqing (515), the Incense Army—which led to the downfall of the Yuan dynasty—(mid fourteenth century), Xu Hongru (1622), the Eight Trigrams (1813), the Taiping Heavenly Kingdom (1850–64) and the Boxers (1899–1900). See Seiwert 2003 for a detailed account of the place of rebellions in the history of Chinese sectarianism. However, as stressed in Overmyer 1976, most sects in history were *not* involved in political opposition or rebellion.

cross each other and turn around, link up, pass each other, collide, expand and influence each other, reaching to the edges of society, without ever covering it completely. It is difficult to draw a clear line between what is within the state and what is outside it. 'The extra-institutional is co-extensive with the state … it is structuring, not only deforming.'[32] It is within such a system, and not outside it, that *qigong* groups were formed and expanded.

Chinese state organisation deploys itself ritually, through formal and informal personal exchanges between official functionaries and the administered. The *performance* of organisation is more important than its content. Participation in exchanges with officials implies the harmonisation and the recognition of mutual obligations between actors and with the state. Most *qigong* masters, by participating in this practice, with its exchange of gifts, favours, goods and prestige, as well as the performance of obedience, to varying degrees integrated themselves in the state order. This ensured them the overall tolerance of the state and the personal support of leaders with whom they cultivated reciprocal relationships. The indeterminacy of the *qigong* category allowed them to infiltrate the state organisation while building their own organisations.

The case of *qigong* thus reveals a dynamic that is often contrary to the processes of individualisation and institutional differentiation characteristic of Western paradigms of modernity. This begins with the dispositions and orientations nurtured by the body practices themselves. Western sports and physical training produce power at the point of friction between discrete material bodies. Muscles are trained against the resistance of external objects. The body's power is measured against disembodied targets. Physical, mental, emotional and moral abilities are the subject of separate training regimens. Chinese body technologies, on the other hand, reveal an opposite tendency: the concentration of all forms of power into the cosmic centre of the body, usually named *dantian*, the elixir field beneath the navel, evoking metaphors of the alchemical furnace in which heterogeneous elements are forged into a single elixir, itself a sign of the primal unity of the Tao. Collecting, cultivating and concentrating energies leads to an inner connection with the ultimate cosmic Power. The energies to be collected are not only inside the body but outside as well, including the powers of the sun,

---

32 Chevrier 1995: 171.

moon, trees, animals, other people and symbols: hence the attempts to draw on and fuse the different traditions of Taoism, Buddhism, Confucianism, martial arts, medicine and science. Power is generated not through friction but through fusion, through entering into a mutually transforming resonance with the object: absorbing the energy of a tree, for instance, does not involve pushing against it: rather, relating to the tree in such a manner that the flow of energies within it passes to the body of the practitioner.

Such a disposition carries to an extreme the relational orientation of Chinese culture. *Qigong* masters' obsession with cultivating relationships with officials goes beyond the instrumental pursuit of legitimacy and the protection of personal interests: connecting to and absorbing leaders' prestige and political power is a natural extension of the process of collecting, cultivating and concentrating cosmic energies. Likewise the practitioner seeks to absorb the master's Extraordinary Powers. The same tendency was at work in the Chinese state itself, in its inclination to harness and absorb the powers of the *qigong* movement: the public health potential of mass exercises, the military potential of paranormal abilities, the economic potential of the *qigong* training and healing market.

The intermediate space of *qigong* was thus not autonomous. It was simultaneously co-opted by the state and popular groups: each tried to use *qigong* for its own ends. If the state encouraged the development of *qigong* circles and gave them institutional support, it was as an instrument of its objectives in health, science and national identity. Its support for the construction of a unified national *qigong* sector aimed to co-opt and control it. In exchange, popular *qigong* groups obtained an institutional legality and legitimacy that permitted their massive expansion. *Qigong* could thus prosper by combining the institutional support of the state and the dynamism of popular groups.

While the *qigong* movement promoted ideas that were deviant or even heterodox by the standards of Marxist orthodoxy, the public behaviour of most *qigong* advocates, masters and practitioners followed the norms of orthopraxy,[33] cultivating webs of reciprocal

33 Anthropologist Erika Evasdottir, in her study of Chinese intellectuals (2004), defines orthopraxy as 'the express formulation of *action* to conform to commonly held standards'. Based on Evasdottir's conceptualisation, I take orthopraxy to mean the collective performance of political order—an order which is not the product of an outside or transcendent law, but the fruit of the harmonised *performance* of

relations with officials, and outwardly displaying deference to the social and political order. Falungong, on the other hand, broke this logic of interpenetration. By the mid 1990s Falungong began to cease participating in the ritual organisation of the post-Mao state system. After coasting on the *qigong* boom and benefiting from the political legitimacy and networks of the China Qigong Research Society, which had played an instrumental role in launching him as a national celebrity in *qigong* circles, Li Hongzhi, having attained a sufficiently large following and reputation, withdrew from the association in 1996. By putting an end to his collaboration with state-sponsored *qigong* associations he placed himself outside the circuit of personal relations and financial exchanges through which masters and their organisations could find a place within the state system. Instead he sought to establish an autonomous social body, the great body of the *Fa*, in which each disciple becomes a *fa*-particle,[34] in which the practitioners' bodies were the theatres of both personal spiritual struggle and of the apocalyptic battle between the demonic old world and the righteous *Fa*.

Falungong was not content to continue a quiet existence in a grey zone of non-legality, like other unregistered groups. While refusing to engage with the state according to its rules, Falungong endeavoured to remain at centre stage, offering the power of its *fa* to society and even to the state, organising spectacular public 'experience-sharing' gatherings and, through its protests against critical media, opposing any attempt to diminish its social influence. Falungong sought to replace the bidirectional flow of power of the interpenetration paradigm with a unidirectional flow, from Li Hongzhi outward to society.

Through the public militancy of his followers, Li Hongzhi openly disrupted the state system's collective performance of order. Without explicitly condemning the Party, he blatantly refused to participate in the state's ritual deployment of power through patronage, co-optations and underhanded deals aiming to integrate all actors into the system. As argued by Jason Kindopp, 'Within the context of modern authoritarian rule, even seemingly innocuous

---

the actors themselves, including both the rulers and the ruled. In orthopraxy order ceases to exist when the actors themselves cease to perform it.
[34] See for example Dafa xuehui, 'Jinji xingdongqilai hufa' [Urgently arise to defend the Fa], <http://faluncanada.net/fldfbb/notice990720.doc>, 21 July 1999 (accessed 4 June 2005).

acts can present formidable challenges to the regime's authority and potentially impair its ability to govern … challenging the regime does not require an assault on its institutions of coercion, but merely acting in a way that violates the prescribed ritual.'[35] Positioning himself outside this system of relations, basing himself on a doctrine of moral and spiritual purity, Li Hongzhi created a centre of moral legitimacy that was independent from state authority, setting the stage for a conflict cast in terms of the unfolding of an apocalyptic struggle between the 'good' *fa* and the 'evil' oppressors.

The non-violence of Falungong militancy accentuated the dichotomy between the two protagonists. Its symbolic power was all the more disruptive: the Zhongnanhai demonstration, where thousands of adepts quietly surrounded the heart of the Party for a whole day, evoked images of a siege or of strangling. Through this act Falungong projected the image of a powerful alternative order, capable of mobilising the masses, and *which was not afraid* of the CCP. Until today political authority in China is only partially exercised through a machinery of control and repression, and more so through the subjective perception and fear of its power. The reinforcement of such impressions, through propaganda and the spectacular performance of power, is thus crucial. The Zhongnanhai demonstration threatened to shatter the fear of the people and to transfer symbolic power onto Falungong. Thus a Chinese practitioner who converted to Falungong after the demonstration told me, in a menacing tone: 'if the Party dares to act against Falungong, Li Hongzhi will show his power.' The repression campaign, which to many harked back to the political struggles of the Cultural Revolution, was precisely designed to revive this fear in the minds of the populace.

FROM SOCIALIST UTOPIANISM TO RELIGIOUS ESCHATOLOGY

The interpenetration paradigm favoured by the *qigong* movement and the polarisation favoured by Falungong are directly linked to the eschatology of the two movements: *qigong* envisioned the gradual accomplishment of a paranormal utopia within the current social order, and so tried to avoid tension with society and the

---

35 Kindopp 2002: 260, based on Havel 1985: 23–96.

state; whereas Falungong apocalypticism eschewed the prevailing 'demonic' order, and saw tension as an opportunity for the public display of an alternative cosmic order[36] which would emerge victorious over ridicule, criticism or repression. How can we understand the shift from the former to the latter?

'*Qigong* fever' has been explained by scholars as a post-Cultural Revolution phenomenon which filled a bodily, emotional, social, cultural, moral or spiritual void left by the end of Maoism. Besides the practical and economic solution *qigong* could bring to the medical needs of the population,[37] Thomas Ots[38] and Evelyne Micollier[39] have pointed to the emotional release offered by spontaneous movements *qigong*. Nancy Chen has described the creation of an alternative mental world, outside of the state and politics, during *qigong* practice.[40] Going further, Jian Xu has argued that *qigong* opened a space for the desire of power and fantasy, responding to a need to reinvent a body other than the Maoist body.[41] Zhu Xiaoyang and Benjamin Penny have noted that collective and charismatic *qigong* gatherings replaced the mass rituals of Maoism, but in a depoliticised mode.[42] Elsewhere, Zhu Xiaoyang[43] and Elizabeth Hsu[44] have considered *qigong* as a response to the spiritual crisis of the 1980s. Thomas Heise has noted that, along with '*qigong* fever', China experienced several other waves during the 1980s: 'culture fever', 'national studies fever', 'Confucian fever', expressing a new questioning of national identity.[45]

Indeed *qigong* was intensely connected with the political, social and cultural realities of the surrounding society. It was deeply involved in political networks; with ideological issues of scientism and modernism; with identity definition and nationalism; with the living traditions it was actively seeking to transform; and with the first stages of China's market reforms. The *qigong* movement is a prism through which many strands of the rapidly unfolding story of

---

36 See Gentz 2004.
37 Penny 1993: 179.
38 Ots 1994: 126.
39 Micollier 1999.
40 Chen 1995: 361.
41 Xu 1999.
42 Zhu and Penny 1994: 7.
43 Zhu 1994 [1989].
44 Hsu 1999.
45 Heise 1999: 110.

post-Mao Chinese society come together. It occurred in a society that was undergoing several successive shocks: the collapse of political utopianism, marked by the end of the Cultural Revolution and then by the failure of the 1989 student democracy movement; the deployment of bureaucratic rationalisation and technocracy; the rediscovery of the nation's cultural heritage; the rush to Westernisation; finally the dismantling of the unit system and the rapid shift to a consumer society celebrating money and hedonistic pleasure—all within two decades.

During this period of rapid social transformation the evolution of *qigong* was inseparable from the changing expressions of utopianism in the People's Republic. In the 1950s modern *qigong* was created as part of a movement to modernise, institutionalise and popularise traditional medical and health technologies, itself a contribution to the larger utopian project of creating the New China—a liberated nation proud of its past and of its traditions stripped of the dross of feudalism and superstition, and a new race of strong and healthy bodies actively involved in the construction of the modern state.

During the Mao years, however, *qigong* was subsumed within the broader political history of the time, its fortunes entirely dependent on changing ideological winds, political campaigns and institutional projects within which its role was insignificant. It was only at the end of the 1970s that the *qigong* movement began to acquire an autonomous momentum. On the one hand the movement, made possible by ideological changes and boosted by senior Party leaders, was still dependent on wider political forces changing society; on the other *qigong* opened a range of possibilities in the realms of experience, knowledge, culture and social association that enabled it to offer an alternative path of personal and social regeneration in the wake of the collapse of the Maoist revolution.

Indeed, after the disillusionment of the Cultural Revolution utopian hopes had begun to devolve into cynicism and apathy. In their initial years Deng's reforms were an attempt to give a new lease of life to utopian energy, through a state-directed campaign to modernise the country and develop the economy on the more pragmatic basis of scientism and technologism. 'Science and technology were regarded as the "magic" ingredient that could automatically transform and modernise the Chinese economy and society', writes Yeu-Farn Wang in his study of Chinese science policy. 'The image of science could be conjured up as an appealing approach to mobilising mass support, [the] promise being that science, progress and modernisation would all be brought by the new times.'[46] The *qigong* of the 1980s can be seen as an alternative, popular reflection of this converted utopianism: in the new social reality, in which meaningful action was no longer possible, utopia could be achieved in and through the body. The materiality of the body, the technicality of the practices and their cost-efficiency made *qigong* fit well with the new priority placed on scientism. For practitioners *qigong* was thus a reaction to nihilism, a space in which agency was possible; for technocrats and political leaders it became a new utopian frontier. Through the *qigong* movement popular agency and political strategies could once again be joined together.

Having been engulfed in a collective fusion with Mao Zedong during the Cultural Revolution, people could, by practising *qigong*, rediscover their own bodies and subjectivities.[47] At the level of the individual body, the practice of *qigong* could produce profound sensations and experiences that often led to a heightened sense of health, empowerment and understanding. These changes could produce a radical transformation in the practitioner's relationship with his or her body and with the world, and a sense of connection with cosmic power that was absent in the alienated routines of disenchanted socialist–industrial culture.

Through exploring the inner universe of the body and directing the circulation of its energies, entering mystical realms through trances and visions, and connecting themselves, through a master, to ancient esoteric traditions, practitioners could enter an alternate world from the monotonous, regimented life of the unit and its totalitarian, industrial–bureaucratic organisation of bodies.[48] For those who weren't politically ambitious, the unit offered little hope for personal development or advancement, limited contact with the outside world and little space for personal subjectivity. However, in the cracked concrete yards of housing compounds and between the scraggly bushes of urban parks practising *qigong* could open endless new horizons of experience and knowledge. Here the body became a receptacle and a conduit of traditional wisdom and mystical symbols. Hitherto unknown forms of energy inside and outside the body could be experienced, monitored, directed and emitted,

46   Wang 1993: 100.
47   See Ots 1994.
48   See Chen, 1995.

leading to a sense of better health and, often literally, of heightened power. *Qigong* offered a way of personally appropriating and embodying this new world of knowledge, power and experience—an alternative to the alienating world of the unit, but one which could be legitimately and openly pursued under the guise of physical fitness.

As a mass movement, *qigong* multiplied such experiences of health and power in millions of bodies, whose number grew exponentially, presaging the day when, eventually, all of China, and even the whole world, would experience and participate in the transformation—leading to universal health, the spread of superhuman and paranormal abilities on a wide scale, and the eventual end of disease and suffering. Such fantasies drew on the tradition of utopian consciousness which had been fostered through forty years of Communism and Maoism—but one which, after the failure and pain of the Cultural Revolution, was turning inwards, into the body, into tending its sufferings, into a mass movement which didn't contest the structure of social relations but spread from body to body, dreaming that all would change once each body had been transformed. At the same time, by holding on to the Marxist teleology of the march of historical progress, *qigong* tempered the sudden fall from Maoist utopianism.

Because the effects of *qigong* could be viscerally felt by the practitioner, soothing and curing illness and pain, and providing experiences of power and knowledge, *qigong* could stimulate the enthusiasm of the masses of all social and educational backgrounds. *Qigong* practice and healing offered an avenue for releasing and working out the pains of the Cultural Revolution, which, following the Chinese tendency to somatise, were verbally unspoken but embedded in people's bodies.[49]

Qigong also offered a way to construct an alternative memory—one that was rooted in embodied experience, that restored a personal and collective link to the past, and that provided a new ideal and sense of purpose. Indeed thirty years of revolutionary campaigns had broken or strongly weakened the ties of memory with the past. Personal memories were of pain and suffering; collective memories, after so many ideological campaigns and flip-flops, had lost their mobilising power. The trend was to collective amnesia.

---

[49] Ots 1994; also, on somatisation in Chinese culture, with particular reference to the post-Cultural Revolution period, see Kleinman 1986.

Qigong, on the other hand, reconciled the scientism of mainstream modern Chinese thought with pride in the achievements of Chinese culture. *Qigong* thus legitimised the restoration of the collective memory of Chinese traditions while holding forth the promise of a revolutionary Chinese science, one which would restore Chinese civilisation and wisdom to its true dignity and propel it to the vanguard of world scientific discovery. All of this was made possible by a phenomenon that was unprecedented in the annals of modern science: a love affair between part of China's scientific community and the charismatic masters and their political supporters, which would continue until 1995.

For intellectuals and scientists, *qigong* thus offered a path of *reconciliation* which promised to resolve the contradictions which had been tormenting China's identity since the beginning of the twentieth century: modernist scientism and ambivalence toward the West, the pride of an ancient civilisation and shame at its current weakness. It is this promise which attracted so many Chinese intellectuals, scientists and political leaders, inciting them to promote practices often disdained by the literati in Chinese history. For *qigong* was an intellectual and official movement as much as popular one, a movement from the top downwards as much as from the bottom up. Though different sensibilities were expressed in different contexts—the trances of 'spontaneous movements' and visions of gods during meditation were downplayed in the more educated *qigong* circles, which attempted to replace 'superstitious' beliefs with rational explanations[50]—they coexisted within *qigong* circles without any real conflict until the very end of the 1980s. Thus famous *qigong* masters such as Yan Xin and Zhang Hongbao, who had a university education, were able to reach a broad audience from élite as well as popular backgrounds.

For Party leaders and state officials—many of whom personally experienced the transformation of their bodies through practising *qigong* themselves or through being treated by *qigong* masters—*qigong* thus offered the promise of national empowerment vis-à-vis the West, not only through creating a healthier, stronger, paranormal race of men, but also through developing a new system of knowledge both more advanced than that of the West and unfathomable for uninitiated foreigners. Qian Xuesen and others saw in *qigong* the

50   See Ots 1994: 124, 131; DF 39: 12–14; Zhang Honglin 1996.

key to a renewed and reinvigorated Marxism based on the mind-body dialectic. Socially as well as ideologically *qigong* helped to heal wounds from decades of political and ideological struggle which had lasted throughout the twentieth century and culminated with Maoism. It also offered a new vision of the future, one that was distinctly Chinese, empowering millions of individuals who could put it into practice through their daily exercises.

Qigong fever rose during the 1980s and reached its peak at the end of the decade, around the same time as the movement for political liberalisation that climaxed in the Beijing spring of 1989. There was neither convergence nor opposition between these two parallel movements. *Qigong* and political liberalism were two different responses to the post–Mao nihilism: the student movement was the last gasp of political utopianism, a popular mobilisation to bring about change through political means, in which the protesters drew inspiration from the Party's and Mao's own revolutionary history and rhetoric.[51] *Qigong*, on the other hand, which drew on nationalist and technical discourses, was in tune with a transitional phase in the Chinese state's gradual move from revolutionary idealism to technocratic management through science and technology. After 1989, then, while the movement for democracy was effectively extinguished, and faith in Marxism definitively shattered, *qigong* continued to flourish for some time, enjoying the support of political leaders who saw in *qigong* a new and harmless alternative faith as a protection against both nihilism and politicisation.

In this transitional phase, after the failure of material revolution, utopia became a magical fantasy, shifting 'back to heaven' through *qigong*: although the *qigong* movement dreamed of a future paradise in this world, the means for achieving it were mostly magical. In this respect similar to the Boxer movement of the beginning of the twentieth century, *qigong*'s solution to the conflict between Chinese tradition and modernity, in a context where the latter was already victorious, was Chinese superiority as a fantasy, manifested through the magical powers of the body.

However, by the 1990s the movement towards wholesale Westernisation and capitalism had become so overwhelming that *qigong* dreams of reconciling science, tradition and utopian ideals fell by the wayside. Interest in creating a distinctive Chinese science

---

51 Pieke 1996; see also Ci Jiwei 1994: 11.

faded, as power in the Chinese scientific community shifted from the more nationalist military establishment to civilian institutions increasingly engaged in international exchanges and interested in applying universally-recognised standards and methods.[52] The idealised body was now that of the hedonistic consumer of fashion, beauty products, plastic surgery and sexual pleasure.[53] Traditional culture became a commodity, a resource to extract and package for the booming markets of tourism, leisure and health.[54]

In the new context the *qigong* movement was led to a point of bifurcation.[55] Much of the movement followed the trend of the times, towards increased commodification and commercialisation within a framework of bureaucratic regulation. The market for *qigong* was considerable—but the entrepreneurial business practices of many *qigong* masters triggered controversies over 'fakes', 'forgeries' and 'swindling'. Such issues were concerns of public discourse about most types of market commodities in China, at a time when consumer rights and principles of business accountability and integrity were still new to the emerging Chinese economic culture. Such practices dissolved the utopian élan of the *qigong* movement, making *qigong* masters appear no different from other profit-hungry businessmen. Tainted by controversy and under renewed attack by the scientific community, political backing for commercialised *qigong* dwindled.

In this context Li Hongzhi, who had founded Falungong as a *qigong* method in 1992, attacked the overall direction of the *qigong* movement, calling instead for a rejection of hedonism and for a morality that invoked both the asceticism of ancient spiritual masters and the altruism of the Maoist era. The primary goal of practice became spiritual accomplishment and entering the 'Falun world', while this world became the stage of an apocalyptic moral battle between demonic forces and the Great *Fa*. Where *qigong* allowed the fusion of practices and fantasies of health, prosperity and spirituality, and involved opening the body to the diffused energies of the

---

52 See Wang 1993: 115–41.
53 Brownell 1998; Johansson 1998.
54 See for example Cingcade 1998.
55 Robert Weller has described this type of bifurcation as symptomatic of the emergence of what he calls a 'split-market culture' in which religious groups, in the transition to a capitalist market economy, either accept or reject its amoral individualism (Weller 1999: 83–105).

cosmos—'collecting *qi*' from trees, the sun and the moon, sending and receiving *qi* between practitioners, dabbling in all types of techniques, symbols and concepts—Falungong drew a line between the sensual pleasures of a hedonistic society and the spiritual rewards, through suffering, of exclusive cultivation. Falungong appealed to widespread concerns about morality and corruption and proposed a radical alternative to mainstream hedonism and materialism.

For thirty years after 1949 altruism had been instilled in the Chinese people to make them into obedient subjects of the Party. Feeling fooled, most of them had given up on revolutionary altruism, and accepted the Party's new promises of hedonistic gratification. Now, marginalised by the ruthless laws of the market, many people once again felt cheated by the proponents of prosperity. Traditional discourses of selflessness and morality, which have deep resonance in Chinese culture, and had, for a time, been co-opted by Communist ideology, were now captured by Falungong. Falungong became the voice of the disillusioned, of those who shook their fingers at society's betrayal of moral and altruistic ideals.

The moral exhortations of Li Hongzhi, which are reminiscent of the moralism of the Chinese sectarian tradition,[56] resonated strongly among practitioners. Li Hongzhi went against the grain of post-Maoist cynicism which, forsaking communist ideals, considers the profit motive the sole mover of men, and of the Hollywood-inspired hedonism of Chinese pop culture incarnated by television and music stars. Falungong's success in mobilising millions of practitioners showed that morality still struck a powerful chord in a country that, in past eras, had made virtue the pillar of its civilisation, and nurtured nostalgic memories of the selfless ethic of the early revolutionary period. Falungong morality, however, was perceived by its followers as of an entirely different nature from the empty and hypocritical moralistic discourse of state propaganda. The free teaching, the warm and supportive atmosphere of the practice and sharing sessions, the discipline of the volunteer trainers, were perceived as signs of an authentic virtue which had become hard to find. Where the simple, honest and virtuous person was often ridiculed and abused by co-workers, Falungong raised this suffering to the level of a heroic spiritual struggle in which the individual was to resign him or herself and bear the blows, each in-

---

[56] On the importance of morality in the sectarian teachings of the sixteenth and seventeenth centuries, see Overmyer 1999: 274, 282.

sult and each wound being a gift of 'white matter' that would help one move a step higher toward celestial perfection. All the more so if a practitioner was verbally or physically abused while defending the *Fa*. Morality was now the central issue, displacing the typical *qigong* concerns with science, paranormal abilities and tradition.

In *qigong*, discourses of morality *did* have a place, following the traditional view of Chinese body cultivation in which morality is seen as an essential aspect of disciplining the body and of controlling its desires and energies, and as a condition for attaining higher-level powers of *gongfu*.[57] But morality was embedded in the discourses and practices of the body; it was not central to the *qigong* movement's vision. Morality was a means, not an end; it grew out of a concern with one's own body rather than for social conditions. On the one hand, then, *qigong* had marked a shift away from revolutionary self-sacrifice to a greater focus on the inner life of the body; on the other hand, traditional discourses of morality re-emerged through the cultivation of body discipline.

In Falungong these discourses became the *dominant* theme, structuring the body discipline itself, and tying it to an apocalyptic eschatology which resonates with medieval texts describing the imminent destruction of the world before the appearance of the True Lord Li Hong, who will inaugurate a new era of joy and longevity.[58] To the body exercises and spiritual concepts of *qigong*, Li Hongzhi added a social critique based on moral fundamentalism. The evolution toward moral predication reinforced the tendency to politicisation. Falungong discourses of morality extended beyond body discipline to social criticism, social problems being perceived

57 On the place of morality in the teachings of Yan Xin and Li Hongzhi, see Ownby 2000. On the embodiment of virtue in classical Chinese thought, see Czikszentmihali 2004.

58 The name Li Hongzhi evokes the name of this saviour, Li Hong; with the final character *zhi*, the name Li Hongzhi can be read as 'the will to be Li Hong'. I have not been able to verify allegations that Li Hongzhi, originally named Li Lai, changed his name to inscribe himself into this tradition, which is not mentioned by himself or Falungong followers, some of whom do, however, consider him to be the Maitreya. Falungong's apocalyptic ideology can be traced back to the Buddhist eschatology of the *kalpas* or universal cycles, which, in Chinese heterodox sects, have pointed to social chaos and corruption as foreboding the end of the present *kalpa* inaugurated by the Sakyamuni Buddha, and have preached paths to salvation and preparation for ushering in the new *kalpa*. On the Li Hong prophecies, see Seiwert 2003: 82–4, 86–9; Seidel 1969–70; and Zürcher 1982: 3. On the Li Hong tradition in the Triads, see ter Haar 1993: 156–62, and ter Haar 1998: 254–7.

in China as the result of a decline in the morality of the people in general and of government leaders in particular.

The response of the state reinforced this antagonistic dynamic, confirming the vision of a world divided between the 'saved' disciples of Li Hongzhi and the world possessed by demons. Furthermore, the repeated protests by followers, both before and after the official crackdown, at newspaper offices, around Zhongnanhai, on Tiananmen Square—which could lead only to a hardening of the CCP's entirely predictable response within the logic of the Chinese political system—seem calculated to draw official power into a moral battle pitting the demonic oppressor against the suffering martyrs.

The isolation, the harassment and the cruelty suffered by followers in mainland China are seen as evidence of the demonic forces of society rising up against the Great Law, and as salutary trials along the disciple's quest for 'merit'. In such a context it becomes easier to understand why many Falungong adepts are fearless of persecution: it validates their doctrine and brings them closer to the salvation promised by Li Hongzhi.

CONCLUDING REMARKS

The popularity of *qigong* and Falungong phenomena have typically been explained in terms of Chinese people's need for cheap health care and their thirst for faith in a context in which traditional religious institutions had virtually disappeared from the cities. These are certainly important factors, and they have been analysed in the preceding pages. But they do not explain how *qigong* could have become a mass *fever* affecting people at all levels of society, from senior Party leaders to common workers, and how this craze could have involuted into the tragic confrontation around Falungong. The answer lies in how strands of Chinese religion, modern ideological currents and political networks intersected during the twisted phases of socialist China's evolution. At the point when traditional culture had been destroyed, *qigong* conjoined reinvented traditions, a mythologised national past and modernist technological scientism, all of which were incorporated and fused within bodily experience, producing an eruption of charisma and merging individual subjectivities with the utopian trajectory of the body politic. As voluntarist idealism dissolved into the consumerist gratification of desire, it was mirrored and contested by an embodied apocalypticism, the lament of an unfulfilled traditional virtue and revolutionary morality. Drawn onto a moral battlefield, the state would, in the early twenty-first century, turn back to Mao-era mythology and Confucian ethics: that, however, is another chapter in the unfolding drama of body, virtue and power in modern China.

APPENDIX

ON THE SOURCES USED FOR THIS STUDY

Since the 1999 crackdown a wealth of information on Falungong has been available in Western languages, notably on the internet, much of which is propaganda by either the Chinese authorities or by Falungong sources. There has also been a flurry of academic articles,[1] reports on human rights abuses during the repression[2] and books written for the general public,[3] but in-depth scholarship on the Falungong issue remains rare. The notable exceptions are David Ownby's[4] and Benjamin Penny's[5] ongoing research, both of which link Falungong to earlier traditions in Chinese religious his-

[1] See notably the thematic issue of *Nova Religio* edited by Catherine Wessinger (2003, vol. 6 no. 2); Leung 2002 on CCP-Falungong relations; Powers and Lee 2002 on the propaganda strategies used by both sides; Tong 2002a on the organisational structure of Falungong; Palmer and Ownby 2000, Palmer 2003 and Porter 2003 on Falungong practitioners in North America; for sociological approaches, see Madsen 2000; Chan 2004 (NRMs, sects and cults); and Lu 2005 (religious economy theory); on legal aspects, see Edelman and Richardson 2003; Keith and Lin 2003; Cheung 2004; on political aspects, see Nancy Chen 2000 and 2003a; Ching 2001; Shue 2002; Thornton 2002; Kang Xiaoguang 2002; on the methods of repression, see Tong 2002b; on the controversy over psychiatric internment of Falungong practitioners, see Munro 2000, 2002a and 2002b and Lee and Kleinman 2002; for general analysis, see also Vermander 1999 and 2001.

[2] Amnesty International, 2000, *The Crackdown on Falungong and Other So-called 'Heretical Organizations'*, <http://web.amnesty.org/library/Index/engASA17011 2000> (accessed 31 May 2005); Human Rights Watch, 2002, *Dangerous Meditation: China's Campaign against Falungong*, New York: Human Rights Watch, <http://hrw.org/reports/2002/china/> (accessed 31 May 2005); Falungong Human Rights Group, 2002, *The Falungong Report*, Buford, GA: Golden Lotus Press; Matas, David and David Kilgour, 2006, *Report into Allegations of Organ Harvesting of Falun Gong Practitioners in China*, <http://investigation.go.saveinter.net> (accessed 10 October 2006).

[3] Hua and Han 1999; Zhang and Gong 1999; Kang Xiaoguang 2000; Schechter 2000; Adams *et al.* 2000; Chang 2004.

[4] Ownby 2000, 2003a, 2003b and forthcoming.

[5] Penny 2002a, 2002b, 2003 and forthcoming.

tory, as well as Noah Porter's anthropological study of Falungong practitioners in the United States, which also discusses in some depth many of the controversial issues surrounding the movement.[6] But little is yet known of the story of the crucial first years of Falungong, between its founding in 1992 and the official crackdown starting in 1999, during which the movement emerged from obscurity and enjoyed exponential growth, and during which it took an increasingly radical posture toward the state. This book has begun to fill that gap, by recounting the story of those years and, most important, showing how Falungong was born and first grew within the matrix of the *qigong* sector, but then broke away from it and embarked on a collision course with the CCP.

On *qigong*, a voluminous scholarly literature has been produced in China, especially in the late 1980s and early 1990s. Most of these works participated in the project of the *qigong* movement itself, which aimed to create a modern technology of the body derived from ancient Chinese wisdom. These studies thus focus on the technical dimension of *qigong* practices, mostly in three areas: (1) the extraction of body technologies from the classical medical and religious literature, their classification, their systematisation and their explanation;[7] (2) the empirical observation of the chemical, physical, biological or clinical effects of the body technologies on human subjects, animals, vegetals, or chemical samples;[8] (3) finally, philosophical systems, conceptual elaborations and 'scientific' theories on the techniques and their effects.[9]

As a popular healing tradition, *qigong* was studied by five Western medical anthropologists in the 1980s and 1990s: Thomas Ots,[10] Evelyne Micollier,[11] Thomas Heise,[12] Elizabeth Hsu[13] and Nancy Chen.[14] Ots and Chen have stressed how, through *qigong*, practi-

---

6   Porter 2003.

7   See for example Li Yuanguo 1987; Zhang Wenjiang and Chang Jin 1989; Li Zhiyong 1988; Zhang Youjun *et al.* 1996.

8   See for example Wang Jisheng 1989; Liu Shanglin 1999.

9   See for example Lu Liu 1994; Liu Zhidong 1993; Qian Xuesen 1996, 1998a and 1998b.

10   Ots 1994.

11   Micollier 1995, 1999 and 2004.

12   Heise 1999.

13   Hsu 1999.

14   Nancy Chen 1995 and 2003b. Following anthropological convention, Chen uses pseudonyms to refer to some of the main figures in the *qigong* movement.

tioners appropriate their bodies and enter alternative worlds free from the pressures and limitations of the state, work and family. The phenomenological approach adopted by Ots has also been applied by Haruhiko Murakawa's[15] study of the bodily experiences of three *qigong* masters. Micollier has examined the relationship between *qigong* and emotion, showing how some types of exercises trigger emotional release, whereas others can help to control emotions. Nancy Chen's research into the treatment of '*qigong* deviation' in Chinese psychiatric hospitals describes the contested field in which extreme experiences or abnormal behaviour triggered by *qigong* practice become the subject of negotiations between affected individuals, family members and psychiatrists, sometimes leading to internment and medical management.[16] She has also examined gender issues in the *qigong* milieu.[17] Micollier and Hsu have studied the interactions between *qigong* masters and patients in Guangzhou and Kunming, as well as the concepts of illness and healing expressed in different therapeutic settings. Hsu also describes the transmission of a secret *qigong* lineage by a master to his brother-in-law, and the impact of family relationships on the transmission.

These studies help us to understand the rich experiences of *qigong* practitioners as they feel the results of their training and interact with others. But while they have mainly focused on specific, local cases, this book has attempted to show how millions of unique, individual trajectories and therapeutic encounters came together as a movement, and to explain the movement's inexorable slide into the religious and political spheres.

The historical data in this work is primarily taken from the following types of documentary sources, almost all of which were published in China: Chinese newspapers; *qigong* magazines; books and articles by *qigong* chroniclers; books on *qigong* masters and methods; internal documents of *qigong* organisations; and *qigong* reference works. Since most of these articles, books and documents are authored by individuals who were deeply involved with the *qigong* movement, either as its key actors and advocates, or as its most vocal opponents, the accuracy of the data can be questioned, especially in view of the polemical or propagandistic nature of much of the

---

15 Murakawa 2002.

16 Chen 2003b: 77–106. Several such cases are also described in the psychiatric literature; see for example Xu 1994; Shan 2000; Lee 2000; Leung *et al.* 2001.

17 Chen 2002.

material. By comparing the accounts of supporters and adversaries of the movement, however, in most cases I have found no discrepancy in the presentation of the key events, figures and political relationships. Controversy raged over whether the purported paranormal powers of *qigong* masters were real, or whether trends in the *qigong* milieu were beneficial or dangerous to society—but not on the historical facts. That the political networks of the *qigong* sector extended far into the heights of the government hierarchy, for instance, was generally admitted by all sides—and, of course, publicised by *qigong* advocates as proof of legitimacy, while critics had to refrain from naming names, for fear of offending powerful *qigong* supporters, as long as the latter remained in positions of influence.

In the Falungong case, opposing claims about the alleged health benefits or dangers of Falungong practice are outside the scope of this study; however, some of the key events, such as Li Hongzhi's change in birth date registration, or his presence in Beijing immediately prior to the Zhongnanhai demonstration, are the subject of wide discrepancies in interpretation, depending on whether the document emanates from Falungong or Chinese official sources. In these cases I present both versions, while sometimes giving precedence to what I judge to be the most plausible account. Here the difficulty is compounded by the fact that in some cases the versions presented in Falungong sources have changed with time. Where I have found such occurrences, they are discussed in footnotes. Only when the Falungong issue will have receded farther into the past, and future generations of historians will have access to sources that are still classified as highly sensitive, will it be possible to reconstruct the full story.

The Chinese mass media, and notably the press, are an important source as much for the impact the reports had on the *qigong* movement as for the events actually being reported. For instance, the significance of the *Sichuan Daily*'s 11 March 1979 report on Tang Yu, a child who could allegedly read Chinese characters with his ears, is not so much the phenomenon in itself—it was certainly not the first time in history that stories of someone with strange or miraculous powers had circulated in the Chinese countryside—but the fact that this story was picked up by an official Party newspaper with the explicit support of the Provincial Party Secretary, giving the story an aura of both political and scientific legitimacy, which could be interpreted by readers as meaning that investigating and reporting on such phenomena was permitted and even encouraged by CCP authorities. This newspaper report is thus considered by both supporters and detractors as a foundational moment which triggered China's paranormal craze. Other newspaper reports also represented turning points in the history of the *qigong* movement. '*Qigong* fever' was indeed very much a phenomenon triggered and amplified by the mass media. The '*qigong* grandmasters' such as Yan Xin and Zhang Hongbao owed much of their fame to the media which, in the 1980s, rushed into the *qigong* wave. But in the 1990s it was these same media which provided a tribune to the opponents of *qigong*, offering wide publicity to the polemic surrounding the phenomenon. And it was again the media which, as instruments of official propaganda, spearheaded the anti-Falungong campaign in the summer of 1999. In many ways, then, the story of the *qigong* movement is the story of the media coverage of *qigong* and paranormal phenomena, of the social impact of this coverage, and of the struggles behind the scenes to ensure that such coverage be either positive or negative.

The Chinese media possess a considerable but highly ambiguous power, as mediators between the official and popular worlds. On the one hand they are state propaganda organs in an environment in which the circulation of information is, in theory, strictly controlled. In this context the information they diffuse is perceived as being, if not 'objectively' correct, at least 'politically' correct, and in line with the Party's will. Theoretically, whether a story is covered, and the angle of coverage, reflects the government's views on the story. Reporting by the Chinese media connotes more than mere facts: it communicates the mind of the authorities. Stories given positive coverage are thus seen as 'safe', while it is politically dangerous to be associated with those that are given negative coverage.

However, at the same time the media were increasingly subject to the laws of the marketplace: the pressure to attract readers was great in a context of fierce competition between newspapers, even though they were all owned by the state. As a newspaper editor told me, a Chinese paper has 'two bosses': the Party and the public. In such a context, sensational stories that could fascinate the reader, such as the miracles of *qigong* masters, were highly susceptible to being reported, especially when the phenomenon was presented as a 'scientific fact'. Mass media coverage of *qigong* was thus a crucial concern for both promoters and adversaries of *qigong*. Almost all of the turning points in the movement's development and decline were either provoked or exponentially amplified by press and television coverage.

The same can be said, but to a lesser degree, of the specialised *qigong* press, which is another major source of data for this study.[18] These popular monthly, bimonthly, or quarterly magazines were the main medium for the circulation of information within *qigong* circles. By the early 1990s there were a dozen national specialised *qigong* periodicals. As pillars of the *qigong* sector, they linked up different masters, denominations, researchers, journalists, businesses serving the *qigong* market, and practitioners, followers and enthusiasts at all levels. *Qigong* magazines contained articles presenting various masters and methods; discussions of classical texts and theoretical concepts; reports on laboratory experiments and other investigations; practical advice on problems encountered during practice; practitioners' healing testimonies; reports on events and activities within *qigong* circles; advertisements for training workshops and *qigong*-related products; and editorials presenting the official line on correct and unhealthy trends in the *qigong* sector. Through these magazines the different actors in the milieu, from leading figures to the grassroots of ordinary practitioners, exchanged news, ideas and information, thus forming a nationwide community sharing a common discourse, which was conscious of itself, its hopes and its interests.

While the mass media created *qigong*'s national celebrities, these specialised magazines had a certain influence on the rise and reputation of different masters and denominations. A master wanting

18   The main *qigong* magazines were: *Qigong*, published from 1980 by the Zhejiang Institute of Chinese Medicine; *Qigong and Science* (Qigong yu kexue), published from 1982 by the Guangdong Qigong Science Research Society; *Chinese Qigong* (Zhonghua qigong), published from 1983 by the All-China Association of Chinese Medicine's Qigong Science Committee; *China Qigong* (Zhongguo Qigong), published from 1984 by the Beidaihe Qigong Hospital; *Qigong and Sports* (Qigong yu tiyu), published from 1985 by the United Front Work Department of the Shaanxi Provincial Party Committee; *Oriental Science Qigong* (Dongfang Qigong), published from 1986 by the Beijing Qigong Society; and the *International Qigong News* (Guoji qigong bao), published in Xi'an from 1994 by the International Qigong Science Federation. See Despeux 1997: 279–80; see also WH: 600–19 for a listing of other, more obscure magazines. Most if not all of these magazines were shut down in the years following the 1999 crackdown on Falungong.

to come out of obscurity would seek coverage in *qigong* magazines, in order to earn recognition of his denomination throughout
the *qigong* sector. The role of these specialised magazines in the
legitimation of masters and denominations was made all the more
important by the fact that these magazines maintained the same
type of relationship with the Party-state as other Chinese media.
Whatever was published in a *qigong* magazine would be perceived
as having been approved by the authorities, and thus as enjoying
a certain degree of political support and legitimacy. Most of these
magazines belonged to a state-sponsored *qigong* association. Their
editorial boards were theoretically responsible for ensuring the
ideological orthodoxy of the contents. Thus the specialised *qigong*
press was supposed to orient the ideological evolution of the *qigong*
sector along the lines dictated by the CCP.

But in practice the *qigong* press paid only lip service to ideological orthodoxy. Magazine content often flagrantly contradicted
the rare editorials presenting the official line. Only *Oriental Science Qigong* (*Dongfang qigong*), the Beijing Qigong Society's official
magazine, regularly published editorials and speeches by the officials
of the state-sponsored *qigong* associations, stressing the need to respect Party ideology, and tended to publish articles which, relatively
speaking, did not stray too far from materialist orthodoxy.

Another source of data are books by *qigong* chroniclers: accounts
published by individuals who were active players in the *qigong* sector or in the polemics against it. The best of this category is *Swirls of
Qi over the Celestial Realm*[19] by Zheng Guanglu, a *qigong* and martial
arts master who tells the story of '*qigong* fever' from its beginnings
in the 1950s to the Yan Xin craze and the beginnings of disillusionment in the movement by the end of the 1980s. While not a
scholarly study, Zheng's account, based on his own experiences,
on interviews with other figures in the movement, and on press
reports, provides a wealth of data on the *qigong* milieu of the 1980s,
especially through anecdotes and personal recollections which
are hard to find elsewhere. Written by an active participant in the
qigong craze who has taken his distance without joining the fierce
anti-*qigong* polemic, Zheng's book conveys with both sympathy
and objectivity how the enthusiasm, the conflicts and the crises of
the *qigong* movement during the 1980s were perceived and debated

19 ZGL.

within the *qigong* milieu. Another useful source is *1995: The Great Qigong Controversy* by Li Jianxin and Zheng Qin,[20] two journalists who, despite their position in favour of *qigong*, provide, in a virtually raw and unedited state, a good quantity of testimonies and interviews with key actors in the polemic, including data and opinions supporting the anti-*qigong* camp. Other actors whose works I have used include *qigong* propagandist turned *qigong* master Ji Yi,[21] and anti-paranormal polemists Yu Guangyuan,[22] He Zuoxiu[23] and Sima Nan.[24]

Books on *qigong* masters and *gongfa*, and internal documents on denominations, are another source of information. The main denominations published one or several works on their master, his or her method, philosophy etc. Works on Yan Xin and Zhang Hongbao, and the voluminous works of Li Hongzhi are rich in relevant data. The internal documentation of these groups is also a precious source of otherwise unavailable material: the *Tantric Qigong Bulletin*,[25] newsletter of Zangmigong published on a single A3 photocopied sheet; the *Guidance for Life Science*,[26] internal journal of Zhonggong, as well as the Zhonggong trainers' manuals; not to mention the copious tracts and literature disseminated by Falungong on the internet and in photocopied form, are replete with data on the organisation of denominations. *Qigong* reference books, especially *The Complete Book of Contemporary Chinese Qigong* edited by Wu Hao, director of the domestic policy office of the *People's Daily*, were also a mine of essential data for this study.[27]

---

20 QDL.
21 Ji Yi 1990a, 1991 and 1993.
22 Yu Guangyuan 2002.
23 He Zuoxiu 2002.
24 Sima Nan 2002.
25 *Zangmi qigong xinxi*.
26 *Shengming kexue daobao*.
27 WH. The book, organised as an encyclopaedia, contains four parts covering methods, literature, masters and organisations. The first part presents 161 *gongfa*. The second part is a bibliography of 389 Chinese books on *qigong*. The third part contains biographic entries on 556 masters, and the fourth provides brief descriptions and contact details for 182 *qigong* associations. This book was used as a basis for creating computer databases on *qigong* masters and associations, to which I then added data from other sources. It should be noted, however, that *The Complete Book…* is not critically edited: the entries under each category seem to have been directly submitted by the different denominations. The accuracy of the data cannot be verified. Furthermore, entries are not standardised in terms of form or

Finally, the internet has become an increasingly rich source of data.[28] Most of our story occurred before widespread adoption of the internet in China, and Falungong was the first *qigong* group to use it systematically as a tool for disseminating information.[29] Currently most of the content of Falungong websites is related to the post-1999 repression. On *qigong*, some Chinese sites, most of which are now closed, contained news reports on events in the *qigong* circles, official policy statements, and interesting debates on future trends of the *qigong* movement.[30] Yan Xin's[31] and Zhang Hongbao's[32] web pages were also useful sources of information. In recent years some individuals have also posted detailed chronologies and historical materials on the internet.[33]

---

content, making it difficult to compare different masters or organisations. Finally, the choice of entries includes several major lacunae: for example, Yan Xin, by far the most famous master, is not included in the directory, while at least a dozen of Zhang Hongbao's principal disciples have separate entries. This may perhaps be attributable to the fact that Yan Xin was exiled to the United States at the time the book was being compiled.

28 Barend ter Haar has created an English-language site which contains a critical and almost exhaustive description of most websites and publications on *qigong* and Falungong in European languages: 'Falungong: Evaluation and Further References', <www.let.leidenuniv.nl/bth/falun.htm>.

29 The main portal for Falungong is <www.falundafa.org>, which contains links to several other Falungong sites.

30 See notably <www.qg100.com/news>, closed in 2003.

31 The best Yan Xin sites, several of which I consulted at the end of 1998, had disappeared by 2002. The current website of the International Yan Xin Qigong Association is <www.yanxinqigong.net>.

32 <www.goldkylin.net>, closed in 2003.

33 Notably Ji Shoukang (see JSK), who, judging from his comments in the online documents, which aim to provide data on the history of *qigong* in Hebei province, appears to have been actively involved in *qigong* circles in that region; and Tu Jianhua (see TJH), whose chronology of events and press reports on the paranormal controversies was initially posted on the 'Scientific Atheism Net' but then appeared in the *qigong* section of the website of the International Noble Academy (<www.nobelac.com>), a Toronto-based organisation of Chinese scientists interested in nano-technology, non-equilibrium statistical physics, Chinese music, science fiction, piano and *qigong*, among other disciplines.

BIBLIOGRAPHY

ABBREVIATIONS USED IN REFERENCES

Mass circulation newspapers and magazines

BQB   *Beijing Qingnian Bao* [Beijing Youth News], Beijing.

BR   *Beijing Ribao* [Beijing Daily], Beijing.

BWB   *Beijing Wanbao* [Beijing Evening News], Beijing.

ET   *Dajiyuan shibao* [Epoch Times], in many countries and online.

GM   *Guangming Ribao* [Guangming Daily], Beijing.

GR   *Gongren Ribao* [Workers' Daily], Beijing.

HW   *Renmin Ribao Haiwaiban* [People's Daily Overseas Edition], Beijing.

HX   *Huaxi Dushibao* [West China Metropolis], Chengdu.

JKB   *Jiankang Bao* [Health], Beijing.

KR   *Keji ribao* [Science & Technology Daily], Beijing.

KX   *Keji Xinwen* [Science & Technology News], Beijing.

MB   *Ming Bao* [Light], Hong Kong.

NF   *Nanfang Zhoumo* [Southern Weekend], Guangzhou.

RR   *Renmin Ribao* [People's Daily], Beijing.

SB   *Chengdu Shangbao* [Chengdu Economic News], Chengdu.

SGB   *Sichuan Gongren Bao* [Sichuan Workers' News], Chengdu.

SR   *Sichuan Ribao* [Sichuan Daily], Chengdu.

TR   *Tianjin Ribao* [Tianjin Daily], Tianjin.

XTY   *Xin Tiyu* [New Sport], Beijing.

ZDB   *Zhongguo Dianzi Bao* [China Electronics News], Beijing.

ZJS   *Zhongguo Jingji Shibao* [China Economic Times], Beijing.

ZQB   *Zhongguo Qingnian Bao* [China Youth News], Beijing.

ZTB   *Zhongguo Tiyu Bao* [China Sports News], Beijing.

ZZ   *Ziran Zazhi* [Nature], Shanghai.

Qigong magazines and newsletters

DF   *Dongfang Qigong* [Oriental Science Qigong], Beijing.

QG   *Qigong* [Qigong], Hangzhou.

QK   *Qigong yu Kexue* [Qigong and Science], Guangzhou.

QL   *Qilin Wenhua Huicui* [Flowering of Qilin Culture], Chongqing.

SMK   *Qigong yu Shengming Kexue* [Qigong & Life Science], Beijing.

TY   *Qigong yu Tiyu* [Qigong & Sports], Xi'an.

ZG   *Zhongguo qigong* [China Qigong], Beidaihe.

ZM   *Zangmi qigong Xinxi* [Tantric Qigong Bulletin], Tieli (Heilongjiang).

Frequently cited works by Li Hongzhi

Changchun   'Wei Changchun Falun dafa fudaoyuan jiefa', see Li Hongzhi 1994.

Essential Points   *Falun Fofa – Jingjin yaozhi*, see Li Hongzhi 1999c.

Europe   *Falun fofa – zai Ouzhou fahui shang jiangfa*, see Li Hongzhi 1999b.

Explanations   *Zhuan Falun fajie*, see Li Hongzhi 1997b.

North America   *Falun Fofa: zai Beimei shoujie fahui shang jiang fa*, see Li Hongzhi 1999a.

Sydney   *Falun Fofa – zai Xini jiangfa*, see Li Hongzhi 1996b.

USA   *Falun Fofa – zai Meiguo jiangfa*, see Li Hongzhi 1997a.

ZFG   *Zhongguo Falungong*, see Li Hongzhi 1993.

ZFL   'Zhuan Falun', see Li Hongzhi 1998a.

ZFL II   *Zhuan Falun (juan er)*, see Li Hongzhi 1995a.

Other frequently cited documents

CME   'A Chronicle of Major Events of Falun Dafa', <http://www.clearwisdom.net/emh/articles/2004/8/27/chronicle.html> (accessed 27 July 2006); translated from Chinese version: <http://www.zhengjian.org/zj/articles/2004/3/2/26013.html>; first part also available at <http://www.pureinsight.org/pi/index.php?news=1996>.

IYXQA International Yan Xin Qigong Association, Section à l'Université de Sherbrooke, 'Introduction au qigong traditionnel chinois et au qigong de Yan Xin', photocopied document, *c*. 1995.

JG   'Jiu guojia dui qigong he teyigongneng yanjiu de jiben zhengce: yu Cui Yongyuan zai tanxin' [Regarding the state's basic policy on qigong and Extraordinary Powers: heart-felt words for Cui Yongyuan], <www.qg100.com/news>, accessed October 2001.

JSK   Ji Shoukang, 'Zhongguo qigong shiliao chuji' [Draft historical materials on Chinese qigong], sections I–IX, <http://www.chinaqigong.net/qgb/wrbz/index.htm>.

LH   'Lishi huigu' [Looking back at history], photocopied Falungong document, script of a radio programme broadcast outside China, *c.* 2000.

QDL   *1995: Qigong da lunzhan*, see Li Jianxin and Zheng Qin 1996.

TJH   Tu Jianhua, 'Teyigongneng de licheng (yi, 1979–1988)' [The story of Extraordinary Powers (I. 1979–1988)], <http://www.nobelac.com/wqsweb/paperforWQS/miracal1.htm>, accessed 1 January 2005.

WH   *Zhongguo dangdai qigong quanshu*, see Wu Hao (ed.) 1993.

YPFX   Yi Pi Falungong Xueyuan [A group of Falungong practitioners], 'Jielu Changchun jishaoshu ren de yinmou' [The plot of a tiny minority of Changchun people unveiled], internal document, Falungong, *c.* 1999.

ZGL   *Qi juan shenzhou*, see Zheng Guanglu 1991.

BIBLIOGRAPHY

Adams, Ian, Riley Adams and Rocco Galati, 2000, *Power of the Wheel: The Falungong Revolution*, Toronto: Stoddart.

Agren, Hans, 1975, 'Patterns of Tradition and Modernization in Contemporary Chinese Medicine' in Arthur Kleinman (ed.), *Medicine in Chinese Cultures: Comparative Studies of Health Care in Chinese and Other Societies*, Washington, DC: Department of Health, Education and Welfare—Public Health Service—National Institutes of Health, pp. 37–51.

Aijmer, Goran and Virgil K.Y. Ho, 2000, *Cantonese Society in a Time of Change*, Hong Kong: The Chinese University Press.

Bakken, Børge, 2000, *The Exemplary Society: Human Improvement, Social Control, and the Dangers of Modernity*, Oxford University Press.

Bastid-Bruguière, Marianne, 1998, 'Liang Qichao yu zongjiao wenti', *Tōhō gakuhō*, 70: 329–73.

Beijing Qigong Yanjiuhui (ed.), 1989, *Qigong xin gongfa gongli xiangjie* [Detailed explanations on new qigong methods and theories], Beijing: Shehui kexue wenxian chubanshe.

Beijing shi tongjiju [Beijing Municipal Statistical Bureau], 2000, *Beijing tongji nianjian 2000* [Beijing Statistical Yearbook 2000], Bejing: China Statistics Press.

Bell, Mark and Taylor C. Boas, 2003, 'Falun Gong and the Internet: Evangelism, Community, and Struggle for Survival', *Nova Religio*, 6(2): 277–93.

Benson, Herbert, 1975, *The Relaxation Response*, New York: William Morrow.

——, 1996, *Timeless Healing: The Power and Biology of Belief*, New York: Simon & Schuster.

Brownell, Susan, 1995, *Training the Body for China: Sports in the Moral Order of the People's Republic*, University of Chicago Press.

——, 1998, 'The Body and the Beautiful in Chinese Nationalism: Sportswomen and Fashion Models in the Reform Era', *China Information*, XIII(2/3): 36–57.

Bruun, Ole, 2003, *Fengshui in China: Geomantic Divination between State Orthodoxy and Popular Religion*, Copenhagen: NIAS Press.

Campbell, Colin, 1972, 'The Cult, the Cultic Milieu and Secularization' in Michael Hill (ed.), *A Sociological Yearbook of Religion in Britain*, London: SCM Press.

Chan, Cheris Shun-ching, 2004, 'The Falungong in China: A Sociological Perspective', *China Quarterly*, 179: 665–83.

Chang, Maria Hsia, 2004, *Falungong: The End of Days*, New Haven, CT: Yale University Press.

Chau, Adam Yuet, 2005, *Miraculous Response: Doing Popular Religion in Contemporary China*, Stanford University Press.

Che Guocheng and Ke Yuwen, 1997, 'Zhongguo gongchandang he renmin zhengfu zhongshi qigong (shang)' [The Chinese Communist Party and the People's Government place importance on qigong (I)], DF, 66: 21–4.

Chen Bing and Deng Zimei, 2000, *Ershi shiji zhongguo fojiao*, Beijing: Minzu chubanshe.

Chen, Hsi-yuan, 1999, 'Confucianism Encounters Religion: The Formation of Religious Discourse and the Confucian Movement in Modern China', PhD diss., Harvard University.

Chen Linfeng, 1988, *Zhongguo huiliangong* [China qigong of the lotus wisdom], Xi'an: Xi'an jiaotong daxue chubanshe.

——, 1993, *Huixue congshu (di 1–5 juan)* [The Study of Wisdom collection (books 1–5)], Changchun: Changchun Chubanshe.

Chen, Nancy, 1995, 'Urban Spaces and Experiences of Qigong' in Deborah Davis, Richard Kraus, Barry Naughton and Elizabeth Perry (eds), *Urban Spaces in Contemporary China*, Cambridge University Press and Washington, DC: Woodrow Wilson Center Press, pp. 347–61.

——, 2000, 'Cultivating Qi and the Body Politic', *Harvard Asia Pacific Review*, 4(1): 45–9.

——, 2002, 'Embodying Qi and Masculinities in Post Mao China' in Jeffrey N. Wasserstrom and Susan Brownell (eds), *Chinese Femininities/Chinese Masculinities: A Reader*, Berkeley, CA: University of California Press.

——, 2003a, 'Healing Sects and Anti-Cult Campaigns', *China Quarterly*, 174: 505–20.

——, 2003b, *Breathing Spaces: Qigong, Psychiatry, and Healing in China*, New York: Columbia University Press.

Chen Xin and Mei Lei, 1988 [1982], 'Renti teyigongneng yanjiu zai Zhongguo' [Research on Extraordinary Powers of the human body in China] in Qian Xuesen, 1988, *Lun renti kexue* [On somatic science], Beijing: Renmin junyi chubanshe, pp. 258–62.

Chen Xingqiao, 1998, *Fojiao 'qigong' yu Falungong* [Buddhist 'qigong' and Falungong], Beijing: Zongjiao wenhua chubanshe.

Chen Yingning, 2000, *Daojiao yu yangsheng* [Daoism and life cultivation], Beijing: Huawen chubanshe.

Chen Yingning, 1963 [1957], 'Shenjing suairuo jinggong liaoyang fa wenda' [Question and answers on the quiet practice therapeutic method for neurasthenia], *Daoxie huikan* [Journal of the China Taoist Association], 3: 1–28; reprinted in 1967 in book form in Taiwan by Zhenshanmei chubanshe, Taipei.

Cheung, Anne S.Y., 2004, 'In Search of a Theory of Cult and Freedom of Religion in China: The Case of Falungong', *Pacific Rim Law and Policy Journal*, 13(1): 1–30.

Chevrier, Yves, 1995, 'La question de la société civile, la Chine et le chat du Cheshire', *Etudes chinoises*, XIV(2) (Autumn), pp. 154–251.

Ching, Julia, 2001, 'The Falungong: Religious and Political Implications', *American Asian Review*, 19(4): 1–18. Available online at <http://www.rickross.com/reference/fa_lun_gong/falun258.html> (accessed 31 May 2005).

Chong, Woei Lien, 1996, 'Mankind and Nature in Chinese Thought: Li Zehou on the Traditional Roots of Maoist Voluntarism', *China Information*, XI(2/3): 138–75.

Ci Jiwei, 1994, *Dialectic of the Chinese Revolution: From Utopianism to Hedonism*, Stanford University Press.

Cingcade, Mary L., 1998, 'Tourism and the Many Tibets: The Manufacture of Tibetan "Tradition"', *China Information*, XIII(1): 1–24.

Clarke, Isabel (ed.), 2000, *Psychosis and Spirituality: Exploring the New Frontier*, London: Whurr Publishers.

Cohen, Paul A., 1997, *History in Three Keys: The Boxers as Event, Experience, and Myth*, New York: Columbia University Press.

Croizier, Ralph, 1968, *Traditional Medicine in Modern China: Science, Nationalism, and the Tensions of Cultural Change*, Cambridge, MA: Harvard University Press.

——, 1973, 'Traditional Medicine as a Basis for Chinese Medical Practise' in Joseph Quinn (ed.), *Medicine and Public Health in the People's Republic of China*, Washington, DC: US Department of Health, Education, and Welfare, pp. 3–21.

——, 1975, 'Medicine and Modernization in China: An Historical Overview' in Arthur Kleinman (ed.), *Medicine in Chinese Cultures: Comparative Studies of Health Care in Chinese and Other Societies*, Washington, DC: Department of Health, Education and Welfare—Public Health Service—National Institutes of Health, pp. 21–35.

Czikszentmihali, Mark, 2004, *Material Virtue: Ethics and the Body in Early China*, Leiden: Brill.

Dean, Kenneth, 1993, *Daoist Ritual and Popular Cults of Southeast China*, Princeton University Press.

Deng, Zixian and Fang Shimin, 2000, 'The Two Tales of Falungong: Radicalism in a Traditional Form', <www.xys.org/xys/netters/Fang-Zhouzi/religion/2tales.doc> (revised May 2000).

Despeux, Catherine, 1981, *Taiji quan. Art martial, technique de longue vie*, Paris: Guy Trédaniel.

——, 1988, *La moëlle du phénix rouge. Santé et longue vie dans la Chine du XVIe siècle*, Paris: Guy Trédaniel.

——, 1989, 'Gymnastics: The Ancient Tradition' in Livia Kohn, *Daoist Meditation and Longevity Techniques*, Ann Arbor, MI: Center for Chinese Studies, The University of Michigan, pp. 225–61.

——, 1997, 'Le qigong, une expression de la modernité chinoise' in Jacques Gernet and Marc Kalinowski (eds), *En suivant la Voie Royale, Mélanges en hommage à Léon Vandermeersch*, Paris: Ecole française d'Extrême-Orient, pp. 267–81.

Ding Mingyue, 1994, *Wu wei – sanbaizhong teyigongneng shiri tong* [Nonaction: master 300 Extraordinary Powers in ten days], Chengdu: Chengdu keji daxue chubanshe.

Ding Shu, 1993, *Yangmou* [Naked conspiracy], <http://members.lycos. co.uk/sixiang001/author/D/DingShu/YangMo/ymchap16.txt> (accessed 16 January 2004).

Ding,Yijiang, 1998, 'Corporatism and Civil Society in China: An Overview of the Debate in Recent Years', *China Information*, XII(4): 44–67.

Dong, Paul, 1984, *The Four Major Mysteries of Mainland China*, Englewood Cliffs, NJ: Prentice-Hall.

DSM-IV, 1994, *Diagnostic and Statistical Manual of Mental Disorders*, Washington, DC: American Psychiatric Association.

Duara, Prasenjit, 1995, *Rescuing History from the Nation: Questioning Narratives of Modern China*, University of Chicago Press.

DuBois, Thomas, 2005, *The Sacred Village: Social Change and Religious Life in Rural China*, Honolulu, HI: University of Hawaii Press.

Edelman, Bryan and James T. Richardson, 2003, 'Falungong and the Law: Development of Legal Social Control in China', *Nova Religio*, 6(2): 312–31.

Eisenberg, David, 1985, *Encounters with Qi: Exploring Chinese Medicine*, New York: Norton.

Eliade, Mircea, 1959, *Initiations, rites, sociétés secrètes*, Paris: Gallimard.

——, 1968, *Le chamanisme et les techniques archaïques de l'extase*, Paris: Payot.

Eng, Irene and Yi-Min Lin, 2002, 'Religious Festivities, Communal Rivalry, and Restructuring of Authority Relations in Rural Chaozhou, Southeast China', *Journal of Asian Studies*, 61(4): 1259–85.

Epoch Group, 2005, *Nine Commentaries on the Communist Party*, Broad Press Inc.

Esherick, Joseph W., 1987, *The Origins of the Boxer Uprising*, Berkeley, CA: University of California Press.

Evasdottir, Erika, 2004, *Obedient Autonomy: Chinese Intellectuals and the Achievement of Orderly Life*, Vancouver, BC: UBC Press.

Fan Shuren, 1992, 'Qihai mingzhu: Bao Guiwen laoshi chuanlue' [A shining pearl in the sea of Qi: the life of master Bao Guiwen] in *Di san jie Xiao Changming zongshi zongjiao zhexue yantaohui lunwenji* [Proceedings of the Third Conference on the Religious Philosophy of Patriarch Xiao Changming], edited by Zhongghua minguo Tiandejiao zonghui and Zhonghua minguo Tiandijiao zonghui, Taipei, pp. 185–96.

Fang, Ling, 2002, 'Les médecins laïques contre l'exorcisme sous les Ming: la disparition de l'enseignement de la thérapeutique rituelle dans le cursus de l'Institut impérial de médecine', *Extrême-Orient Extrême Occident*, 24: 31–46.

Feuchtwang, Stephan, 2002, *An Anthropological Analysis of Chinese Geomancy*, Bangkok: White Lotus.

—— and Wang Mingming, 2001, *Grassroots Charisma: Four Local Leaders in China*, London: Routledge.

Flower, John Myers, 2004, 'A Road is Made: Roads, Temples, and Historical Memory in Ya'an County, Sichuan', *Journal of Asian Studies*, 63(3): 649–85.

Foucault, Michel, 1988a, 'Technologies of the Self' in *Technologies of the Self: A Seminar with Michel Foucault*, edited by L.H. Martin, H. Gutman and P.H. Hutton, London: Tavistock, pp. 16–49.

——, 1988b, *The History of Sexuality, Vol. I*, translated by Robert Hurley, New York: Vintage.

Frank, Adam D., 2006, *Taijiquan and the Search for the Little Old Chinese Man: Understanding Identity through Martial Arts*, London: Palgrave Macmillan.

Friedman, Edward, 1983, 'Einstein and Mao: Metaphors of Revolution', *China Quarterly*, 93: 51–75.

Gentz, Joachim, 2004, 'The One Discourse that Pervades All: Concurrent Constructions of an Ideal Order in the Fight Between the CCP and Falungong', paper presented at the XVth Congress of the European Association of Chinese Studies, 28–29 August, Heidelberg.

Gernet, Jacques, 1981, 'Techniques de recueillement, religion et philosophie: à propos du jingzuo néoconfucéen', *Bulletin de l'Ecole française d'Extrême-Orient*, LXIX: 475–93.

Gladney, Dru, 1991, *Muslim Chinese: Ethnic Nationalism in the People's Republic*, Cambridge, MA: Harvard University Council on East Asian Studies.

Goldfuss, Gabriele, 2001, *Vers un bouddhisme du 20e siècle. Yang Wenhui (1837–1911), réformateur laïque et imprimeur*, Paris: Collège de France, Institut des Hautes Etudes Chinoises.

Gong Yuzhi, 2002, 'Zongxu' [General preface] in Yu Guangyuan, *Wo shi Yu Guangyuan* [I am Yu Guangyuan], Beijing: Zhongguo shidai jingji chubanshe, pp. 1–6.

Goossaert, Vincent, 2000, *Dans les temples de la Chine. Histoire des cultes, vie des communautés*, Paris: Albin Michel.

——, 2003, 'Le destin de la religion chinoise au 20e siecle', *Social Compass*, 50(4): 429–40.

Gu Hansen, 1980a, 'Juexin dakai qigong kexue shenmi de damen' [Firmly resolve to open the great mysterious gate of qigong science], QG, 1(1): 4–5.

———, 1980b, 'Shengming xinxi kexue chutan – renti shoufa liti xinxi de tansuo' [Preliminary scientific investigation on vital information: exploration on information sent by the hand outside the human body], ZZ, 3(8): 563–65.

———, 1980c, 'Qigong "waiqi" wuzhi jichu de yanjiu' [Research on the material basis of 'external qi'], ZZ, 3(10): 747.

Gulik, Robert van, 2003 [1961], *Sexual Life in Ancient China*, Leiden: Brill.

Guo Lin, 1980a, *Xin qigong liaofa (chujigong)* [New qigong therapeutic method (Beginning level)], Hefei: Anhui kexue jishu chubanshe.

———, 1980b, *Xin qigong fangzhi aizheng fa* [A new qigong method for cancer prevention and therapy], Beijing: Renmin tiyu chubanshe.

Guo, Zhouli (ed.), 1989, *Di'er jie guoji qigong huiyi xueshu lunwenji* [Collected academic papers of the second international qigong conference], Xi'an: Tianze chubanshe.

Guojia tongjiju [State Statistical Bureau], 1998, *Zhongguo tongji nianjian 1998 nian (di 17 hao)* [China Statistical Yearbook 1998 (no. 17)], Beijing: China Statistical Publishing House.

Haar, Barend ter, 1992, *The White Lotus Teachings in Chinese Religious History*, Leiden: Brill.

———, 1993, 'Messianism and the Heaven and Earth Society: Approaches to Heaven and Earth Society Texts' in David Ownby and Mary Somers Heidhues (ed.), *'Secret Societies' Reconsidered: Perspectives on the Social History of Modern China and Southeast Asia*, Armonk, NY: M.E. Sharpe.

———, 1998, *Ritual and Mythology of the Chinese Triads: Creating an Identity*, Leiden: Brill.

———, 2001, 'Falungong: Evaluation and Further References', <http//www.let.leidenuniv.nl/bth/falun.htm>.

Havel, Vaclav *et al.*, 1985, *The Power of the Powerless: Citizens against the State in Central-Eastern Europe*, Armonk, NY: M.E. Sharpe.

He Zuoxiu, 1996a, 'Weishenme shuo "renti teyigongneng" shi jiade?' [Why do I say that the 'extraordinary functions of the human body' are a hoax?], KX, 3(39): 8–11, 22.

——— (ed.), 1996b, *Wei kexue baoguang* [Pseudo-science exposed], Beijing: Zhongguo shehui kexue chubanshe.

———, 1999, 'I Do not Approve of Teenagers Practicing Qigong', *Chinese Law and Government*, 32(5): 95–8. Translation of article published in *Qingshaonian keji bolan*, 19 April 1999.

———, 2002, *Wo shi He Zuoxiu* [I am He Zuoxiu], Beijing: Zhongguo shidai jingji chubanshe.

Heberer, Thomas, 2002, 'Social Associations – China' in David Levinson and Karen Christensen (eds), *Encyclopedia of Modern Asia*, New York: Scribners (Thomson Gale), vol. 5, pp. 241–3.

Heelas, Paul, 1996, *The New Age Movement: The Celebration of the Self and the Sacralization of Modernity*, Oxford and Cambridge, MA: Blackwell.

Heise, Thomas, 1999, *Qigong in der VR China: Entwicklung, Theorie und Praxis*, Berlin: Verlag für Wissenschaft und Bildung.

Hertz, Ellen, 1998, *The Trading Crowd: An Ethnography of the Shanghai Stock Market*, Cambridge University Press.

Hervieu-Léger, Danièle, 1993, *La religion pour mémoire*, Paris: Le Cerf [English translation by S. Lee published as *Religion as a Chain of Memory*, Cambridge: Polity, 2000].

———, 1998, *Le pèlerin et le converti*, Paris: Flammarion.

———, 2001, *La religion en miettes ou la question des sectes*, Paris: Calmann-Lévy.

——— and Jean-Paul Willaime, 2001, *Sociologies et religion. Approches classiques*, Paris: Presses Universitaires de France.

Hess, David J., 1993, *Science in the New Age: The Paranormal, its Defenders and Debunkers, and American Culture*, Madison, WI: University of Wisconsin Press.

Hillier, S.M. and J.A. Jewell, 1983, *Health Care and Traditional Medicine in China, 1800–1982*, London: Routledge and Kegan Paul.

Hobsbawm, Eric and Terence Ranger (eds), 1983, *The Invention of Tradition*, Cambridge University Press.

Hsu, Elizabeth, 1999, *The Transmission of Chinese Medicine*, Cambridge University Press.

Hu Chunshen, 1989, *Zhonghua qigongxue* [The study of Chinese qigong], Chengdu: Sichuan daxue chubanshe.

Hu Haichang and Hao Qiyao (eds), 1989, *Qigong kexue wenji* [Compilation on qigong science], Beijing: Beijing ligong daxue chubanshe.

Hu Meicheng, 1981, 'Qigong mingcheng de youlai' [The origin of the term qigong], QG, 2(1): 42–3.

Hu Yaozhen, 1959, *Qigong ji baojian gong* [Qigong and health-preserving gong], Beijing: Renmin weisheng chubanshe.

Hua Chu and Zhong Han, 1999, *Falungong Fengbao* [The storm of Falungong], Hong Kong: Pacific Century.

Hunter, Alan and Kim-Kwong Chan, 1993, *Protestantism in Contemporary China*, Cambridge University Press.

Ji Yi, 1990a, *Da qigongshi chushan – Zhang Hongbao he tade gongfa mizong* [The qigong grandmaster comes out of the mountains: Zhang Hong-bao and the esoteric secrets of his qigong method], Beijing: Hualing chubanshe.

——, 1990b, *Zhongguo shengong jiemi* [The secrets of miraculous qigong revealed], Beijing: Hualing chubanshe.

——, 1991, *Chao shengming xianxiang* [Phenomena transcending life], Bei-jing: Zhongguo guangbo dianshi chubanshe.

——, 1993, *Qi zai Zhongguo – shinian Zhongguo qigong dachao xiemi* [Qi in China: revelations on ten years of the great qigong wave], Beijing: Guoji wenhua chuban gongsi.

Jiang Weiqiao, 1974 [1917], *Yin shizi jingzuofa* [Master Yin Shi's sitting meditation method], Taibei: Xinweiyi chuban gongsi.

——, 1981 [1956], 'Tantan "qigong zhiliaofa"' [About 'qigong therapy'] in Tao Bingfu and Yang Weihe (eds), 1981, *Qigong liaofa jijin* [Outstand ing selections on qigong therapy], Beijing: Renmin weisheng chuban-she, pp. 12–19 [Originally published in *Zhongyi zazhi*, 10 (1956)].

—— and Liu Guizhen, 1958, *Qigong liaofa, di yi ji* [Qigong therapeutic method, first volume], Beijing: Renmin weisheng chubanshe.

Johansson, Perry, 1998, 'White Skin, Large Breasts: Chinese Beauty Prod-uct Advertising as Cultural Discourse', *China Information*, XIII(2/3): 59–84.

Johnson, David, 1995a, 'Introduction' in David Johnson (ed.), *Ritual and Scripture in Chinese Popular Religion*, Berkeley, CA: Publications of the Chinese Popular Culture Project.

——, 1995b, 'Mu-lien in *Pao-chüan*: The Performance Context and Reli-gious Meaning of the *Yu-ming Pao-chuan*' in David Johnson (ed.), *Ritual and Scripture in Chinese Popular Religion*, Berkeley, CA: Publications of the Chinese Popular Culture Project, pp. 55–103.

——, Andrew Nathan and Evelyn Rawski (eds), 1983–5, *Popular Culture in Late Imperial China*, Berkeley, CA: University of California Press.

Jordan, David K. and Daniel L. Overmyer, 1986, *The Flying Phoenix: As-pects of Chinese Sectarianism in Taiwan*, Princeton University Press.

Kane, Daniel, 1993, 'Irrational Belief among the Chinese Elite' in Mabel Lee and A.D. Syrokomla-Stefanowska (eds), *Modernization of the Chi-nese Past*, Sydney: Wild Peony, pp. 152–65.

Kang Xiaoguang, 2000, *Falungong shijian quan toushi* [The full story of the Falungong incident], Hong Kong: Mingbao chubanshe.

——, 2002, 'The Political Effects of the Falun Gong Issue', *Chinese Education and Society*, 35(1): 5–14.

Ke Yunlu, 1989, *Da qigongshi* [The great qigong master], Beijing: Renmin wenxue chubanshe.

——, 1993, *Miandui qigongjie. Qigong xiulian de aomi yu wuqu* [Facing the qigong sector: mysteries and errors in qigong cultivation], Beijing: Zuojia chubanshe.

——, 1994, *Shengming teyi xianxiang kaocha* [Investigation on extraordinary life phenomena], vols 1–3, Beijing: Jinri Zhongguo chubanshe.

——, 1995a, *Xin jibingxue* [The new pathology], Beijing: Zhongguo chubanshe.

——, 1995b, *Qigong xiulian de aomi yu wuqu* [Mysteries and errors in qigong cultivation], Beijing: Jinri Zhongguo chubanshe.

——, 1996, 'Renti teyigongneng zhenwei zhibian' [Controversies on the true or false nature of extraordinary powers of the human body], ZG, 71: 28–32.

——, 1997a, *Zhongguo qigong Daqushi* [The great trend of Chinese qigong], Beijing: Xinhua chubanshe.

——, 1997b, *Faxian Huangdi Neijing* [The discovery of the *Yellow Emperor's Classic of Internal Medicine*], Beijing: Zuojia chubanshe.

Keith, Ronald C. and Zhiqiu Lin, 2003, 'The "Falungong Problem": Politics and the Struggle for the Rule of Law in China', *China Quarterly*, 175: 623–42.

Kindopp, Jason, 2002, 'China's War on "Cults"', *Current History*, September: 259–66.

Kleinman, Arthur (ed.), 1975, *Medicine in Chinese Cultures: Comparative Studies of Health Care in Chinese and Other Societies*, Washington, DC: Department of Health, Education and Welfare—Public Health Service—National Institutes of Health.

——, 1981, *Patients and Healers in the Context of Culture*, Berkeley, CA: University of California Press.

——, 1986, *Social Origins of Distress and Disease: Depression, Neurasthenia, and Pain in Modern China*, New Haven, CT: Yale University Press.

Kohn, Livia (ed.), 1989, *Daoist Meditation and Longevity Techniques*, Ann Arbor, MI: Center for Chinese Studies, The University of Michigan.

——, 1992, *Early Chinese Mysticism: Philosophy and Soteriology in the Daoist Tradition*, Princeton University Press.

——, 2002, 'Quiet Sitting with Master Yinshi: The Beginnings of Qigong in Modern China' in *Living with the Dao: Conceptual Issues in Daoist*

Practice, Cambridge, MA: Three Pines Press, E-Dao series. Revised version of 'Quiet Sitting with Master Yinshi: Medicine and Religion in Modern China', *Zen Buddhism Today*, 10 (1993), 79–95.

—— (ed.), 2004, *Daoism Handbook*, Leiden: Brill.

Komjathy, Louis, 1996, 'Qigong in America' in Livia Kohn (ed.), *Daoist Body Cultivation*, Cambridge, MA: Three Pines Press, pp. 203–36.

Krippner, Stanley, 1984, 'Afterword' in Dong, Paul, *The Four Major Mysteries of Mainland China*, Englewood Cliffs, NJ: Prentice-Hall, pp. 206–9.

Kwang, Mary, 1999, 'China Exposes Falungong Structure', *The Straits Times Interactive* (Singapore), 28 July 1999, <http://straitstimes.asia1.com.sg/>.

Kwok, D.W.Y., 1965, *Scientism in Chinese Thought: 1900–1950*, New Haven, CT: Yale University Press.

Lagerwey, John, 1997, 'Rituel taoïste et légitimité politique', *Bulletin de l'Ecole française d'Extrême-Orient*, 84 (1997): 99–109.

Lampton, David M., 1977, *The Politics of Medicine in China: The Policy Process, 1949–1977*, Folkestone, Kent: Wm. Dawson and Sons.

Lan Sheng, 1999, 'Gongheguo wushinian qigong beiwanglu' [Restrospective on qigong during fifty years of the People's Republic], *ZG*, 118: 4–8.

Latour, Bruno and Steve Woolgar, 1986, *Laboratory Life: The Construction of Scientific Facts*, Princeton University Press.

Lee, Sing, 2000, 'Chinese Hypnosis can Cause Qigong-Induced Mental Disorders', *British Medical Journal*, 320(7237) (18 March 2000): 803.

—— and Arthur Kleinman, 2002, Psychiatry in its Political and Professional Contexts: A Response to Robin Munro, *Journal of the American Academy of Psychiatry and the Law*, 30(1): 120–5.

Leslie, Charles and Allan Young (eds), 1992, *Paths to Asian Medical Knowledge*, Berkeley, CA: University of California Press.

Leung, Beatrice, 2002, 'China and Falungong: Party and Society Relations in the Modern Era', *Journal of Contemporary China*, 11(33): 761–84.

Leung, K.P., T. Yan and L.S.W. Li, 2001, 'Intracerebral Haemorrhage and Qigong', *Hong Kong Medical Journal*, 7(3): 315–18.

Li Hongzhi, 1993, *Zhongguo Falungong (xiuding ben)* [China Falungong (revised edition)], <www.falundafa.org/book/chicg.htm>.

——, 1994, 'Wei Changchun Falun dafa fudaoyuan jiefa' [Explaining the Fa to the Falun Dafa assistants in Changchun] in *Falun Dafa yijie* [Explanation of the meaning of Falun Dafa], <www.falundafa.org/book/chigb.htm>.

——, 1995a, *Zhuan Falun (juan er)* [Turning the Dharma Wheel (vol. 2)], Beijing: Zhongguo shijieyu chubanshe.

——, 1995b, *Falun Dafa yijie* [Explanation of the meaning of Falun Dafa], <www.falundafa.org/book/chigb.htm>.

——, 1996a, *Falun Fofa (Dayuanman fa)* [The Buddha-Law of the Dharma Wheel (Method of the Great Attainment)], <www.falundafa.org/book/chigb.htm>.

——, 1996b, *Falun Fofa – zai Xini jiangfa* [The Buddha-Law of the Dharma Wheel. Dharma talk in Sydney], publisher unknown.

——, 1997a, *Falun Fofa – zai Meiguo jiangfa* [The Buddha-Law of the Dharma Wheel. Dharma talk in the United States], Hong Kong: Falun fofa chubanshe.

——, 1997b, *Zhuan Falun fajie* [Turning the Dharma Wheel explained], Hong Kong: Falun fofa chubanshe.

——, 1998a [1994], 'Zhuan Falun' [Turning the Dharma Wheel] in *Falun Dafa* [Falun Dafa], Hailaer: Neimenggu wenhua chubanshe.

——, 1998b, *Falun Fofa (Zai Changchun fudaoyuan fahuishang jiangfa)* [The Buddha-Law of the Dharma Wheel (Dharma talk for the Dharma assembly of the Changchun assistants)], <www.falundafa.org/book/chigb.htm>.

——, 1998c, *Falun Fofa (Zai Ruishi fahuishang jiangfa)* [The Buddha-Law of the Dharma Wheel (Dharma talk at the Dharma assembly in Switzerland)], <www.falundafa.org/book/chigb.htm>.

——, 1999a, *Falun Fofa – zai Beimei shoujie fahui shang jiangfa* [The Buddha-Law of the Dharma Wheel. Dharma talk at the first North American Dharma assembly], Xining: Qinghai renmin chubanshe.

——, 1999b, *Falun Fofa – zai Ouzhou fahui shang jiangfa* [The Buddha-Law of the Dharma Wheel. Dharma talks at the European Dharma assemblies], Xining: Qinghai renmin chubanshe.

——, 1999c, *Falun Fofa – Jingjin yaozhi* [The Buddha-Law of the Dharma Wheel. Essential points for progressing], <www.falundafa.org/book/chigb.htm>.

——, 1999d, *Falun Fofa – zai Xinjiapo fahui shang jiangfa* [The Buddha-Law of the Dharma Wheel. Dharma talk at the Singapore Dharma assembly], Hong Kong: Falun fofa chubanshe.

——, 1999e, 'My Statement', *Chinese Law & Government*, 32(6): 26–7. Translation of 'Wode yidian shengming', originally in Li Hongzhi 1999c, but removed from online editions subsequent to 2004; translation taken from Chinese-language posting on <www.chinesenewsnet.

com, duowei xinwenwang>; also found on 22 May 2005 at <www. prism.gatech-edu/~ph279cl/GB/jwen.html>.

——, 2000 [1994], 'Brief Biography of Li Hongzhi, Founder of Falungong and President of the Falungong Research Society', *Chinese Law & Government*, 32(6): 14–23. Translation of 'Zhongguo Falungong chuangshiren, Falungong yanjiuhui huizhang Li Hongzhi xiansheng xiaozhuan' in *Zhongguo Falungong*, Zhongguo guangbo dianshi chuban gongsi, 1994.

Li Jianxin and Zheng Qin, 1996, *1995: Qigong da lunzhan* [1995, the great qigong controversy], Chengdu: Sichuan wenyi chubanshe.

Li Liyan, 1998, *Sima Nan hai huozhe* [Sima Nan still lives], Beijing: Zhongguo qingnian chubanshe.

Li Lun, 1989, *Yan Xin qigong xianxiang* [Yan Xin qigong phenomena], Beijing: Beijing gongye daxue chubanshe.

Li Peicai, 1988, *Zhongguo chaoren – shenqi de teyi gongneng* [China's superman: the miraculous Extraordinary Powers], Beijing: Jiefangjun chuabanshe.

——, 1989, *Da ziran de linghun – Ji ziran zhongxin gongfa chuanshouzhe Zhang Xiangyu* [The soul of nature: Zhang Xiangyu, teacher of the Qigong of Nature's Centre], Beijing: Changhong chuban gongsi.

Li Ping, 1998, *Qigong yu Zhongguo wenhua* [Qigong and Chinese culture], Xi'an: Shaanxi renmin jiaoyu chubanshe.

Li Yuanguo, 1987, *Qigong jinghua ji* [Collection of essential texts on qigong], Chengdu: Bashu shushe.

Li Zhiyong, 1988, *Zhongguo qigong shi* [History of Chinese qigong], Changsha: Henan kexue jishu chubanshe.

Liang, Shifeng, 1988, *Dongjing qigong* [Miraculous qigong of motion and stillness], Hong Kong: Guangdong gaodeng jiaoyu chubanshe; Yiyao weisheng chubanshe.

Lin Hai, 2000, 'Qigong yu kexue de 20 nian' [20 years of qigong and science], <www.qg100.com/bjzm/>.

Lin Housheng, 1988, *Qigongxue* [The study of qigong], Qingdao: Qingdao chubanshe.

Lin Zhongpeng, 1988, *Zhonghua qigongxue* [The study of Chinese qigong], Beijing: Beijing tiyu xueyuan chubanshe.

Liu Guizhen, 1957, *Qigong liaofa shixian* [Applications of qigong therapy], Shijiazhuang: Hebei renmin chubanshe.

——, 1981 [1957], *Qigong liaofa shixian* [Applications of qigong therapy], Shijiazhuang: Hebei renmin chubanshe (revised version of 1957 edition).

Liu, Huajie, 2004, *Zhongguo lei kexue: cong zhexue yu shehuixue de guandian kan* [Alternative sciences in China, seen from a philosophical and sociological perspective], Shanghai: Shanghai jiaotong daxue chubanshe.

Liu, Kwang-Ching and Richard Hon-Chun Shek (eds), 2004, *Heterodoxy in Late Imperial China*, Honolulu, HI: University of Hawaii Press.

Liu Shanglin (ed.), 1999, *Zangmi gongfa xueshu yanjiu II* [Academic studies on Zangmi Gong II], Harbin: Harbin gongcheng daxue chubanshe.

Liu, Xun, 2001, 'In Search of Immortality: Daoist Inner Alchemy in Early Twentieth-Century China', PhD diss., University of Southern California.

Liu Zhidong (ed.), 1993, *Zhang Hongbao Qilin zhexue daodu* [Handbook on Zhang Hongbao's qilin philosophy], Xi'an: Zhonghua chuantong wenhua jinxiu daxue.

Lü Feng, 1993, 'Dongfang wenhua de shengteng' [The rise of Oriental culture] in Liu Zhidong (ed.), *Zhang Hongbao Qilin zhexue daodu* [Handbook on Zhang Hongbao's qilin philosophy], Xi'an: Zhonghua chuantong wenhua jinxiu daxue, pp. 192–233.

Lu Liu, 1994, *Qi Dao* [The Dao of Qi], Shanghai: Sanlian shudian.

Lü, Xiaobo and Elizabeth Perry (eds), 1997, *Danwei: The Changing Chinese Workplace in Historical and Comparative Perspective*, Armonk, NY: M.E. Sharpe.

Lü Yulan and Cheng Xia, 1988, *Dangdai qigong daguan* [The magnificent spectacle of qigong today], Beijing: Wenyi chubanshe.

Lu, Yunfeng, 2005, 'Entrepreneurial Logics and the Evolution of Falungong', *Journal for the Scientific Study of Religion*, 44(2): 173–85.

Ma Xisha and Han Bingfang, 1992, *Zhongguo minjian zongjiao shi* [History of Chinese popular religious sects], Shanghai: Shanghai renmin chubanshe.

MacKerras, Colin (ed.), 1998, *Dictionary of the Politics of the People's Republic of China*, London: Routledge.

Madsen, Richard, 1998, *China's Catholics: Tragedy and Hope in an Emerging Civil Society*, Berkeley, CA: University of California Press.

——, 2000, 'Understanding Falungong', *Current History* (September 2000): 243–7.

Maspero, Henri, 1971 [1937], 'Les procédés de "nourrir le principe vital" dans la religion taoïste ancienne' in Henri Maspero, *Le Taoïsme et les religions chinoises*, Paris: Gallimard, pp. 480–589. [English translation published as *Taoism and Chinese religion*, Amherst, MA: University of Massachusetts Press, 1981].

Mauss, Marcel, 1967 [1947], *Manuel d'ethnographie*, Paris: Payot.

——, 1979 [1935], *Sociology and Psychology*, London: Routledge and Kegan Paul.

Micolllier, Evelyne, 1995, *Un aspect de la pluralité médicale en Chine populaire: Les pratiques de Qi Gong – Dimension thérapeutique/dimension sociale*, PhD diss., Université de Provence (Aix-Marseille I).

——, 1999, 'Control and Release of Emotions in Qigong Health Practices', *China Perspectives*, 24: 22–30.

——, 2004, 'Le qigong chinois: enjeux économiques et transnationalisation des réseaux, pratiques et croyances', *Journal des anthropologues*, 98–9: 107–46.

Miller, H. Lyman, 1996, *Science and Dissent in Post-Mao China*, Seattle, WA: University of Washington Press.

Ming Zhen (ed.), 1988, *Yan Xin kexue qigong* [Yan Xin's scientific qigong], Hong Kong: China Books Press.

Miura, Kunio, 1989, 'The Revival of Qi: Qigong in Contemporary China' in Livia Kohn (ed.), *Daoist Meditation and Longevity Techniques*, Ann Arbor, MI: Center for Chinese Studies, The University of Michigan, pp. 331–58.

Morris, Andrew D., 2004, *Marrow of the Nation: A History of Sport and Physical Culture in Republican China*, Berkeley, CA: University of California Press.

Munro, Robin (ed.), 1989, *Syncretic Sects and Secret Societies: Revival in the 1980s*, thematic issue of *Chinese Sociology and Anthropology*, 21(4) (summer 1989).

——, 2000, 'Judicial Psychiatry in China and its Political Abuses', *Columbia Journal of Asian Law*, 14(1): 106–20.

——, 2002a, 'On the Psychiatric Abuse of Falungong and Other Dissenters in China: A Reply to Stone, Hickling, Kleinman, and Lee', *Journal of the American Academy of Psychiatry and the Law*, 30(2): 266–74.

——, 2002b, 'Political Psychiatry in Post-Mao China and its Origins in the Cultural Revolution', *Journal of the American Academy of Psychiatry and the Law*, 30(1): 97–106.

Murakawa, Haruhiko, 2002, *Phenomenology of the Experience of Qigong: A Preliminary Research Design for the Intentional Bodily Practices*, PhD diss., California Institute of Integral Studies.

Naquin, Susan, 1976, *Millenarian Rebellion in China: The Eight Trigrams Uprising of 1813*, New Haven, CT: Yale University Press.

——, 1981, *Shantung Rebellion: The Wang Lun Uprising of 1774*, New Haven, CT: Yale University Press.

——, 1985, 'The Transmission of White Lotus Sectarianism in Late Imperial China' in David Johnson *et al.* (eds), 1983–5, *Popular Culture in Late Imperial China*, Berkeley, CA: University of California Press, pp. 255–91.

Nedostup, Rebecca, 2001, 'Religion, Superstition and Governing Society in Nationalist China', PhD diss., Columbia University.

O'Leary, Stephen, 2001, 'Falun Gong and the Internet', *Online Journalism Review*, <www.ojr.org/ojr/ethics/1017964337.php> (accessed 1 October 2003).

Ostrov, Benjamin C., 1991, *Conquering Resources: The Growth and Decline of the PLA's Science and Technology Commission for National Defense*, Armonk, NY and London: M.E. Sharpe.

Ots, Thomas, 1994, 'The Silenced Body: The Expressive *Leib*: On the Dialectic of Mind and Life in Chinese Cathartic Healing' in Thomas Csordas (ed.), *Embodiment and Experience: The Existential Ground of Culture and Self*, Cambridge University Press, pp. 116–36.

Overmyer, Daniel, 1976, *Folk Buddhist Religion: Dissenting Sects in Late Traditional China*, Cambridge, MA: Harvard University Press.

——, 1999, *Precious Volumes: An Introduction to Chinese Sectarian Scriptures from the Sixteenth and Seventeenth Centuries*, Cambridge, MA: Harvard University Press.

Ownby, David, 2000, 'Falungong as a Cultural Revitalization Movement: An Historian Looks at Contemporary China', lecture given at Rice University, 20 October, <http//www.ruf.rice.edu/~tnchina/commentary/ownby1000.htm>.

——, 2003a, 'A History for Falungong: Popular Religion and the Chinese State since the End of the Ming Dynasty', *Nova Religio*, 6(2): 223–43.

——, 2003b, 'The Falungong in the New World', *European Journal of East Asian Studies*, 2(2): 303–20.

——, forthcoming, *Falun Gong and China's Future*, Oxford University Press.

Palmer, David A., 2001a, 'Falungong: la tentation du politique', *Critique internationale*, 11: 36–43.

——, 2001b, 'The Doctrine of Li Hongzhi. Falungong: Between Sectarianism and Universal Salvation', *China Perspectives*, 35: 14–24.

——, 2002a, 'Le qigong au carrefour des "discours anti". De l'anticléricalisme communiste au fondamentalisme du Falungong', *Extrême Orient Extrême Occident*, 24: 153–166.

——, 2002b, 'La fièvre du qigong. Guérison, religion et politique en Chine, 1949–1999', PhD diss., Ecole Pratique des Hautes Etudes.

——, 2003a, 'Modernity and Millenialism: From Qigong to Falungong', *Asian Anthropology*, 2: 79–110.

——, 2003b, 'Le qigong et la tradition sectaire chinoise', *Social Compass*, 50(4): 471–80.

——, 2004, 'Cyberspace and the Emerging Chinese Religious Landscape—Preliminary Observations' in Françoise Mengin (ed.), *Cyber China: Reshaping National Identities in the Age of Information*, New York: Palgrave MacMillan, pp. 37–50.

——, 2005a, *La fièvre du qigong. Guérison, religion et politique en Chine, 1949–1999*, Paris: Editions de l'Ecole des Hautes Etudes en Sciences Sociales.

——, 2005b, 'L'Etat et le sectarisme en Chine contemporaine' in John Lagerwey (ed.), *Religion et politique en Asie*, Paris: Les Indes Savantes.

——, 2006, 'Body Cultivation in Contemporary China' in James Miller (ed.), *Chinese Religions in Contemporary Society*, Santa Barbara, CA: ABC-CLIO.

——, forthcoming a, 'Religion and Social Agency in China: Divisions and Multiplications' in Gilles Guiheux and K.E. Kuah-Pierce (eds), *Emerging Social Movements in China*.

——, forthcoming b, 'Heretical Doctrines, Reactionary Secret Societies, Evil Cults: Labelling Heterodoxy in 20th Century China' in Mayfair Yang (ed.), *Chinese Religiosities: The Vicissitudes of Modernity and State Formation*, Berkeley, CA: University of California Press.

——, forthcoming c, 'Tao and Nation: Li Yujie's Appropriation of Huashan Taoism' in David Palmer and Liu Xun (eds), *Between Eternity and Modernity: Taoist Tradition and Transformation in the 20th Century*.

Palmer, Susan, 2003, 'From Healing to Protest: Conversion Patterns Among the Practitioners of Falungong', *Nova Religio*, 6(2): 348–64.

—— and David Ownby, 2000, 'Falun Dafa Practitioners: A Preliminary Research Report', *Nova Religio*, 4 (October 2000): 133–7.

Penny, Benjamin, 1993, 'Qigong, Daoism, and Science: Some Contexts for the Qigong Boom' in Mabel Lee and A.D. Syrokomla-Stefanowska (eds), *Modernization of the Chinese Past*, Sydney: Wild Peony, pp. 166–79.

——, 2002a, 'The Body of Master Li', Australian Religious Studies Association, <http://users.senet.com.au/~nhabel/Lectures/penny.pdf> (accessed 19 May 2005).

——, 2002b, 'Falungong, Prophecy and Apocalypse', *East Asian History*, 23: 149–68.

—— (ed.), 2002c, *Religion and Biography in China and Tibet*, Richmond, Surrey: Curzon.

——, 2003, 'The Life and Times of Li Hongzhi: Falungong and Religious Biography', *China Quarterly*, 175: 643–61.

——, forthcoming, *The World of Master Li: The Religion of the Falun Gong.*

Perry, Elizabeth, 1980, *Rebels and Revolutionaries in North China, 1845–1945*, Stanford University Press.

—— and Stevan Harrell (eds), 1982, *Syncretic Sects in Chinese Society* (in two volumes), *Modern China*, 8(3 and 4).

Pieke, Frank, 1996, *The Ordinary and the Extraordinary: An Anthropological Study of Chinese Reform and the 1989 People's Movement in Beijing*, London: Kegan Paul.

Pitman, Don A., 2001, *Toward a Modern Chinese Buddhism: Taixu's Reforms*, Honolulu, HI: University of Hawaii Press.

Porkert, Manfred, 1974, *The Theoretical Foundations of Chinese Medicine*, Cambridge, MA: MIT Press.

——, 1975, 'The Dilemma of Present-Day Interpretations of Chinese Medicine' in Arthur Kleinman (ed.), *Medicine in Chinese Cultures: Comparative Studies of Health Care in Chinese and Other Societies*, Washington, DC: Department of Health, Education and Welfare—Public Health Service—National Institutes of Health, pp. 61–75.

Porter, Noah, 2003, *Falungong in the United States: An Ethnographic Study*, MA thesis, University of South Florida, electronic version available at <http://www.lib.usf.edu/ETD–db/theses/available/etd-06122003-113105/> (accessed 31 May 2005); book version available from <www.dissertation.com>.

Powers, John, and Meg Y.M. Lee, 2002, 'Dueling Media: Symbolic Conflict in China's Falungong Suppression Campaign' in Guo-Ming Chen and Ringo Ma (eds), *Chinese Conflict Management and Resolution*, Westport, CT and London: Ablex, pp. 259–74.

PureInsight.org, 2002, 'Summary of Health Surveys Conducted in Mainland China to Assess Falungong's Effect on Healing Illness and Maintaining Fitness, Summarized by Dafa Disciples in North America', <http://www.pureinsight.org/pi/articles/2002/3/11/841.html> (accessed 31 May 2005).

Qian Xuesen, 1981a, 'Kaizhan renti kexue jichu yanjiu' [Developing fundamental research in somatic science], ZZ, 4(7): 483–88.

——, 1981b, 'Xitong kexue, siwei kexue yu renti kexue' [System science, cognitive science and somatic science], *Xinhua wenzhai*, 3 (March 1981): 214–21.

——, 1982, 'Some Theoretical Ideas on the Development of Basic Research in Human Body Science', *Psi Research* (June): 4–15.

——, 1987, 'Some Papers were Reviewed and Supported by Professor Qian XueSheng [*sic*]', web page containing the copies of two handwritten review notes by Qian Xuesen on Yan Xin's experiments at Qinghua University, <http://www.interlog.com~yuan/yanqian.html> (accessed January 1999).

——, 1988, *Lun renti kexue* [On somatic science], Beijing: Renmin junyi chubanshe.

——, 1996, *Renti kexue yu xiandai keji fazhan zongheng guan* [A broad view of somatic science and the development of modern science and technology], Beijing: Renmin chubanshe.

——, 1998a, 'Jianli weixiang qigong xue' [Establishing a phenomenology of qigong] in Yan Xin, *Yan Xin fangtan lu* [Interviews with Yan Xin], Beijing: Zhongguo youyi chuban gongsi, first preface, pp. 1–8.

——, 1998b, 'Zai tan renti kexue de tixi jiegou' [Further comments on the structure of the system of somatic sciences] in Yan Xin, *Yan Xin fangtan lu* [Interviews with Yan Xin], Beijing: Zhongguo youyi chuban gongsi, second preface, pp. 9–13.

—— et al., 1989, *Chuangjian renti kexue* [Establishing somatic sciences], vol. 1, Chengdu: Sichuan jiaoyu chubanshe.

Qin Chongsan, 1959, *Qigong liaofa he baojian* [Therapy and health preservation by qigong], Shanghai: Shanghai kexue jishu chubanshe.

Qin Hui, 1990, *Yan Xin chuanqi* [The legend of Yan Xin], Guangzhou: Huacheng chubanshe.

Quinn, Joseph (ed.), 1973, *Medicine and Public Health in the People's Republic of China*, Washington, DC: US Department of Health, Education, and Welfare.

Renmin tiyu chubanshe (ed.), 1981, *Qigong jingxuan* [Compilation on Qigong], Beijing: Renmin tiyu chubanshe.

Robinet, Isabelle, 1979, *Méditation Taoïste*, Paris: Dervy Livres.

——, 1990, 'Nature et role du maître spirituel dans le taoïsme non liturgique' in Michel Meslin (ed.), *Maître et disciples dans les traditions religieuses*, Paris: Editions du Cerf, pp. 37–50.

——, 1995, *Introduction à l'alchimie intérieure taoïste. De l'unité et de la multiplicité*, Paris: Editions du Cerf.

Schechter, Danny, 2000, *Falun Gong's Challenge to China: Spiritual Practice or 'Evil Cult'?*, New York: Akashic Books.

Schipper, Kristofer, 1993, *The Taoist Body*, Berkeley, CA: University of California Press.

——, 1997, 'Rediscovering Religion in China', communication to the symposium 'Modern Society and the Science of Religion'.

Seidel, Anna, 1969–70, 'The Image of the Perfect Ruler in Early Taoist Messianism: Lao-tzu and Li Hung', *History of Religions*, 9(2 and 3): 216–47.

Seiwert, Hubert, 2003, *Popular Religious Movements and Heterodox Sects in Chinese History*, Leiden: Brill.

Shahar, Meir, 2001, 'Ming Period Evidence of Shaolin Martial Practice', *Harvard Journal of Asiatic Studies*, 61(2): 359–413.

Shan, Huaihan, 2000, 'Culture-Bound Psychiatric Disorders Associated with Qigong Practice in China', *Hong Kong Journal of Psychiatry*, 10(3): 12–14.

Shanghai shi qigong liaoyangsuo jiaoyanzu, 1958, *Qigong liaofa jiangyi* [Lectures on qigong therapy], Shanghai: Keji weisheng chubanshe.

Shanghai shi Huangpu qu Dongchang diduan yiyuan [Shanghai Municipal Huangpu District Dongchang Hospital] *et al.*, 1976, *Liangong shiba fa* [Eighteen methods of gong practice], Shanghai: Shanghai tiyu chubanshe.

Shao Yong, 1997, *Zhongguo huidaomen* [Sects and secret societies in China], Shanghai: Shanghai renmin chubanshe.

Shue, Vivienne, 2002, 'Global Imaginings: The State's Quest for Hegemony and the Pursuit of Phantom Freedom in China: from Heshang to Falungong' in Kristina C. J. Kinnvall (ed.), *Globalisation and Democratization in Asia*, London: Routledge, pp. 210–29.

Siegler, Elijah, 2006, 'Chinese Traditions in Euro-American Society' in James Miller (ed.), *Chinese Religions in Contemporary Society*, Santa Barbara, CA: ABC-CLIO, pp. 257–80.

Sima Nan, 1995, *Shengong neimu* [The backstage of miraculous qigong], Beijing: Zhongguo shehui chubanshe.

——, 2002, *Wo shi Sima Nan* [I am Sima Nan], Beijing: Zhongguo shidai jingji chubanshe.

—— and Li Liyan, 1998, *Taiyigong heimu. Hu Wanlin yu « Faxian Huandi Neijing* [The dark truth about the Taiyi Palace: Hu Wanlin and the Discovery of *The Yellow Emperor's Classic of Internal Medicine*], Beijing: Zhongguo shehui chubanshe.

Siu, Helen F., 1990, 'Recycling Ritual' in P. Link, R. Madsen and P. Pickowicz (eds), *Unofficial China: Popular Culture and Thought in the People's Republic*, Boulder, CO: Westview.

Song Shaoming, 1988, *'Shenren' Zhang Baosheng teyigongneng jishi* [The Extraordinary Powers of the 'Miracle Man' Zhang Baosheng], Beijing: Zhongguo wenlian chuban gongsi.

Strickmann, Michel, 1996, *Mantras et Mandarins. Le bouddhisme tantrique en Chine*, Paris: Gallimard.

Sumrall, Shannon Larry, 1998, *Alternative and Complementary Medicine: A Focus on Qigong*, MA thesis, Medical Anthropology, University of Mississippi.

Tai, Hsüan-chih, 1985, *The Red Spears, 1916–1949*, transl. R. Suleski, Ann Arbor, MI: Centre for Chinese Studies, The University of Michigan.

Tao Bingfu (ed.), 1994, *Xinban Guo Lin xin qigong* [New edition of Guo Lin's new qigong], Beijing: Tongxin chubanshe.

—— and Yang Weihe (eds), 1981, *Qigong liaofa jijin* [Outstanding selections on qigong therapy], Beijing: Renmin weisheng chubanshe.

Tao Zulai, 1990, *Qigong, kexue yu xiandai wenming* [Qigong, science and modern civilization], Beijing: Huaxia chubanshe.

Tarrow, Sydney, 1994, *Power in Movement: Social Movements, Collective Action and Politics*, New York: Cambridge University Press.

Taylor, Kim, 2001, 'Civil War in China and the New Acumoxa' in Elizabeth Hsu (ed.), *Innovation, Convention and Controversy in Chinese Medicine*, Cambridge University Press.

——, 2002, '"Improving" Chinese Medicine: The Role of Traditional Medicine in Newly Communist China, 1949–1953' in A.K.L. Chan, G.K. Clancey and H.-C. Loy (eds), *Historical Perspectives on East Asian Science, Technology and Medicine*, Singapore: Singapore University Press and World Scientific Publishing, pp. 251–63.

——, 2005, *Chinese Medicine in Early Communist China, 1945–63: A Medicine of Revolution*, London: Routledge.

Thornton, Patricia M., 2002, 'Framing Dissent in Contemporary China: Irony, Ambiguity, and Metonymy', *China Quarterly*, 171: 661–81.

Tong, James, 2002a, 'An Organizational Analysis of the Falungong: Structure, Communications, Financing', *China Quarterly*, 171: 636–60.

——, 2002b, 'Anatomy of Regime Repression in China: Timing, Enforcement Institutions, and Target Selection in Banning the Falungong, July 1999', *Asian Survey*, 42(6): 795–820.

Touraine, Alain, 2002, 'The Importance of Social Movements', *Social Movement Studies*, 1(1): 89–95.

Troeltsch, Ernst, 1960, *The Social Teachings of the Christian Churches*, translated by O. Wyon, vol. 1, New York and Evanston, IL: Harper Torchbooks.

Unschuld, Paul, 1985, *Medicine in China: A History of Ideas*, Berkeley, CA: University of California Press.

——, 1992, 'Epistemological Issues and Changing Legitimation: Traditional Chinese Medicine in the Twentieth Century' in Charles Leslie and Allan Young (eds), *Paths to Asian Medical Knowledge*, Berkeley, CA: University of California Press, pp. 44–61.

Vermander, Benoît, 1999, 'Law and the Wheel: The Sudden Emergence of Falungong: Prophets of "Spiritual Civilisation"', *China Perspectives*, 24: 14–21.

——, 2001, Looking at China through the Mirror of Falungong, *China Perspectives*, 35: 4–13. Available online at <http://www.cefc.com.hk/uk/pc/articles/art_ligne.php?num_art_ligne=3501> (accessed 31 May 2005).

Walder, Andrew, 1986, *Communist Neo-Traditionalism: Work and Authority in Chinese Society*, Berkeley, CA: University of California Press.

Wallis, Roy, 1979, *Salvation and Protest: Studies of Social and Religious Movements*, New York: St Martin's Press.

Wang Buxiong and Zhou Zhirong, 1989, *Zhongguo qigong xueshu fazhanshi* [History of the development of academic qigong], Changsha: Henan kexue jishu chubanshe.

Wang Chien-ch'uan, 1995, 'Tongshan she zaoqi lishi (1912–1945) chutan' [Preliminary discussion of the early history of the Tongshanshe], *Minjian zongjiao*, 1: 57–81.

Wang Jisheng, 1989, *Zhongguo qigong xinlixue* [The psychology of Chinese qigong], Beijing: Zhongguo shehui kexue chubanshe.

Wang, Yeu-Farn, 1993, *China's Science and Technology Policy: 1949–1989*, Aldershot: Avebury.

Weber, Max, 1995, *Economie et société, vol. 1: Les catégories de la sociologie*, Paris: Plon.

Weller, Robert, 1994, *Resistance, Chaos and Control in China*, Seattle, WA: University of Washington Press.

——, 1999, *Alternate Civilities: Democracy and Culture in China and Taiwan*, Boulder, CO: Westview Press.

Wile, Douglas, 1992, *Art of the Bedchamber: The Chinese Sexual Yoga Classics Including Women's Solo Meditation Texts*, Albany, NY: SUNY Press.

—— 1996, *Lost T'ai-chi Classics from the Late Ch'ing Dynasty*, Albany, NY: State University of New York Press.

Wortzel, Larry M., 1999, *Dictionary of Contemporary Chinese Military History*, Westport, CT: Greenwood Press.

Wu Hao (ed.), 1993, *Zhongguo dangdai qigong quanshu* [The complete book of contemporary Chinese qigong], Beijing: Renmin tiyu chubanshe.

Wu Xutian (ed.), 1992, *Yan Xin dashi zai beimei* [Grandmaster Yan Xin in North America], Chengdu: Chengdu keji daxue chubanshe.

Xie Huanzhang, 1988, *Qigong de kexue jichu* [Scientific foundations of qigong], Beijing: Beijing ligong daxue chubanshe.

Xinhua News Agency, 1999, 'Two Documents Concerning the Banning of the Research Society of Falun Dafa', *Chinese Law & Government*, 32(5): 31–2. Translated from HW, 23 July 1999, p. 1.

Xu, Jian, 1999, 'Body, Discourse, and the Cultural Politics of Contemporary Chinese Qigong', *Journal of Asian Studies*, 58(4) (November): 961–91.

Xu, Shenghan, 1994, 'Psychophysiological Reactions Associated with Qigong Therapy', *Chinese Medical Journal*, 107(3): 230–3.

Yan Xin, 1988, *Huaxia shengong* [The miraculous gong of China], Beijing: Qinghua daxue chubanshe.

——, 1996, *Yan Xin qigong tongzi changshou jiubu gong – di yi bu* [Yan Xin Nine-Step Qigong of the Longevity of the Child – first stage] (audio-cassette), Canada: Editions Lotus.

——, 1998, *Yan Xin fangtan lu* [Interviews with Yan Xin], Beijing: Zhongguo youyi chuban gongsi.

——, n.d., *Santé et longévité: le qigong en Neuf Etapes*, photocopied document.

Yang, C.K., 1961, *Religion in Chinese Society: A Study of Contemporary Social Functions of Religion and Some of their Historical Factors*, Berkeley, CA: University of California Press.

Yang, Mayfair Mei-hui, 1994, *Gifts, Favors, and Banquets: The Art of Social Relationships in China*, Ithaca, NY: Cornell University Press.

——, 2000, 'Putting Global Capitalism in its Place: Economic Hybridity, Bataille, and Ritual Expenditure', *Current Anthropology*, 41(4).

Yang Meijun, 1986, *Dayan qigong* [Great Goose Qigong], Hong Kong: Peace Books.

Ye Xiaoqing, 2002, 'Regulating the Medical Profession in China: Health Policies of the Nationalist Government' in A.K.L. Chan, G.K. Clancey and H.-C. Loy (eds), *Historical Perspectives on East Asian Science, Technology and Medicine*, Singapore: Singapore University Press and World Scientific Publishing, pp. 198–213.

Yin Shizi [Jiang Weiqiao], 1962 [1955], *Huxi xijing yangsheng fa* [Method of cultivating life by practising stillness through breathing], Hong Kong: Taiping shuju. Originally published in *Xin zhongyiyao*, 8 (August 1955). Extracts also published in Tao Bingfu and Yang Weihe (eds), 1981, *Qigong liaofa jijin* [Outstanding selections on qigong therapy], Beijing: Renmin weisheng chubanshe, pp. 19–23.

Yu Guangyuan, 1982, 'Psi he tade bianzhong – renti teyigongneng' [Parapsychology and its mutant: Extraordinary Powers of the human body], *Zhongguo shehuikexue* [China Social Science], 14 (March 1982): 31–45.

——, 1996, 'Bu neng shi wo xinfu "teyigongneng"' [It is impossible to make me believe in 'Extraordinary Powers'], KX, 3(39): 6.

——, 2002, *Wo shi Yu Guangyuan* [I am Yu Guangyuan], Beijing: Zhongguo shidai jingji chubanshe.

Zhang Bangshen, 1992, 'Yan Xin zaonian de chengzhang' [Yan Xin's growth during his childhood] in Wu Xutian (ed.), *Yan Xin dashi zai beimei* [Grandmaster Yan Xin in North America], Chengdu: Chengdu keji daxue chubanshe, pp. 303–7.

Zhang Hongbao, 1993, 'Shengming qiyuan yu yundong guilu' [The origin of life and the laws of movement] in Liu Zhidong (ed.), *Zhang Hongbao Qilin zhexue daodu* [Handbook on Zhang Hongbao's qilin philosophy], Xi'an: Zhonghua chuantong wenhua jinxiu daxue, pp. 137–53.

——, 2001, 'Wode jianli' [My resume], <www.goldkylin.net/zunshipian/ zunshijianli> (accessed July 2001).

Zhang Honglin, 1989a, '"Waiqi" langchao zhong de fansi' [Thoughts on the 'external qi' wave], QK, 69.

——, 1989b, '"Waiqi" shizhi sanping: qianda Fu Shijing tongzhi' [Three criticisms on the nature of 'external qi': a humble answer to comrade Fu Shijing], ZG, 5 (1989), reproduced in ZGL: 243–53.

——, 1996, *Huan qigong benlai mianmu* [Return to the original face of qigong], Beijing: Zhongguo shehui kexue chubanshe.

Zhang Mingwu and Sun Xingyuan, 1982, *Qigong zikong liaofa* [Qigong self-control therapy], Shandong kexue jishu chubanshe.

Zhang Weiqing and Qiao Gong, 1999, *Falungong chuangshi ren Li Hongzhi pingzhuan* [Li Hongzhi: the founder of Falun Dafa], Carle Place, NY: Mirror Books.

Zhang Wenjiang and Chang Jin, 1989, *Zhongguo chuantong qigongxue cidian* [Dictionary of traditional Chinese qigong], Taiyuan: Shanxi jiaoyu chubanshe.

Zhang Xiaoping, 1993, *Zhonghua qibao – 'Wanfa guiyi gong' michuan zhenjing* [China's miraculous jewel: the true scriptures of the secret transmission of the 'Qigong of the Union of the Myriad Schools'], Beijing: Huayi chubanshe.

Zhang Yaoting, 1998, '1996 nian jiang shi qigong shiye you chengjiu de yinian' [The year 1996 will be a year of successes for the qigong cause] in Yan Xin, *Yan Xin fangtan lu* [Interviews with Yan Xin], Beijing: Zhongguo youyi chuban gongsi, fifth preface, pp. 21–5.

Zhang Youjun, Li Huaiyan, Zhu Pengfei and Zhang Guifa (eds), 1996, *Zhongguo qigong Daquan* [The complete book of Chinese qigong], Tianjin: Tianjin renmin chubanshe.

Zhang Zhenhuan, 1988a, 'Zhang Zhenhuan tongzhi zai Zhongguo qigong kexue yanjiu zhongxin chengli dahui shang de jianghua' [Speech by comrade Zhang Zhenhuan at the founding meeting of the China Qigong Science Research Centre], DF, 11: 2–3.

——, 1988b, 'Address Given by Zhang Zhenhuan at a Meeting Held to Celebrate the Formation of the Chinese Qigong Scientific Research Association' in Zhu Xiaoyang and Benjamin Penny (eds), 'The Qigong Boom', *Chinese Sociology and Anthropology*, 27(1) (fall), pp. 13–20. Original version published in ZG, 3 (1988).

——, 1988c, 'Zhenzhengde kexue tansuo shi wusuo weijude' [There is nothing to fear in true scientific research] in Qian Xuesen, *Lun renti kexue* [On somatic science], Beijing: Renmin junyi chubanshe, pp. 169–76.

——, 1989, 'Cong guojia jiaowei zhongshi qigong de jiaoxue shuoqi' [Speaking of the importance placed on qigong teaching by the State Education Commission], DF, 16: 2–3.

——, 1999, *Zhang Zhenhuan wenji: renti kexue bufen* [Works of Zhang Zhenhuan: somatic science section], Beijing: Guojiwenhua chubanshe.

—— and Tao Zulai, 1989, 'Guanyu fazhan dangdai qigong de jidian sikao' [Some thoughts on developing contemporary qigong] in Hu Haichang and Hao Qiyao (eds), *Qigong kexue wenji* [Compilation on qigong science], Beijing: Beijing ligong daxue chubanshe, pp. 1–11.

Zhao, Dingxiu, 2001, *The Power of Tiananmen: State-Society Relations and the 1989 Beijing Student Movement*, University of Chicago Press.

Zhao Jinxiang, 1986, *Zhongguo hexiangzhuang qigong* [Chinese Flying Crane Qigong], Beijing: Beijing chubanshe.

——, 1987, *Zhongguo hexiangzhuang qigong tujie* [Illustrated guide to Flying Crane Qigong], Hong Kong: Joint Publishing.

——, 1993, 'Hexiangzhuang jianjie' [Introduction to the Flying Crane posture] in WH: 453.

Zhejiang sheng zhongyiyao yanjiusuo [Zhejiang Provincial Research Institute of Chinese Medicine and Pharmaceuticals], 1959, *Qigong liaofa* [Qigong therapeutic method], Beijing: Renmin weisheng chubanshe.

Zheng Guanglu, 1991, *Qi juan shenzhou* [Swirls of qi in the divine realm (China)], Chengdu: Chengdu chubanshe.

——, 1995, *Zhongguo qigong wushu tanmi* [The secrets of Chinese martial arts qigong], Chengdu: Sichuan renmin chubanshe.

Zheng Ping, 1994, 'Fengyu fenjin ershisi nian' [Twenty-four years of struggle through winds and storms] in Tao Bingfu (ed.), *Xinban Guo Lin xin qigong* [New edition of Guo Lin's new qigong], Beijing: Tongxin chubanshe, pp. 302–8.

Zhou Qianchuan, 1959, *Qigong yao'er liaofa yu jiuzhi piancha shoushu* [Yao'er qigong therapy and the surgical treatment of deviations], Taiyuan: Shanxi renmin chubanshe.

——, 1961, *Qigong yao'er liaofa quanshu* [The complete book of yao'er qigong therapy], Hong Kong: Xianggang taiping shuju.

——, 1967 [1959], *Qigong liaofa Emei shi'er zhuang shimi* [The secrets of the twelve postures of the Emei school of qigong therapy explained], Hong Kong: Shiyong shuju.

Zhu, Xiaoyang, 1994 [1989], 'Spirit and Flesh, Sturm und Drang', translation of an article published in *Shidai* (October 1989) in Zhu Xiaoyang and Benjamin Penny (eds), 'The Qigong Boom', *Chinese Sociology and Anthropology*, 27(1) (fall), pp. 35–47.

—— and Benjamin Penny (eds), 1994, 'The Qigong Boom', *Chinese Sociology and Anthropology*, 27(1) (fall): 1–94.

Zito, Angela, 1997, *Of Body and Brush: Grand Sacrifice as Text/Performance in Eighteenth-Century China*, University of Chicago Press.

—— and Tani Barlow (eds), 1994, *Body, Subject and Power in China*, University of Chicago Press.

Zürcher, Erik, 1982, '"Prince Moonlight": Messianism and Eschatology in Early Medieval Chinese Buddhism', *T'oung Pao*, LXVIII: pp. 1–75.

INDEX

acupuncture (针灸, *zhenjiu*), 34, 36, 47, 50n15, 176

Aerospace Medical Engineering Institute/Institute no. 507 (航天工程医学研究所/507 所, Hangtian gongcheng yixue yanjiusuo/507 suo), 68n97, 71, 74, *83*, 161

All-China Medical Qigong Science Research Society (全国医学气功科学研究会, Quanguo yixue qigong kexue yanjiuhui), 59, 75, *83*, 175

All-China Society for Chinese Medicine (全国中医学会, Quanguo zhongyi xuehui), 59, 79

Aromatic Qigong (香功, Xianggong), 13

Bao Guiwen (包桂文), 50

Baoding Qigong Hospital, 37n29

barefoot doctors, 95, 137

becoming inflamed and falling into a spell (走火入魔, *zouhuo rumo*), 158–9

Beidaihe Qigong Sanatorium (Hospital) (北戴河气功疗养院, Beidaihe qigong liaoyangyuan), 1, 36–7, 38–9, 43, 58, 75, 80, 82, *83*, 312n18

Beijing Association for Science and Technology (北京科学技术协会, Beijing kexue jishu xiehui), 57

Beijing Haidian District Qigong Science Research Institute (北京市海淀区气功科学研究所, Beijing shi haidian qu qigong kexue yanjiusuo), 147

Beijing Institute of Education, 68

Beijing International Qigong Services Co. Ltd (北京国际气功服务有限公司, Beijing guoji qigong fuwu youxian gongsi), 218

Beijing Labour Union (北京市总工会, Beijing shi zong gonghui), 57

Beijing Normal University, 40, 64, 69

Beijing Qigong Research Society (北京气功研究会, Beijing qigong yanjiuhui, BQRS), 30, 57, 75, 154, 175, 192, 312n18, 313

Beijing Society for Chinese Medicine (北京中医学会, Beijing Zhongyi xuehui), 80

Beijing University, 64, 69, 144, 147, 162

Beijing University of Medical Sciences, 159

Beijing University of Science and Technology, 146–7

Benson, Herbert, 78

Bi Xuejing (碧雪景), 40

bigu fasting (辟谷, *bigu*), 106, 133, 144, 151, 159, 201

Bodhidharma (菩提达摩), 39

Bodhisattva (菩萨, *pusa*), 175, 179, 238, 254

Book of Changes, the (周易, 易经), 2, 18, 79, *93*, 96, 109, 114, 153, 236

Bronze Bell Qigong (铜钟气功, Tongzhong qigong), 39–40

Buddhas (佛, *fo*), 92, 145, 152, 175, 180, 232, 233, 235, 237, 238, 254, 262, *see also* Sakyamuni

Buddhism and Buddhists: 11, 24, 119n43, 125; Li Hongzhi/Falungong and, 124n51, 220n3, 221, 224, 225, 226, 230, 232–3, 236, 246, 248, 262–3, 283, 304n58; and *qigong*, 5,